THE HUNDREDTH YEAR

Books by *JOHN D. BERGAMINI*

THE TRAGIC DYNASTY

A History of the Romanovs

THE SPANISH BOURBONS

The History of a Tenacious Dynasty

THE HUNDREDTH YEAR

The United States in 1876

by John D. Bergamini

G. P. Putnam's Sons
New York

Library of Congress Cataloging in Publication Data

Bergamini, John D
   The Hundredth Year

   Bibliography: p. 341
   Includes index.
   1.   United States—History—1865–1898. I.   Title.
E661.B5   1976   973.8'2   75–44328   13Dec'79

Contents

January 1, Washington

ALL comers were welcome to the New Year's Day reception at the White House, in accordance with a fine democratic tradition going back to the first years of the Republic. The man of medium height and few words presiding over the receiving line was President Ulysses S. Grant, at once gracious and poker-faced, dignified and vulnerable, heroic and commonplace. The youngest person ever elected chief executive, Grant at fifty-three showed only a touch of corpulence and gray hair after seven years in office. He was dressed in a solemn black suit, the male uniform in this so-called Gilded Age, preferred alike by corporation heads and labor agitators. Grant's white kid gloves proclaimed that he was a gentleman; an undone button on his waistcoat hinted that he was not completely comfortable at a formal occasion.

Assisting the President in the oval Blue Room, with its crystal chandeliers and French vases, were his wife, a generous collection of live-in relatives, and the Cabinet officers and their ladies. The first lady wore a black silk gown trimmed in orange. A stoutish, cheerful, animated woman, Julia Grant also had a little silver in her glossy black hair, and she had never quite overcome her nervousness at being slightly cross-eyed. She looked over admiringly at her husband, with whom she had a relationship of teasing affection and complete harmony. Mrs. Fred Grant stood next to her mother-in-law. Dressed in bright pink silk and lace, she closely resembled her sister, the celebrated Mrs. Potter Palmer of Chicago society. Her husband, not so long out of West Point, was a colonel serving on General Sheridan's staff in the West. Behind the presidential group were arrayed the seven Cabinet officials according to rank, beginning with Secretary of State Hamilton Fish and his formidable wife. The ladies wore silk and velvet gowns in respectfully subdued colors, all except Amanda Belknap, the wife of the secretary of war, who was outstanding in "one of Worth's wonderful suits" in light blue and gold.[1] The murmurs about Mrs. Belknap today would in two months' time give way to a nationwide outcry against her.

The first guests to be received at 10:30 A.M. were the ministers of foreign countries, some of them resplendent in court uniforms. Then came the lesser department officials, whose bows became deeper as the more junior the rank, the justices of the Supreme Court, members of Congress, and special delegations like veterans of the Mexican War. Military uniforms were in profusion, a noticeable feature all during Grant's administration. The visitors entered the north portico of the White House into a spacious vestibule and proceeded down a hall past portraits of several of the presidents. In the Red Room a marine band in scarlet coats played favorites of the day. On entering the larger blue and gold reception room, each caller was announced to Grant by the marshal of the District of Columbia.

At 1 P.M. the general public were admitted. Not a few female department clerks, wearing carefully pressed plain alpaca dresses and their fanciest hats, braved the crush along with society dowagers. Many veterans stood in line, predominantly Union men, but proud Confederates too. No blacks ever attended these receptions, "thus showing themselves modest and not aggressive," according to Mrs. Grant, who did give orders that they not be turned away.[2] Most visitors received only a presidential handshake, some a nod of recognition, a few a smile of remembrance. When Grant appeared to be tiring, the doors were closed at 2 P.M., and the reception ended. Later in the day the President took his customary stroll down Pennsylvania Avenue, once again acknowledging gravely the salutes of his fellow citizens.

The prerequisites of the presidency brought a peculiar satisfaction to Grant. For much of his life a social failure, then lofted to fame as a military genius, the general in the White House received the services of scores of domestics and subordinates, as well as the flattering attentions of the rich and the well-born. It was all a far call from the weatherboard Ohio cabin where he was born. He now enjoyed fine horses and carriages and a grand mansion, which Mrs. Grant had done over with brocades and lace and gilt in an effort to dispel the gloomy era of Mrs. Lincoln. Both the Grants liked to entertain, mixing ceremony with conviviality. His weekly receptions were on Thursdays; hers on Saturdays. Usually each week there was a dinner for thirty-six, prepared by an Italian chef whom Mrs. Grant had installed in place of the general's quartermaster, and occasionally the first family gave lavish banquets, the courses numbering over thirty and the cost more than $1,000, as during the successive visits of Prince Arthur of England and the Grand Duke Alexis of Russia. Julia Grant displayed as many pearls and diamonds as royalty.

Most evenings President Grant was a whiskey and cigars man, enjoying the company of a masculine group more remarkable for their abilities to tell a good story than for their mental attainments. Perhaps it was a deep sense of inferiority that made the outwardly self-possessed general avoid the well-educated and the blunt-spoken and surround himself with wily politicians and flashy business operators. More than anything, Grant's misjudgment of men made his administration the most corrupt in the nation's history. He was stubbornly loyal to his friends, to his repeated misfortune, and he let himself be betrayed also by his many thievish relatives who mixed into politics. The unprecedented number of twenty-five men sat in his Cabinets, one after another. The most flagrant grafters in this procession were eventually ousted by Grant with great reluctance, while, what was worse, the few upright men were replaced with alarming alacrity. The press made a cliché of the phrase "the collapse of official morality."[3] Apologists for the President said he was really only a scapegoat in an era of general moral deterioration and of almost hysterical acquisitiveness. The stolid military hero can be made out as the victim of forces he did not fully understand and certainly did not control—namely, the Industrial Revolution.

If Grant chose to be thoughtful on New Year's, 1876, he had worries other than his graft-ridden bureaucracy. The country since 1873 was in its greatest depression to date, with business failures in the thousands and unemployment in the millions. The whole policy of Reconstruction in the South seemed a disaster, the state governments in shambles, the blacks still oppressed, and the whites increasingly enraged. Out in the West the Indians were on the point of open revolt.

Grant could also reflect upon positive accomplishments, as he had done in his seventh State of the Union message in December. Foreign policy was comfortably uneventful. Inflation was not a concern, the budget was balanced, and the national debt was small. Americans were rapidly populating a whole continent, building an unrivaled communications system, and amassing wealth of all sorts. The public school system was the envy of the world.

In 1876 the Grants knew to their disappointment that the general would be denied a chance to repeat his electoral triumphs of

1868 and 1872. The President's unprecedented third-term ambitions were common knowledge, although he had spoken only of responding to an "imperative duty" to remain in office. In December a Democratic majority in the House had grimly resolved that any "departure from the time-honored two term custom would be unwise, unpatriotic, and fraught with peril to our free institutions."[4] Republican conventions in such key states as New York and Ohio registered a like disenchantment with another term of "Grantism."

Beyond official Washington, the beginning of 1876 was celebrated variously in cities and villages from coast to coast. Often there was a midnight torchlight parade, while Cleveland, befittingly for the capital of the oil barons, had a bonfire of twenty barrels of petroleum. People later filled the churches or filled the saloons. On New Year's Day the well-to-do gave at homes, lesser versions of the presidential reception, and pensioners, orphans, and the institutionalized poor frequently received special meals or other charitable bounties, as the newspapers reported. For unchronicled millions of Americans it was just another harsh winter day, another year of hard times.

Perhaps no city as a city brought in the holiday so enthusiastically as Philadelphia, which was preparing to play host to a huge Centennial Exhibition in honor of the Declaration of Independence and a hundred years of national progress. Midnight in the country's second largest metropolis was greeted by the sounding of the whistles, sirens, and bells of all the ships, factories, and churches around—"the most extraordinary sound ever heard," according to John Lewis, an English-born grocer from New York City.[5] He was on hand later when the mayor of Philadelphia made a patriotic speech at Independence Hall, which was brightly illuminated, as were John Wanamaker's department store and other city landmarks. Historically uniformed military companies fired salutes, and gangs of boys threw firecrackers. Marching clubs paraded the streets, some with banners reminding Congress that the Centennial still needed $1,500,000 in federal funds. The depot church was filled to overflowing with rapt followers of the celebrated revivalists Dwight L. Moody and Ira Sankey. In the morning the sober made excursions to Fairmount Park to tread the muddy paths and inspect the unfinished buildings of the great exposition.

January 3, Chicago

THESE were times when one could start a metropolitan newspaper with a few thousand dollars' capital. Impressed with the success of the New York *News* and the Philadelphia *Star* selling at a penny a copy, instead of the usual two or four cents, Melville E. Stone turned out the first regular issue of the Chicago *Daily News* this morning and confirmed a new trend in journalism. Himself a downstate preacher's son who became a city reporter at age sixteen, Stone began his enterprise with little except the help of an experienced correspondent and a loan of $5,000 from a young Englishman who insisted on the title of associate editor and the privilege of doing no work. The newspaper was only four pages at first, five columns to a page, and it was remarked for the brevity of its news items, for its flair, and for its political independence, even to the point of siding with labor on occasion. One problem for the one-cent pioneer was a shortage of pennies in Chicagoans' pockets, and Stone resorted to such promotional devices as getting merchants to price goods at 59 cents or 99 cents. When his original partners left, Stone brought in a young politician named Victor Lawson, who knew how to sell advertising and boosted the circulation to 20,000 at the end of the year. A dozen years later circulation stood at 200,000, and Stone sold out to Lawson for $350,000, having built up one of the most saucily brilliant newspapers of the Midwest.[1]

Compared to today, the newspapers of 1876 were far more numerous, far more varied in character, and far more influential on public opinion, in the absence of other media. Six hundred dailies were in existence, and ten times that number of weeklies and semiweeklies, and the increase in the numbers of newspapers continued for some time to outstrip population growth, for the press learned to make itself so popular as to be virtually universal. Towns of a few hundred people had to have their weeklies, and even frontier settlements, barely established, soon boasted their embattled editors, to the amazement of Europeans.

While the New York *Sun* achieved a record circulation of 220,000 the day after election day in 1876, there were only six daily newspapers in this period that usually had a run between 50,000 and 100,000 copies. These were, in descending order:

Daily News (New York)
Sun (New York)
Herald (Boston)
Public Ledger (Philadelphia)
New Yorker Staats-Zeitung
Times (New York)

The presence of the German-language newspaper on the list reflected the prominence of that group of immigrants and the fact that 10 percent of all newspapers were foreign language.

New York City with its more than twenty dailies was the newspaper capital. For years, first in circulation was the *Daily News*, a one-cent mass-appeal broadsheet, undistinguished by style or content and closely responsive to Tammany Hall. Sometimes surpassing it in press run, the two-cent *Sun* under the editorship of Charles A. Dana was likewise Democratic in politics but more sensational in content and keener in its editorial edge; it was a newspaperman's newspaper, in which the reporter was king in developing human-interest stories. Neither of these, however, had anything like the prestige of the *Herald,* now under James Gordon Bennett, Jr., the spoiled, erratic, heavy-drinking young man-about-town who had succeeded his famous father in 1872. With more advertising revenue than any other paper, the *Herald* was hailed here and abroad as the most news-filled of all the dailies. Moreover, Bennett liked to boast, "I make news,"[2] and he consistently spent more money than anyone to achieve sensational scoops, a couple of the greatest in 1876. With half the circulation of the others, the *Times* in this era was in between periods of great owners, but, for all its colorlessness of format and content, its fierce Republican partisanship paid off in this election year, out of all proportion seemingly. New York intellectuals preferred the *Tribune,* once Horace Greeley's organ, now under the editorship of Whitelaw Reid, who was determined to start a trend toward "independent" journalism—that is, newspapers which did not lie, conceal, or slander for sake of party. Also noteworthy was the New York *World,* much quoted, which deliberately kept its circulation at 20,000 on the conviction that such was the number of people around who mattered.

Elsewhere in the country, the Boston *Herald* and the Philadelphia *Public Ledger* rivaled the top New York papers in size. Massachusetts' Springfield *Republican* was so levelheaded and fair-minded that it led the list of little newspapers most frequently cited in other newspapers. Chicago's *Tribune* in this era was influential editorially, but it was small compared to the now-defunct *Inter Ocean*, which asserted proudly that it was "Republican in everything; independent in nothing." The biggest newspaper in the South was the staunchly Democratic Louisville *Courier-Journal*, soon to be displaced by the Atlanta *Constitution*, which changed ownership in 1876 and also this year acquired the services of a young journalist, Joel Chandler Harris, whose Uncle Remus stories became nationally famous.[3]

Most of the country's 1,400 periodicals catered to the interests of special groups, whether iron and steel producers, locomotive engineers, missionaries, librarians, stamp collectors, or various cultists. *Frank Leslie's Illustrated News* was the most popular picture magazine, with its sixteen pages weekly containing telling, often shocking woodcuts of the latest crimes and other events. *Harper's Weekly* was another, slightly more dignified miscellany that had a circulation of 160,000 and the best cartoonists, especially Thomas Nast. *Harper's Monthly* was the most successful magazine with articles of general interest, closely followed by *Scribner's*, while Boston's *Atlantic Monthly* and the *North American Review* were considered more intellectual.

The freedom enjoyed by the press here and the power it wielded never failed to impress European visitors. They found American newspapers more concerned with straight news, speedily and accurately reported, than with style, literary form, wit, or even viewpoint. An English journalist observed that Americans would put aside a newspaper representing their own politics in favor of one giving the "latest and fullest items of events."[4] Yet, by American standards of today, almost all newspapers then appeared to be aggressively partisan in their editorial politics. Most indulged in crusades of one sort of another. Many were so sensational, so relentlessly prying, and so tasteless as to bear comparison to the underground newspapers of the 1960s. The sheer numbers of newspapers a hundred years ago allowed huge diversity, imaginative reporting, and earnest argumentativeness, in pleasant contrast with today's noncompetitiveness, blandness, and nonthink.

The transatlantic cable was only ten years old in 1876, with all it meant for quick reportage. The Associated Press was now firmly a monopoly. Personal interviews were still a novelty resented by many men in public life. Evening papers were just becoming more numerous than morning ones, and the first Sunday editions were appearing. Editors were paid $25 to $50 and reporters $15 to $30 a week, but only one college, Cornell University, offered a certificate in journalism (for a liberal arts program plus work in the printing shop). So much was still in the offing before the modern newspaper came into being: the later 1870s brought the telephone, the typewriter, halftone illustrations instead of woodcuts, and full-page ads; the 1880s saw the introduction of the linotype, syndicated columns, and comics. Joseph Pulitzer was only a twenty-nine-year-old reporter in 1876, not without a role to play this year, and William Randolph Hearst was a boy of thirteen.

Journalism was more freewheeling and fun before the advent of supermechanization and commercialization. The Chicago *Daily News,* bravely launched this January 3, soon found that its news items were being stolen time after time by its chief competitor, the *Post and Mail,* owned by the McMullen brothers, Stone's former employers. Stone resorted to the ploy of printing a bogus story about a famine in Serbia. The mayor of Sovek was quoted as saying, "Er us siht la Etsll iws nel lum cmeht," translated as "The municipality cannot aid." The *Post and Mail* duly copied the quotation, which spelled backwards "the McMullens will steal this sure." Stone's rivals were virtually laughed out of business and sold out to him within two years for a mere $15,000.

January 4, Albany

GOVERNOR Samuel J. Tilden remained quietly working in his book-lined study in the executive mansion while a clerk read his voluminous annual message to the legislature at the Capitol. The sixty-one-year-old Democrat knew that his call for reduction of taxes and the state debt would find support among the senators and assemblymen, but he could not expect the Republican majorities to applaud his lengthy and somewhat gratuitous denunciation of the Grant administration. Yet he dwelled on the shame of the scandals in Washington, federal waste and mismanagement, and the evils of Reconstruction in the South. As expected, the New York *World,* its editor friendly to the Democrats, took up his call for a housecleaning under the headline TILDEN AND REFORM. Tilden promptly emerged as the leading candidate for the Democratic presidential nomination in 1876.[1]

Far from being a man of the people, Tilden was uncommonly intellectual and the richest candidate so far in history. His neighbors in New Lebanon, New York, remembered little about him except his bookishness as a youngster. He attended Yale and the College of the City of New York, but sickness forced him to prepare for the bar on his own. In his maturity a collector and connoisseur of books and art, Tilden was to leave $2,000,000 to a trust which, together with the Astor and Lennox bequests, was the basis for the establishment of the New York Public Library.

"A man of letters among men of the world," Tilden was also very much "a man of the world among men of letters."[2] For thirty years he had been a highly successful corporation lawyer and investment broker, receiving fees at one time or another from perhaps half the railroads of the Northeast.

Tilden made no effort to conceal his gilded life-style, maintaining a fashionable residence at 15 Gramercy Park in Manhattan and a mansion called Greystone in Yonkers. As governor in Albany he rented for himself another mansion at $10,000 a year, although this sum took the whole of his official salary and the state allowed him only $4,000 for rental. This house at 138 Eagle Street, purchased by the state in 1877 for $45,000 and the executive mansion ever since, was at various times labeled "the handsomest building in Albany" and "a dismal abode."[3] In any era it was a singular sight with its square, round, and octagonal towers, its wrap-around veranda, its huge portico, and its two iron greyhounds *couchant* at the gates. Tilden promptly added extensive gardens to the original property and a commodious stable for his seven carriages. The governor rode horseback daily in nearby Washington Park, affecting a tailored sealskin suit in the raw winters. Inside the mansion were a formal parlor dominated by a portrait of Tilden on an easel and a study decorated with busts of famous men, filled to the ceiling with books, and littered on every chair and table with documents and newspapers. In these and other rooms on the first floor it was easy to hold a reception for 1,500 people, as Tilden had recently done in honor of the poet John Greenleaf Whittier.

Any picture of Tilden as the dilettante quickly yields to that of the most professional of politicians. He had first made his mark in the Van Buren administration of the 1830s, and at twenty-six he was elected an assemblyman. Unlike most successful politicians of his day, Tilden did not have a military record from the Civil War. State chairman of New York's Democrats as of 1866, two years later Tilden was already being talked of as presidential material. Not much of an orator but rather a behind-the-scenes organizer, the politician was seldom seen on the platform, just as the lawyer rarely appeared in the courtroom.

A landslide victory in 1874 made Tilden governor. Once an ally of Tammany Hall, or at least at its mercy, he made political capital by taking up the prosecution of the Tweed Ring, the machine of the most notorious boss in the history of New York. Later he went after the Canal Ring, a group of upstate politicians of both parties whose mismanagement of the waterways cost the state some $30,000,000.

Many of Tilden's associates in boardrooms and at banquet tables considered the millionaire lawyer *déclassé* for being a Democrat. Tilden's blithe explanation was that as a theorist and as a friend of the masses he distrusted the Republicans as a "party of self-seekers."[4]

For all his impressive qualifications as a "reformer" and for all his driving ambition, Tilden was personally something of a "cold fish." Tall and spare, he had pinched, shallow features and the disability of one permanently paralyzed eyelid. All his life he had known ill health, suffering a stroke while governor, and because of his frailty, he had remained a bachelor. "A tired old man" was an exaggerated impression of him by a young observer in 1876,[5] for actually he was an overworker, as well as meticulous, orderly, and demanding of others. None of these traits were endearing ones, and Tilden's chief biographer concedes that he was precisely "lacking in those human qualities—kindly sympathy, good fellowship, sociability, and warm-heartedness."[6] He was "admired, not liked."[7]

Actually, two of Tilden's greatest defects of character remained to be revealed in this year of a disputed election: his secretiveness and his utter indecisiveness. Already he had nicknames aplenty— Slippery Sam or Sealskin Sammy, for example, vying with the Sage of Gramercy Park.

While Tilden's January 4 message served to make him the leading contender, from the outset of the year the politicians and press weighed the assets and liabilities of several others. The great orator Senator Thomas F. Bayard of Delaware would be the choice of the South. Governor Thomas A. Hendricks of Indiana was the darling of Western radicals. Then there was General Winfield Scott Hancock, a war hero and a man whose very name had a special ring to it in the Centennial year. Yet the tight-faced, soft-spoken New York governor had the biggest name, the most money, and his state the largest bloc of electoral votes.

January 10, Washington

TAKING the headlines from Governor Tilden, Representative James G. Blaine of Maine electrified the House with a speech opposing the grant of amnesty to ex-president of the Confederacy, Jefferson Davis, on the grounds that he was "the author, knowingly, deliberately, guilty willfully of the gigantic murders and crimes of Andersonville." The orator, warming to his subject, described the notorious Confederate prisoner of war camp as more infamous than the Spanish Inquisition or the St. Bartholomew's Day Massacre.[1] Blaine's reopening of Civil War rancors, his "waving the bloody shirt," drew stormy applause in the galleries and from his Republican colleagues, while both Northern and Southern Democrats sat in silent fury until they could reply.

The Forty-fourth Congress, sitting in its second session since December, had a Republican majority in the Senate, but the House of Representatives for the first time in sixteen years was controlled by the Democrats as a result of the sweeping national reaction against Grantism in the midterm election of 1874. The Republican Blaine had been replaced in the speakership by the Democrat Michael Kerr, and, in the nature of things, Southerners, many of them ex-Confederates, held most of the committee chairmanships—a generally distressful situation, according to a rising Republican member, James A. Garfield of Ohio. Because of Reconstruction, there were still seven black representatives and one senator, all Republicans.

James Randall of Pennsylvania, the number two Democratic leader, had introduced the Amnesty Bill, which removed office-holding liabilities for the remaining 750 ex-Confederate officers

[23]

and officials not covered by a similar act of 1872. Randall had also sponsored a bill limiting the presidential term to six years. In this election year a number of constitutional amendments were put forward relative to the electoral process, as, for example, an Iowan's proposal that the President and Vice President be elected directly by the people, without recourse to the electoral college. The House had already gone on record with its anti-third-term resolution. Further, both houses of Congress were debating the so-called Twenty-second Joint Rule of 1865, which provided that either body could reject the electoral vote of any given state, something that had been done in 1868 and 1872, when control of the Congress was not split between Republicans and Democrats.[2] The possibility of a disputed election in 1876 was in the air.

It seemed appropriate to stress national harmony in the Centennial year. Accordingly, the House had unanimously passed a resolution urging its members not to "unnecessarily disturb the patriotic concord now existing and increasing, nor wantonly revive bitter memories of the past."[3] Then Blaine made his intemperate attack on Jefferson Davis, in the guise of amending Randall's Amnesty Bill. Sheer maliciousness, presidential ambitions, and a desire to distract public attention from the scandals of the Republican administration appeared to be Blaine's motivations.

If Blaine sought to provoke countervituperation by the Democrats, he completely succeeded. The Northern leader Samuel S. "Sunset" Cox led off by questioning the intentions of "his Majesty of Maine."[4] Later the respected Southern spokesman Benjamin Hill of Georgia took up the bait. He would have done well to rest with his dignified declaration to the effect that "we came here . . . to reopen no strife," but Hill went on to denounce Reconstruction in general, to argue that if Jefferson Davis were a criminal then Grant deserved twenty years for the Whiskey Ring scandal, and to charge that the Union prison at Elmira, New York, had been fully as barbaric as Andersonville.[5] The last charge was denied by a New York Democrat, causing recriminations in the ranks of his own party, to Blaine's obvious delight. Blaine later attacked the wartime records of Cox and Hill, his nasty sneers often convulsing the galleries with laughter. Cox now referred to him as "the honorable hyena from Maine."[6] Soon the Northern press was full of atrocity stories involving the Confederacy such as had not been published in a decade, and the Amnesty Bill was dead.

Jefferson Davis, the man whose name provoked all the clamor, was currently living in New Orleans, where he pursued business ventures that involved the Mississippi Valley and occasionally brought him to England. Informed by a friend of the attacks by the "foul mouth coward" Blaine, Davis replied late in January that "is is not, however, among those who braved the hazards of battle that unrelenting vindictiveness is to be found. The brave are generous and gentle; it is the skulkers of the fight, the Blaines, who display their flag on an untented field. They made no sacrifice to prevent the separation of the States—why should they be expected to promote the confederation and good will essential to their union?"[7] Later in a public statement Davis declared he had "no claims for pardon," not having changed his convictions before, during, or after the war.[8] One absurdity in all these wranglings was evident in a letter from a colonel to the editor of the Richmond *Daily Dispatch:* "My Lord, if we can forgive Davis for what he did to us, can't you Radicals [Republicans] forgive him?"[9] One serious consequence was that Davis' home state, Kentucky, stuck by its resolution, adopted earlier, not to participate in the Philadelphia Centennial "until there shall be universal amnesty."

Jefferson Davis' dignified rejoinders did not lessen the sensation caused by Blaine's attacks, and the Maine representative thus focused attention on himself as the leading Republican presidential candidate. Nor did press investigation of his less than heroic background serve to diminish his appeal. Of fifth-generation Scotch-Irish parentage, Blaine had been born in Pennsylvania in 1830. Like Tilden, he had attended Yale briefly, but financial straits forced him to take up schoolteaching in Kentucky, where he married a fellow teacher from Maine. Down South Blaine was secessionist, low-tariff, and soft-money, but he reversed himself completely on these issues after he settled in his wife's hometown of Augusta, Maine. He took bar examinations, bought into an influential local newspaper, and became rich. Now a Republican, he went from the Maine legislature to the House of Representatives, serving there fourteen years, six of them as speaker.

Forty-six at the beginning of 1876, Blaine was physically well proportioned and had a commanding presence with his bright brown eyes, his sculpted beard, and his full head of hair just beginning to gray. He had poise and also a breezy geniality. His skills as a parliamentarian were considerable, as were his gifts as an orator, since he had mastered a youthful speech impediment.

Terms applied to Blaine by his enemies, and by many historians, include clown, boor, hypocrite, arrogance personified, consummate actor, and the greatest opportunist ever. A contemporary made this apt observation about Blaine: "There has never been a man in our history upon whom so few people looked with indifference. He was born to be loved or hated."[10]

In January, 1876, Blaine was clearly willing to fan sectional hatreds to advance his political career. Nor he did shirk from stirring up animosity between Catholics and Protestants by introuucing an amendment to the Constitution barring financial aid to sectarian schools, all the while enjoining Bible reading in the public system.[11] Willing to gain votes by deliberately antagonizing the South and the Northern city Irish, Blaine had all the courage of his demagoguery.

January 10, New York

ANOTHER speech given this day caused less sensation than Blaine's, but its implications were far more revolutionary. The improbable, almost spectral orator was the eighty-five-year-old Peter Cooper, a beloved New York figure, even if slightly comic with his billowing white hair and beard, his bifocals, and his air cushion, which he carried around to assure comfort whenever he sat down. The place was Cooper Union, the hall that was the speaker's major benefaction to his fellow citizens. The audience, which included many of this institution's students, was composed largely of working people—German cigar makers, Jewish garment cutters, Irish construction men, Italian stevedores, blacks, Poles, and hundreds of unhyphenated, ordinary Americans. The enemies that Cooper attacked in his address were the lawmakers of both major parties, Wall Street, and the "money power." These were to blame for not providing work for "the tens and hundreds of thousands in enforced idleness" and for having the effrontery to talk about jailing "tramps."[1] Extreme radicals might mutter that the millionaire Cooper did not attack capitalism itself, but nonetheless, if capitalism were to receive any jolt in the Centennial year, it would be from this man and from the mass meetings he inspired.

Cooper's listeners could ponder the nearly incredible circumstance that the old man's lifetime virtually spanned that of the Republic itself. Born in New York City in 1791, the third year of Washington's presidency, Cooper had received the barest minimum of formal schooling before going to work as an apprentice to a carriage maker. In business for himself by the time he was twenty, he at one time ran a grocery store opposite the later site of Cooper Union. Then he invested in a mill making glue, the label "glue manufacturer" sticking with him all his life. His real fortune, however, was made as an iron and steel producer, after he established a works in Canton, Maryland. Cooper's name would be in the history books just for his having designed and built the first American railroad engine, the Tom Thumb, which was about the size of a present-day handcar. Subsequently, he constructed the largest blast furnaces in the country.

Cooper's worth was just over $2,000,000, and accordingly, his endowment of Cooper Union with $900,000 during his lifetime was truly generous philanthropy. The institute was opened in 1859 to give workers what Cooper himself had been denied—a free education in the arts and sciences, especially engineering, chemistry, and practical architecture. Besides classes, Cooper Union provided New York's first free public reading room and was a unique forum for lectures and speeches of general interest, such as the one given by Cooper himself this Monday evening.

To the chagrin of his close business associates and relatives, Peter Cooper embraced political radicalism with a magnificent determination and persistence. He was one of the few illustrious Americans who befriended labor before the Civil War. Even before the depression of 1873 Cooper was moving toward the managed currency doctrines that became known as Greenbackism.

Cooper told his worker audience that they should not strike as a remedy to wage cuts and layoffs; they should "rather pity their employers than throw unnecessary difficulties in their way." He was opposed to the current eight-hour-day movement, reasoning that "for myself I have given in labor and attention to business more than twelve hours a day through a large portion of a long life." Rather than defy the wage system, Cooper argued, workers should form producers' cooperatives of their own.[2] Leftists of the day could rightly label Cooper's vision of a nation of small producers as essentially reactionary, but they overlooked the fact that Cooper was one of the few convincing critics of the economic and political aggrandizement of big corporations, the banks, and foreign bondholders. He also pointed out "the persistent class legislation of Congress since the War,"[3] at a time when only a few Marxists saw this. It is to the octogenarian's credit that the older he got, "the more radical his views became, the more passionately and intensely did he espouse them."[4] Eventually, he did not even shrink from the word "revolution," avowing that "there may at some future date be a whirlwind precipitated against the moneyed men of this country."[5]

Two months after his Cooper Union speech, Cooper was formally endorsed by the Greenback Party of New York State as a candidate for president of the United States—an alternative to a Tilden or a Blaine. Cooper did not commit himself but continued to give his lectures against the money power. At New Haven on March 31, for example, hundreds were turned away from an enthusiastic meeting addressed by the "grand old man,"[6] who once allowed that in his advanced years he had fewer aches and pains than he did as a delivery boy.

The Greenback movement was the historic convergence of the activities of three groups: intellectuals theorizing over the financial ills of the country; workers seeking an expanding economy; and farmers facing declining prices.[7] The literary advocates of a managed currency argued that instead of retiring or curtailing the wartime paper money in circulation, as "hard-money" traditionalists advocated, the government should print more greenbacks and thus become deliberately inflationist. Closely tied in was the panacea of the "interconvertible bond": holders of paper money, rather than redeem it in gold, would instead purchase government bonds paying only 3.6 percent interest. The expectation was that all interest rates would be forced down from such current levels as 12 percent.

Originally, the soft-money intellectuals found mass support primarily from the labor movement, but the depression of 1873 all but wrecked the unions. They turned elsewhere and found a ready response from farmers hurt by a long-term cycle of decreasing prices. The wholesale price index for farm products had gone from 140 in 1866 to 89 in 1876. The farmers were also raising hell about the exorbitant rates charged them by the railroads and grain elevators. Agrarian discontent found expression in the organization of the Patrons of Husbandry and the proliferation of local Granges throughout the country, especially in the Midwest. The several thousand Granges were not a political party but a pressure group. They successfully lobbied in several states to obtain controls on the middlemen in the form of legal maximum rates for the transportation and storage of grain. Such interference with free enterprise was fought desperately by the railroad and elevator companies, and their lawsuits finally reached the Supreme Court, which heard arguments in January, 1876, in the famous test case of *Munn* v. *Illinois.* Fourteen months later in a landmark decision of this era the Court held that "when private property is devoted to public use, it is subject to public regulation." It was the Grangers' great victory.[8]

Grange activities did not fully satisfy the more militant farmers, who resorted to local third parties under assorted "reform" and "antimonopoly" labels. A national conference of such soft-money groups in March, 1875, adopted the party name "Independent," but "Greenback" became the popular term. Several leading participants in this and other meetings, realizing the futility of a political party based on self-appointed reformers, set out to build grass-roots support by organizing clubs and larger constituencies pledged to the Independent Party. They were very successful in the West, where in several states conventions were held to endorse candidates for state offices and to elect delegates to a national presidential-nominating convention scheduled for May 17, 1876. The Illinois Farmers Association and the Indiana Grange came very close to endorsing the new crusade.

In some states, notably Ohio, the Democratic Party headed off the Greenback threat only by holding early conventions and running soft-money candidates. This strategy was impossible in New York where hard-money ideas dominated the Democratic organization. It was in this context that New York's Greenbackers turned to Peter Cooper for leadership. Their convention in Syracuse on March 15 denounced "the great money and corporate interests" that controlled Governor Tilden.[9]

January 16, Madrid

THERE were two minor war crises during the second Grant administration, both involving Spain and its insurrectionary colony

Cuba. The present crisis began with the notorious Dispatch Number 266 of Secretary of State Fish to Minister to Spain Caleb Cushing on November 5, saying that "the time was at hand when it may be the duty of other Governments to intervene" in the Cuban situation.[1] The tension was brought out into the open today when the Spanish foreign minister, summoned Cushing to his office and asked him point-blank, "What is the precise thing he [Fish] would wish Spain to do under the circumstances?"[2] Cushing was noncommittal, but he hastened to telegraph Washington that if the United States took unilateral action, "there will be war, and a popular though desperate one on the part of Spain." He elaborated in a letter the same day: "Many of the most thoughtful men in Spain really long for a foreign war as the only effective remedy for the domestic dissensions which now distract the country."[3]

Long before our Civil War certain Americans had cast covetous eyes on Cuba. Then the Great Cuban Insurrection of 1868 focused public attention on the threatened American business interests on the island, to say nothing of the ferociousness of the Spanish efforts to suppress the revolt. Secretary Fish in Dispatch Number 266 complained of both the barbarities and "the inability of Spain to maintain peace and order on an island lying at our door."[4]

Spain itself had been going through such revolutionary turmoil as to make resolution of its Cuban problem a secondary consideration. The past decade had seen successively the overthrow of the Bourbon dynasty, the abdication of a trial Italian king, the proclamation of a republic, the outbreak of anarchist rebellions, and the beginning of a civil war when the right-wing Carlists seized the northern provinces and proclaimed a dissident Bourbon as king.[5]

Just when the Spanish government was at its shakiest in the fall of 1873, a Spanish naval commander seized a filibustering vessel, the *Virginius*, which was illegally flying the United States flag as it headed to join the Cuban insurrectionists. The crew and passengers of the ship, Americans mostly, were taken to Santiago de Cuba, given farcical courts-martial, and then thirty of them were executed by firing squads. The *Virginius* incident produced an uproar of protest in the United States, which massed its warships at Key West and sent an ultimatum to Spain. The regime clinging to power in Madrid had no choice but to be very conciliatory, and it promptly paid an indemnity of $80,000 to the families of the victims and promised to punish those responsible, never actually doing so.

Fear that a new *Virginius* type of incident might occur was one thing that prompted Secretary Fish to adopt such a strong stance against Spain at the turn of 1876. Also, he was apprehensive that more American estates in Cuba might be seized or "embargoed." And, as he said in Dispatch Number 266, "even some new act of exceptional severity in Cuba may suddenly produce a feeling and excitement which might force events which this Government anxiously wishes to avoid."[6] While Fish worried about things that might "force events," the administration was really doing just that in asking the European powers to put pressure on Spain. Moreover, the United States Navy was mobilizing for fleet exercises at Port Royal, South Carolina, and at Key West, and Admiral John L. Worden of the European squadron had been ordered to move two ships westward to Lisbon and two back across the Atlantic "as if on your own authority and without attracting attention if possible."[7]

Acknowledging the initiative of Secretary Fish, Britain flatly declined to intervene against Spain in a note of January 25, and the other powers indicated their sympathy with the embattled nation by refusing to say or do anything. Something of a counterreaction took place among thoughtful Americans: it suddenly seemed a terrible mistake to invite European cooperation in solving a New World problem in view of the whole Monroe Doctrine.[8]

Failing to get a response abroad, Grant and Fish found almost complete apathy at home to the war crisis. Seemingly, in times of severe depression, a foreign adventure might distract the masses, but there were no Cuba protest meetings as in 1873. The press made no effort to drum up hysteria, in complete contrast with the "yellow journalism" that produced the Spanish-American War over Cuba twenty-two years later. The House of Representatives took note of the crisis only to the extent of resolving on January 19 that the State Department should reveal Dispatch Number 266 and other correspondence, and then it went determinedly back to investigating the administration's domestic scandals. The staff officers in the Navy Department expressed their vast relief that the Navy's obsolete collection of monitors would not face the suicidal prospect of fighting modern Spanish cruisers,[9] Even Minister Cushing undercut his bellicose chief Fish by independently adopting an interpretation of Number 266 as an invitation to negotiations rather than as a summons.

Most of all, Spain's conciliatory but firm attitude dissipated the tensions. At the beginning of 1875 the Bourbons had been restored in the person of Alfonso XII, and the new government rapidly brought the Carlist War to a conclusion. On February 3 the Spanish government felt strong enough to send a note to the powers rejecting Fish's accusations and characterizing the Cuban revolt as having degenerated into brigandage led by foreigners. Almost complete agreement was reached on the matter of the embargoed American plantations in Cuba on May 16, and a Calderón-Cushing protocol announced the next year provided that Americans in Cuba would not be tried by court-martial unless found with arms in their hands and even then would have the right of counsel and appeal. Meanwhile, the Cuban insurrection had been suppressed by massive force.

An interesting footnote on Spanish-American relations was the arrival of the pretender Don Carlos in New Orleans from Mexico in late June. The press was studiously indifferent to the itinerary of this reactionary prince, although Bennett and New York society did give him a dinner at Delmonico's.

The Cuban crisis in perspective was just another chapter in the story of the expansionist foreign policy of Grant and Fish being consistently frustrated by the indifference of Congress and the public. The President's fondest dream, the annexation of Santo Domingo, had been blocked by the Senate in 1869. Likewise, proposals to buy the Virgin Islands from Denmark fell on deaf ears. Although Americans for decades, officially and unofficially, had schemed to secure the building of an isthmian canal, in 1876 Ferdinand de Lesseps and French interests began active operations in Panama without provoking any reaction in the United States. Generally, the American public was too self-preoccupied and too isolationist to seek adventures in the Caribbean, or Hawaii, or Samoa, or Africa, or China, as later events of the year would show.

January 18, Mauch Chunk, Pennsylvania

MICHAEL J. DOYLE'S first mistake was to be Irish; his second, to be a coal miner; his third, to be a labor militant; and his final one, to be all these at a time of national hysteria directed against the "Molly Maguires," a reputed secret society of criminals that was being relentlessly exposed and prosecuted by the most aggressive capitalist in eastern Pennsylvania, Franklin B. Gowen. This dreary Tuesday in this grimy little mining hamlet Doyle went on trial for the murder of John P. Jones, a foreman of the Lehigh and Wilkes-Barre Coal Company.

Since the great famine of 1846 the Irish had been pouring into the United States by the hundreds of thousands, and being considered the dregs in the hierarchy of immigrants, they found themselves in the worst job situations, like coal mining. "No Irish need apply" signs regarding employment symbolized the widespread popular prejudice against the newcomers. The press was not at all loath to pander to a stereotype view that all Irish were drunks and brawlers who had no respect for any law except their own secret codes and who went from the confessional to renewed crimes with hypocritical Catholic consciences.[1]

The greatest imaginable opportunities for exploiting Irish labor existed in the coal-mining region of some 500 square miles just west of Philadelphia. It was a high-risk, get-rich-quick industry in which ownership was increasingly centralized and management increasingly concertized in dictating prices and wages. A few mineowners had mansions on the hills behind the mining towns, but most were absentees living in Rittenhouse Square or Fifth Avenue or even London's West End. Their agents, English or Welsh, took full advantage of the labor surplus, bringing in strikebreakers almost at will. Their private army authorized by the legislature, the Coal and Iron Police, broke the heads of troublemakers. The Irish mining families lived in company houses, rickety hovels with one room on the first floor and two on the second. They were completely at the mercy of their employers, being paid on a piecework basis of something like 60 cents for a carload of coal, forced to buy their own blasting power at the company's triple-value price, and obliged to get all commodities from a company store or "pluck me" (many miners were so manipulated that they never saw cash wages). Schooling for the children was out of the question, for at six they were working as slate pickers, after which they progressed to gatekeepers, mule drivers, miners, and then, perhaps, back to the trash-culling job, if they happened to live to old age. Mining accidents were frequent and ghastly, such as the 111 men and boys who suffocated at Avondale in 1869 (so as to avoid proposed safety legislation, the companies blamed the disaster on the Molly Maguires).

The first attempts at unionization of the coal miners were defeated by every foul tactic of divide and rule that the owners could devise, but in 1868 under the leadership of John Siney a Miners Benevolent Association got going and soon won the allegiance of 30,000, or 85 percent of the miners in the region. A successful strike the next year led to a promising agreement with the owners pegging wages to the price of coal. Then came the panic of 1873, which brought drastic wage reductions and layoffs. Credit at company stores was cut off at Christmastime, 1874. The "long strike" ensued between December and June, 1875. Siney opposed the strike but was arrested anyhow on conspiracy charges. After some miners tried to return to work and were blocked by the others, the militia was called out. In the end the Miners Benevolent Association was completely smashed. Subsequently, it was charged that the Molly Maguires forced the continuance of the hopeless strike, after which they resorted to a crime wave.

Since 1862 Schuylkill County did seem to have a huge number of unsolved murders, to say nothing of instances of arson and robbery. That same year the local press began talking of the mysterious Molly Maguires as responsible for the killings, and by 1864 the amount of lurid publicity persuaded the archbishop of Philadelphia to name and denounce this group in a pastoral letter. While no one agreed on the exact origin of the Mollies, it was taken for granted that they were related to secret soceieties that arose in oppressed Ireland, possibly as far back as 1562. One widely accepted legend was that a young woman of the nineteenth century named Molly Maguire, who wore giant pistols at her thighs, rode about with a gang of Irish youths disguised in women's clothes and meted out popular justice against landlords and their agents. The existence of such a Mafia-like group in the coalfields was supposedly proved by the pattern of the killings, such things as threatening letters telling people to get out of the area, ambushes on lonely roads, and the bringing in of strangers to do the dirty work (a contemporary practice of the Ku Klux Klan). The cover for the Molly Maguires was believed to be the Ancient Order of Hibernians, chartered by the state in 1874, ostensibly a fraternal organization with a network of lodges in Irish communities. That this order provided money for the defense of accused Mollies was regarded—unreasonably—as one indication of its complicity in crime. Such a degree of public paranoia developed that by 1874 the *Miner's Journal* of Pottsville could soberly aver that the Molly Maguires "commenced in Boston and now extended all over the country, controlling all the nominations of the Democratic Party in our cities and in some parts of the country."[2]

A few sane observers were willing to link the crime wave in eastern Pennsylvania with labor problems rather than with Irish lawlessness. Clearly evident now is that when the Miners Benevolent Association was at its strongest in the years after 1868, the violence greatly diminished. The chief spy for the owners admitted that there was "very little killing whilst the union stood."[3]

The man most responsible for the Molly Maguire trials, Franklin B. Gowen, boasted in an 1877 report to the stockholders of his company that he had spent $4,000,000 to save the country "from the arbitrary control of an irresponsible union" and "from the domination of an oath-bound association of murderers."[4] What if he had spent the four millions on maintaining miners' wages instead of cutting them? Even the conservative press suspected that Gowen was out to make himself dictator of the coalfields by sheer ruthlessness against the union and even other operators. The forty-year-old Gowen, half Irish but Protestant, was the son of a rich Philadelphia merchant and had attended fancy Eastern schools. After failing as a coal mine operator, he became district attorney of Schuylkill County in 1862 and gained more experience than convictions during the early crime wave. Then he went from the position of counsel for the Philadelphia and Reading Railroad Company to becoming its president in 1869, initiating a policy of combining transportation of coal with the actual ownership of coal mines. Gowen soon gained control of about one-third of the fields and embarked on complicated schemes in the industry of pressuring, pooling, and price-fixing. Bad times in 1873 made him need new triumphs to placate his stockholders. Even after crushing the Miners Benevolent Association, he was determined to break any resurgence of unionism by raising the Molly Maguire bugbear. He was well fitted to lead a self-righteous campaign. A handsome six-footer with curly brown hair, he was forceful, daring, cynical, and magnetic personally.

In the renewal of violence in Schuylkill County after the defeat of the long strike, one of the most flagrant episodes was the murder in broad daylight of the mine foreman John P. Jones on the railroad station platform at Lansford on September 3, 1875. A student told of seeing the deed committed by two gunmen, a farmer reported three strangers leaving the area, and within a day a posse had surprised and captured Michael J. Doyle, Edward Kelly, and James Kerrigan while they were picnicking in the mountains. Only a ruse by a quick-thinking sheriff saved the three from a lynching, after the Shenandoah *Herald* invited one editorially with the words "the law cannot reach this evil . . . violence is the only means."[5]

The three accused in the Jones murder asked for separate trials, and that of young Doyle began January 18. He had able lawyers for his defense, but not the battery of talent that the railroad and coal companies provided the prosecution. Two hundred witnesses gave largely circumstantial evidence linking him to the scene and weapons of the crime, and the jury readily found him guilty of murder in the first degree on February 1. Doyle's lawyers suspected not only that the prosecution had been using Kerrigan as an informer against him but also that the prosecution had been somehow privy to their plans for his defense.

The second trial at Mauch Chunk in the Jones murder, that of Edward Kelly beginning on March 27, was marked by the excitement attendant on the publicizing of Kerrigan's confession. After being kept in solitary confinement, he decided to turn state's evidence in return for clemency and made up a plausible story that he had merely pointed out the victim and acted as guide for the escaping gunmen Doyle and Kelly. The previous life of the thirty-year-old diminutive Kerrigan was a hard-luck story of abandonment at age three, no schooling, brutal years in the mines, and, currently, desperate dissipation to the neglect of his large family. In his favor was only his nickname, Powderkeg, earned after he won a place at a winter's fire by standing his ground after throwing into it a barrel of blasting powder.

The most sensational part of Kerrigan's testimony was that the Jones killing had been an exchange of favors with men of another town so as to secure the murder of Yost, a policeman who had once given Kerrigan a beating. He told of meetings in a Tamaqua saloon where the murders were plotted, always careful to show that his own cognizance of events was not accompanied by criminal acts. The culprits were identified as officials of lodges of the Ancient Order of Hibernians. "That is the order of the Molly Maguires and nothing else," he declared, to the satisfaction of the prosecution and of Gowen behind the scenes.[6]

On April 16 Kelly was sentenced to be hanged for the Jones murder after the twenty-four-year-old Irishman was found guilty by a jury of men with the names George, Everett, Koons, Deleker, Nothstein, Knoll, Serfose, Graves, Smith, Rehrig, Mechos, and Snyder. The testimony of eyewitnesses plus Kerrigan's confession made the case against him seem overwhelming, although there were a few slipups. One witness identified Kelly's brother John as the murderer.

The two convictions of alleged Molly Maguires convinced many of the existence of a widespread conspiracy. The Bethlehem Steel Company announced that it would fire any who remained members of the Hibernians, and in much-publicized incidents priests refused the sacraments to families associated with that society. Actually, Gowen was just beginning his crusade, and he had one of the star informers of all time in reserve.

January 24, Hartford

THE members of the "Monday Evening Club" sat around the lushly furnished Victorian parlor in the new and expensive house of Gingerbread Gothic and enjoyed the reading performance of their host, a shaggy-headed man of medium height with intense eyes, nervous gestures, and a nasal snarl of a voice. Mark Twain delivered himself of a piece he had just written called "The Facts Concerning the Recent Carnival of Crime in Connecticut." As his surroundings indicated, the forty-year-old author was comfortably off financially, and in a certain mood he could call himself "the busiest white man in America and much the happiest."[1] The guests were delighted with the latest creation of their local literary celebrity, which was described as "serious in intent though vastly funny and splendidly, brilliantly read."[2]

Actually, the "Carnival of Crime" was most significant for revealing the darker side of the humorist. It was one of many outward signs of his struggles with his Presbyterian conscience which achieved peculiar intensity in 1876. The story told of the author-narrator's being jolted out of his contentment by the coming of a grotesque dwarf who proceeded to remind him of shameful aspects of his past that he thought no one knew about, such as his backbiting his friends. The accused ended up killing his acuser and subsequently felt free to embark on an orgy of murder of enemies and innocents alike. This strange self-indictment of Twain's was published in the June issue of the *Atlantic Monthly* by his close friend and editor William Dean Howells, who called it a "powerful allegory."[3]

It was Howells who wrote about this time that the "Clemenses are whole-souled hosts with inextinguishable money and a palace of a house."[4] The nineteen-room mansion of brick and sandstone at 351 Farmington Avenue was a far cry from the small wooden house in Hannibal, Missouri, where Mark Twain had grown up as Samuel L. Clemens. Like Governor Tilden's newly acquired residence in Albany, the Twain house was a contemporary extravaganza of turrets, chimneys, balconies, and verandas rising high under a red tile roof—"part steamboat, part medieval stronghold, and part cuckoo clock."[5] To run such an establishment required the attentions of six servants. The interiors reflected the tastes of Mrs. Clemens, a fragile, cultivated woman from Elmira, New York, whom Mark Twain married in 1870 and worshiped for a lifetime. The style of living, the best food and drink available, proclaimed that the provincial husband had made it big. Yet he was the sort of man who, as his family grew, gave up his study to be a nursery and made do with the billiard room.

The story that first brought attention to Mark Twain as a writer was already eleven years old—"The Celebrated Jumping Frog of Calaveras County." Then, in 1869, appeared his *Innocents Abroad,* a seemingly artless combination of humor and facts garnered from Twain's excursion to Europe. Later *Roughing It* contained colorful reminiscences of his earlier trip to the Far West as a prospector, after which Twain had worked for the San Francisco *Call* and returned to the East via the Isthmus of Panama.

Twain's *Gilded Age* of 1874 (in collaboration with Charles Dudley Warner) was an essay in contemporary history that sold 120,000 copies in a few years. Although President Grant attended the successful adaptation of the book to the stage, many people found this side of Twain too irreverent, and accordingly, the directors of the Centennial avoided inviting Twain to contribute to their celebrations. In 1875 the *Atlantic Monthly* serialized his "Old Times on the Mississippi," a wonderfully humorous and nostalgic account of his early days as a steamboat pilot, and afterward the Westerner had the satisfaction of being accepted in the New England literary set. He was the highest paid of Howells' contributors at $20 a page. His great popularity as a lecturer also provided a sizable income.

Between major projects at the beginning of 1876, Twain gave himself over alternately to moody self-torturing and pessimistic assessments of the state of the country. He had just finished *Tom Sawyer* and awaited its publication with increasing frustration as one delay followed another. About this time he dashed off for the benefit of his intimate circle a wildly ribald piece called "1601 or Conversation as It Was by the Social Fireside in the Time of the Tudors."

Twain's political aberrancy as the Centennial approached had found expression in a fall article in the *Atlantic* in which he argued that the votes of men of talent should count five times those of ordinary citizens. The greed, vulgarity, and corruption that he had satirized in *The Gilded Age* deeply upset him, but he chose to blame them on the ignorance of the immigrant masses rather than on the upper class. In April, 1876, he excitedly belabored these ideas at both lunch and dinner with his friends Annie Fields and her husband, attacking "this wicked, ungodly suffrage where the vote of a man who knew nothing was as good as the vote of a man of education and industry; this endeavor to equalize what God made unequal was a wrong and a shame."[6] First, he talked of wishing the government overthrown and later of being so ashamed to be an American that he intended to go to England. Twain's current antidemocratic sentiments, so at variance with those of the radical champion of the people in later years, may be excused as the soul-searchings of a perfectionist rather than the simplistic reactions of a snob.

During another visit Annie Fields was also made privy to Mark Twain's personal turmoil. He told her that his life was "one long apology" for which he spent hours on his knees begging forgiveness. Dwelling on his Southern heritage, he characterized his past as a sorry mess of "ignorance, intolerance, egotism, self-assertion, opaque perception, dense and pitiful chuckheadedness."[7] Such confessions were at once a phase Twain was going through in 1876 and one side of his basic personality. His women friends and his wife always knew of Twain's sensitive nature, his self-doubt, and his boyish craving for approval and affection. Men might see in him only excitability, outspokenness, and a huge sense of the absurd.

The solid, respectable Howells, who was a foil to Twain's volatility and flamboyance, came to appreciate both sides of his friend's character. He wrote in *My Mark Twain:*

> His casual acquaintances might know him, perhaps, for his fierce intensity, his wild pleasure in shocking people with his ribaldness and profanities, or from the mere need of loosing his rebellious spirit in that way, as anything but exquisite, and yet that was what in the last analysis he was. . . . One could not know him well without realizing him the most serious, the most humane, the most conscientious of men.[8]

That Mark Twain was not just a funny man must have struck some of those first exposed to his "Carnival of Crime" on a cold Monday night in late January.

January 25, Washington

THE House of Representatives voted an appropriation of $1,500,000 to complete the buildings at the Philadelphia Centennial Exhibition so that it could open in solvency and on schedule on May 10. Sectional animosities and congressional parsimoniousness yielded to patriotic pride and pocketbook optimism regarding the success of the country's first and the world's sixth international fair. Philadelphia's sixty acres of display of the arts and sciences could not fail to outdo London's Crystal Palace of 1851 with nineteen acres or Paris' Exposition of 1867 with thirty-one.

Credit for the idea of a general Centennial celebration belonged equally to a world-traveling general and to a sentimental

Ohio mathematics teacher. Philadelphia was quick to assert its preeminent role in the nation's birth, and this city and the state of Pennsylvania undertook to raise $1,500,000 for a national exposition. In 1872 Congress allowed the establishment of a private Centennial corporation and authorized its board of directors to sell $10,000,000 in stock at $10 a share, this in addition to Pennsylvania's money. Congress also voted half a million for a United States building. President Grant then proclaimed the enterprise to be an international exhibition, and in 1873 Secretary Fish issued invitations to thirty-nine countries, all agreeing to participate. That European monarchies were willing so to honor the American Republic caused pleased surprise.

By the beginning of 1876 the Philadelphia fair was taking definite physical shape despite financial uncertainties. The two largest buildings were completed, but elsewhere there was a chaos of unpaved walks, unpacked boxes, and unfinished architecture. The directors bravely gave a banquet for Washington officialdom in Horticultural Hall. That the management was and remained untainted by accusations of financial skulduggery was something of a novelty for the times. The president of the board was General Joseph Hawley, honor college graduate, owner of the Hartford *Evening News*, onetime governor of Connecticut, and congressman up for reelection in the fall. It was Hawley's task to persuade Congress and President that the most magnificent exposition ever to be held needed an outright federal grant if it were to open.

One and a half million dollars, which is about two minutes' federal outlay in 1976, was even in 1876 a mere one-hundredth of the national budget, but nonetheless, in the week before January 25 numerous Congressmen rose in protest against any appropriation for the Centennial. Some considered the whole enterprise a gaudy extravaganza. Narrow constitutionalists said that such an expenditure was illegal. The government had no business subsidizing a private corporation with the people's money in depression times. The most impassioned opposition came from Southerners still smarting from Blaine's taunts during the debate on the Amnesty Bill. Many Southern states had already refused outright to participate at Philadelphia. The Virginia state legislature, for example, prodded by its governor and leading newspaper to spend $10,000 for a pavilion, voted it down. The Columbia, South Carolina, *Daily Register* throughout the year snorted about "the

Centennial of Northern Independence," explaining that "the poor enslaved South is not free, it is tied to the North by brute force."[1]

Proponents of the expenditure, largely Republicans, eventually overwhelmed the naysayers with an outburst of grandiloquence to the effect that the exhibition was exactly what was needed to dispel sectional animosities and promote national cohesion. In the words of a Kansan orator, a nation which spent "four millions a day in war can afford a million and a half once a hundred years to render civil wars impossible." It was argued further that spending by Centennial travelers, native and foreign, would stimulate the economy and that the educational benefits of the world's fair would be incalculable. Accordingly, on January 25 the Republican minority in the House was joined by enough Northern Democrats to pass the bill, 146 to 130, but only after the economy-minded had been placated by an amendment, which infuriated General Hawley, providing that the government must be fully repaid from the Centennial proceeds before the stockholders were. The bill cleared the Senate without difficulty, and President Grant promptly signed it into law on February 16 with a special quill made from the plumage of an American eagle.[2]

"Centennial mania" began to grip the country. Businessmen were eager to use Centennial themes in their advertising, promoting everything from patriotic pancakes to red, white, and blue stockings. The nationwide press started publishing a spate of readers' odes and essays on 1776, and it increasingly reported the progress at Philadelphia. Readers were informed of things in prospect for them to see, such as the arm and hand of Bartholdi's Statue of Liberty, the whole to be a gift from the French Republic. Somebody somewhere was contributing George Washington's false teeth as an exhibit, and Queen Victoria and her daughters had sent embroidery from the royal hands. The mechanics of putting on the fair received attention, such things as granting the soda-water concession for $50,000 and that for popcorn for $7,000.

General Hawley's Centennial Commission faced up to many difficulties with determined efficiency. Soda water without ice would not do, and there appeared to be a genuine threat of an ice shortage in view of the extremely mild winters on the Delaware and Hudson rivers. A whole bay full of ice was obtained from faraway Maine to assure customer comfort during the notoriously hot Philadelphia summer. The commission pressured the railroads to make their contribution to the success of the national enterprise by building additional lines and by offering attractive fares. Ticket reductions of up to 30 percent promised that travelers could come from New York for $3, from St. Louis for $18, and from San Francisco for $136. One of the greatest problems for the commission was the blindness of the United States Customs Service to the spirit of it all and their levying the usual high duties on the swelling shipments of foreign products to be displayed and sold in Philadelphia.

The commission had to deal with touchy questions of ecology and vice, deciding, for example, not to grant a peanuts concession because of litter. Likewise, smoking was to be banned on the fairgrounds to the satisfaction of religious groups, but so was the sale of religious literature. The puritans did not succeed in getting a prohibition against alcoholic beverages, although on-premises sales were restricted to weak beer and wine. The Catholic Total Temperance Union promptly announced that it would supply free ice water to Centennial visitors, and one surviving result of its determination and of contemporary taste is a structure in the form of a Greek temple from which statues of biblical and patriotic heroes look down on twenty-six drinking fountains.

The most controversial decree of General Hawley and his fellow directors was that the exhibition would be shut tight on Sundays. Whatever their real feelings about the consequent loss of attendance, they bowed to the dominant sabbatarianism of one hundred years ago. Protestant fundamentalism, ready to find expression from 10,000 pulpits, was too strong for the secularist feelings of many newspapers and the Catholic or Continental custom of Sundays-to-be-enjoyed.[3] The most violent feelings on the whole subject came from the labor press. The *Socialist* began its publishing career by editorially bemoaning the impossibility for the starving millions to benefit from the Centennial and predicting financial disaster for its promoters. With the $1,500,000 of the taxpayers' money that he won in January, General Hawley was more optimistic.

January 31, Red Cloud Agency

THE drama of the day at this Indian Bureau outpost on the desolate western edge of Nebraska was that there was no drama. The deadline passed for the roving bands of Indians to report to the Sioux reservation or be considered hostiles. Runners had been sent into the virtually uncharted Black Hills and Bighorn Mountains to serve the government's ultimatum. Chief Crazy Horse of the Oglala Sioux, located near Bear Butte, sent back a message that the bitter cold and deep snow made it impossible to move his people. Chief Sitting Bull of the Hunkpapa Sioux, whose camp was near the mouth of the Powder River, replied vaguely that he might show up during "The Moon When the Green Grass Is Up." Actually, the Indians seemed determined to fight as never before, and for its part, Washington had not really expected them to comply and was getting war plans under way.

In the post-Civil War era the Indians numbered about 270,000. Many groups were so decimated by white men's diseases as to have no will to resist the westward movement, which brought 1,000,000 settlers beyond the Mississippi in the decade after 1860 and 2,500,000 in the next decade. Some tribes had fought and lost already, like the Navaho of Arizona. Some accommodated themselves peacefully like the Pueblo of the Southeast and the Crow of Montana, who would be the Army's auxiliaries in the latter area in 1876. The remaining potential hostiles, fewer than 100,000, were the Apaches in the Southwest, the Paiute and Modoc in the Northwest, the Nez Percé in the Rockies, and the Sioux, Cheyenne, Arapaho, and Comanche on the Great Plains.

The largest tribe of the Great Plains, the Sioux, had once ranged from Arkansas to the Canadian border. The migration of whites to California and Oregon in the 1840s had the effect of pushing them north of the Platte River, and later it became policy to keep them well above the route of the Union Pacific Railroad. The crisis of the 1870s arose when the Sioux were crushed as in a vise with the frontier moving both westward from Minnesota and Dakota and eastward from Idaho and Montana.

The Sioux could have given the government a great deal of trouble during the Civil War but did not, at least until the end. In the postwar era "the Indian policy of the United States . . . vacillated between beating the Indians to death and loving them into submission."[1] The spirit of 1865 was exemplified by a general's orders to his subordinates that "you will not receive overtures of peace and submission from the Indians but will attack and kill every male Indian over twelve years old."[2] A three-pronged campaign against the Sioux, remarkably like that of 1876, ended in a fiasco, and in 1866 a Captain William J. Fetterman, who made a Custer-like boast that he could ride through any number of hostiles, was massacred with his entire command.

Advocates of a peace policy now gained ascendancy, and in 1868 the Treaty of Fort Laramie was concluded with the Sioux— the only Indian treaty whereby the United States gained nothing. Fort Laramie in easternmost Wyoming was the starting-off place for the Bozeman Trail to the Montana goldfields, which the government tried to protect with a series of forts northward. The Indians now secured the abandonment of these forts, they kept the surrounding hunting grounds as an enormous "unceded territory," and they got all of present-day South Dakota west of the Missouri River as a Sioux reservation that could not be encroached on by whites or ever alienated except by the vote of three-quarters of the male Indians. This treaty was signed by Chief Red Cloud, who was invited East to be regaled and impressed with military reviews, as well as to be exhibited like a freak to an assemblage at Cooper Union. Sitting Bull and Crazy Horse did not assent.

Genocide against the Indians was considered neither humane nor practical. "Rather it was an impulse to civilize the Indians that dominated military attitudes as it dominated public sentiment and governmental policy."[3] The hope of idealists in the Indian Bureau was to get the Indians onto reservations, preferably out of the path of white settlement, to protect them, to feed them, and to domesticate them. The Indians did not necessarily share this ideal, as Chief Gall indicated in 1868:

> We were born naked and have been taught to hunt and live on the game. You tell us that we must learn to farm, live in one house, and take on your ways. Suppose the people living beyond the great sea should come and tell you that you must stop farming and kill your cattle and take your houses and lands, what would you do? Would you not fight them?[4]

Nonetheless, thousands of Sioux did attempt to take up a peaceful existence on their reservation.

The Indian Bureau ran about sixty posts, among which the large Red Cloud Agency was supposed to supply about 12,000 Oglala Sioux, northern Cheyenne, and northern Arapaho with food, blankets, horses, and even hunting rifles. Unfortunately, in the Grant era the Indian Bureau was staffed largely with political hacks, spoilsmen, and outright swindlers. Investigations later revealed that agents on a salary of $1,500 a year were making as much as $15,000 a year by adulterating food, diverting supplies, and defrauding the Indians in other ways. It is altogether probable that if the "hostile" Sioux had left their hunting grounds and submitted in the winter of 1875–76, they would have faced dire conditions of hunger and exposure, for a little-publicized document of the government dated February 28, 1876, admitted the desperate "deficiency of supplies at the Red Cloud Agency, Nebraska."[5]

Sitting Bull had taunted the "agency Indians" in the past with the words "Look at me—see if I am poor or my people either. . . . You are fools to make yourselves slaves to a piece of fat bacon, some hard tack, and a little sugar and coffee."[6] Although their main wish was to be left alone, the roving bands were not altogether peaceful, occasionally making raids on outlying settlements and more often on pacified Indians like the Crows. Many male Sioux had it both ways, leaving their women and children to be fed at the agencies while they went off to join Sitting Bull during the summer. Often they returned to boast of their exploits, steal supplies, and abuse the Indian agents.

The sins of the savages were as nothing compared to the systematic encroachments of the white man. Gold-mining settlements in western Montana brought the population of that area to 15,000 in 1876, and their desire was accessibility from the east rather than just from the west. Such a link would be provided by the completion of the Northern Pacific Railroad, which in 1873 had reached Bismarck, Dakota Territory. The panic of 1873 delayed the completion of this line for six years, but government surveyors continued working in the Yellowstone River area, in violation of the 1868 Treaty. Colonel George Armstrong Custer's 7th Cavalry was involved in two successful skirmishes in support of the surveyors, adding to his already excessive confidence. At stake from the Indians' point of view were the last remaining good buffalo hunting lands, following a decade of insane decimation of the herds elsewhere.

A far greater threat to the Sioux than the "Iron Horse" was the gold rush of 1875 into the Black Hills, which lay in the middle of their reservation. This area was sacred to the Indians, the center of their world where among the holy mountains they could commune with their gods. Here at Bear Butte the Indians held annually a great meeting, and a recent council had decreed the death penalty to anyone who revealed the mineral wealth to be found in the area, originally conceded to the Sioux as worthless. It was Custer again who led a reconnaissance expedition into the Black Hills in 1874 and was responsible for publicity that there was "gold at the grass roots."[7] By the summer of 1875 some 800 white prospectors were in the area; by winter the invaders had grown to 15,000. President Grant ordered the Army to arrest the encroachers; but the newspapers treated the temptation as irresistible, and civil courts released men as fast as they were apprehended.

A commission was sent to buy the Black Hills, a commission typically composed of a senator, a bishop, an Army officer, and a trader. In vain they offered up to $6,000,000 (one mine alone in the area later produced $500,000,000 worth of ore). They were lucky to get away with their lives, as several thousand armed and angry Indians milled about. An envoy of Chief Crazy Horse named Little Big Man rode in, brandishing revolvers, and shouted, "I will kill the first chief who speaks of selling the Black Hills."[8]

The magic of gold was simply too strong in the calculations of American and European bankers, in the imaginings of the press, and even in the hopes of the unemployed for the Grant administration to resist the pressures. The President, who had recently insisted that the Indians be represented at the Centennial and had spoken of the advantages of civilization dictating that we be "lenient towards the Indians,"[9] now appointed a new commissioner of Indian affairs, William Smith, who, untypically for this civilian office, agreed with the Army that Indian policy should once again be to "*whip* them into subjugation."[10] On November 23, 1875, there took place in the executive offices a meeting of the President, the Indian commissioner, his boss, Secretary of the Interior Zachariah Chandler, Secretary of War William W. Belknap, and Generals Philip H. Sheridan and George Crook. Their decision was to force the Sioux away from the unceded territory and to open up the Black Hills. Their excuse for breaking the treaty was the sporadic raids of the roving bands. Chandler's ultimatum to the Sioux to report to the agencies by January 31 or be classified as hostile and their failure to do so were just part of the "scenario carefully worked out at the White House on November 23."[11]

Possibly, the roving bands did not respond to Washington's demand because they considered it just another idle threat. Possibly, they realized its implications and bravely accepted the prospect of the all-out struggle being forced on them. In the past the Indians practically never rose above their tribal rivalries, they never accorded their chiefs the authority white men thought they had, and they never pursued a strategy beyond glory, plunder, and revenge. Now they would behave differently. This winter, as if they expected the Apocalypse, the Sioux and their allies bought more guns than usual, and too late the government banned such sales on January 18, an indication that Washington's left hand did not always know what its right was doing. In any case, the uneasy truce of 1868 was over.

February 1, Washington

ONE issue enthralled the country in 1876 as none other. It was the preoccupation of boards of directors, of labor meetings, of Grange picnics, of all political conventions, of barrooms, of everyone except, perhaps, Southerners, Indians, and a few other minorities who had more pressing particular concerns. The issue was utterly bread and butter, yet utterly dull, complicated, and unexplainable except by a few economists, and even they never quite came to grips with it either then or later. The very name of the issue was formidable: the resumption of specie payments, as provided by a law of January, 1875. Opposition to the Resumption Act was immediate, continuing, and heated, pitting soft-money believers against hard-money traditionalists. One of the main reasons Kerr had been elected speaker of the House over other Democrats was that he was a hard-money man, and on this day he fulfilled his purpose by refusing even to recognize the soft-money congressman from Tennessee, John Aitken, who was trying to reopen the currency question with a resolution against resumption. Aitken and his supporters were plainly infuriated by Kerr's action or, better, inaction, and there appeared the prospect of a hopeless split in the Democratic Party as it prepared to go into the election of 1876.[1]

The United States had technically been off the gold standard since 1862. To meet the costs of fighting the Civil War, the North had issued $430,000,000 in paper money or greenbacks. About $350,000,000 of these United States notes were still in circulation in 1876. The question was how, when, and if the government would redeem them in specie—that is, gold. Distrust of paper money meant that greenbacks were quoted at less than par in the money market. In Western frontier posts, for example, Army personnel were paid in greenbacks and they received 10 percent less goods from local merchants than if they offered specie.

The Resumption Act of 1875 provided that the country would return to a strict gold standard in its international and domestic payments by January 1, 1879. It was expected that the remaining greenbacks would be absorbed by the Treasury.

The hard-money or "honest money" people who insisted on resumption were conventionally identified as Easterners, businessmen, and creditors. Class lines such as this did matter, but for many the issue was one of duty more than clear self-interest. In the words of one writer, "paper money is the ruin of all morality; specie is philosophy, morality, and religion."[2] The moral argument was buttressed by standard economic theory, such as the murky work of Professor A. L. Perry of Williams College which went into twenty editions. The rising young Republican Congressman James A. Garfield summed up the conservative case in the February, 1876, issue of the *Atlantic Monthly:* as long as there is paper money in circulation, the economy is artificial. President Andrew D. White of Cornell backed him up in addresses to Congress and the Union League Club, giving a scholarly dissertation on the evils of paper money in France during the Revolution.

Replying to Garfield and White in the April issue of the *Atlantic Monthly,* a Professor Baird reasoned that anything is money that functions like money, that the currency was the people's servant, not master, and that Britain provided an example of a judicious use of both specie and paper.[3] Nonacademic soft-money people were predominantly Westerners, smaller capitalists like farmers, and debtors. They suspected some sort of "gold conspiracy," especially after Jay Gould and other Wall Street speculators had been caught in a bald-faced attempt to corner the gold market on the famous "Black Friday" of 1869. They murmured about foreign and domestic holders of government bonds, who had bought with paper money or at a large discount, being repaid now in specie. At the other extreme a farmer who contracted a debt in greenbacks might have to pay it back at a rate equivalent of $1 instead of 80 cents, if resumption took place; this would be "rank injustice and, in many cases, ruin."[4]

Most soft-money advocates were not "inflationists," as their enemies chose to call them. There were a few genuine inflationists, people who sincerely believed that the Treasury should resort to the printing press even more than it had, and there were even a few repudiationists, extreme radicals, who would, in effect, expropriate the bondholders. Peter Cooper, for example, although a leader in soft-money circles, drew the line against such proposals, declaring, "I am as much opposed to an irredeemable currency and an inflated and irresponsible paper currency as I ever was."[5] A managed currency, instead of abrupt and heavy-handed resumption, was Cooper's solution.

Since the panic of 1873, the country had been in a deep depression, evident in the fall in railroad construction from 7,500 miles in 1872 to 1,600 in 1876. The causes of the recession historians attribute to unhealthy speculation in railroads, overexpansion of business, and the big drop in European demand for American farm products. In 1874 the Grant administration did release into circulation $26,000,000 more in greenbacks, and some soft-money advocates pointed to this way of putting money into people's hands as a method of reviving the economy. On the other hand, hard-money believers, especially the religious press, saw 1873 as God's retribution for extravagance and paper money.

At the time of the panic the Republicans had been split between hard- and soft-money factions, but the Resumption Act, a carefully worked-out compromise, had successfully reunited them. It did not take money altogether out of politics in 1876, as they hoped, for *all* Democrats were willing to make an issue of it. Conservative Easterners, like Tilden and Speaker Kerr, essentially opposed resumption on technical grounds, not principle. The radical Western Democrats feared contraction much more deeply, to the point that they would repeal the 1875 act and delay resumption indefinitely, and a few were outright inflationists. These were the lines drawn when Speaker Kerr on February 1 refused to give the floor to Aitken of Tennessee, in an effort to avoid a public acknowledgment of how badly the Democrats were split on the currency issue.

Subsequent behind-the-scenes efforts at compromise failed, and the Democrats were destined to thrash out the money question at their June convention.

To keep these matters in the context of 1876, it should be stressed that inflation was not the overriding political concern it is in the 1970s, nor did the Grant administration use the national budget or the tax system to affect economic conditions. While the Civil War had raised the national debt to $2.8 billion, every year from 1875 to 1893 the Treasury had an excess of revenue over expenditure, and this was applied to debt reduction. The financial experts at least had the sense not to curb the money supply by salting away the surplus in the vaults.

February 8, St. Louis

THE President's private secretary, General Orville E. Babcock, was put on trial for complicity in the dealings of the Whiskey Ring, a group of distillers and politicians that had defrauded the government of millions. The suspicion that official corruption reached right into the White House stunned the nation.

Far from reacting with shame or seeking to disinvolve himself, President Grant angrily denounced Babcock's detractors and "expressed his determination to go to St. Louis, to start either this evening or tomorrow" for the purpose of testifying in Babcock's behalf.[1] Secretary of State Fish led the group that succeeded in dissuading Grant from such a desperate action. Only Secretary of the Navy George Robeson, himself a blatant corruptionist, half-heartedly backed the wishes of his chief.

General Babcock was one of the Civil War careerists of whom Washington had a surfeit. He had met Grant at the siege of Vicksburg and became his chief military aide. Later, as Grant's private secretary, the congenial forty-year-old, with his pleasant blue eyes and ruddy hair, lived and dined at the White House and also at the Grants' summer house at Long Branch, New Jersey. With his desk in the reception room outside of the executive office, Babcock was in a position to screen all communications and callers seeking the President.

The picture of Babcock as the President's watchdog suggests that of Haldeman and Nixon a hundred years later. The Whiskey Ring revelations have many striking parallels with Watergate, despite the fact that they concerned graft rather than political dirty tricks. Elaborate cover-up attempts and the use of hush money are similarities that come to mind. And just as Watergate seemed but part of a dreary chain of official wrongdoing, so the Whiskey Ring was readily dubbed "ring" by a generation already numbed by the Tweed Ring, the Canal Ring, the Customs House Ring, and so forth.

The Whiskey Ring was less the creation of an evil genius than the inevitable result of the spoils system of politics, invented, perhaps, by Jacksonian Democrats but no less eagerly used by Lincoln, Grant, and the Republicans. What had begun with giving jobs to the party faithful in the Internal Revenue Department and their accepting petty graft from the distillers ended up as big business, and the pretense of aiding Republican campaigns was lost in the scramble to build private fortunes. By the 1870s the country's largest distilleries in St. Louis were shipping out three times as much spirits as they paid excise taxes on, and they used part of the annual $1,000,000 of which they defrauded the government to bribe a whole army of officials from local inspectors to the chief clerk of the Treasury Department. One widespread practice was the use of counterfeit revenue stamps. Honest distillers who complained against the competition were silenced by blackmail and harassment, as were honest bureaucrats trying to manage on their nominal official salaries.

Putting Dracula in charge of the blood bank—again a familiar phrase in 1974—might have been used a century earlier, when Grant named another general-politician, John A. McDonald, supervisor of the Internal Revenue headquarters in St. Louis. Scandal was already being rumored, and Grant's appointment drew the heated opposition of many Missouri Republicans, notably ex-Senator Carl Schurz, a German-born liberal. "I know General Grant better than any of them," said McDonald, "and I shall be appointed."[2] Thereafter McDonald did, indeed, bring the operations of the Whiskey Ring to smooth-running perfection. The master grafter saw the need of one final piece of protection against exposure, and that is why Babcock was brought into the ring, the perfect man not only to intercept warnings to Grant but also to alert St. Louis of any new investigators sent out by the

Treasury Department from Washington. Diamond stickpins and cigar boxes full of large bills to the total amount of, perhaps, $25,000 were the rewards given the President's secretary, according to later testimony by McDonald. Babcock found excuses to make several trips to St. Louis and enjoyed there the companionship of a ring-enlisted courtesan known as Sylph.

President Grant's trusting innocence in the face of his close friends' persistent and gross criminality was at once pathetic and damnable. When the chief executive visited St. Louis in 1874, he stayed at the Lindell Hotel as McDonald's guest and accepted from him a pair of fine carriage horses complete with gold-trimmed harnessing. Yet, if Grant had any real idea of what was going on, he would not have appointed a political zealot secretary of the treasury, as he did when he named Benjamin Bristow to that post in June of the same year. A Kentucky-born lawyer with a good war record and some local fame for prosecuting the Ku Klux Klan, Bristow was a dynamic hulk of a man with piercing eyes and cropped hair and beard; he was utterly honest and utterly committed to replacing the spoils system with an uncorruptible civil service.

Bristow's first investigations into organized tax evasion drew a blank since St. Louis had been mysteriously warned. Only after Bristow had devised whole new codes and hired a whole corps of secret inspectors did he gain the evidence needed to break the Whiskey Ring. The proof was overwhelming, and even Grant was moved to scrawl on the back of a letter to Bristow, "Let no guilty man escape."[3] The secretary promptly released this phrase to the press, and it had a sustained, if increasingly hollow, ring over the months ahead.

Bristow got indictments against 350 persons, including McDonald. Their trials dragged on over much of 1875, and the sustained press coverage began to dismay Republican leaders facing an election. Babcock and others around the turn of the year sought to instill suspicions in Grant's mind that Bristow was so single-mindedly seeking the presidential nomination for himself that he was willing to discredit the whole administration, that he was, in effect, trying to build up an image of himself as more of a reformer than Tilden ever thought of being. After some heated face-to-face exchanges, Grant began to acknowledge his secretary of the treasury only with scowls, but he did not dare fire him.

Nonetheless, Grant's reactions were almost foolhardy when

Bristow's investigations began to implicate Babcock. He summarily dismissed from office a former senator who had been the successful prosecutor of the chief clerk of the Treasury, and he authorized the attorney general to issue a circular depriving local district attorneys of the power to grant immunity from prosecution to individuals who turned state's evidence. The implication seen by the press was that the administration did not want any new informers testifying against the President's secretary. Existing evidence against Babcock included the "Sylph" letters, mysterious warnings sent from the White House to St. Louis under that name. Babcock temporarily gulled Grant into believing that blackmail and a woman's honor were at the base of the letters. Eventually cornered, Babcock requested a military trial as due his official status, and Grant obligingly appointed one. The civilian prosecutors refused to turn their evidence over to this tribunal, and, accordingly, Babcock found himself before a regular court in St. Louis on February 8.

Such was the atmosphere in St. Louis that Babcock's conviction appeared a certainty. Grant's personal intervention probably saved him. Thwarted in his hope to testify in person, Grant on February 12 submitted to three hours of interrogation in the executive office by the principals in the case in front of Chief Justice Morrison Waite, and the resulting deposition in favor of Babcock duly impressed the Missouri jurors, who at length found Babcock "not guilty" on February 24. McDonald and two others had already been sentenced to prison and scores of lesser fry had been fined.

Babcock's vindication was giddy but short. He spoke to cheering well-wishers outside his courtroom, and later, as champagne flowed at a reception at the Lindell Hotel, the general accepted a purse of several thousand dollars to defray the costs of his defense. A congratulatory telegram arrived from the President. Two days after Babcock returned to the White House to resume his duties, however, he was dismissed, following a long closeting with Grant. Secretary Fish and Republican reformers had expressed their dismay at the possibility of Babcock's staying on. After Grant appointed his friend inspector of lighthouses, Babcock disappeared from public view. His name received a few brief headlines several years later when his death in a storm at Cape Canaveral was reported.

February 8, Chicago

FROM Army headquarters of the Division of the Missouri General Philip A. Sheridan telegraphed General Alfred Terry in St. Paul and General George Crook in Omaha to begin preparations for a campaign against the Sioux Indians. Following the White House conference of November 23 and the expiration of the agreed-upon ultimatum to the "roving bands" January 31, the civilians in the government abdicated further responsibility. Secretary of the Interior Chandler notified Secretary Belknap down the street in Washington that "said Indians are hereby turned over to the War Department for such action on the part of the Army as you may deem proper under the circumstances."[1] Now the generals in the West laid plans for the convergence of three columns on the hostiles under Sitting Bull and Crazy Horse—a strategy that "failed spectacularly."[2] Given the state of the Army, nothing was surprising.

With Grant in the White House, the four-star rank of General of the Army fell to William Tecumseh Sherman, the hero of the Atlanta campaign, now an awesome sixty-year-old with slightly wild eyes and unruly graying hair, one of the most blunt and most cerebral of American militarists. After William Belknap became secretary of war, however, Sherman found that he often learned of War Department developments from the newspapers, and he had huffily moved his headquarters from Washington to St. Louis, where he still sulked in early 1876. The brilliant Sherman was consulted, but the civilian secretary and staff officers held the purse strings over the line commanders.[3]

Sherman's three stars and lieutenant generalcy had been inherited by Sheridan, the most effective Union cavalry leader of the war, who for fourteen years was to direct virtually all the Indian fighting from Montana to New Mexico from his Chicago headquarters. Sheridan was unpopular with many of his officers, one of whom, Crook, declared that Sheridan's "supposed genius turned his head" and "caused him to bloat his little carcass with debauchery and dissipation."[4] Brigadier General Crook, a veteran of harrying the Apache, commanded the Department of the Platte with headquarters at Omaha. The other part of Sheridan's Division of the Missouri concerned with fighting the Sioux was the Department of Dakota, based on St. Paul and headed by Briga-

dier General Terry, an able officer as well as a rich bachelor and
dilettante, whose subordinates included the flashy Colonel
George Armstrong Custer.

In a sense the power of 40,000,000 white Americans was being
thrown in 1876 against several thousand Indians. The entire Regular Army, however, outnumbered Sioux braves only about 10 to
1. Such was the prejudice against a standing army in this country
that after the Civil War the Regular Army was cut almost immediately to 50,000 and by 1876 to 25,000, at which size it stayed until
the Spanish-American War of 1898. To be exact, while Congress
had banned recruitment beyond 25,000 enlisted men, in 1876
there were actually on the rolls 2,151 officers and 26,414 others.
The authorized strength was twenty-five regiments of infantry,
ten of cavalry, five of artillery, one battalion of engineers, and various supporting units including the West Point cadets.[5]

The postwar period was known as the Regular Army's Dark
Ages, and at times its very existence was in doubt. In 1876 venerable New York Congresssman Fernando Wood proposed that the
War Department be abolished altogether since the Army "per-
forms none of the legitimate functions of our Government in
times of peace."[6] The chairman of the Senate Military Affairs
Committee this year questioned promotions or rewards to officers
for "making assault on the Indians," arguing, "Congress had not
declared war on the Indians. If the Senate will not recognize glory
in Indian warfare, there will not be any glory in Indian warfare."[7]
His counterpart in the House, Henry B. Banning of Ohio, joined
in attacking the Army mystique, as well as calling for reductions in
numbers and salaries. Following his lead, the Democratic House
on June 1, by a vote of 123 to 82, passed a bill paring the cavalry
regiments from ten to eight, the infantry from twenty-five to
twenty. Only the fact that the Senate was Republican blocked the
measure at this time. The Democrats' vendetta against the military reflected the resentment of Southerners that one-quarter of
the Army was still stationed in the ex-Confederate states in connection with Reconstruction. They accused the Grant administration of exploiting the Indian menace to keep a large standing
army for political purposes in 1876. In a couple of crucial votes
the Army's strength was left unimpaired only because Texans voted as Westerners rather than as Southerners.

To get a picture of the 1876 Army, which the press at the time
frequently satirized as something out of comic opera, it must be

[56]

remembered that its 430 companies were spread among 200 posts. In the East there were only three military installations with more than 300 soldiers apiece. Many posts had only 50 men fit for duty at any given time. The Hollywood movie version of "Fort Apache" strongly built, as well as liberally manned, fades before General Sherman's 1874 report: "Some of what are called military posts are mere collections of huts made of logs, adobes, or mere holes in the ground, and are about as much forts as prairie dog villages might be called forts."[8] The Army would have liked better, consolidated installations but was thwarted by congressional parsimony and the refusal of local politicians to part with existing facilities. Right before 1876, for example, the military wanted a fort in the heart of the lands of the Sioux, for, in the words of a general, "building posts in their country demoralizes them more than anything else except money and whiskey."[9] The Indians, again contrary to Hollywood, almost never assaulted outposts, even the most ramshackle ones.

One thing the Army had a surplus of was officer material. At the end of the Civil War there were, for example, 135 major generals. Virtually all these had temporary or brevet rank, and in the process of adjustment to postwar conditions three regular major generals survived. Others found themselves among the 75 regular colonels, of whom the high percentage of 31 were on staff duty in Washington. A colonel's pay was fixed at $3,500 in 1870, and he faced heavy out-of-pocket expenses for uniforms and transfers, as well as suffered the discount on paper money. The 445 second lieutenants received a salary of $1,400, and even this was too much for Congressman Banning, who declared in 1876 that "small salaries are best for young officers who know little of the real value of money. It teaches them to avoid extravagance and to practice economy."[10] The sluggish nature of promotion in the postwar Army meant that a second lieutenant could not expect to become a colonel for at least thirty-three years. This fact, which accounts for the number of graybeards among the junior officers that one sees in photographs of the Indian campaigns, indicated that many officers were really too old to be fit for active duty.

Referring to the enlisted men, the New York *Sun* reported in this period that "the Regular Army is composed of bummers, loafers, and foreign paupers."[11] At $13 a month for privates and with terms of five years, the ranks did contain a predominance of unskilled laborers, half of whom were foreign-born. Conditions in the service were so inhuman that only the most desperate victims of the depression turned to it, but even then recruitment never lagged. Punishments, officially banned, still included spread-eagling, confinement in a sweatbox, suspension by one's limbs, and marching with a knapsack full of bricks. Medical facilities were sadly lacking, owing to both governmental stinginess and professional incompetence. A minimum of the soldier's time was spent in training, a maximum in performing manual labor, such as building roads and forts. One result of the outrageous system was that the annual turnover among enlisted men was almost half the Army's strength; the desertion rate was an extraordinary one-third. A preponderance of inexperienced men was inevitable.

The role the maligned and neglected United States Army played between the Civil War and the Spanish-American War—enforcing Reconstruction, fighting Indians, and later suppressing strikes—made it "not so much a little army as a big police force."[12] Yet the Washington generals sounded as if a foreign enemy were their only concern. The Franco-Prussian War of 1870–71 particularly stirred the imaginations of deskbound strategists, but they accomplished no modernization beyond the introduction of fancy Prussian-type helmets with plumes. Unprepared in fact to fight a conventional war, the Army was insistently unready in theory to fight the unconventional war forced on it by the Sioux in 1876.

The first thing the Army failed to do was to achieve an element of surprise against the Sioux by waging a winter campaign, when Sitting Bull and Crazy Horse would be immobilized in their camps. General Sheridan sensed the need for this, declaring that "unless they are caught before early spring, they cannot be caught at all," but he soon resigned himself to summer operations.[13] Heavy snows were a factor in delaying the dispatch of supplies by railroad to the advance posts, but part of the problem was the usual dilatoriness and red tape in Washington that provoked one officer to exclaim that a field commander had as much control over his logistics "as a coroner in Cincinnati."[14]

A second failing was in reconnaissance and intelligence. Army headquarters at first believed the Sioux chiefs' camps to be 200 miles east of where they actually were. More fatal was the miscalculation of the number of hostiles, some scoffers estimating them as few as 75, most guesssing around 750, and a rare alarmist expecting several thousand.

Mobility was the Army's third lack in countering the elusive tactics of the Indians. A typical military expedition in the Great Plains was like a dog on a chain, "with the length of the chain irresistible, beyond it powerless," according to one officer, referring to the complete dependence on wagon trains for supplies.[15] Even cavalry ended up guarding their own transport columns more than anything else. Infantry, which had superior firepower, were particularly slow-moving.

Lacking all the prerequisites for catching the Sioux by surprise, Generals Sheridan, Terry, and Crook in their consultations after receiving orders on February 8 decided on the alternate tactic of converging on the enemy with three columns: one under Crook was to go north from Fort Fetterman in Wyoming; a second under Colonel John Gibbon was to march eastward from western Montana; and a third, Custer's 7th Cavalry mainly, was to proceed westward from Fort Abraham Lincoln, situated outside Bismarck on the western edge of Dakota. They were confident that any of the three columns was strong enough to block the Sioux trying to escape.[16] What they did not know was that the Sioux did not intend to run away.

The first column to get started was that of the dynamic, no-frills veteran Indian campaigner General Crook, who left Fort Fetterman on the North Platte River on March 1, even though the weather was 23 degrees below zero. His cavalry and infantry slogged northward in makeshift wool and fur outfits until they almost reached Montana. Indians were sighted, and Crook now made the first mistake of dividing his force and sending ahead Colonel Joseph J. Reynolds, a onetime crony of President Grant, currently in some disgrace for Army contractor scandals. Reynolds found a village of northern Cheyenne and Oglala on the Powder River and attacked it without warning. In the words of Wooden Leg, "our tepees were burned with everything in them and I had nothing left but the clothes I had on."[17] Eventually, the Indians counterattacked, and Reynolds made the second mistake of abandoning the position after destroying the large stores of ammunition, robes, and meat. This action deprived General Crook of the chance of using the village as a base, and he had to retreat ignominiously back to Fort Fetterman. The Indians were now both alerted and full of new confidence.

Meanwhile, Colonel Gibbon was moving westward with all the troops he could muster. The "Montana column" reached Fort Ellis in a blinding snowstorm on March 28. Visiting a nearby Crow camp, Gibbon was able to enlist a number of valuable scouts, and his expedition then marched down the Yellowstone River, reaching the mouth of the Bighorn April 19. There the news was received that General Crook was stalled in the south until May. As for Custer's 7th Cavalry, they had not even started their march westward—their commander was in Washington, testifying before a congressional committee investigating the scandalous administration of Indian affairs.

February 9, Boston

THE reek of the Whiskey Ring and other scandals penetrated even to Harvard Yard and to the home at 91 Marlborough Street of Henry Adams, historian, editor, and aesthete. On this quiet, snowless Wednesday night he wrote an English friend, Charles Gaiskell, about his disappointment with teaching and added:

> Politics too are miserably out of joint. Our organization has been secretly effected and is ready to act, but is in doubt what it ought to do, and although we have unquestionably the power to say that any given man shall not be President, we are not able to say that any given man shall be President. Our first scheme was to force my father on the parties. This is now abandoned, and we have descended to the more modest plan of pushing one of the regular candidates, or splitting the parties by taking one of their leaders . . . we mean to support the present Secretary of the Treasury, Bristow, for the Presidency, provided he will give us any sort of assurance that he will if necessary accept an independent nomination from us.[1]

The secret organization of Republican liberals that Adams talked about was his first essay into politics and would, indeed, affect the outcome of the election.

Of the most distinguished lineage in the United States, Henry Adams was a great-grandson of the second President, John Adams, who, simultaneously with his foe Thomas Jefferson, contrived to die on July 4, 1826, the exact half centennial of independence. His son John Quincy Adams, sixth President, lived to

1848, and in turn his son Charles Francis Adams played a not-inconsiderable role in politics. Mentioned in Henry's letter as a presidential possibility, Charles Francis had already been a Free Soil candidate for Vice President in 1848, but he had won his greatest repute as the dignified and forceful American minister to Britain during our trying relationship with that country in the Civil War years. Probably no man would have excited as much enthusiasm among progressive-minded intellectuals of both parties in 1876 as Charles Francis Adams.

The fourth-generation Adamses, Charles Francis' sons, included a second John Quincy, born in 1833, who confined himself largely to Massachusetts state politics—as a Democrat. Henry's middle brother, a second Charles Francis, born in 1835, devoted his life to business and scholarship equally, serving at different times as president of the Union Pacific Railroad and president of the American Historical Society. He was beloved by historians of this era of the "robber barons" for his ho-hum Boston Brahmin appraisal of the latter: "I have known, and known tolerably well, a good many "successful' men—'big' financially—men famous during the last half century, and a less interesting crowd I do not care to encounter."[2]

Henry, the youngest son, Boston-born (1838) and Harvard-educated like all the rest, shared his brother's sniffy attitude toward society and seemingly devoted his life to proving his delicate sensibilities and refined tastes. The year 1876 was crucial in his career for three reasons: it was his last full year of teaching; he also left the editorship of the *North American Review* under controversy; and he meddled in partisan politics for the first time—and the last.

After service as his father's private secretary in both London and Washington, in 1870 Adams chose to try the isolated life of an assistant professor of history at Harvard. For a few he must have been a very inspiring teacher, and he is credited with conducting the first true seminar. In his own words, "no text books existed, the professor refused to profess, and the students read what they pleased and compared their results. As pedagogy, nothing could be more triumphant."[3] The country's first three doctorates in history were awarded to his favorite students, who in 1876 collaborated with him in the publication of *Essays in Anglo-Saxon Law* (he described this to Gaiskell as "fearfully learned. . . . You cannot read it, and I advise you not to open it").[4] His best student and closest friend was Henry Cabot Lodge, for whom Adams in 1876 secured a teaching position, asking Charles Eliot, the president of Harvard, to allow Lodge to teach a course "rival" to Adams' own in American history, since Lodge was "federalist and conservative" while he considered himself "democratic and radical."[5]

Social life in Boston "would have starved a polar bear," Henry Adams once allowed.[6] Late in 1876 he expanded this theme to Gaiskell:

> There is no society worth the name, no wit, no intellectual energy or competition, no clash of minds or of schools, no interests, no masculine self-assertion or ambition. Everything is respectable, and nothing amusing. . . . Dr. Oliver Wendell Holmes, who does the wit for the city of three hundred thousand, is allowed to talk as he will—wild atheism commonly—and no one objects.[7]

Another time to the same correspondent he boasted: "I mean to irritate everyone to a frenzy by . . . declaring a university education to be a swindle."[8] Adams' strictures are somewhat puzzling in view of his own modest success in teaching and in view of the fact that Harvard was undergoing its greatest renaissance in two centuries under the leadership of Eliot. In any case, Adams moved back to Washington the next year and devoted himself exclusively to writing, first as a historian of the early Federal period and later as a medievalist in love with French cathedrals.

While at Harvard, Adams was chief editor of the *North American Review,* an esoteric rival of the *Atlantic Monthly* and *Harper's Monthly.* He appeared also to enjoy this work, constantly writing associate editor Lodge about it in 1876 and displaying a humorous familiarity with him (*e.g.,* "I did not steal *Review* books. I stole your books").[9] Toward the end of the year Adams and Lodge lost their editorships for printing the most trenchant of articles called "The Whiskey Ring"; their publishers apparently had vested interests in other than the truth.

It is, of course, perfectly consistent that Adams in his February 9 letter to Gaiskell gave his presidential preference to Benjamin Bristow, the giant killer of the Whiskey Ring and Babcock. Adams was no hero worshiper, however, and wrote Lodge on February 17 relative to Bristow: "We must have a man who cares nothing for party or he will betray us."[10] On the same idealistic theme he communicated on February 14 with Carl Schurz, ex-senator, a Republican who refused to support Grant in 1872, and the obvious leader of any splinter-Republican maneuverings in 1876, that "we can found a new party and are content to bring the Democrats into power as the only means of reorganizing politics. To this he added, contradicting his earlier avowal to Gaiskell, "I am willing to sacrifice my father to such an object if necessary."[11] Schurz would have his day later in the year, and so would Charles Francis Adams, while Henry Adams would give up in frustration.

February 14, Washington

FILING their papers at the Patent Office within a few hours of each other, Alexander Graham Bell and Elisha Gray each applied for a caveat in the invention of the telephone. A caveat was a document affirming that someone was on the verge of making an invention, and it was important for establishing precedence if there was litigation. The clerks happened to process Bell's application first, so that it was he who was granted the patent on March 7, four days after his twenty-ninth birthday.

"Such a coincidence has hardly happened before," Bell rather ingenuously said of his and Gray's filing the same day.[1] Fully a year earlier the inventor had written that "it is a neck and neck race between Mr. Gray and myself who shall complete our apparatus first."[2] Actually, neither man had succeeded yet in transmitting the human voice audibly.

Bell did succeed within a month, and Elisha Gray became the classic inventor's hard-luck story, as he later found out in the courts. His own partner was philosophically accurate about him when he said that "of all the men who *didn't* invent the telephone Gray was the nearest."[3] Gray's efforts, incidentally, were inspired by a current novelty, the so-called lover's telegraph, or two tin cans and a string. A sometime professor at Oberlin and sometime employee of the Western Electric Company of Chicago, Gray did well for himself anyhow, making a fortune in the millions from other inventions. The trickiness of the whole business of being first with a technological discovery is further illustrated by the fact that Germany has a statue to Philipp Reis as "inventor of the telephone."[4] He was another scientist of the same era who was on to the right principle without making it work.

Almanacs rush in to assign a particular year to inventions. In 1876, for example, we are told, accurately enough, that a cigarette-making machine came into being, and the Bissell carpet sweeper was demonstrated at the Centennial Exhibition. Also at the Philadelphia fair, allegedly, the first dynamo-powered electric lights. In fact, the principle of the dynamo and working models came years earlier, and electric lights of the modern incandescent sort had to wait until Edison in 1879. The typewriter was another case in point. E. Remington and Sons, the arms manufacturers, put their Model 1 on the market in 1876, but the invention belongs to Christopher Sholes, who made usable machines in the 1860s, and it was not until Remington Model 2, with a shift key and both capital and lower-case letters, that the invention caught on with newspaper writers and others in the early 1880s.[5]

Inventions, according to Marxists and some sociologists, come not so much because individual geniuses exist as because the times are ready for them. Bell's difficulties marketing the telephone would somewhat belie this theory.[6] Yet the public in this era was ready for almost anything, expecting one technical marvel after another. *Popular Science,* which began publishing in 1872, catered to this enchantment.

The popular preoccupation with new gadgets should not obscure contemporary achievements in pure science that demonstrated that the United States was reaching a par with countries like Britain and Germany. This year, for example, the work of the Yale professor Josiah W. Gibbs, "On the Equilibrium of Heterogeneous Substances," was a great theoretical breakthrough and established him as a father of the science of physical chemistry. Gibbs was associated with such a widespread and productive fraternity of scientists in his field that they were inspired to found the American Chemical Society on April 6, 1876.

February 16, Lynn, Massachusetts

"FIVE years old, sir" was George Brown's reply when the strapping, self-possessed young man was asked his age by A. Bronson

Alcott, the seventy-six-year-old father of Louisa May Alcott and philosopher of transcendentalism. Brown's strange answer was explained as the number of years he had known his spiritual "mother," Mary Baker Glover, whose circle Alcott was meeting for the first time at one of their "Sunday sittings at her house."[1] As the visitor from Concord described it in his diary:

> I find her followers thoughtful and devout, without cant or egotism, students of life rather than of books, and a promising company. The slightest touch of mysticism mingling with their faith renders them more interesting, and Mrs. Glover's influence appears to be of the happiest character.[2]

In meeting these people who called themselves Christian Scientists, Alcott has the rare privilege of virtually being a witness to the founding of a new religion. The year 1876 was when the denomination became formally organized, and it was also when Mrs. Glover made the personal decision that gave her the name she is remembered by—Mary Baker Eddy.

Alcott had written Mrs. Grover (*sic*) on January 17 "thanking her for her remarkable volume entitled *Science and Health,* which I have read with profound interest."[3] The philosopher's critique of her book was at variance with that of scores of clergymen, who from their pulpits and in the press were denouncing the presumption of a woman, a divorced woman at that, to meddle in theological matters. That Mrs. Glover was a "seeress of divine things" actually enhanced Alcott's respect. He found her to be "one of the fair saints" with "a faith in Spirit transcending any contemporary whom I have been fortunate to meet," and he resolved to "cultivate further acquaintance with a person of such attractions mentally and spiritually."[4]

Fifty-five when she met Alcott, Mary Baker had been born in Concord, New Hampshire, the sixth child of a family that could afford to give her an extensive and liberal education. From an early age she published poems and prose in New England journals, acquiring a literary style and a reputation as an unconventional woman. She married first a South Carolina builder, Major George Washington Glover, but was widowed within a year. For a while she taught school near Concord. Her second marriage to a dentist named Daniel Patterson ended in divorce in 1873, after he had deserted her in Lynn, Massachusetts, and she sued on grounds of adultery.

Mrs. Glover's strong religious bent had been remarked even in her childhood. At age twelve she disputed a point of theology with the local Congregational elders. Her transcending conversion did not come until thirty years later after she had fallen on an icy street in Lynn and was critically ill for three days. She had the Bible opened, and the passage of Matthew 9:2 revealed to her the secret of divine healing. From this time "the Bible was my textbook," with great new meanings for her.[5]

Four years after her crisis Mrs. Glover wrote her own textbook, a pamphlet which included her basic challenge: "In the nineteenth century I affix for all time the word Science to Christianity . . . and call upon the world to battle on this issue."[6] In 1872 she began her longer work, *Science and Health,* which finally appeared in late 1875 after many difficulties finding a publisher. George Brown and another student put up the $1,500 necessary to get slightly more than 1,000 copies produced, for Mrs. Glover was stubbornly averse to contributing a cent of her own money to the sacred undertaking. Sales were disappointing, 235 copies between November and May, 1876; 424 more by the end of the year. She bitterly blamed the publisher Kennedy for the many typographical errors which caused people to joke about her "pure teachings."[7] When the two students recovered some of their investment by keeping the proceeds of a sale of 600 remaindered copies in 1877, they were added to the increasing list of her "enemies."

The substance of Mrs. Glover's religious philosophy was the primacy of mind over matter. Her conviction led her to write such things as "we have no evidence of food sustaining life, except false evidence."[8] Her central concern was "metaphysical healing," according to Alcott, who added that "her cures have been many."[9] Anyone could perform the miracles of Christ by spiritual understanding and by reading her book. If antimatter, she was by no means antimoney, and she candidly advertised *Science and Health* as an "opportunity to acquire a profession by which you can accumulate a fortune."[10]

While no fortune came her own way, Mrs. Glover did make a comfortable living as a writer and teacher. She bought her seven-room house at 8 Broad Street in Lynn in 1875 for $5,650. Classes were held in the parlor, a conventionally decorated room with gray wallpaper, a crimson carpet, lace draperies, and black walnut furniture. Upstairs were bedrooms for herself and her students.

The attic was Mrs. Glover's seldom-seen study. Here she could retreat to her rocker, her writing table, her Bible, and her favorite framed inscription, "Thou Shalt Have No Other Gods Before Me." The floor was usually strewn with papers, but there were always fresh flowers, her one extravagance.

In the spring of 1876 Mrs. Glover had five students, eight by the end of the year. She had tried reaching larger audiences by hiring Templars Hall, but the Sunday meetings there were disrupted by Spiritualists, who, as Alcott noted, were quite antithetical in their beliefs to hers. Confining her activities to the house on Broad Street, Mrs. Glover decided to dignify her following with the name Christian Science Association, choosing July 4 to make this dispensation. In the same parlor five years later she founded the first Church of Christ, Scientist and soon after the Massachusetts Metaphysical College.

At the beginning of 1876 Mrs. Glover's foremost disciple, and some suspected her chief romantic attachment, was the thirty-three-year-old Daniel H. Spofford, whose previous career was that of farmboy, Union soldier, and shoemaker. After reading one of Mrs. Glover's works and studying with her, Spofford began practicing cures in Lynn. Such was his devotion, however, that on April 11 he agreed to work full time for the Christian Science Publishing Company, in effect becoming a door-to-door salesman of *Science and Health.* Into Spofford's lucrative practice stepped a new convert, Asa Gilbert Eddy. Another farm-reared New Englander, Eddy had been a sewing machine salesman in East Boston, until he availed himself of a cure by Mrs. Glover. Then a three-week course with her sufficed to let him hang out his shingle reading "Dr. A. G. Eddy Christian Scientist"—the first such bold sign in history, to Mrs. Glover's great satisfaction.

On July 14 Mrs. Glover had a "violent seizure," as she described it in a letter to her cousin Harriet. Dr. Eddy was called, and he immediately brought her out of it. "Never before had I seen his real character, so tender and yet so controlling," she wrote. "Hattie, you would change your views of him if you were to read him spiritually." This incident, of romantic significance, also pointed up a great paradox of Mrs. Glover's situation, that she, the faith healer, was prone to fits of hysteria, when she would scream with passion or shake with fear or fall unconscious. Her own explanation of her problem was contained in a letter of February 24 to the same cousin: "I feel the weight of sick folks terribly since my book is at work."[11] What she was saying was that her own sickness was caused by unseen people seeking help from her and taxing her strength. She believed that for a person to cast his or her ills on her by mental effort was worse than robbery.

A neighbor who had dealings with Mary Baker Glover during this spring later said of her that "she was a crank but the purest-minded woman I ever knew."[12] Before two years were out gossips could add a third marriage and murder to the list of her real and imagined unconventionalities.

Lynn, Massachusetts, was also the hometown of Lydia Pinkham, creator of an elixir for women's troubles. In May, 1876, her son, Dan Pinkham, brought several thousand handbills to New York as the beginning of a successful effort to market the product on a national scale. Although "Lydia Pinkham's Compound" contained 18 percent alcohol, it was endorsed by the Women's Christian Temperance Union.[13]

February 19, London

THE scandals of the Grant administration carried even beyond our shores into our embassies abroad. The United States minister to the Court of St. James's, General Robert C. Schenck, finally submitted his resignation, after being under fire for some time for his involvement in the shady dealings of the Emma Mine Company. Controversies had also discredited Schenck's predecessor and would soon swirl around his designated successor.

The main qualification of General Schenck for the first-ranking diplomatic post appeared to be that he was a personal friend of President Grant. He also had a fine war record and had served in Congress. Affability and dignity were assets for his new job, and two vivacious daughters in their teens helped ingratiate Schenck into London society.

Schenck would long be remembered in Britain, not for the scandal involved in his leaving, not for his considerable diplomatic attainments, and not even for giving lavish parties. His enduring contribution was introducing the game of poker to the smart set. Far from content to play and instruct at weekly late-night sessions at the American ministry, Schenck with supreme insouciance saw to the publication in 1871 of a volume written by him called *Draw Poker*. His pioneer exposition of the game included these passages:

> In the game of poker every player is for himself and against all others; and to that end will not let any of his cards be seen nor betray the value of his hand by change of countenance or any other sign. It is a great object to mystify your adversaries up to the 'call,' when hands have to be shown. To this end it is permitted to chaff or talk nonsense, with a view of misleading your adversaries as to the value of your hand without unreasonably delaying the game.
>
> To 'bluff' is take the risk of betting high enough on a poor hand, or a worthless one, to make all the other players lay down their hands without seeing or 'calling' you.[1]

It is not difficult to imagine what a sensation Schenck's opus caused in circles where playing fair and good sportsmanship were supposed to be bywords. A few British clergymen publicly protested the book.

Part of the appeal of poker was that it was a game from the American West, which was also associated with gold mines, such as the Emma Mine in Utah. Soon after coming to London, Schenck was approached by the British owners of this enterprise, who offered him 10,000 pounds' worth of stock in return for listing him on a promotional prospectus as a trustee and director of the Emma Mine. Schenck later lied to Secretary Fish when he said he paid "dollar for dollar" for the stock, for, in effect, he had received a bribe. The propriety of the American minister's lending his name and title to the company was almost immediately questioned, but Schenck explained directly to President Grant that he was acting to protect other American shareholders as well as to make some money for himself to defray the unexpectedly high private costs of the London diplomatic post. Grant replied that Schenck had the right to invest as he saw fit but recommended that he give up his managerial status in the company, advice which the minister took after some delay.

Some years later the Emma Mine foundered financially, and its victimized stockholders angrily took their grievances to the newspapers and courts on both sides of the Atlantic. Schenck's name came up frequently in witnesses' testimony. Suspicious letters by him were published. London was shocked in early February when the *Times* announced that the President's friend was being investigated by committees of both houses of Congress. Although Grant and Fish considered making a serious defense of Schenck, they were quite relieved to receive his resignation on February 19. Schenck sailed from Liverpool on March 4. While Schenck had forthrightly admitted that his usefulness in London was over, on his return to Washington he insisted on facing the House investigating committee and succeeded in clearing his name of gross misconduct. Nonetheless, he was censured for imprudence.[2]

Schenck's predecessor as minister to Britain had also left under a cloud, not because he was a speculator but because he was a historian. John Lothrop Motley was, in fact, one of America's two or three most distinguished historians, as a result of his multivolume labor *The Rise of the Dutch Republic*. His republican convictions persuaded him that it was unseemly for an American to wear traditional court costume at Queen Victoria's receptions, and his behavior caused a flurry of ill feeling. Sensing Motley's unpopularity in London, the Grant administration asked for his resignation and secured Schenck's confirmation by the Senate within forty-eight hours of nominating him. The embarrassing situation was then compounded when Motley refused to resign and had to be ordered to quit the scene. Incidentally, the problem of what to wear at court was easily solved for Schenck, who always appeared in his general's uniform.

The administration's efforts to find a successor to Motley and Schenck produced yet another disaster. Ideally, the new minister would be a man of good reputation, some private means, and no political connections. Richard H. Dana seemed to fit this bill, as the world-famous author of *Two Years Before the Mast,* a work already hailed as a classic of realism. The announcement of Dana's nomination on March 6 was greeted with enthusiasm in the London press, and Dana's fellow New England Brahmins and liberal Republicans generally were momentarily mollified by this unexpected inspiration of Grant and Fish. The choice was opposed, however, by the machine politicians, who found the author's political independence intolerable. Dana's enemies proceeded to dig up the preposterous old accusation that he had plagiarized the work of Wheaton in writing his justly admired *Elements of International Law*. A legal suit regarding this charge had been in the courts for years and would drag on for some time before Dana was exonerated. Citing all the adverse publicity, the head of the

Senate Foreign Relations Committee, Senator Simon Cameron of Pennsylvania, asked Grant to withdraw Dana's name, and when the President refused, the committee ordered Dana to appear at a hearing. After announcing that he would not answer any questions "touching his honor," Dana did submit to the senators' probing and made a thoroughly bad impression by his outspokenness. Thereafter the committee rejected the nomination, Senator Cameron offering his opinion that it was just as well that the country not be represented abroad by "one of those damned literary fellows."[3]

After two or three other men had refused the post, Attorney General Edwards Pierrepont finally agreed to fill the London vacancy, having tired of his labors in Washington prosecuting the Whiskey Ring. Ostensibly, the administration was doing the right thing by sending the highly respectable New York lawyer to London, but actually some political conspiring was involved. Into Pierrepont's post of attorney general, strategic in an election year, moved Alphonso Taft, who had briefly served as secretary of war. Into the War Department came none other than Senator Cameron's son J. Donald Cameron, whose bare forty years of age and inexperience did not matter compared to his family's importance in Pennsylvania Republican affairs. As for the new minister to Britain, Pierrepont, he arrived at Liverpool by coincidence on the Fourth of July and was immediately guest of honor at a civic luncheon. He made a speech, "signifying nothing," as he was prompt to assure Secretary Fish. His tenure in London was suitably uneventful. He was remembered for the remark that "a Minister cannot live here on less than $45,000 a year."[4]

The generous British response to the Centennial Exhibition signified the good state of Anglo-American relations. The British sent their finest artworks to Philadelphia and a rich selection of their manufactures, as well as a few mementos of their august fifty-seven-year-old ruler. Later in the year two of the most eminent British scientists would make memorable visits to the United States.

The enmities between Britain and the United States that had arisen during the Civil War were largely dissipated with the settlement of the *Alabama* claims in 1872. An international arbitration commission, in a landmark case of peaceful diplomacy, had awarded the United States a few million dollars' money damages from Britain for the depredations of British-built Confederate commerce raiders. Schenck's poker experience at bluffing, perhaps, had come into play when the United States originally demanded "indirect damages" or, in other words, asked Britain to pay the entire costs of the war, because the commerce raiders had prolonged it. New enmities would arise later when the Irish vote became more important and "twisting the British lion's tail" became popular politics. In 1876, however, about the only difficulty between the two nations was Britain's unwillingness to extradite two American forgers. President Grant, the State Department, and Congress devoted reams of paper to their frustrations, but they realized all along that the British refusals were grounded in legalisms, not obstinacy or hostility.[5]

February 22, Princeton

IN the first dated entry into his *Index Rerum,* college freshman Thomas Woodrow Wilson copied a brief newspaper item to the effect that governments took $1.4 billion each year from the people of Christendom in order to maintain standing armies. The future twenty-eighth President began this "commonplace book," largely a collection of quotations from famous men, with the aim of developing his writing style and of providing himself with ready ammunition for his literary and debating activities. Wilson also kept a diary for about half of 1876, in which he revealed himself to be more bookish than fun-minded, as well as more of a Democrat than a democrat.

Wilson's *Index* was written in shorthand, which he learned before coming to college. It begins alphabetically with "America, Burke on." He was very biased toward English statesmen and literary figures, and his long list of fiction writers under "Authors" contains scarcely an American name. The strictly reared young Presbyterian put in an entry "Bad Habits, How to break oneself of," and prescribed for himself "keep busy." Under "English Composition" Wilson wrote that it was "dreaded by teachers, hated by pupils" and that "very few pupils acquire any facility of expression until they gain it from experience outside the classroom."

Wilson's book had a minimum in it about the politics of the day. There is an entry on "English and American Officials," taken from a London newspaper, which blandly asserts that "no hint of corruption is ever brought against an English public man," whereas "the men of highest character and greatest ability in the United States" shun politics, thus abandoning the field to corruptionists. Wilson's American heroes were not contemporaries but men like Jackson, Webster, and Calhoun. These are quoted at length on the subject "Union, the," and these same passages a year later find their way into a speech Wilson made to the American Whig Society, a hundred-year-old debating club, one of two at Princeton. "Hear now the noble Webster speak," declared the young orator at one point.[1]

The American Whig Society was the very center of Wilson's existence at Princeton until he began writing for the weekly *Princetonian,* which itself just began publication in June of this year. The next winter he won second prize for his declamation on "The Ideal Statesman," telling his audience that government was too important to be left to "petty lawyers" or "narrow-minded politicians."[2] He and his fellows sharpened their intellects on such topical questions as Mormonism, Boss Tweed, the Third French Republic, and "That the Indians Should Not be Driven Out of the Black Hills."

One of the most scholarly presidents and one noted for the clarity and brilliance of his writings, Wilson indulged in unnecessary self-deprecation as a freshman. "I am nothing as far as intellect goes," he wrote in his diary, "but I can plod and work."[3] His education was essentially self-education. Wilson's formal recitations in English, French, mathematics, and Greek he treated as a distraction from his independent reading, which in 1876 included Addison, Milton, Shakespeare, Macaulay, Boswell, Goldsmith, and Dante. What he called "studying" averaged three hours a day, except in examination periods.

As the son of a minister, as a Southerner, and as a slightly built young man in frail health Wilson had his particular problems as a beginning Princetonian. His father was a Presbyterian divine of some distinction in theological circles, whose work had taken him from Staunton, Virginia, where Woodrow was born in 1856, to Georgia, South Carolina, and currently Wilmington, North Carolina. Accordingly, young Wilson had intense memories of the Civil War and Reconstruction. He was the eldest son, with two older sisters and a younger brother. In his youth he was called Tom and he signed up for debates at Princeton as "T. Wilson," but soon he let himself be persuaded by one of his sisters that his middle name, Woodrow, carried more distinction.

Wilson's mother, more loving than demanding, once voiced her concern that the fifteen-year-old was "not a favorite" among his peers.[4] He apparently constructed an elaborate fantasy world for his solace, assigning to himself and his few friends and relatives English-sounding titles of nobility and commands in a fictional navy. He even wrote a constitution for his dream kingdom. In the mature person the earlier pastimes found expression in Wilson's admiration for English institutions and his successful effort in writing a new charter for his debating society. That Wilson would one day be a senator was a confident expectation of one of his boyhood acquaintances.

At Princeton Wilson's life was circumscribed by his reading and church activities. "Loafing" is a word that guiltily creeps into his diary occasionally, but it seemed to embrace long walks and serious talks with his colleagues rather than pool halls or theaters. A Sunday might find him reading the Bible first thing, then taking in three successive sermons in different churches. When he spoke out for the first time at a prayer meeting, he was pleased at his absence of awkwardness.

"Failure in athletic sports does not detract from the excellence of the college," wrote freshman Wilson in 1876.[5] As a spectator Wilson with dogged loyalty would follow Princeton's seemingly constant defeats by the likes of Yale and Amherst. Later he would become more involved as a team manager. But on this Washington's Birthday night in his Princeton boardinghouse the young Virginian found an outlet for his talents only in making entries into his *Index Rerum*.

February 23, Liverpool

THE Cunard ship *Germanic* steamed out of port on the evening tide bound for America. Its sailing was too soon for ex-Minister Schenck to make passage. On board were Americans returning to the United States and foreign emigrants, including a twenty-nine-year-old Polish man, Henryk Sienkiewicz. Five days previously Sienkiewicz had been given a gala farewell at the Warsaw railway station by his friends and relatives, many envious that he was escaping the oppressions of Russian-ruled Poland. "I should sooner believe almost anything than that I should journey to America" was his own reaction.[1]

The nineteenth-century drama of masses of Europeans coming to the promised land is a familiar one. Sienkiewicz, however, was by no means a typical emigrant in his background, his intentions, or his subsequent career. From a family of impoverished gentry, but well educated, he was a rising young writer and a fixture of Warsaw intellectual circles, especially that of the moderately wealthy Count Chlapowski and his opera-singer wife, Madame Helene Modjeska, to whom Sienkiewicz was romantically attached. One winter's night in late 1875 at the Chlapowskis' house the talk had turned to America and the excitement of the approaching Centennial. The group was acquainted with the classic accounts of such New World critics as De Tocqueville and Dickens and also with two recent books by Polish travelers, the latter filled with romantic exaggerations particularly about California. All talked of wanting to settle in this country, and the count suddenly proposed that they found a communistic colony on the model of Brook Farm, promising to back it financially as well as to draw up its regulations. It ensued that Sienkiewicz and another were sent off in advance to find a suitable site for the utopia. His trip was paid for through an arrangement that he would write a series of articles on America for *Gazeta Polska*.

Sienkiewicz traveled in first-class luxury on the Cunard steamship, putting up with nothing more than the rough wintry weather, eccentric fellow passengers, and bad renditions of Chopin in the saloon. His first impressions of the American travelers were not good: they wore their hats to meals and read newspapers with their feet on the table. The journalist and Polish patriot in Sienkiewicz also made him acutely aware of the miserably harsh circumstances of the Poles and other emigrants in steerage below. Later he was to write a moving story about shipboard emigrants, based on his firsthand knowledge and called "In Search of Bread."

The total of 169,986 immigrants reaching this country in 1876 represented a distinct drop from the peak of 459,803 in 1873. Because of the depression, the higher figure was not matched again until 1880. In the 15 percent of the American population that was foreign-born, the largest national groups at this time were the Germans, the Irish, the Canadians, and the Scandinavians. Only a little more than 4 percent of the immigrants came from central, southern, and eastern Europe, which would include Sienkiewicz's fellow Poles. The great exodus of millions from this area did not come until the end of the century.[2]

For Sienkiewicz, arrival in New York did not mean undergoing frightening difficulties with the immigration authorities at Castle Garden but merely brazening it out with a $2 bribe to a customs official. The voyager carried a revolver, brass knuckles, and a sword cane. Apart from his hotel, which had a "magnificent lobby," Sienkiewicz found very little to like at first. "New York not only did not enthrall me," he wrote off to his Warsaw newspaper, "it disappointed me."[3] After describing the numbers of ownerless pigs roaming the streets, the Polish visitor declared,, "I have never seen a more untidy city."[4] He also decided that "American cuisine is the worst on earth."[5] Some of the big buildings and their workings inside impressed him, notably the *Herald* tower and the Post Office, and he was awed by the volume of transactions on Wall Street, which otherwise he likened to an "insane asylum."[6] He was most offended by the commercial hustle and bustle everywhere: "Business, business, business from morning to night, that is all you see, read, and hear."[7] He also found Americans as persons boorish, crude, and cocksure, reporting that men of all classes dressed badly, chewed tobacco incessantly, and whittled with penknives at everything in sight, possibly as a "screen for stupidity."[8]

If most of Sienkiewicz's broad descriptions were of a sort to produce distaste for America in his readers, his specific reports of conditions under which new immigrants lived were enough to discourage any further arrivals from Poland. He wrote of New York having the "scum of the proletariat of all nations," with people living "overcrowded in houses which are wretched and dirty beyond description" and daily facing "starvation, cold, and want" as well as "all kinds of diseases."[9] To get away from the misery of the port cities to the West, the immigrant unfortunately needed as much as or more money than the cost of his passage from Europe. There was not even much hope of joining the Army, he noted, since it was held to a maximum of 25,000 men.

Sienkiewicz himself did go West eventually, and the utopian community was duly established in California. His later experiences in 1876 caused him to change his views of America completely, with a somewhat paradoxical result: he wrote every encouragement for Poles to come here; he himself went back.

March 2, Washington

PRESIDENT GRANT was due to have his portrait painted this Thursday morning at Henry Ulke's studio near the White House, so that when he came downstairs for breakfast, he brought his overcoat with him. An early caller was Benjamin Bristow; the secretary of the treasury was the first to tell Grant that the day before in the House grave charges had been brought against Secretary of War William W. Belknap, involving his and his wife's accepting graft in the sale of Army post traderships. Getting up from breakfast, Grant encountered at the door Zachariah Chandler, secretary of the interior, and a very shaken, haggard, swollen-eyed, and almost incoherent Belknap, who therewith offered his resignation. Still intent on going to the artist's, the President did not go upstairs to his office but sent for a draft of a letter of acceptance, which he personally changed somewhat, writing upon a mantel. The President was to explain later: "I understood that he was expecting an investigation that he would avoid by resigning; that the facts, if exposed, would not damage him so much as his wife. He spoke of his dead wife too. . . . So I wrote him a letter accepting the resignation." Taking up his hat once again, Grant was detained for another fifteen minutes by two very agitated senators, Justin S. Morrill and Oliver P. Morton. Finally, Grant walked leisurely to Ulke's and sat for more than an hour, betraying no unusual emotion in his face, by the painter's later recollection. Only after receiving the full shocking details of the Belknap affair at noon did Grant show any agitation, taking off the whole afternoon to go walking with his son by the riverbank behind the White House. Whether he realized it or not, by permitting Belknap's resignation, Grant was allowing an accused criminal to escape justice.[1]

Coming just one day after General Babcock's dismissal in the aftermath of the Whiskey Ring investigations, the Belknap resignation was the most sensational scandal in the whole sordid history of the administration. Carl Schurz wrote sadly to a friend: "It is painfully apparent to every candid man that the machinery of government is fairly honey-combed with corruption. The Republic stands before the world in an attitude of unprecedented humiliation and shame."[2] Some of the press was less sober-minded. "Washington Has Written a Dime Novel,"[3] crowed the New York *Herald* after a week of fast-breaking reports of the wheeling and dealing, the triumphs and tears of Belknap and his two wives.

William W. Belknap, New York-born Princeton graduate, might have lived out his days as a lawyer in Keokuk, Iowa, but for the Civil War, which brought him to eminence as a major general serving with General Sherman in Georgia. In the course of his campaigning, Belknap also met the ravishing and vivacious Tomlinson sisters from Kentucky, and he married the elder after a brief courtship. Once again in 1870 he was lifted from the obscurity of being collector of internal revenue in Iowa to be named secretary of war. For the next six years Belknap played a major role in such administration policies as keeping federal troops in the South. Although he had the "air of an unctuous politician,"[4] Belknap was a solid, good-looking man with fine, full blond hair and beard—a suitable foil for each of his two radiantly attractive wives.

The first Mrs. Belknap figured prominently in the March, 1876, revelations because it was she who had, years before, struck up a friendship in Cincinnati with the wife-to-be of one Caleb P. Marsh. In 1870 the Belknaps found themselves summering nearby the Marshes at Long Branch, and later Mrs. Belknap, suffering a prolonged illness, stayed with them in New York. Gratitude, perhaps, impelled her one day to tell Marsh to apply for one of the post traderships on the frontier, assuring him in advance of her husband's approval and also coyly suggesting that she be given a cut of the profits. The arrangement was duly made for Marsh to have, *in absentia,* the lucrative Fort Sill tradership, and Marsh in turn sent her remittances.

Shortly thereafter Mrs. Belknap died. The husband promptly married her sister, the widowed Mrs. Bowers, who always seemed to be with the Belknap-Marsh ménage in these years. One evening the new Mrs. Belknap, with her sister's baby in her arms, dramatically confronted Marsh with her knowledge of the financial deal, and he promised to continue the remittances, sending them directly to Belknap, presumably to be held in trust for the child. The payments totaled $25,000 over six years.

It was unlikely that Amanda or "Puss" Belknap kept much money in savings accounts for her stepchild or for any other reason, in view of her predilection for expensive jewelry, fancy carriages, and party giving. The second wife was determined to be the number one hostess in Washington, and she attained her aim. She had all the dazzling beauty, insinuating charm, and fascinating cleverness for the role. The secretary thoroughly relished his wife's success.

The first vague accusations against Belknap involving Indian post traderships were made in an article in the *Herald* on February 10, an article which ended asking how much he "made in the Sioux country, starving the squaws and children."[5] The President's brother Orvil was also named as part of this "Indian Ring." Subsequently, a man named John S. Evans, who originally owned the Fort Sill tradership and was kept on to run it, got disgusted with the whole arrangement whereby he sent the profits to Marsh. He confessed, pointing the finger at Marsh, and in turn Marsh was frightened into appearing before a House committee on March 1 and telling everything. Mrs. Marsh and Mrs. Belknap apparently had had a falling out, and, in a confrontation of all of them the night before, Marsh was dissuaded by his wife from perjuring himself with an alibi that Mrs. Belknap had concocted. Mrs. Marsh's vamping at the committee hearing was so outrageous that some of the members had to look away or absent themselves.

The committee in question, the House Committee on Expenditures in the War Department, was headed by a Southern Democrat, Heister Clymer, who, incredibly, had been Belknap's roommate at Princeton. The wife of another committee member, Joseph Blackburn of Kentucky, had been a girlhood friend of Mrs. Belknap, and it came out that Mrs. Belknap had visited the Blackburns, her sister's child in her arms, and begged for their assistance the night before. Nonetheless, on the afternoon of March 2, Clymer, trembling and wretched, addressed the rapt and solemn House and, after reviewing the coincidence of Marsh's revelations and Belknap's resignation, moved that his former chum be impeached. In the brief debate Blackburn said

[79]

forcefully that no man in "exalted station" should "shelter himself from investigation by interposing the dishonor of his wife."[6]

Reactions in Washington to the Belknap scandal varied according to one's sex and politics. Representative Blaine appeared ashen over this new blow to the prospects of a Republican's winning in November. Senator Thomas F. Bayard exploded: "I cannot afford to dress my wife as these Cabinet Minister's wives are dressed."[7] The ladies of officialdom, however, rallied to Mrs. Belknap's defense, reasoning that her husband was using her, rather than vice versa. It was reported that Mrs. Belknap was prostrated with grief and fever. Mrs. Grant asked the Cabinet wives to be kind.

Three days after that dramatic Thursday Washington gossip became so strong that the Belknaps planned to flee to Belgium, a country with which we had no extradition treaty. The Marshes had already removed themselves to Canada. Accordingly, a warrant was sworn out, and Belknap was put under house arrest. The ex-secretary allegedly broke down in tears at the sight of guards outside his home at 2022 G Street, which ironically was next door to the Babcocks' house. Later, after Belknap was arraigned in police court, he was permitted to post bond, and the guards left. Mrs. Belknap began to flaunt around in her carriage again, and sympathy for her diminished.

The administration used every device of intimidation and legal maneuver to block and delay Belknap's impeachment. Charges were made against Clymer, the committee chairman, for being an ex-Confederate. The House finally did submit five articles of impeachment on April 3, and the trial began in the Senate on April 17. In the upper house all during May the most bitter debate raged over jurisdiction, whether a resigned Cabinet member could be tried and punished for crimes in office. Democratic Senator Bayard led those claiming the Senate's competence, the Republicans Morton and Conkling those denying it. Belknap himself, appearing at the hearings, was relaxed, almost carefree, and openly appreciative at the legal witticisms tossed out.

When the Senate ultimately voted that the trial should proceed, the tally indicated that the prosecution would not get the two-thirds vote necessary to convict. The final vote on August 1 was 35 against, 25 for acquitting Belknap. Of the 25 for acquittal all but 3 admitted that they considered the man guilty but balked on the issue of jurisdiction. The whole performance was *bouffe* à la Offenbach "and hardly could have been made more so 'by music and dance by all of the company' at the end."[8]

Instead of spending three years in jail and paying double indemnity to the government, his fate if convicted, William W. Belknap settled down to a comfortable law practice in the nation's capital, and he continued to support his wife's high style here and abroad. Outwardly a man of sunny disposition, he once was quoted as voicing regret that his "chivalric" resignation was taken to be an admission of real guilt on his part. Amanda Belknap occasionally dominated the social news, showing up at an inaugural ball in a particularly spectacular gown or at the beach in a particularly daring bathing suit.

March 4, Camden, New Jersey

TWO decades had passed since the publication of his *Leaves of Grass* and one since he was fired from his job in Washington by a secretary of the interior who found his poetry immoral. Centennial America tried to ignore Walt Whitman but did not succeed, largely because English admirers upheld his claim to greatness. To one of these Whitman wrote of his circumstances at age fifty-seven:

> My physical condition physically is pretty much the same—no worse at least most decidedly. I get out nearly every day, but not far and cannot walk from lameness—make much of the river here, the broad Delaware, crossing a great deal on the ferry, full of life and fun to me—get down there by our horse cars, which run along near my door—get infinite kindness, care, and assistance from the employees on these boats and cars.[1]

The poet's good spirits would be rewarded this year both personally and professionally.

Whitman had suffered a stroke in 1873, and as late as March, 1876, he wrote a friend that "my physique is entirely shattered—doubtless permanently—from paralysis and other ailments."[2] Actually, as another acquaintance noted, he had "mended decidedly"[3] of late, and by the end of the year he was chafing to make up for three years of enforced idleness.

The solitary invalid had had to lodge at his brother George's house in Camden, a factory city in New Jersey across from Philadelphia. The brother, destined to become prosperous, was insensitive to Walt Whitman's talents and needs. He paid board to his relative "just the same as at an inn" and "in the same business spirit."[4] With a yearning eye to "a pleasant little cheap lot" he had bought in 1873, he wished "to put up for myself this little 3 or 4 room house for the rest of my days, independently, in a sort. I suppose it would cost 700 or 800 dollars."[5] Lonely, he admitted that he did not experience or anticipate "pinching want,"[6] and daily existence had its pleasures like playing with his dog Tip and his baby nephew. In one letter he happily recorded a wine and dinner party "filled with animated talk," where there were only four women and "no men-critters but me."[7]

In May Whitman wrote insistent letters to the editor of the *Herald* to get him to print his "Song of the Exposition," a refurbished poem of five years earlier for which he wanted $50. His main concern, however, was the publication of a Centennial edition of his own complete works in two volumes entitled *Leaves of Grass and Two Rivulets*. This author's edition was to sell for $10. He was his "own publisher and book seller" because the New York book agents had "successively, deliberately, badly cheated me."[8] After an edition of 150 was exhausted by midsummer, he became impatient for more copies to send on approval to his overseas friends. Once he received a group subscription check for 25 pounds, including 5 pounds from Tennyson.

Since the turn of the year letters had been appearing in English newspapers chiding America for persecuting its great poet and leaving him in a condition of penury. More stung than ashamed, the American press rose to the controversy. The Springfield, Massachusetts, *Republican,* for example, attacked the "loose talk" that Whitman was a "neglected martyr" and assured world public opinion, lamely, that he was "not yet in want." Whitman himself stoked up the fire, writing to the *West Jersey Press* that, while he was not starving, he had to publish "to keep the wolf from my door."[9] More philosophically, in the same letter of March 4 in which he described his health, he admitted that "I have learned to feel *very thankful* to those who attack and abuse and pervert me—that's perhaps (besides being good fun) the only way to bring out the

[82]

splendid ardor and friendships of those, my unknown friends, my best reward."[10]

One criticism of Whitman was of his "having broken down the barriers between decency and dirtiness," the words of an American editor.[11] Aside from whatever sexual license people chose to read into Whitman, his untraditional style and ungenteel approach to poetics also offended current taste. The comfortably romantic, conventionally metered Bayard Taylor felt safe to parody Whitman in an 1876 piece. Josiah Holland of *Scribner's* wrote that Whitman was "radically wrong . . . a literary eccentric," reacting to the author's *Democratic Vistas* in which he argued that European models and surface virtuosity were no substitute for native forms and heartfelt ideas.[12]

Americans were blind to Whitman's gifts as an innovator in style and as a celebrator of democracy because, in part, they were so put off by his morals. Similarly, Edgar Allan Poe was dismissed twenty-seven years after his death as an alcoholic and dope addict. Some of Whitman's English admirers, by contrast, were more entranced with his liberated stance on sex than with his broader message. One who sent four pounds in January wrote: "Dear Friend, you have so infused yourself that it is daily more possible for men to walk hand in hand over the whole earth."[13] Bram Stoker, the author of *Dracula,* had also been moved to communicate with his far-off mentor in similar words: "How sweet a thing it is for a strong healthy man with a woman's eyes and a child's wishes to feel that he can speak so to a man who can be, if he wishes, father and brother and wife to his soul."[14]

If Whitman's male suitors in England remained at a distance, not so his greatest female admirer there, Anne Gilchrist, who translated the passion in his poetry into a need for her. The poet was the dismayed recipient of this effusion on February 25: "Soon, very soon I come, my darling . . . this is the last spring we shall be asunder. O, I passionately believe there are years in store for us. . . . Hold out a little longer for me, my Walt." His reply of March 17 said affectionately but clumsily that he did not wish her to subject herself to American "crudeness," but she was not dissuaded.[15] Shortly after writing Mrs. Gilchrist, he met the office boy at his brother's business, a youth named Harry Stafford. Shaking off his sense of ailing, he became a frequent guest at the country place of Stafford's parents.

March 8, New York

A JURY brought a verdict against "Boss" William M. Tweed in a civil suit to recover for the city $6,500,000 he had stolen. Tweed had never confessed to anything. If he had talked, half the respectable politicians of New York might have been implicated. Just months before, the *Times* had a headline COULD EVEN MR. TILDEN AFFORD TO HAVE TWEED'S STORY TOLD?[1] The verdict and the speculation were somewhat futile since Tweed had disappeared.

The Tweed Ring was the first modern city machine, and in fact, it has ever since been considered the very model of municipal corruption for the sheer grandeur and audacity of its operations. The best estimates have Tweed and his henchmen looting the city treasury of about $75,000,000 in the decade before 1871, although some historians say four times as much. In less than three years the city debt rose $50,000,000, virtually all of it for graft. As in the case of the Whiskey Ring, the Tweed Ring was more than one man's villainy. Machine politics were largely a post-Civil War development: the city had outgrown its governmental institutions; old-fashioned civic leaders were pushed aside by political and financial sharpsters; and the influx of foreign immigrants gave an opportunity for vote buying.

William Marcy Tweed, contrary to the stereotype of the social background of a "boss," was born in 1823 into a third-generation Protestant Scots family of considerable means. His father's chairmaking business did not suffice for Tweed's energies, and in his twenties he organized Fire Company Number 6 and used it as a springboard to become a city alderman. His popularity earned him a seat in the House of Representatives by the time he was thirty, but the legislator's role did not suit this natural manipulator. Back in New York, Tweed discovered the possibilities for behind-the-scenes chicanery inherent in the Board of Supervisors, a city watchdog agency established, ironically, by municipal reformers.

Typical of the way the Tweed Ring came to operate was the case of a contractor who bid $6,000 to install electrical fire alarms for the city, only to be told that he would be awarded $450,000 if he returned $225,000 of it to the grafters. The city had to buy its stationery from a Tweed-owned company at a markup of 600 percent. The most famous of the Tweed boondoggles was the County Courthouse, a building in classical style which cost New York $9,000,000, or more than what the country had recently paid for Alaska. Investigations later found such outrages in the the plastering contractor who was getting $50,000 a day by overcharging the city for his work and twice as much to repair it.[2] About a century later Mayor Abraham Beame's task force recommended that the poky little courthouse be torn down, but instead it was put on the National Register of Historic Places, a fitting memorial only to Tweed's crimes against the taxpayers.

How Tweed and his associates got away with it all is the familiar story of the patronage power of Democratic Tammany Hall, which could parade on any occasion 12,000 of the faithful in the so-called Shiny Hat Brigade. The machine made and unmade mayors, it bought judges, and it bribed both Democratic and Republican state legislators. The Tweed Ring infiltrated the police and organized crime with impartial effectiveness. It subsidized 100 newspapers with city advertising and paid off any troublesome journalists.

The mastermind of this brazen, yet complex swindling was obviously a man of unusual ability, shrewdness, and purpose. Tweed was also the soul of joviality, with a smile for everyone. With his hearty personality went an outsize physique: he was almost six feet tall and weighed 280 pounds. Craggy, ruddy, large-featured, he had small, twinking blue-gray eyes and was just beginning to get gray and bald. In sum, he "looked something like God hacked out with a dull axe."[3] Yet coarseness of manner was something Tweed turned on only to set his ordinary followers at ease: with the rich and powerful he could be suavity itself. As a public speaker he was a shambles, but his talents lay elsewhere.

Power for Tweed meant living handsomely. He had his mansion worth nearly $500,000 on the southeast corner of Fifth Avenue and Fifty-third Street, and he also had a country estate in Greenwich, Connecticut, with stables costing $122,000. His steam yacht, the *William M. Tweed,* with a liveried crew of twelve, could accommodate a small orchestra when he entertained in style. At the same time Tweed was a loving family man, an abstainer from liquor and tobacco, and a devout churchgoer. He spent his wealth as freely as he stole it, supporting numerous charities and indulging in such grand gestures as giving $50,000 in 1870 for Christ-

[85]

mas dinners for the unfortunate. This particular action was criticized by the respectable not just because it involved tainted money but because it encouraged thriftlessness in the poor.

The years 1870 and 1871 were when Tweed had everything his way in the city and when even the state Democratic organization seemed his plaything (at the party convention in Rochester Tilden not only was insulted verbally by Tweed men but had his gold watch stolen). Republicans and reformers were scandalized all along, but the boss felt immune enough to utter a much-publicized "Well, what are you going to do about it?"[4]

The cartoonist Thomas Nast and the New York *Times* shared the honors for bringing about the downfall. One of the most celebrated political cartoonists in American history and worth $20,000 a year to *Harper's Weekly,* Nast built up much of his reputation with a scathing series on the Tweed Ring. One of the most famous, called "The Tammany Tiger Loose," showed a toga-clad, smirking Tweed presiding over the slaughter of Christians in a Roman arena. Tweed tried to get Nast off his back, sending an emissary who offered the cartoonist $100,000 to go to Europe "to study art." Replied Nast: "I have decided not to go to Europe. I shall be busy here for some time getting a gang of thieves behind bars."[5] Incidentally, Nast cartoons of 1870 and 1874 were the origin of the Democratic Donkey and Republican Elephant, subsequently adopted by the major parties as their official symbols.

The long, almost private vendetta of the *Times* against Tweed became a public crusade only after the newspaper obtained incriminating financial vouchers from a disgruntled Tweed supporter. Civic-minded reformers were now joined in their anti-Tweed campaign by conservative elements, who were alarmed at the links between Tammany and "the dangerous classes" and who sought to limit the suffrage. Anti-Tammany people won the November, 1871, elections.[6] Tilden emerged as a reformer. Investigations multiplied, and scores of prominent members of the machine fled abroad.

Tweed did not flee, a point stressed by his lawyers. He was arrested in late 1871 and underwent several court trials. At one point he was declared guilty of fifty-three criminal offenses, sentenced to twelve years, and fined $12,500, only to have another court in 1875 reverse the finding and release him. He was promptly rearrested in a civil suit brought by the state and held in the Ludlow Street jail on $3,000,000 bail.

The ever-charming, ever-flush Tweed was treated in jail like an honored guest, being taken daily on a northerly carriage ride so that he could have a constitutional in Central Park and then eat his dinner at the mansion. On December 4, 1875, Tweed, in the company of his son and two wardens, came home and went upstairs to talk to his wife. When the son reported him missing, the wardens made a show of searching the house and then called the police, ten minutes or several hours after the fact, according to different interpretations of what happened. In any case, Tweed was gone, having made his escape over roofs and down a coal scuttle at the end of his block. The police offered a reward of $10,000, and people reported seeing him from North Carolina to Texas, Canada to England. Actually, the boss was across the Hudson River in a house on the Jersey Palisades, and he was still there on March 8, 1876, when the jury found against him to the extent of $6,500,000 and thus made his return to the city as a free man impossible.

March 10, Boston

ALTHOUGH his patent on the telephone had been approved in Washington three days before, Alexander Graham Bell still had not been able to make his mechanism work. He kept tinkering away at the transmitter in two garret rooms on Exeter Place he rented for $16 a month. His assistant, Thomas Watson, a skilled young mechanic, had run wires from their laboratory down a hall and through two closed doors into Bell's bedroom. Late this Friday afternoon he was adjusting the receiver when suddenly he heard it loud and clear: "Mr. Watson, please come here. I want to see you!" If the explanation is true that Bell had just spilled acid on his pants, he showed remarkable restraint of language. Watson came bounding in and exclaimed, "I can hear you. I can hear the *words*."[1]

Three countries can claim Bell, the inventor of the telephone. He was born in Scotland on March 3, 1847, and became the third generation of his family to teach speech. Having attended the University of Edinburgh, he was studying at the University of

London when he came into contact with an electrical scientist intimately connected with the invention of the telegraph and also with a philology professor who experimented with producing humanlike sounds on tuning forks. Becoming an expert in both fields, Bell had the genius to see the possibility of combining wires and sounds.

In 1870 Bell emigrated to Canada, a change of climate prescribed by a doctor for his tuberculosis. At Brantford, Ontario, he taught Mohawk Indians, using a system of "visible speech" devised by his father whereby the action of the vocal cords is indicated in written characters for each sound. He combined this work with experiments in electricity, so that now Canada claims responsibility for his great invention, having issued commemorative stamps in 1974.

Bell's reputation as a speech instructor brought him an invitation from the Boston Board of Education, and in 1872 he began teaching at the new School for the Deaf. At the same time he gave private lessons to a five-year-old deaf-mute boy, whose father, Thomas Sanders, let Bell board at his house and use his cellar for his puttering. Another acquaintance, later his wife, was a deaf-and-dumb girl named Mabel Hubbard, the daughter of an energetic lawyer with an eye to patents, Gardiner G. Hubbard.

Both Sanders and Hubbard gave Bell support in his experiments, insisting that he give priority to the musical or multiple telegraph, a device for reproducing many sounds simultaneously in which they saw real commercial possibilities. Hubbard made his prospective son-in-law promise to work on the multiple telegraph four days a week from nine to two. The inventor did so but also secretly pursued his greater interest, the telephone. Mabel Hubbard pouted that he put in too many hours at night in his laboratory and once coquettishly sent him a picture of a great white owl.

Bell had long understood the problem: "If I can get a mechanism which will make a current of electricity vary its intensity as the air varies in its density when a sound is passing through it, I can telegraph any sound, even the sound of speech."[2] By 1874 he was able to design an instrument for Watson to make. A year later, by lucky accident, Watson was hitting a reed in the malfunctioning mechanism and succeeded in producing an undulating current. The first human sounds were thereafter produced electronically, sounds that were neither clear nor strong. In September Bell wrote out the specifications for his patent—in Brantford.

All along he had been solving subproblems, as, for example, the diaphragm necessary for the transmitter. Once he tried using an ear from a corpse obtained from a doctor.

When he won the race with Gray for the patent, Bell was anything but modest, telling his father that now he was "sure of fame, fortune, and success, if I can only persevere in perfecting my apparatus."[3] Pleased for her fiancé, Mabel Hubbard foresaw difficulties. The president of Western Union was backing Gray, and he was "almost the most important man in the country and willing to spare no expense, honest or dishonest, to conquer you." She added an interesting political note in her letter of March 3: "Just now too when Belknap's iniquity, coming after all those other stories and scandals, makes us feel as if there were no justice in such a sink of corruption as Washington."[4]

Bell's persistence finally produced the moment of "Mr. Watson, please come here. I want to see you." Later the two men regretted that he had not said something more high-sounding. Scholars have found no convincing evidence for the historical thesis of Lily Tomlin that the occasion had homosexual overtones.

March 28, Washington

THIS evening President Grant complained of such blinding headaches that his physician was called. The doctor informed the press the following morning that the chief executive was suffering from "neuralgia of the brain" brought on by physical exhaustion. Capital rumor mills decided incorrectly that Grant had had a severe stroke. The headache attacks continued through the spring, and Grant made fewer public appearances, he received fewer visitors, and he left the White House more often to go for strolls. Callers found the President gray-faced and subdued, but he clung to his usual cigar and would become amiable over his whiskey.[1]

Grant's illness was news, but it caused no great alarm, despite the fact that the country did not have a vice president. The administration's first Vice President, Schuyler Colfax, had departed the scene under a cloud after his implication in the Crédit Mobilier scandal of 1873, a grandiose bit of robbery, whereby railroad directors and politicians despoiled the Treasury of millions in connection with the building of the transcontinental railroad. Grant's second Vice President, Henry Wilson, had died in office in November, 1875. By existing law, if Grant himself had died in April, 1876, he would have been succeeded by the president pro tem of the Senate, Senator Thomas Ferry. Next in line would have been Speaker Kerr, who himself died in August. A more careful system of presidential succession, with appointed vice presidents, would await almost the nation's bicentennial.

If Grant's indisposition at his time was psychosomatic, one did not have to look far for the causes. Eight years of unprecedented wrongdoing in both Washington and Wall Street had reached a crescendo this year in the Babcock, Belknap, and Schenck affairs. Grant may not have felt personally responsible, but he certainly had reason to feel betrayed. He was quoted by a newspaper earlier in the month: "I have heard it said frequently that if I had no other virtue it would not be said of me that I did not stand by my friends. But my friends must not try my forbearance too far."[2]

The Democratic House of Representatives went after the faltering administration with growing confidence and partisan determination in the crucial election year. Investigations abounded, the House concerning itself with everything from Cuban policy to Indian affairs. Rather insensitively, the House passed a resolution on April 3 questioning the legality of Grant's absences from the seat of government, whether it was to go to Long Branch in the summer or to the West in 1874. In reply, Grant felt impelled to issue a lengthy message on May 3 accusing Congress of trying to usurp the discretion of a coordinate branch of government and then reciting the absence record of all seventeen of Grant's predecessors in office.[3] Nor did even Mrs. Grant escape censure: the President was particularly incensed that his enemies tried to make out an expensive European watch given her by a general as a political rather than a personal gesture.

The *Herald* reported Grant exclaiming about two weeks after his illness' "I wish to Heaven the 4th of March 1877 was at hand."[4] This outburst about his wanting to get through his term of office was at least reassuring to those who still feared that the President might seek a third term, a possibility that was not completely discounted until May, when Grant announced his plans for a post-White House trip around the world.

As for Grant's preferences at the upcoming Republican nominating convention, he felt it improper to endorse anyone openly. Nor would he publicly disown any Republicans, although his distaste for Representative Blaine and Secretary of the Treasury Bristow were taken for granted. His most loyal supporters at the Capitol, Senators Conkling of New York and Morton of Indiana, each had reason to hope for the presidential blessing, but perversely, Grant probably favored more upright types like Secretary Fish, who did not want the honor, or Minister to France Elihu Washburne, who did. Sick, his power slipping, Grant kept most of his thoughts to himself, but so he had when he was the greatest military hero and vote getter in memory.

March 29, Washington

THE capital was overrun with self-serving generals and ex-generals during Grant's two terms, and congressmen, especially Democratic congressmen, had lost patience with them. Yet today, at the hearings of Heister Clymer's House committee, the members were visibly impressed with the star witness, George Armstrong Custer, the "boy general," the Civil War hero who had never lost a gun or flag, and was now reputedly the greatest Indian fighter in the Army.[1] At thirty-seven, Custer was awesomely handsome with long, curly blond hair, bright-blue eyes, and an intensity of expression on his windburned face. Six feet tall, weighing about 165 pounds, with broad shoulders and a lithe figure, he looked admirable in his tailored black coat, white vest, and gray trousers, but those present may have imagined him, as in the newspaper engravings, wearing a rakish black hat and gauntlets of his own design, a buckskin jacket, and the regulation striped pants and boots of the cavalryman.

Custer was in Washington not so much to glorify the Army as to disparage the War Department, not so much to preach hatred of the Sioux as to show how the Indians had been defrauded by a "ring" of post traders. The Democratic-dominated committee's aims were frankly partisan as the impeachment proceeding against Belknap got under way, and Custer obliged them on the witness stand by offering his opinion that the disgraced secretary of war had profited personally from the corrupt operations of the Fort Sill and other traderships. His direct knowledge of what went on at Fort Abraham Lincoln led him to believe that not only were the Indians the victims of short supplies but also the Army's own officers and enlisted men were being systematically cheated in their purchases. He testified that Belknap exiled or punished military personnel who complained. Finally, Custer was led on by Chairman Clymer to implicate the President's brother, Orvil Grant, telling of his coming to Bismarck and being involved in such shady dealings as the sale of stolen government goods.

Subsequently, the Republicans on Clymer's committee were able to discredit some of Custer's testimony as hearsay, even producing direct refutations of his reports about Orvil Grant in the way of communications from his commanding officer, General Terry. They characterized the constant marks of mutual admiration between Custer and the Democrats as motivated by political ambitions.

A native of Ohio, Custer had won an appointment to West Point and was graduated in 1861 when he was twenty-two, being at the bottom of his class scholastically but at the very top for physical strength, horsemanship, and marksmanship. He was sent right into the First Battle of Bull Run and thereafter distinguished himself for daring and brilliance as a cavalry leader. A general by the time he was twenty-three, he and the Michigan Brigade played an important role at Gettysburg. By the war's end he was divisional commander of the Union van, he received the Confederates' white flag at Appomattox, and he was rewarded with the table upon which Grant wrote the surrender terms.

From his temporary rank of major general of volunteers, Custer reverted in peacetime to his permanent rank of lieutenant colonel in the Regular Army. Hence he was officially "Colonel Custer," although often addressed out of respect as "General Custer." In the late 1860s he became identified in the public mind as the colorful second-in-command of the 7th Cavalry Regiment, which was transferred from the South to the frontier. He led the 7th in late 1868 in the controversial Battle of the Washita during which 103 Indians were slaughtered in the course of an hour. Civilian critics questioned why he had attacked the friendly village in the first place. It was with this action partly in mind that the liberal reformer Wendell Phillips declared in 1870: "I only know the names of three savages upon the plains—Colonel Baker, General

Custer, and at the head of all—General Sheridan." (Colonel Eugene M. Baker was responsible for another scarcely provoked massacre of 173 Indians that year.)[2]

An officer as aggressive and self-advertising as Custer inevitably had his worshipers and his detractors. He himself liked to talk of what he called "Custer's luck," which some took to be the modest reward of courage while others attributed it to his being Sheridan's pet. He was called "a supreme egotist," to which it was replied that his self-esteem was fully warranted.[3] Friendly newspapers reported that the men in the 7th admired his bravado; contrarily, a colleague declared that he was a "cold-blooded, untruthful, and unprincipled man who was universally despised by the officers of his regiment."[4]

Custer's ambition extended far beyond a frontier Army post. Right after the war, he had toyed with the idea of going to Mexico to fight for Benito Juárez against the French-supported Emperor Maximilian. A Democrat, he had made known his opposition to Reconstruction in the South, and he had accompanied President Andrew Johnson in 1866 on a train trip campaign against the Radical Republicans. At this time the youthful, good-looking war hero heard voices from crowds suggesting that he himself run for president. On several occasions later during his long service with the 7th Cavalry, Custer made speeches to his Crow scouts in which he impressed on them the possibility that he might be Great Father one day. Whatever his political dreams, Custer assiduously kept himself in the limelight. In 1874 he published a book, called *My Life on the Plains*, which went beyond reminiscence to recommendations about Indian policy.

During the winter of 1875–76 Custer was far from the frontier, indeed; he was in New York City enjoying the social whirl with his wife, Elizabeth, like himself exceptionally attractive physically and charmingly outspoken. At one luncheon in honor of the glamorous young couple Custer made a long-remembered boast that his regiment alone could whip all the Indians on the Plains at once. One of Custer's most important sponsors was James Gordon Bennett of the *Herald*. That newspaper published a hardly anonymous piece of Custer's critical of Belknap early in the year. He was also in the process of negotiating a lucrative contract to go on the lecture circuit.

Reporters caught up with the Custers on February 13 at Chicago's Palmer House, the new fashionable hotel built by merchant-prince Potter Palmer, whose fame was considerably less than that of his exotically alluring wife, recently returned from visiting her sister, Grant's daughter-in-law, in Washington. Custer had received orders to return at once to Fort Abraham Lincoln to lead one of the three columns against the Sioux. He spoke wistfully to his interviewers about his dissipated dreams of settling down to "solid comfort" in civilian life but showed enthusiasm for the task of tracking down Sitting Bull. Asked if she had qualms, Mrs. Custer replied with Army wife gallantry, "Not in the least."[5]

Custer went on to Bismarck by special train, but his military preparations there were soon interrupted by an urgent summons from Clymer that he come to Washington. In a letter to Clymer on March 16 Custer proposed to send written opinions, but the chairman insisted on a personal appearance, even if it meant postponing the expedition. In due course Custer returned to the East and took the witness stand on March 29, the day after Gibbon's column reached Fort Ellis, twelve days after Crook's defeat on the Rosebud.

One can plainly see how Custer was being used by the Democrats, but one can only speculate how Custer may have hoped to use his politician friends. During all the lionizing he received in Washington, as earlier in New York, was he encouraged to think, perhaps, that he was just one more victorious battle away from the Democratic presidential nomination?

April 2, Paris

THE second independent show of the group of French artists known as the Impressionists or Irreconcilables opened at the Durand-Ruel gallery and was promptly labeled a "disaster" by Albert Wolff, the distinguished critic of *Le Figaro*. His review continued:

> The inoffensive passer-by, attracted by the flags that decorate the façade, goes in, and a ruthless spectacle is offered to his dismayed eyes: five or six lunatics—among them a woman—a group of unfortunate creatures struck with the mania of ambition have

met there to exhibit their works. Some people burst out laughing in front of these things. . . . These self-styled artists . . . take up canvas, paint, and brush, throw on a few tones haphazardly and sign the whole thing.[1]

A pleasantly unexpected note in this familiar story of hidebound critics failing to recognize great painting was that two Americans in Paris, Henry James and Mary Cassatt, came to the exhibition and admired it thoroughly. The reaction of these two sophisticated expatriates was scarcely a true measure of the level of art appreciation among Americans and, in fact, emphasized the degree of their isolation from their fellow countrymen. Yet the state of fine arts for Americans was not so backward as might be supposed.

The 252 paintings the Impressionists exhibited at the 1876 show would, of course, later command huge prices as masterpieces of a vital new movement. The woman mentioned was Berthe Morisot, whose husband was barely dissuaded from challenging Wolff to a duel. The twenty-four Degas paintings included one done during his American visit of four years earlier, "The Cotton Exchange in New Orleans." Wolff contended that Degas' works were lacking in "certain qualities called drawing, color, execution, control" and that Renoir's faces resembled a "mass of flesh in the process of decomposition with green and violet spots."[2] Among the fifteen Renoirs was his celebrated "Dancing at the Moulin de la Galette."

Henry James in an article called "Parisian Festivity," which appeared in the New York *Tribune* on May 13, informed his readers that the new show contained "no dangerous perversities of taste" and was "decidedly interesting." The thirty-three-year-old American writer was wise enough to concede that "the effect of it is to make me think better than ever of all the good old rules which decree that beauty is beauty and ugliness ugliness." James did hedge somewhat with a comment that the group's "doctrines strike me as incompatible with the existence of a first-rate talent."[3] His article was one of a series of twenty he did about Paris for Whitelaw Reid of the *Tribune*. James had no doubt about his own talent, and when the editor complained that the articles were possibly too polished and urbane, he replied, "If my letters are 'too good' I am honestly afraid they are the poorest I can do, especially for a newspaper!"[4]

This year Henry James was twitted by his brother for looking down on Americans back home "from your gilded and snobbish heights." The slightly older William James, later famous as philosopher of pragmatism, was currently an assistant professor of physiology at Harvard at $1,200 a year and had just improvised a new laboratory for Psycho-Physics, which would be a landmark in the development of experimental psychology. In the friendly letters he exchanged with Henry abroad, William put his finger on his brother's problem when he warned him not to let "your style become too Parisian and lose your hold on the pulse of the great American public to which after all you must pander for support."[5] Henry James' difficulty would always be that he was too refined, too cosmopolitan. In June the *Atlantic Monthly* began serializing his novel *The American*, in which the straightforward rich Westerner Christopher Newman is bested in his encounter with effete, corrupt French society. Such a plot was not likely to please many patriotic Americans, and moreover, James "committed perhaps the greatest sin" in writing about "people who do not have to work."[6] Although hailed at twenty-two as a master of short stories, James had not achieved success or contentment as a writer working in either Boston or New York. Paris also failed to satisfy him. "The longer I live in France," he wrote William, "the better I like the French personally but the more convinced I am of their bottomless superficiality."[7] He moved to London in the fall.

James' fellow exile Mary Cassatt had a far profounder experience with the French Impressionists and would remain in Paris forever. The daughter of a rich family from Allegheny City, a fashionable suburb of Philadelphia, she was allowed to dabble in painting at the Pennsylvania Academy of Fine Arts, but her family was shocked when she insisted on studying in Paris and treating art as her profession. One of her paintings was accepted by the Salon of 1872, the year she turned twenty-eight. Then she saw a Degas drawing in a window: "It changed my life. I saw art then as I wanted to see it."[8] Her new perceptions appeared in a portrait of her sister that the Salon of 1875 rejected as too light-toned and atmospheric. It was slight satisfaction but instructive that the Salon of 1876 accepted the same canvas redone with an acceptably darker palette. The Impressionists' show this year hastened her emancipation, and a new rejection by the salon in 1877 and her meeting an admiring Degas completed the process. She never bothered with the salon again and exhibited with the Impressionists, beginning with their most crucial show of 1879. In her own words, "finally I could work with absolute independence without concern for the eventual opinion of a jury. . . . I detested conventional art. I began to live."[9]

Mary Cassatt's conversion to modernism in art in 1876 and 1877 was entirely unchronicled as far as America was concerned then, nor was there even awareness in this country after she established her place as a minor master in the Parisian art market in the 1880s with such paintings as "Mother and Child." At the very end of the century, when she returned to the United States for the first time since 1874, the Philadelphia *Ledger* had only this to say: "Mary Cassatt, sister of Mr. Cassatt, president of the Pennsylvania Railroad, returned from Europe yesterday. She had been studying painting in France and owns the smallest Pekinese dog in the world."[10] Aside from her own stature as a painter, Mary Cassatt did eventually have a great impact on art in this country as the encourager of purchases of French Impressionists by rich Americans like the Havemeyers and Mrs. Potter Palmer.

Mary Cassatt was not the only expatriate American artist in 1876 to win a later reputation. In London James Abbott McNeill Whistler was at the top of his career, starting work on his sensational Peacock Room about September 11. The twenty-year-old John Singer Sargent, who visited the United States for the first time in 1876, returned to Paris this year to strike up a close friendship with Claude Monet and to begin his climb to becoming society's favored portraitist with acceptance of a canvas by the Salon of 1877. As far as Cassatt was concerned, Sargent sold out to the Philistines, but no one could fault his amazing technical skill and a suavity that was more severe than sentimental.

Moreover, the era had an unusual share of major painters seeking their fortunes more or less successfully in the United States. The forty-six-year-old Albert Bierstadt was widely recognized as the greatest landscapist of the American West, and in 1876 many visitors made a pilgrimage to his Hudson River estate. John La Farge, another noted landscapist, won a commission this year to do a mural for Boston's Trinity Church and began a new career of religious painting. The not-yet-thirty Albert Pinkham Ryder was now well past the threshold of his great experiments with fantasy. Winslow Homer, his senior by a decade, had long enjoyed the patronage of *Harper's Weekly* and was currently exhibiting the first of his marine masterpieces, "Breezing Up." Homer, Bierstadt, and

La Farge would all be shown at the Centennial, as well as Louis C. Tiffany and Thomas Moran. Thomas Eakins, thirty-two and once a fellow student with Cassatt, would have an unfortunate experience with the Philadelphia Exhibition bureaucrats: his monumental "Clinic of Dr. Agnew" was rejected as a work of art and relegated to the medical exhibits.[11]

Clearly, the United States had great artistic talents, but the country was hesitant to recognize them, and it lacked insitutions to support them. The nation's inferiority complex about its painters was evident at the Centennial, where people crowded to see the foreign offerings but not the native. Many visitors had never seen any art before except chromos, and their lack of sophistication produced such amusing episodes as the case of the Republican farmer who became incensed at an English canvas called "Ulysses and His Friends" because he thought the depiction of the shepherd surrounded by pigs was a slam at President Grant.

Boston's Museum of Fine Arts first opened its doors on July 4, 1876. New York's Metropolitan Museum was six years older, its existence in part the result of Boss Tweed's civic pride.

April 10, New York

AT age seventy-two, the merchant prince Alexander T. Stewart died in his marble mansion on Fifth Avenue, leaving a fortune of $50,000,000. A few days later a weathy citizen walking by 39 East Thirty-fourth Street had this comment: "I saw a great crowd of the roughest class of people gazing at A. T. Stewart's house and waiting to see the funeral. Suppose they find it hard to believe that a man who can conquer millions cannot escape death."[1] The nationwide press made much of the story, less by way of mourning than by way of moralizing about the passing from the scene of the richest American to date.

Contrary to romanticized stories of his rise from Irish poverty, steerage passage, and the job of errand boy, Stewart had been born near Belfast in comfortable circumstances, attended Trinity College in Dublin briefly, and owned his own dry goods business in New York at the age of twenty-two. By the time of the great

Irish famine of 1846 he could afford to send a boatload of relief supplies to his native land. During the Civil War his income reached $2,000,000 a year. The huge mart he erected at Chambers Street and Broadway soon sufficed only for his wholesale business, so that he built an even larger store on the block bounded by Ninth and Tenth streets, Fourth Avenue and Broadway. This emporium, a five-story iron building, was reportedly the largest retail establishment in the world. His mansion was considered one of the most handsome private residences in the country and housed a large art collection. At the time of his death Stewart was the benefactor of numerous charities, the most noticed being the palatial home for working girls under construction at Thirty-second Street and Fourth Avenue.[2]

In his prime, Stewart was remembered as a thin, undersized man with coarse reddish hair, sharp features, and "slate eyes of almost unbelievable coldness."[3] He had few close friends, forbidding as he was. He was superstitious enough to worry that there were thirteen guests at dinner the Sunday before he died. Since none of his children had survived infancy, he left his fortune entirely to his wife, except for a few bequests to trusted subordinates. One of his clerks, with mixed awe and hurt, remembered that the big boss had spoken to him only twice, once to reprimand him for making "shiftless looking bundles" and the other to lecture as he unwound some excess wrapping: "Never waste even a piece of string. Waste is always wrong."[4]

While the majority of newspapers glorified the story of A. T. Stewart into the triumph of American opportunity and free enterprise, a few, like the newly founded *Socialist*, had some grave reservations:

> We grant that A. T. Stewart was very diligent and economical, but so were the ten thousand employees in his reach. . . . He took great care to have them very diligent and very economical. But has any one of them turned out rich? . . . Thousands were ruined by competition with him who had his talents but not his capital . . . even in his charities we recognize a constant tendency to enable working people *to live on lower wages*. [italics in original][5]

Stewart was a largely frustrated force in Republican politics. President Grant was impressed enough by him to nominate him for secretary of the treasury, but his confirmation was prevented, ostensibly because of an old law barring from that office importers of merchandise and more likely because of the unpopularity of his connections with the Tweed Ring and the corrupt Judge Henry Hilton. Stewart was also thwarted in his ambition to run for mayor of New York. In all these dealings, the Jewish banker Joseph Seligman had been ahead of Stewart, so to speak: he was first offered the Cabinet post; he had turned down the mayoralty; and he had helped oust Tweed. Accordingly, the Irish millionaire spitefully transferred his enterprises' business from Seligman's bank.

The dignity of Stewart's passing was eventually marred by two sensational events. Judge Hilton came to manage his estate, including the department store and also Stewart's $2,000,000 interest in the Grand Union Hotel, the largest hotel in fashionable Saratoga, New York. Banker Seligman arrived in Saratoga in his private railroad car in the summer of 1877 and was refused admission to the Grand Union on the basis of his faith. Whether or not Seligman deliberately sought such a confrontation, the press suddenly discovered anti-Semitism and indulged in speculation about the status of New York's rich Jews, as did the Jews themselves. In the furor Stewart's emporium underwent a boycott, and it was eventually forced to sell out to John Wanamaker's.[6]

Two and a half years after Stewart's death his body was stolen from his grave in the churchyard of St. Marks-in-the-Bouwerie at Second Avenue. Police energy and the offer of a reward failed to produce any clues to the crime until a letter reached Mrs. Stewart from Canada a few months later relating how her husband's body had been taken away in a grocer's cart to a secret location in northern Manhattan. She received this assurance: "Except that the eyes have disappeared, the flesh is as firm and the features as natural as on the day of interment and can therefore be instantly identified."[7] The thieves demanded $200,000 but settled for $20,000, surrendering the remains on a lonely road in Westchester. Subsequently, Stewart was buried under the dome of the Garden City Cathedral in a vault that had a spring mechanism to set off warning bells if there was any tampering by intruders.

Fear of ghouls on the part of the rich reached the point that when William H. Vanderbilt died about a decade after Stewart, his crypt was opened and inspected by a watchman at fifteen-minute intervals. The inheritor of $90,000,000, William Vanderbilt gained everlasting notoriety for his "the public be damned" outburst, but he was just a plodding second-generation millionaire, compared to his glamorous father, Cornelius Vanderbilt, the first railroad king.

Cornelius or Commodore Vanderbilt was very much on people's minds in 1876, for it was revealed soon after Stewart's death in April that a richer man was dying. A watch of cardplaying reporters began to camp out across the street from his mansion at 10 Washington Square. Vanderbilt had gone from borrowing $100 from his mother in 1801 to buy a barge to building an empire that embraced about one-fiftieth of the nation's railroads. By the mid 1870s the Commodore had largely retired from his business ventures and devoted his last years to blasphemous harassment of his doctors, hymn singing (his favorite was "I Am Poor, I Am Needy"), and the sponsorship of eccentric sirens like Victoria Woodhull. Almost daily throughout the summer and fall of 1876 the newspapers reported how many hours the old man slept, how much he coughed, and how he reacted to his champagne or brandy. He finally died in the first days of 1877, leaving almost twice as much money as Stewart had.

America had got used to its millionaires, and the press played counting games with their numbers and their fortunes. Historical analysts of the era later delved deeper, concluding that Stewart was one of the last to make it really big as a merchant capitalist and that Vanderbilt represented a dying breed that ran railroads as well as speculated in them. The flashy Wall Street types like Jay Gould and Jim Fisk were also a passing phenomenon. The most multi of multimillionaires of the future were industrial capitalists like John D. Rockefeller and Andrew Carnegie and banker capitalists like J. P. Morgan, men well on their way in 1876, even if less well known than A. T. Stewart.[8]

April 15, New York

LIVING emperors were even more exciting than deceased millionaires, and elusive emperors doubly so. The harbor forts fired salutes, passing ships blew whistles, and the band on the wharf struck up the Brazilian national anthem as the government-owned steamer *Alert* pulled into the Battery. The crowd stopped cheering only when it became apparent that the eagerly anticipated guest of the country, Dom Pedro II of Brazil, was not aboard.

"The Emperor is in Brazil; I am only a private citizen," Dom Pedro told Secretary of State Fish, who had come on board the British steamship *Hevelius* in New York's Narrows and invited the ruler to partake of an elaborate official welcome. So Dom Pedro stayed on the *Hevelius* until it reached its usual berth in the East River, having savored the Manhattan panorama like any new visitor. With his stoutish empress at his side carrying a satchel, he then disembarked to the applause of a few bystanders and without ado took a cab to the Fifth Avenue Hotel, where an apartment awaited them. For this beginning and for subsequent royal successes in eluding ceremonial, America's most distinguished and most thoroughgoing tourist in 1876 earned the title the "Artful Dodger."[1]

Dom Pedro's reputation preceded his arrival in New York. Ruler since 1840 of the largest Latin American country, he had won attention as a conscientious and enlightened reformer, especially for decreeing the emancipation of the slaves in Brazil in 1871. Restless, somewhat worn out by cares of state, concerned to get medical treatment for his wife, and confident that his daughter would face no trouble as regent in his absence, Dom Pedro found the Centennial Exhibition the ultimate enticement to visit this country. During the late March sailing from Rio de Janeiro the fifty-year-old ruler soon relaxed and became the "liveliest and jolliest" of the passengers, according to a companion at the captain's table, James J. O'Kelly, a reporter for the *Herald* that the ever-resourceful Bennett had sent to be on hand.[2] Serious-mindedness, however, was more the mark of the Brazilian emperor, as Americans learned from their newspapers, for he spent mornings in his cabin studying Sanskrit with a tutor and on deck read Shakespeare with an American woman traveler to help his English. As per the plainly antique joke, O'Kelly was embarrassed not to be able to furnish Dom Pedro with very many stanzas of "The Star-Spangled Banner," which the royal scholar wished to render into Portuguese.

Two days after Dom Pedro's back-door arrival in the city, the New York *Times* "confessed" that "our people do not entertain a very high reverence for kings and emperors, as kings and emperors go," but that "a monarch so liberal, enlightened, and practical as Dom Pedro must command the respect of all sensible men."[3] Actually, many Americans were intensely flattered by the visit of the scion of the Bourbon, Hapsburg, and Braganza dynasties. Uncrowned or dethroned royalty had been here, like Louis Philippe and Joseph Napoleon, but apart from the visit of the exotic King Kalakaua of Hawaii a few years previously, this was the first time that reigning royalty had graced the shores of the Republic. Few sour notes crept into the press. The Columbia, South Carolina, *Daily Register* at first sneered that Dom Pedro's departure from Brazil was a "well-conceived sanitary measure" in view of the 536 yellow fever deaths in that country in the past two weeks, but eventually this journal relented enough to publish a half-effusive, half-deprecatory poem called "Brother Jonathan to Dom Pedro," which included these lines:

> Hail Equator-crowned Braganza
> Hail Centennial Big Bonanza
> I wave welcome to your clipper
> Lift aloft your royal flipper.[4]

During his three-month stay in this country, Dom Pedro gravely saluted many thousand Americans with his "royal flipper." Always genial, never pompous, he went about his role as tourist with an astonishing intensity. He and the empress left their hotel the Saturday night of their arrival for a performance of *Henry V* at the Booth Theater, and thereafter he showed a willingness to see any kind of stage performance. Sunday morning he worshiped at St. Patrick's Cathedral, the original one on Mott Street, and then rounded out the day by attending a Moody-Sankey revival meeting, where he sat next to the evangelists on the stage with his silk hat resting on top of the umbrella clutched between his knees. The next day the emperor revealed his wont to start sightseeing at such an early hour as seven, sightseeing for him meaning such places as Bellevue Hospital, P.S. 14, and the *Herald* office.

Because he wanted to see the West Coast before the weather became hot, Dom Pedro left New York after only three days in the city. He traveled in a special Pullman car, with stopovers at hotels in major cities, like Salt Lake City, whose Mormon institutions excited a critical curiosity in him. The "Artful Dodger" managed to gain his rooms at the Palace Hotel in San Francisco on April 25 before a gala reception committee in Oakland realized that he was no longer on the scheduled train. Thereafter, Chinatown, the new university at Berkeley, schools, and factories claimed the attention of the royal visitor, who surveyed the Pacific for the first time from the Cliff House and pronounced San Francisco's bay to be grand but less magnificent than Rio's.

A rapid return journey on the transcontinental railroad enabled Dom Pedro to lend his official presence to the opening of the Centennial Exhibition in early May. Before going to Philadelphia, he spent a few days in Washington, where he paid whirlwind visits to the Naval Observatory and the Smithsonian Institution early the first morning and made a formal call at the White House in the afternoon. He had an interview with his particular hero, General Sherman. Later he made the acquaintance of some of President Grant's enemies by visiting the Capitol and listening to the Belknap impeachment proceedings from the diplomatic gallery of the Senate.

The emperor's energy, his relentless schedule, and his predilection for technology pleased Americans greatly. People did not always respect his privacy, but for his part Dom Pedro allowed that he did not mind the stares of the citizenry and the attentions of officialdom as long as they did not waste his time. Another thing that the press reported with increasing delight was his innocent way of asking questions about everything, questions that often embarrassed his hosts but questions that were well intended and practical-minded. It is not surprising that someone dubbed Dom Pedro "Our Yankee Emperor."[5]

April 17, Pittsburgh

THE bloc of socialist delegates stormed out of the National Labor Conference amid "volleys of the most cowardly epithets."[1] They were protesting the meeting's voting a pro-Greenback resolution. Far from stirring enthusiasm among the working class, the Pittsburgh conference symbolized the nearly complete disappearance of organized labor from the American scene in the 1870s. Ironically, the socialists profited from their experience to achieve unity of all existing factions.

The organizing of American workers on more than a local scale had been a phenomenon of just the past two decades. The national union of machinists and blacksmiths for example, had been established in 1859 and conducted a successful strike against the Baldwin locomotive works the next year. Unionization received a marked impetus from the Civil War: workers reacted against their failure to share in the general prosperity, which saw prices rise 76 percent while wages went up only 50 percent. Seventeen national unions came into being in the seven years after 1863. Also, employees needed to counter the sudden flourishing of employers' associations dedicated to keeping the ten-hour day and to breaking strikes by the use of a mutual slush fund.

The proliferation of big unions and also of citywide trade assemblies was matched by the appearance of a single countrywide organization claiming to speak for labor, the National Labor Union, which held yearly conventions beginning with one in Baltimore in 1866. This organization took the lead in pressuring state legislatures to pass eight-hour-day laws, such as New York's in 1867. When the administration consented to an eight-hour day for federal employees in 1868, officials of the National Labor Union dissuaded President Grant from exacting a corresponding wage cut. The 1868 convention of the National Labor Union was the first to demand the creation of a Department of Labor.

The National Labor Union never achieved anything like the power of the later AFL, for example. The central office was too poor to send even one delegate to the Congress of the International in 1868, although they did affiliate with Marx's organization two years later. The successive American congresses did not deal effectively with the problems of black workers or women workers. The local unions were left free to practice racial discrimination, and most did. The 1869 congress denied a seat to the influential suffragist Susan B. Anthony on the grounds that she used scab labor and paid less than union wages.[2] When the leadership of the National Labor Union became deeply committed to Greenbackism, the national and local unions decided that the organization was too political and lost interest, the cigar makers, for example, disaffiliating altogether in 1870.[3]

The panic of 1873 wrecked the American labor movement at all levels, demonstrating the paradoxical law that union activity is strongest in times of prosperity. The New York *Times* rather gleefully reported that membership in the city's unions declined from

45,000 in the early 1870s to 5,000. Instead of the thirty national unions at the beginning of the decade, only eight or nine listed themselves in the pages of the labor press in 1876. Many unions had previously been financially involved in cooperative enterprises; these now failed one after another.

The Pittsburgh labor conference of April, 1876, was a last effort to rally the working class and revitalize the remnants of the National Labor Union.[4] The call for the meeting came from two Pennsylvania-based organizations: one was the two-year-old semi-secret Junior Sons of '76, which was politically oriented and interested in running labor candidates for all offices right up to the presidency; the other was the Knights of Labor, which was a completely secret order dedicated to labor solidarity against the employers. Prominent in both groups was John M. Davis, editor of the Pittsburgh *National Labor Tribune,* and he was readily elected permanent chairman of the conference. Pennsylvanians were in a majority generally among the 136 delegates from twenty states. No unions were represented as such; only four delegates had attended previous such congresses. Even granted the current disarray of the American labor movement, the conference was a sorry representation of it. The one fresh element was the socialists.

Before the conference began its deliberations in Lafayette Hall, the socialist delegates had met around the corner in Washington Hall to plot a common strategy. Most of them from the New York area and many German-born, the socialists were venturing in force across the Allegheny Mountains and participating in the English-speaking labor movement for the first time. Their spokesman was the twenty-four-year-old Irishman Peter J. McGuire, an outstanding graduate of the Cooper Union night school, a member of the wood joiners union, and a fiery orator.

When the full conference got around to passing resolutions, McGuire offered one favoring the government's lending money to the working class to form cooperatives. This passed initially by a vote of 67 to 27, but then, made aware that they were endorsing a socialist proposal, the delegates reversed themselves and tabled the resolution by a vote of 56 to 51. In vain, the socialist delegates cried parliamentary fraud.

The next resolution that came up put the conference foursquare against resumption and for the interconvertible bond—Greenbackism pure and simple. McGuire and his sympathizers heaped scorn on such "financial trickery," but the proposal was carried by a majority of 55 to 47. Besides themselves with indignation, the twenty-three socialists now insisted on leaving. Before McGuire reached the doors, a delegate made a slur about a "small clique who had no sympathy with the laboring man." The Irishman probably would have started swinging, but Chairman Davis hastily explained that the insult was not specifically directed at him. The socialists' enemies had no monopoly of indelicacy of sentiments: the *Socialist* was quick to characterize the Pittsburgh majority as "the lickspittles of petty capitalists."

Their principled opposition to Greenbackism was one thing that placed American socialists beyond the fringe of native radicalism. Their reasoning was curiously self-denying—namely, "that greenbacks and bonds bearing a low rate of interest were questions that properly belonged to bankers, merchants, and employers" and that a labor meeting "could not logically consider these subjects."[5] More cynically it could be said of the socialists at Pittsburgh that they had a chance to "practice their best trick of withdrawing from any meeting they could not dominate."[6]

The remaining delegates in Pittsburgh continued voting resolutions. One that showed the unseen hand of the Knights of Labor called on workers "to organize under one head, each for all and all for one, upon a secret basis"—a proposal hardly calculated to attract the unions and unionists already out in the open.[7] The conference proved itself to be very conservative on the matter of politics, rejecting a committee resolution favoring a genuine workingmen's party and substituting a declaration that "independent political action is extremely hazardous and detrimental to labor interests."[8] The "existing political parties," meaning just the two major ones, "can be made the vehicle for the attainment of our ends." Having already offended the socialists and the trade unionists, the conference now succeeded in alienating political activists, such as the Sons of '76.

The last accomplishment of the Pittsburgh labor conference was to set up a committee of fifteen to think up more resolutions and to prepare for future annual meetings. None was ever held. The era of general conferences of all elements involved in the labor question was over. The political activists, the secret organizers, the trade unionists, and the socialists were destined to go their separate ways at a time when the employers' antilabor offensive was at its strongest.

April 18, Washington

ACTING the statesman, President Grant this day vetoed a bill that would have cut his successor's salary to $25,000 from the present $50,000. The bill was another maneuver in the current harassment of the executive branch by the legislative.

Three years previously majorities in Congress had doubled the presidential salary to $50,000 and then raised their own from $5,000 to $7,500. Public indignation over what the press labeled the "Salary Grab Act" forced the repeal a few months later of the legislators' pay hike but not the executive's. Now, in his new veto message, Grant conceded that "no one having a knowledge of the cost of living in the national capital will contend that the present salary of Congressmen is too high," but he also pointed out that originally a congressman's pay was one-thirtieth of the presidential salary, while currently it was one-tenth of the existing $50,000, not to speak of one-fifth of the proposed $25,000. "Twenty-five thousand dollars does not defray the expenses of the Executive for one year, or has not in my experience," Grant continued. "It is not one fifth in value of what it was at the time of the adoption of the Constitution in supplying needs and wants."[1]

Compared to Grant's $50,000, his Cabinet secretaries got $8,000 (the vice president, if there had been one, would deserve a slight bonus with $8,500). In 1876 there were only seven Cabinet posts—State, War, Treasury, Justice, Post Office, Navy, and Interior. Agriculture, at present represented by a commissioner, would not get Cabinet status until 1889, Labor even later.

The other most highly paid officials were Supreme Court justices at $17,500 and the eleven top ministers abroad, who got from $17,500 to $12,000. Sherman, a full general, and Porter, a full admiral, received $13,000 each. Chester A. Arthur, later President, drew $12,000 as customs collector of the City of New York,[2] half again as much as his Treasury boss was paid and about twelve times what Herman Melville, the novelist, was getting as one of his customs inspectors.

For the fiscal year ending June 30, 1876, the government's total revenue was $283,500,000, of which $148,100,000 came from customs receipts, $116,700,000 from excises, and less than $1,000,000 from income taxes (in 1976, according to an estimate of February, 1975, the revenue will be $297.5 billion, of which

$4.3 billion will derive from customs, $32.1 billion from excises, with most of the rest from income taxes). Running a considerable surplus, the Grant administration spent only $158,200,000 in its next to last year, with a breakdown as follows: Civil and Miscellaneous, $67,000,000; War Department, $38,100,000; Navy Department, $19,000,000; Indian affairs, $6,000,000; and Pensions, $28,300,000 (in the 1976 budget, military expenses account for $94 billion, veterans' benefits for $15.6 billion).[3]

April 24, Washington

INTERRUPTING normal debate in the House, Representative James G. Blaine rose to a point of order and defended himself against charges in the press that he had secretly profited from the sale of worthless railroad bonds. He declared that his relationship with the railroads in question had been "open as the day" and read letters from railroad officials exonerating him. Blaine accused the Democrats in the "Confederate" House of seeking to discredit him politically just as they were discrediting the administration, but all the while Blaine knew that it was primarily other Republicans who were instigating the attacks, Republicans jealous of his front-running status for the presidential nomination.[1] Blaine's reply to the charges was "manly, truthful, and exhaustive," wrote James A. Garfield in his journal,[2] but the House thought otherwise and ordered an investigation.

Blaine's shady railroad dealings, insofar as they were revealed in 1876, began in 1869, when he promoted and sold bonds for the Little Rock and Fort Smith Railroad while speaker of the House. The Arkansas line went bankrupt, and Blaine was left with a bundle of worthless bonds on his hands, but he managed to dispose of these to other railroads, like the Union Pacific, which took $75,000 in paper value and gave or lent him $64,000 in return. Details of these transactions through a Boston firm were contained in letters preserved by a clerk named James Mulligan, and the leaking of the "Mulligan Letters" in the New York *Sun* and other newspapers kept Blaine's name on the front pages all through May and into June. What was not brought to light until later was that during Blaine's entire fifteen-year tenure in Washington he had received money or stock from virtually every railroad that was given land grants or other aid from the government, for a total sum approaching $200,000.

The tip-offs for the newspaper exposés of Blaine were eventually traced to associates of Blaine's chief opponents in the Republican Party, like a brother-in-law of Senator Morton, a publisher friend of Secretary Bristow, and a reporter friend of Governor Rutherford Hayes of Ohio. Blaine himself initially blamed Senator Conkling, who was probably the most innocent.

After fifteen years in power nationally, the Republican Party was ridden with factions. In the first part of the Grant administration the dominant group in the party was the Radicals, a name not merited by any sort of social extremism but used pejoratively by white southerners who considered themselves the victims of "radical" Reconstruction after the Civil War. More recently the major Republican group in Congress was known as the Regulars or Stalwarts; led by Senators Conkling and Morton, they essentially supported all of Grant's policies and were rewarded with complete control of federal patronage. Independent of these, in sort of a middle position regarding the spoils system and Reconstruction, were the Half-breeds, mostly in the House, with Blaine as their leader. To the other extreme were Republican liberals who looked to Bristow and thoroughgoing civil service reform.[3]

Blaine was widely quoted in the spring of 1876 as having said, "I have no influence with the present administration. No man has who is not a thief by instinct."[4] Such sentiments did not, of course, endear Blaine to the President or the Stalwarts, and Blaine certainly hoped to put himself at the head of all those who disassociated themselves from Grantism. Yet the Maine representative neither won nor possibly even sought the image of a liberal, particularly in view of his business dealings. Garfield, who sensed or hoped that Blaine was a winner, had reservations about his man. In May he confessed, "He is certainly not the highest type of reformer. Hardly a reformer at all."[5]

No one ever mistook Senator Roscoe Conkling of New York for a liberal. Dispenser of the largest single source of federal patronage in the country, the New York Customs House, Conkling was forthright enough once to say, that "when Dr. Johnson called patriotism the last refuge of a scoundrel he forgot the possibilities contained in the word 'reform.'"[6] New York also had thirty-five electoral votes, the same ones Governor Tilden was promising the Democrats, and the state convention at Syracuse on March 22 had this in mind when it declared that "we present Roscoe Conkling to the National Republican Convention as our choice for President."[7] Conkling had his enemies, like Theodore Roosevelt, Sr., the Union League Club, and ordinary men who disliked Conkling's wealth, his arrogance, and his quarrelsomeness. Yet few would deny his consummate abilities as an orator, one who could be alternately smoothly authoritative or sneeringly satiric. And few would deny that he was one of the handsomest men around, prompting one historian to speculate that if women had had the vote in 1876, Conkling would have been a shoo-in for president. More than six feet tall, Conkling kept himself in shape by boxing, and he affected flamboyantly elegant clothes to set off his full reddish beard and the hyacinth curl over his forehead. His "life of temperance" was such that the state convention took official notice of it[8]; paradoxically, the abstemious, debonair New Yorker was one of Grant's chief after-dinner cronies. A never-forgotten remark by Blaine about Conkling's "turkey gobbler strut" sufficed to make the two enemies, to the point that Conkling's own candidacy was regarded by some as secondary to his desire to block the other.

Oliver Morton of Indiana was closely associated with Conkling as a leader of the Senate Republican Stalwarts, even though the men personally disliked each other. An outstanding wartime governor of his state, Morton had subsequently suffered a stroke, which left him paralyzed and necessitated his being carried to his desk in the Senate chamber. His disability did not detract from Morton's forensic skills, and as a savage baiter of Democrats only Blaine was his equal. As a bold, persistent parliamentarian Morton was responsible for much of the legislation of Reconstruction, and his willy-nilly support of each and every carpetbagger and scalawag in the Southern states promised him the solid support of the party in that region. More power-hungry than venal, the black-haired, spiderlike Morton excited the strong language that only a highly successful politician could: "extremely ambitious and selfish" (Blaine); "totally unfit, both morally and politically" (Garfield); "dreaded" (Hayes); and "an unprincipled demagogue" (Whitelaw Reid).

Also in the Republican stable was the "dark horse"[9] contender Rutherford B. Hayes, governor of Ohio, who had been endorsed as a "favorite son" candidate by his state's convention on March 29. All along the press spoke of Hayes as everyone's second choice, and his candidacy could be interpreted as a lever to get him the vice presidential slot. The choice of Hayes' hometown Cincinnati as the site of the Republican convention seemingly reflected his having appeal without being a threat to anyone else or even identifiable as a Stalwart or Half-breed or Reformer. Actually, since the earliest phases of the campaign, some Republicans were pushing Hayes as a genuine possibility, and no one was more self-consciously diffident about his position than the diary-keeping Ohioan. In April, 1875, he wrote: "Several suggest that if elected Governor now, I will stand well for the Presidency next year. How wild! What a queer lot we're becoming. Nobody is out of reach of that mania."[10] In January, after hearing proposals for a ticket with Hayes for president and Congressman William A. Wheeler of New York as vice president, Hayes sent a letter to his wife, which became ironically famous: "I am ashamed to say who is Wheeler?"[11] As late as the beginning of April he was confessing, "I would be glad if now I could in some satisfactory way drop out of the candidacy."[12]

With Bristow, Conkling, Morton, and Hayes all in the running, Blaine faced numerous strong opponents. None of the others were under the exhausting running fire of the press exposures of Blaine's railroad chicanery. Yet in the minds of friend and foe alike Blaine appeared somehow unbeatable. On May 24 the Chicago *Tribune* predicted a sweeping victory for him.

May 4, Pottsville, Pennsylvania

ARMED militiamen patrolled the streets of this Schuylkill County mining center as the third and most sensational of the year's "Molly Maguire" trials began. Crowds of the curious and the families of the accused milled around in excitement when the four prisoners were brought out in chains. Every seat in the courtroom had been occupied four hours previously. One big surprise followed upon another: the railroad magnate Gowen himself appeared at the prosecution table; a Pinkerton agent told a fantastic tale of his infiltration of the alleged gang of murderers; and Gowen revealed his intention to treat mere association with the Molly Maguires as a criminal offense.

The specific crime under consideration went back to July 6, 1875, at 2 A.M., when Benjamin Yost, a policeman in Tamaqua, was making his rounds and was shot fatally while in the act of climbing a post to extinguish a gaslight. His helper exchanged shots with two fleeing gunmen. Yost's wife and doctor were also immediately on the scene and heard his dying words to the effect that he did not recognize his assailants but that "they were two Irishmen." Yost, of Dutch origin, was unpopular for aiding in the blacklisting of Irish coal miners.[1]

The defendants in the Yost case whom Kerrigan had fingered were James Boyle, twenty-four, generally well regarded although a saloon habitué, later said to be a last-minute substitute in the plot; Hugh McGehan, twenty-one, an abstainer, proud of his physique, blacklisted for union activity; James Carroll, the middle-aged owner of a Tamaqua saloon where the plot was allegedly hatched, the only one of the group who could sign his name; and James Roarity, another middle-aged official of the Hibernians from nearby Coaldale. These men now watched coldly as their jury was selected from among their non-Irish and non-Catholic neighbors. The prosecution succeeded in empaneling some Germans who admitted difficulty understanding English.

While respected lawyers represented the defense, the prosecution as in the earlier cases was composed not only of the district attorney but of high-priced experts hired by the coal and railroad companies. On the second day Franklin B. Gowen himself joined them and took the limelight, which he obviously enjoyed. With his bustling cordon of bodyguards, the president of the Philadelphia and Reading Railroad seemed to be daring his enemies to martyr him. Gowen was entirely confident of success ever since he had brought the Pinkerton agency into his drive against crime and labor, having despaired of the abilities of the constabulary or the Coal and Iron Police. Certain ironies later came to light concerning this detective agency, one of the first in the country when it was founded in 1850. Its founder, Allan Pinkerton, had been a Chartist firebrand in Scotland before fleeing to America. He turned amateur detective work into a successful business, but he was hurt by the panic of 1873, had to borrow money from his employees, and admitted his firm was "failing" just when Gowen came to his rescue with the contract to send agents to the coalfields.[2]

When the district attorney in his opening statement announced that a key witness for the prosecution would be James McParlan, a Pinkerton agent operating in the very midst of the alleged Molly Maguires since 1873, the defense was visibly stunned. As reported in the *Miner's Journal,* "Carroll was as if struck by lightning. He could scarcely get back the breath which seemed to be lost to him. Boyle shook like an aspen, and the other prisoners became grave as judges. A thrill of astonishment went through the audience."[3] McParlan's subsequent testimony did not disappoint them. "Even the calmest recording of his deeds had all the aspects of the wildest fiction."[4]

The Irish-born McParlan had come to the United States ten years before when he was twenty-three and had worked in the New York and Chicago areas in an amazing number of occupations—teamster, deckhand, lumberman, policeman, and bartender—before joining the Pinkertons. A wily and wiry man of five feet eight, he made up for his lack of schooling with his "gift for gab" and other supposedly Irish traits like red hair, twinkling blue eyes, a charming brogue, and physical liveliness. When he began his mission in the coal region, he went right to the likeliest bar and ingratiated himself with its owner by his abilities to sing and dance, to gamble, and to fight with his fists. He also gave himself underworld status by intimating that he had committed a murder and was cheating the government by drawing two veterans' pensions. Within months he had been initiated into the Ancient Order of Hibernians as "James McKenna," and thereafter he became secretary of one of the lodges, being thus enabled to take all the notes he wanted without arousing suspicions.[5]

McParlan alias McKenna corroborated all of Kerrigan's earlier testimony that Yost and Jones had been murdered by seeming outsiders after two different lodges of the Hibernians arranged an exchange of revenge killings. He claimed that McGehan, Carroll, and Roarity together confessed to him their participation in the Yost murder. The Pinkerton agent's story had only a few minor holes in it, as discovered by the defense at the time or perceived later by historians. He hesitated when asked if the conspirators specifically referred to the involvement of the Molly Maguires and said only "we understood what was meant."[6] It may be wondered why, if McParlan was so intimate with the criminal element, he did not know of the plot against Yost before the murder.

One of the strangest aspects of McParlan's story concerned his surviving the vengeance of his associates after they became suspicious of him in the aftermath of the Jones murder trials early in 1876. He wove a tale of brazenly demanding a gang-style trial from a local leader, Jack Kehoe, whom McParlan quoted as saying at one point, "For God's sake have me killed that night or I would hang half the people in Schuylkill County." Yet somehow a gang of men with tomahawks, Kehoe, and another crime leader, both of whom McParlan visited in their homes at this time, all failed to do him in, and McParlan went off to Philadelphia to lay low before returning to testify in May. The supposed Molly Maguire desperadoes showed "unbelievable hesitancy."[7]

The prosecution had built up a generally convincing case of the guilt of Boyle, McGehan, Carroll, and Roarity, and they could have left it that the Yost murder was just a vendetta by a group of unscrupulous men. Instead, almost from the beginning of McParlan's testimony he shifted from the individuals involved to the organizations supposedly directing them and spent hours needlessly describing the institutions and rituals of the Ancient Order of Hibernians. It became apparent that Gowen's aim was to make the Molly Maguires as a group responsible for the crimes and to condemn as criminals any and all persons connected with them. The Philadelphia *Inquirer* revealed this guilt-by-association aspect of the trial when it declared on May 19 that "these cutthroats will be convicted there can scarce be a doubt, and these convictions will be followed by those of some fifteen other assassins of the same Order who are now in jail awaiting trial."[8] The prosecution became blatant in its appeals to the Yost case jury to go beyond the facts of a specific murder and to protect themselves against a social evil. One lawyer said that "if it requires the bold surgery of hanging 10, 50, or 500 Molly Maguires at the end of a rope, let us apply the surgery."[9]

The defense opened its case on May 13 with the statement that "there are only two prosecution witnesses, a professed informer and a professional informer."[10] They were unable to crack McParlan's story but did succeed in impugning Kerrigan's testimony by producing his wife, who declared that on the night of the murder Kerrigan had told her that he himself had shot Yost. Asked by the prosecution if she wanted "to get your husband hung," Mrs. Kerrigan said she only wished "to tell the truth . . . because he picked innocent men to suffer for his crime."[11] The defense scored another point by having the mother of the farmer who claimed seeing the Jones' murderers testify that her son was elsewhere and that he later had been promised a job by the coal company associated with the prosecution.

The dramatic proceedings at Pottsville were interrupted on May 18 by the illness and subsequent death of a juror and were not recommenced until early July. Meanwhile, in the same city on June 27, a separate trial had begun for Thomas Munley, accused of being one of four gunmen who had shot down on September 1 a young English mine foreman, with a reputation for strictness, named Thomas Sanger and a miner, William Uren, who tried to come to his rescue. McParlan testified that the assassins had confided to him all the details of the killing, conveniently after the fact. At this trial Gowen reached the very peak of his eloquence about the nature and consequences of a general Molly Maguire conspiracy, asking, "Of what use would be capital or wealth or industry or enterprise or property" if their administrators and agents doing their duty were "dogged by the assassin" and were "unknowing whether, when they left their houses in the morning, they would not be carried back dead before night?" Only after liquidating all Molly Maguires "we can say: 'Now all are safe in this county; come here with your money'."[12] The defense ably pictured Munley's crime as really that of being a labor militant and stressed that Gowen was confusing the Molly Maguires with the union. One lawyer burst out: "For God's sake, give labor an equal chance. . . . Let it not perish under the imperial mandates of capital in a free country."[13] Nonetheless, Munley received the familiar verdict of guilty of murder in the first degree.

When the Yost trial resumed, the defense argued in vain that the conviction of Munley and attendant publicity had prejudiced the jury against all suspected Molly Maguires. This jury, indeed, took very little time in finding the four guilty.

In retrospect, the verdict against the four as individuals was plausible, but it was far from proven that they acted as members of the Hibernians or as Molly Maguires any more than that they acted as members of the Democratic Party, to which they also happened to belong. Nonetheless, Gowen had completely succeeded in convincing public opinion that some sort of pervasive Molly Maguire evil lurked in eastern Pennsylvania and that more dire measures were needed for its eradication.

May 4, Chicago

LIEUTENANT COLONEL GEORGE CUSTER stepped off the train from the East and encountered a staff officer, who saluted and informed him that he was under arrest, in accordance with a court order sent by the War Department. Later, while Custer was being held in detention at Sheridan's headquarters, a longer wire arrived from Washington demanding an explanation of why he had left the capital without permission.

Having been in New York for the winter social season, Custer had returned to Fort Abraham Lincoln in the Dakota Territory during the middle of February. A month later, the expedition against the Sioux put off, he was back in the East to testify at Clymer's committee hearings. His appearance as a witness took up a week, after which he secured his release by Clymer and set out on his return to the frontier, leisurely, to be sure, for he visited the uncompleted Philadelphia Centennial and consulted with his publishers in New York. Once again he was summoned by Clymer to Washington to offer evidence in the Belknap impeachment proceedings and took the stand on April 28. The following day urgent orders came through from General Terry requiring his presence with his regiment. Custer then tried to secure official orders to leave Washington from General Sherman, who was away, and a requested White House interview that Saturday was put off until Monday. In the anteroom of the President's office at 10 A.M., Custer waited all morning and all afternoon. General Rufus Ingalls, an old friend with whom he was staying in Washington and currently a member of Grant's staff, was unable to persuade the President to see him. Painfully ill since March 28, Grant was particularly miffed at Custer's connivance with Clymer, later telling someone, "I did not mean to allow Custer to smirch the administration." Custer forthwith left for the West on his own.[1]

The arrest of the renowned Indian fighter in Chicago made headlines. Bennett's *Herald*, of which Custer was a protégé, declared that Grant's order "Was the most high-handed abuse of his official power which he has perpetrated yet." Other newspapers, however, spoke of Custer's "presumptuous egotism."[2] Generals Sheridan and Terry rose to his defense, and after many wires had gone back and forth, Washington sent permission for Custer to proceed to Fort Abraham Lincoln, at the same time forbidding him to join the upcoming expedition. His whole career in jeopardy, Custer now wrote Grant directly: "I appeal to you as a soldier to spare me the humiliation of seeing my regiment march to meet the enemy and I not share its dangers."[3] Grant at last relented, after General Sherman joined those interceding for Custer.

Sherman's wire to Terry giving permission for Custer to march with him and the 7th Cavalry contained the words "Advise Custer to be prudent, not to take along any newspapermen, who always make mischief, and to abstain from personalities in the future." Neither grateful nor one to take advice, Custer went ahead with his arrangements for a reporter representing the *Herald* to accompany him. He also confided to a fellow colonel his determination to "cut loose from Terry" during the campaign, obviously so as to seek his own glory, presumably to show up President Grant, and possibly to make himself a political candidate.[4]

General Terry and Colonel Custer did not reach Fort Abraham Lincoln until May 10, and another week passed before the Dakota column marched out. Because of all the delays in their expedition's taking the field in conjunction with General Crook to the South and Colonel Gibbon to the west, they gave an opportunity for thousands more Indians to leave the Sioux reservation to join Sitting Bull and Crazy Horse in what the chiefs were now promising would be a big fight.

On May 17 after a 4 A.M. reveille, the Dakota column paraded forth from Fort Abraham Lincoln, as the post band played "The Girl I Left Behind." The 1,200 men were not paid until that afternoon, when they were well away from the saloons and brothels of Bismarck. Their pack train of more than 1,700 animals stretched for two miles.

The roads were so bad that the Dakota column covered only forty-six miles westward in the first four days. The soldiers were gloomy, but not so Custer, who acted as if he were on a holiday excursion. Accompanied by his four staghounds, Custer often rode far up front hunting elk, and he was the first to spot a few Indians in the distance. Contrary to hopes, however, the expedition did not find any Indian villages when it reached the headwaters of the Little Missouri. On June 1 they had to march through a blizzard, a freak snowstorm that also impeded Crook's and Gibbon's columns.

Gibbon's force of 400 had moved out of Fort Ellis a week before the Dakota column left, scouting eastward. After delays, the Montana column continued along the Yellowstone River, sending ahead the shallow-draft stern-wheel steamer *Far West* to make contact with Terry. The ship met up with the Dakota column on June 8, after it reached the mouth of the Powder River, a murky stream described as "too thick to drink and too thin to plough."[5] Shortly afterward the west and east forces in Terry's command were united at the mouth of the Rosebud River and set up a base camp. A sutler soon had a bar going, and drinks went for $1 apiece.

Custer wrote his last letter to his wife on June 10, boasting that he was about to go into territory that no white man had ever traversed. Always eager to be first, he forgot that Lewis and Clark among others had passed through here and history.

May 6, New York

THE Frenchman Jacques Offenbach, his name almost synonymous in this era with light opera, was another much-noticed foreign visitor to the United States in 1876 and one who left fascinating, largely flattering impressions of this country. Offenbach had enough self-esteem to compare his popularity with that of Dom Pedro, but unlike the Brazilian emperor, he was altogether delighted that his steamship was met off Sandy Hook early this morning by boatloads of well-wishers, musicians, and reporters and that he was greeted at his hotel by a sign WELCOME OFFENBACH and an orchestral serenade.

Although of German-Jewish parentage, Offenbach became the sensation of Parisian music circles in the 1850s and 1860s as the tireless author and impresario of thirty-plus operettas, the most famous of which was *Orphée aux enfers* (once translated by some American as "To Hell with Orpheus"). His works were lively musically and full of sly humor, a vaudevillian mixture of songs and dances with alluring divas and dazzling choruses. Himself something of a caricature of diminutive size and gawkiness, the composer made up for everything with his wit, elegance, and *joie de vivre*. In recent years his operettas had been less popular, suffering from the competition of Johann Strauss, and Offenbach ex-

perienced bankruptcies but also made dramatic comebacks, something he said he found typical and admirable among his American
acquaintances. Given his financial difficulties and his high opinion
of himself, Offenbach in 1876 eagerly accepted an offer to conduct thirty concerts in America at $1,000 apiece, and he had no
doubt he would be as lionized here as he had been in his headiest
days on the Continent. He sailed from Le Havre on April 21 on
the maiden voyage of the sleek French steamship *Canada*.[1]

The very first day he was in New York Offenbach "ran to the
Gilmore Garden"—that is, the Hippodrome. Satisfied with its
"thicket of tropical plants," its waterfalls, and its capacity for 9,000
customers, Offenbach subsequently "won my orchestra" by refusing to conduct until he had been admitted to the musicians
union.[2] His concertmaster was none other than John Philip Sousa.
Opening night, May 11, was, however, a "catastrophe," despite all
the publicity given the illustrious foreigner and the doubled admission prices.[3] A large part of the audience simply walked out
when it became apparent that Offenbach was going to give them
only straight renditions of his own music without chorus line or
cancan. Offenbach did not despair for long and successfully
fulfilled his whole engagement of thirty concerts after cutting
prices and livening up his programs with favorite works of rival
composers, like Weber and Strauss, as well as with a specially composed "American Eagle Waltz." Reviewers in response to his music and conductorship used such words as "elegant," "electric,"
and "delicious."[4] Offenbach's increasing popularity persuaded an
impresario to venture a weeklong series of the famous operettas
at the Booth Theater, beginning with *La Vie Parisienne* on June
12, and another $20,000 was the reward. The staid were less than
pleased with the Frenchman's success, and the New York *Times*
decided that "the *opéra bouffe* is simply the sexual instinct expressed in melody."[5]

Offenbach repaid the ovations he got with literary effusions
about New York, his sense of constant amazement softening a few
criticisms. Initially he put up at the Fifth Avenue Hotel, then a six-
story structure just two years old, and he described it as unlike
anything in Europe, with private baths in each luxurious room
and its lobby an "immense bazaar" containing barber, tailor, book-
seller, and bootblack. "You can find everything . . . except a
person who can speak more than one language."[6] The hotel cost
him $20 a day with four meals. Later he tried a private house on

Madison Square, once again raving about the sheer comforts of central heating, an Edison stock ticker in his room giving the "news of the two worlds," and call buttons that summoned police or firemen or an errand boy.[7]

New York restaurants confounded Offenbach at first—the invariable glass of ice water, the oversized menus, and the waiters' habit of bringing everything at once. After a while he decided that "there are no American restaurants, properly speaking," but that one could dine very well at Brunswick's (French), Delmonico's (Swiss), Hoffmann's (German), Morelli's (Italian), and so forth. Somewhat contradictorily, he then allowed that "the most interesting of all the restaurants" were American bars, *"where you eat for nothing,"* or, more accurately, for a dime drink one could partake of dozens of dishes, which Offenbach meticulously listed, ranging from roast beef to pickles. When he looked askance at businessmen using their hands to gulp this fare down, he was duly informed that in America "time is money."[8]

Playing the boulevardier in Manhattan, Offenbach liked the fact that street names were not constantly changed for political reasons and that there were fewer statues than birdhouses in the "magnificent public squares."[9] He enjoyed a five-cent streetcar ride to Central Park, just completed in 1876 and described by him as "the rendezvous of elegant society." High life was the Frenchman's main interest all during his trip, but he was enough of a social critic to repeat a companion's explanation that a stroller in the park touched his hat or bowed low according to whether his acquaintance's worth was in the thousands or millions of dollars.

Naturally, the Parisian went to all the theater he could. Like Dom Pedro, he saw *Henry V* at the Booth, noting that this house mixed tragedy, comedy, and opera rather capriciously. One could see grand opera at the Academy of Music, but it was not often open. Offenbach found most of the playhouses "admirably arranged" with rising tiers of comfortable seats in the orchestras and balconies, but he commented unfavorably on the Lyceum Theater, where "for the first time the orchestra was placed out of sight of the public, a system which Wagner is trying at this very moment at Bayreuth" (he thought it made for bad acoustics and uncomfortably hot musicians).[10] Among the plays Offenbach saw but reported without much comment was one called *The Mighty Dollar,* which was actually the great hit of the season, although disparaged by the critics.

Still ahead of the French composer were triumphs in Philadelphia and sightseeing at the Centennial and a few other places. And his further comments on America, especially on the arts here, would be memorable.

May 10, Philadelphia

FAVORED by mostly sunny skies, opening day of the Centennial Exhibition took place on schedule and drew the largest crowds in the nation's history. The illustrious on hand were headed by a president and an emperor. Laying aside momentarily political corruption, economic recession, and local rebellion, the press devoted its news columns and editorials to the spectacular achievement at Fairmount Park on the Schuylkill River.[1]

Overnight the solemn city of Philadelphia had been transformed into an expectant, convivial, and cosmopolitan center, its hostelries filled to capacity with tourists from city and farm, politicians of all descriptions, and reporters in unusual number. Signs in several languages appeared, buildings displayed decorations, flags abounded, and seemingly everyone wore motifs in red, white, and blue. It rained all day on May 9 and into the night, but the clouds timed their disappearance for the early-morning moment when the bells of Independence Hall announced the start of festivities. Tens of thousands of people then began to move toward the fairgrounds, jamming ferryboats, trains, horsecars, and private vehicles. By nine o'clock a crowd of more than 100,000 milled around the change booths or stood before the gates, clutching in their hands special passes or the required exact 50-cent admission charge in one silver coin or a bill of that denomination.

The determined clatter of last-minute work on the exhibition could be heard until the turnstiles were opened, and the throng streamed in and hastened toward the plaza between Memorial and Main halls. The first arrivals were soon being rudely pushed by the crowds in the rear. A "fierce conflict" ensued between the police trying to keep order and this "most extraordinary mass of human beings," according to the correspondent of the New York

Times, who took refuge from the fray on one of the turrets on the roof of Main. Hundreds joined him in high perches on buildings, statues, and trees. The frenzy lessened only slightly when the music began, a medley of national airs coming from an orchestra of 150 pieces led by the most renowned American conductor of the day, Theodore Thomas. Sharing the raised platform in front of Main was a choir of 1,500.

Across the crowd from the musicians—that is, in front of Memorial Hall—stood the circular grandstand for the celebrities. The arrival of millionaires such as J. P. Morgan and Cyrus Field created less excitement than that of the great war heroes like Generals Sherman and Sheridan and Admiral Porter. Reporters tried to gauge the relative cheers at the successive appearances of Republican presidential hopefuls—Blaine, Conkling, Fish, and Bristow. The venerable black abolitionist Frederick Douglass had difficulty getting past the guards. The general hubbub gave way to frantic applause when the orchestra struck up the Brazilian national anthem, and Dom Pedro and his empress made their way to seats of honor. Finally came the first fanfares of "Hail to the Chief," and once again a great ovation as the President with Mrs. Grant on his arm arrived on the scene. The chief executive, looking old and careworn, had taken a train to Philadelphia the night before and stayed at a private house. In the morning he had been escorted to Fairmount Park by a brass band and the Boston Cadets. That he wore "just a business suit without gloves" offended the Polish journalist Sienkiewicz.[2]

The official program began with the premiere performance of a "Centennial March" by the celebrated opera composer Richard Wagner, but maestro Thomas' efforts did not stay a great pushing and shoving in the assemblage in the plaza, producing some minor casualties and causing alarm in the grandstand. The President had to order his military escort to join the police in a renewed charge outward. The invocation by a Methodist bishop went largely unheard; the patient could read it the next day in the newspapers, as they could professional criticisms, favorable and not, of the ensuing set pieces especially commissioned for the Centennial. A "Hymn" by Whittier with music by John K. Paine received good-natured applause at appropriate intervals, and the people appeared to appreciate the chorus' rendition of Sidney Lanier's cantata "The Centennial Meditation of Columbia" with music by Dudley Buck.

When it was time for speeches, General Hawley in forceful tones led off with an explanation of the genesis of the Centennial and a prognosis that it would bind the states and nations closer together. He brought President Grant to his feet with the words "I present to your view the International Exhibition of 1876." With characteristic diffidence and deliberation, Grant put on his glasses and pulled from his coat the notes he had labored over himself for many hours. His comments seem genuinely thoughtful and appropriate today, with their stress less on the political triumphs and material gains of a hundred years and more on our attainments in education, letters, and science. The caricature of the cigar-smoking militarist in the White House fades with his humble words: "Whilst we are proud of what we have done we regret that we have not done more." His final sentence, "I declare the International Exhibition now open," was the signal for complete tumult—cheers, unfurled banners, waving hats, the choir rendering the Hallelujah Chorus, artillery salutes, and the echoes of bells and sirens from Philadelphia four miles away.[3]

The opening-day ceremony most familiar in picture-book illustrations of the Centennial was yet to come, as President with Empress and Dom Pedro with Mrs. Grant led the dignitaries to the east entrance of Machinery Hall. Within stood the gigantic Corliss steam engine, its 750 tons capable of producing 1,400 horsepower.

The chiefs of state stood together on a platform before the mammoth contraption, and at a signal each flipped a switch that set it in motion. In turn all the hundreds of dependent machines in the building were brought into action, and the noise of this visual industrial revolution precluded more speeches and discouraged even conversation.

Pale, unrelaxed, President Grant skipped the further ceremonies scheduled that day so he could rest back in the city. The ever-jovial Dom Pedro let himself be mobbed by reporters and bystanders, and he made the best joke of the day. Informed regarding the exact number of revolutions performed by the Corliss engine, he said, "That beats our South American Republics."[4]

Meanwhile, the Empress Theresa, unaccompanied by her husband, was causing a stir by lending her presence to the formal opening of the Women's Pavilion. A group of suffragists over several years had agitated for a maximum of special women's displays at the exhibition and, thwarted by the directors, resorted to raising money for their own building. Their formidable leader, Mrs. Elizabeth Duane Gillespie, now had the satisfaction of escorting the empress on a tour of their achievement with its attractive showcases full of art objects, housewares, clothing, and manufactures produced by the hands of female workers. A woman engineer manned the machine that powered everything, including printing presses for an eight-page magazine called *The New Century for Women*. Philosophical but male visitors to the fair later on, like William Dean Howells, might wonder why the women needed a separate pavilion when the results of their toil where so extensively represented throughout the exhibition, but historians would set apart this special event on May 10 as a clear milestone in the long campaign for female suffrage and the even longer struggle for equal pay for equal work.[5]

The curious crowds milled through the fairgrounds for the rest of the day, the unveiling of some new building or other often setting off a great rush. At five o'clock it began to rain heavily, and chaos was repeated as people returned to their houses and hotels. Admissions opening day were 186,672, of which only about half were paid for, leaving General Hawley both pleased and apprehensive.

May 15, New York

ONE hundred and fifty self-appointed liberal notables met at the Fifth Avenue Hotel to record their disgust with both major parties and to threaten the creation of a third party if a "reform" candidate was not offered on the 1876 ballot in the fall. The politicians muttered, and the press made fun, but when all was said and done, both the Republicans and the Democrats got the message.

The Fifth Avenue Hotel group was composed primarily of progressive elements in the Eastern intellectual establishment. On hand were Edwin Godkin, editor of the *Nation,* and William Cullen Bryant, editor of the New York *Evening Post* and a founding father of the Republican Party in 1854. Two noted college presidents were present, Theodore Dwight Woolsey of Yale and Mark Hopkins of Williams. Charles Francis Adams, Theodore Roosevelt, Sr., John Jay, Thomas W. Higginson, and Cyrus Field were other celebrities of the day, while the conference secretary, young Henry Cabot Lodge, was a name for the future. The one dominant voice, however, was ex-Senator Carl Schurz.[1]

The foreign-born Schurz was something of an anomaly in American politics, and as an out-of-office maverick he needed a sounding board such as this conference to offer his advice to the country. While still in his teens, Schurz had manned the barricades in the German Revolutions of 1848. Emigrating, like Marx and so many of his generation, Schurz reached the United States in the 1850s and found an outlet for his cooling revolutionary ardor in the antislavery movement and then in the fledgling Republican Party. During the Civil War he reached the rank of major general. After a career in newspaper editing in various Midwestern cities, Schurz served as a Missouri senator from 1869 to 1875.

Schurz had broken with the Grant administration over the issue of corruption in government and had been instrumental in persuading a decrepit, failing Horace Greeley, once his editor on the *Tribune,* to run for president in 1872 as a Liberal Republican. Even though the Democrats also endorsed Greeley, Grant won his second term in a landslide of 286 to 62 electoral votes. While this experience showed Schurz that third-party politics could be tricky, even farcical, it established his threat value in the eyes of Republican regulars faced with a closer contest in 1876 than in 1872.

On April 6 Schurz, Bryant, and three others had issued a circular calling for the Free Conference. Republican politicians promptly denounced them as wild-eyed idealists, spoilers, and straddlers. Relative to the last charge of fence-sitting, Schurz replied smartly, "So we have—because the mud is too deep on both sides to drop into." In his view, the voters deserved above all somebody who was not a "mere choice of evils."[2]

Consciousness of the real significance of the Centennial was strong in the minds of the delegates at the Fifth Avenue Hotel. Their published "Address to the Nation" intoned: "In this Centennial year memories of our past history are rising up before us in a new glow of life, forcing upon us comparison of what the Republic once was, what it was intended to be and what it is." The country's present mood after the Grant administration scandals was one of "mortification" and "shame." The solution was a new president, not merely a man of "integrity," but one who had "the courage and the will to weed out evils and replace spoilsmen by honest able officials." Likening themselves to the Founding Fathers, Schurz's notables declared that "theirs was the work of independence, ours is the work of reformation."[3]

Out of the much-publicized meeting came neither party nor candidate. Charles Francis Adams would have suited everyone, if there had really been a will to start an independent movement. Adams saw salvation in the Republicans' nominating Bristow, as did Schurz, who publicly endorsed him a week later. Very few favored the Democrat Tilden, but the others did not deny his credentials as a reformer. More important than the fact that these liberals did not endorse anyone was their promise to hold a new and larger conference if one of their villains was nominated—Conkling or Morton or Blaine.

Essentially, Schurz and his fellow intellectuals were a one-issue pressure group—that of civil service replacing the spoils system. In contempt and with considerable truth, the *Socialist* could say: "Any platform that does not propose something for the starving millions is not worthy of the name 'reform'."[4]

May 17, Philadelphia

"HAVE you been to the Centennial?" was the most frequent conversational gambit of 1876, or at least for Easterners of some means. The figure of 10,000,000 admissions over six months suggests that about 1 in 5 Americans journeyed to see the exhibition at Philadelphia.[1] Dom Pedro, Buffalo Bill, Jacques Offenbach, Mary Baker Eddy, Woodrow Wilson, Ralph Waldo Emerson, Governors Hayes and Tilden were among the known or future celebrities who appeared at one time or another, and numerous groups came, ranging from the West Point Cadets to a delegation of French workers. All year the press was filled with the impressions of different visitors, everything from gee-whiz accounts by schoolboys to diatribes by shocked clergymen. A far from typical but an extremely thoughtful citizen who began a weeklong inspection of the fair on this "dull, drizzling day, somewhat cold and thoroughly unpleasant" was William Dean Howells of Boston.[2]

Editor of the *Atlantic Monthly* for the past five years, the thirty-nine-year-old Howells was as cosmopolitan as only a superbly self-educated Midwesterner could be. Born in Martins Ferry, Ohio, he had worked as a printer and journalist, before a few poems and a campaign biography of Lincoln brought him to the attention of the Boston literary Establishment in the early 1860s. Later a long stint as American consul in Venice gave him a deep appreciation of contemporary European literature. When he took over the *Atlantic Monthly,* he sought to make it more colloquial in style and more national, less regional, in interest. His encouragement of Mark Twain and Henry James was a significant contribution, and Howells would be remembered as a critic as well as a writer. Far more than most of his contemporaries, Howells was aware of the new social forces at work in an industrial society, and he wanted a more realistic, even proletariat-conscious literature. Although he never quite succeeded in his own novels in escaping genteel conventions, sentimental optimism, and a certain moral prudishness, he did remain pleasantly self-critical about these matters. His most popular work, *The Rise of Silas Lapham,* was still a decade away.[3]

Howells came to Philadelphia on "the wonderful Pennsylvania Railroad," and right off he had the perverse thought that its owner, Tom Scott, one of the richest men in the country and considered by many a "despot," had a "right to enslave the public" if his employees could be such models of civility and kindness.[4] The Pennsylvania also ran trains from downtown Philadelphia to a depot opposite the main entrance of the fair, where three platforms and an engine turnaround permitted a trainload of passengers to be unloaded every three minutes. Within the fairgrounds Howells enjoyed the "gay open cars" of the narrow-gauge circular railroad, with riders paying 5 cents for a complete tour or for each stopover at the major buildings. He eschewed the rolling chairs available for foot-weary tourists at 60 cents an hour, resigning them to women with the observation that "very few men have the self-respect required for being publicly trundled about in that manner."[5]

On the first day of Howells' visit "we wandered quite aimlessly about from one building to another."[6] He was struck by the "disorder and incompleteness" and the irony of "keep off the grass" signs on muddy embankments; but he observed much progress over the following week, and he could picture the exhibition at its prime with verdure and flowers. His first Monday there was hot and gave him a "foretaste of what the Philadelphia summer must be." Generally, Howells found "a great deal of beauty in the architecture." He also concluded: "What we found interesting at the beginning, that we found interesting at the end, and this is an advantage to those whose time is short at the Centennial."[7]

Howells' first intensive study was of Memorial Hall or Art Hall. He approached his task with less preciousness than his fellow Bostonian William James, who came to Philadelphia only to see "the English paintings," dismissing all else as "trashy."[8] The editor was indeed scornful of the foreign sculpture in the rotunda, which included a plaster rendition of George Washington "perched on an eagle much too small for him" and a bronze called "Emancipation" with a figure of a black so wildly gesticulating that "one longs to clap him back in hopeless bondage." He did see some wry humor in one of the most popular attractions at the Centennial—a grouping in wax of an alluring Cleopatra in "extreme dishabille," a slave girl, and a parrot, all of which were mechanized. As for the paintings, he considered the German battle pieces outrageously nationalistic, the French and Italian selections second-rate, and the English "most delightful." It was a compliment that the English had sent their best, Gainsboroughs and Reynolds and "modern" pre-Raphaelites as well. With some pride Howells noted that in the American offering "there were not many positively poor and there were many strikingly good," particularly in the way of landscapes.[9] Other visitors reacted to the art displays less dispassionately: the puritanical, for example, were aghast at the pervasive nudity. For many who had not traveled in Europe it was their first exposure to other than chromos, and historians credit the Centennial with giving a perceptible jolt to native efforts in both painting and sculpture.

The bulk of foreign exhibitions were in Main Hall, a building Howells admired for its grace and lightness despite the fact that it was supposed to be the largest structure in the world, some twenty acres in extent. Here three organs and numerous fountains, some spraying perfume, bemused the senses of the tourist as he turned away in disappointment from the as yet bare pavilions of the Russians and Turks to the well-organized, artistic displays of the Scandinavian countries consisting of silverwork, furs, and the like. The section of the khedive of Egypt, stressing archaeology, was also "in perfect order," as befitted a bloodthirsty "slave-driver," in

Howells' estimation. He was disappointed in the "bric-a-brackish-ness" of the Italian and the "shoppiness" of the French *objets d'art,* but once again he was charmed by the English offerings, articles in metal, glass, and tile in the way of "household decoration in which England now leads the world." By contrast, the American contributions were unrivaled in the province of "artificial teeth and all the amiable apparatus of dentistry," to say nothing of gas fixtures. Howells conceded that Nevada silverworking has serious merit and that the show of book-making, which he carefully avoided, by report "did us great honor."[10]

For most Centennial travelers the magnetic attraction was Machinery Hall, whose glass and steel construction had "the beauty of a most admirable fitness for its purpose." Howells was dutifully impressed by the gigantic Corliss engine:

> It rises loftily in the center of the large structure, an athlete of steel and iron with not a superfluous ounce of metal on it; the mighty walking beams plunge their pistons downward; the enormous fly-wheel revolves with a hoarded power that makes all tremble; the hundred life-like details do their office with unerring intelligence. In the midst of this ineffably strong mechanism is a chair where an engineer sits reading his newspaper, as in a peaceful bower. Now and then he lays down his paper and clambers up one of the stairways that cover the framework, and touches some irritated spot on the giant's body with a drop of oil, and goes down again and takes up his newspaper; he is like some potent enchanter.[11]

Otherwise, Machinery Hall gave Howells the "sense of too many sewing machines," although he was pleased to observe American inventors enthusiastically inviting questions about their contrivances. Howells chose to dwell somewhat mockingly on a lady who tended a foot-powered Radiant Flat Iron, but the masses of visitors were impressed by such marvels as huge machines which turned out 180,000 pins in paper cards or mountains of chewing tobacco or whole editions of the New York *Times* and the *Herald.* Aftersight in 1976 makes us wonder how many people noticed such eventual brand-name successes as Otis elevators, Bissell carpet sweepers, and Bell's telephone. The Californian visitor Harris Newmark was aware of history when he reported his "astonishment at seeing a man before an apparatus apparently in the act of printing letters. He was demonstrating a typewriter, and I dictated to my wife half a dozen lines which he rapidly typed on paper."[12]

Howells' leisurely week at the exhibition afforded him many more sights and surprises, like the long row of reaping machines in Agricultural Hall and Iowa's boastful display of rich soils six feet deep in glass cylinders. He made a return visit there just to glimpse "Old Abe," the veteran eagle mascot of a Wisconsin regiment that ate live chickens and bit too friendly strangers. In the United States Building he joined the crowds admiring the memorabilia of George Washington—his clothes, his camp bed, and his weapons—and was moved to make the invidious remark that no present national leaders would be even remotely worthy of such reverence. He pondered photographs and models of American Indians and then ungenerously suggested that their "false and pitiless savage faces" justified the "moldy flour and corrupt beef" that the government was currently giving the Sioux.[13] Howells was more perceptive about the fact that the government had brilliantly succeeded in bringing to the attention of both taxpayers and foreigners its manifold beneficial activities, as evidenced by the equipment of the Post Office Department and the weather instruments of the Army Signal Corps.

The handful of separate foreign buildings at the exhibition did not stir Howells. Even the much admired Japanese house struck him as merely like the pictures. Many historians feel, on the other hand, that the dramatically simple, uncluttered Oriental building had a tremendous salutary effect in the future on American architects and owners of Victorian mini-castles. The New England critic could not "detect at once the beauty or occasion" of most of the small buildings of twenty-four individual states grouped on the crescent-shaped "States Avenue." Their "unrepresentative architecture" disturbed him, except in the case of Mississippi House, which was of rough bark logs covered with Spanish moss and had a picturesquely slack-jawed white Mississippian lounging without and an intelligent black guide within. In the similarly built Old Colony House of Massachusetts the crowds showed a keen interest in the dried apples and corn hanging from the rafters amid the furnishings of John Alden and Paul Revere. "Altogether the prettiest thing I saw at the Centennial" was when Howells witnessed an "old Quakeress" from Pennsylvania sit down at the spinning wheel and demonstrate that it really worked.[14] Howells was close to awareness that "antiques" were becoming a craze, particularly after the Centennial convinced Americans that they had a past.

Howells wrote that "we thought it well during our week at the Centennial to lunch as variously as possible," and he was delighted to be able to eat "cheaply and well" at restaurants of several nationalities, at the Southern Restaurant, and at the Old Colony House, where they served boiled dinners and baked beans. Along with many others he objected to bad coffee at 25 cents at the Vienna Bakery and called the much-advertised establishment Les Très Frères Provençaux "impudently extortionate," guessing that it got its name from the fact that each of the brothers added his own bill to the total.[15] He did not record if he sampled the novelty of bananas in tin foil sold by hawkers for three cents or Charles E. Hires' root beer made on the spot from roots and spices. Nor did Howells' magazine audience hear of the generally appreciated Department of Public Comfort, which boasted not only washrooms but an array of services from letter-writing desks to binocular rentals. He did enjoy "the gaiety of the approaches and surroundings" of the exhibition, meaning, no doubt, that he spent time in "Shantyville," a whole new city thrown up outside the official grounds where one found freak shows, shooting galleries, and cheap eateries. Everywhere Howells was pleased to encounter "honest and well-behaved liveliness."

Summing up his impressions, Howells decided that "a very pleasant thing about the exhibition is your perfect freedom there. There are numerous officials to direct you, to help you, to care for you, but none of them bothers you." One could find enough of interest at the exhibition to spend a whole season there, but "if you have a single day to spend, it is well to go." Finally, this sophisticate admitted, "no one can now see the fair without a thrill of patriotic pride."[16]

May 18, Indianapolis

THE 240 delegates from eighteen states who formed the First National Convention of the Independent Party entered their second day of deliberations with the enthusiasm of crusaders convinced they were bringing about the millennium, not merely celebrating a centennial. Unlike the Fifth Avenue liberals, the Greenbackers were unabashedly launching a third party. By nominating Peter Cooper as their candidate, they gained begrudging recognition from a hostile national press. The *Herald,* for example, conceded that their choice "shows an elevation of tone not often seen in our politics."[1]

The Greenback delegates could be collectively described as some of the best minds in the country or as some of the biggest misfits, according to people's lights. One of the chief organizers of the convention was Moses Field, a wealthy Detroit businessman who had once been a Democratic congressman. Also from Michigan was Richard Trevellick, one of three delegates with impressive credentials in the labor movement. Neighboring Illinois contributed Robert Campbell, celebrated gadfly of the present Congress, and Adlai E. Stevenson, a newcomer to politics destined to be Vice President. Minnesota's fiery publicist Ignatius Donnelly served as the convention's temporary presiding officer, yielding his gavel in due course to the permanent chairman, Thomas Durant, a lawyer and Republican politician from the state of Washington. The party's secretary was Wallace Groom, editor of the New York *Mercantile Journal* and a close associate of Peter Cooper. Also on hand were John Siney, of the Pennsylvania miners; John Drew of New Jersey, a venerable utopian reformer; D. Wyatt Aiken of South Carolina, a leader of the National Grange; and General James B. Weaver of Iowa, a new face who would one day be the party's standard-bearer.[2]

To characterize this group as a farmer-labor party was something of an oversimplification in view of the absence of genuine representatives of the "producing classes" and the presence of so many politicians, lawyers, businessmen, and intellectuals. What united these reformers of diverse economic interests was the panacea of a managed currency. "From the beginning, Greenbackism had the quality of a transfiguring faith, but its quasi-religious nature had never emerged so clearly as it did at Indianapolis."[3]

The true believers had little difficulty writing their party platform, since their principles had been codified at a hundred previous meetings. Their first demand was the "immediate and unconditional repeal of the specie resumption act of January 14, 1875 and the rescue of our industries from ruin and disaster resulting from its enforcement." The present policy of contraction was termed "suicidal and destructive." Their second plank called for the issuance of United States notes, instead of bank notes, as full legal tender and interchangeable at par with bonds bearing interest at not more than one cent a day per $100. The paper money plus the interconvertible bonds "will afford the best circulating medium ever devised."[4]

With the currency planks taking up half the space of the platform, it became evident that the Greenbackers were a single-issue party at this point in their history. Their declaration said nothing of civil service reform, of Reconstruction, of women's rights, or of any political changes. It promised nothing specifically even for the farmers or for labor. Behind this silence lay neither timidity nor apathy, but rather the unquestioning faith that enough greenbacks would bring high farm prices, end unemployment, and cure all ills.

One minor addition to the platform proposed from the floor provided a historical irony. A Michigan delegate moved that "justice demands" that the government redeem its "coin obligations" in "either gold or silver." Since the platform already contained a gratuitous sneer at the "owners of silver mines," the other delegates were confused by the new idea and the motion was tabled. Later they approved it and thus committed themselves to the doctrine of bimetallism, which was to find full expression twenty years hence in the Populist crusade for the free and unlimited coinage of silver at sixteen to one relative to gold. "Only as an afterthought was the most momentous domestic issue of the next quarter century injected into American politics."[5]

Unanimity also marked the Greenbackers' eventual choice of candidate. During the first day the host Indianans maneuvered to put forward their favorite son, Supreme Court Justice David Davis, but, after some acrimonious debate, the majority balked at his lack of commitment to soft-money doctrine.[6] Later New York's Wallace Groom had little difficulty arousing a thunderous endorsement of the octogenarian ironmonger and philanthropist Peter Cooper. In view of Cooper's age and obvious inability to wage an active campaign, some historians have called it a "foolish choice," one reminiscent of the Republican Liberals in 1872 when they picked the doddering Horace Greeley.[7] Yet all would agree that Peter Cooper lent the new party needed respectability and that his convictions were both forceful and tenacious. Nor would any deny that the prospect of Cooper's financing the impoverished Greenbackers carried great weight with the delegates.

[134]

With far more geographical boldness than either major political party would display for decades, the Greenback convention chose as Cooper's running mate Senator Newton Booth of California, a Democratic politician who had fought the railroad interests and other monopolies while governor of his state and had won his seat in Washington over their determined opposition. Many delegates openly expressed the hope that Cooper would resign in favor of his energetic, youthful vice president after leading the party to victory. When tendered the nomination later, however, Senator Booth refused to bolt the Democratic Party, and the party's Executive Committee had to select another man, turning to General Samuel F. Cary of Ohio, an ex-congressman, the representative of the Cincinnati trade unions, one of the original organizers of the Greenback movement, and a good stump orator.[8]

When Peter Cooper was notified of his nomination by New York reporters, his initial reaction was a flat and seemingly final refusal to run. Later he unbent to the extent of agreeing to be candidate if neither major party adopted the Greenback money planks at their upcoming conventions. Responding to an interviewer's baited flattery about his possible political impact as the "great unknown," the kindly old man mused aloud: "God knows I love my country and would cheerfully lay down my life for her in this dark hour of her need." Cooper formally acknowledged the "great honor" paid him by the Independent Party but declared that he had hopes that "wise counsels" might prevail in the other parties. "I therefore accept your nomination conditionally," he wrote. Two weeks later Cooper was informed, perhaps teasingly, by reporters that many predicted some sort of standoff in the election, the decision being thrown into the House of Representatives, and his being the compromise choice. Worried but game, he replied, "I regard my possible selection as President of the United States with positive alarm. . . . God knows I pray against it. . . . But if it must be Cooper, Cooper is prepared."[9]

May 23, Boston

THE first no-hit baseball game was pitched before a crowd of 20,000 by Joe Borden of the local team. Thereafter Borden went into such a slump that he ended up the season as his club's groundskeeper. Nor did the Boston Red Stockings win the pennant this year for the fifth time in a row; rather Chicago took it to the West at last, having had 52 wins and 14 losses.

Like so much else in the Grant era, professional baseball had just gone through a major scandal. Charges were being aired about drunkenness, gambling in and out of the clubhouses, and stealing players from other teams. As a result, the original association of just four years' standing disbanded, and on February 2, behind closed doors at New York's Grand Central Hotel, a group of high-minded promoters joined to found the National League of Professional Baseball Clubs under the presidency of Morgan G. Bulkeley, later governor of Connecticut and U.S. senator. They adopted bylaws standardizing players' contracts, banning liquor and betting, and limiting club franchises to eight cities, four East and four West. Boston won the first league game against the Philadelphia Athletics on April 2. The other teams were the New York Mutuals, Hartford, the Chicago White Stockings, Cincinnati, Louisville, and St. Louis. Within a year it was necessary to suspend New York and Philadelphia from the league for infractions.

Regarding spectator sports generally, football was still a game left to collegians in this era, and basketball was not played until 1891. The newspapers catered to a widespread public interest in professional boxing. In a match billed as the world's heavyweight championship, Joe Goss of England went twenty-seven bare-knuckle rounds with Tom Allen, an American, at Covington, Kentucky, on September 27 before the latter was ruled the loser for fouling. Marquess of Queensberry rules and the John L. Sullivan era were still more than a decade away.

The press also gave coverage to yachting, particularly the twenty-five-year-old *America*'s cup race, which this year took place off Montauk Point on August 11 and resulted in this country's schooner defeating a Canadian challenger in two races. Polo was the rich man's new sport. Introduced at Dickel's Riding Academy in New York in 1874 by Anglophile James Gordon Bennett, the games this year in Newport featured such names as August Belmont and Leonard Jerome. Tennis, another import from England and brought to the United States the same year as polo, was starting to engage genteel society, as was the somewhat earlier discovery croquet.

Popular participatory sports included bowling, as old as Rip Van Winkle; roller skating, a midcentury innovation; and bicycle riding, a more recent phenomenon. The first velocipedes were so crude and uncomfortable as to be known also as boneshakers. Later came the ordinary, which achieved a gear ratio by means of the enlarged front wheel (sometimes 64 inches to the rear wheels' 12 inches), and English models of these were a much noticed exhibit at the Centennial Exhibition. The modern safety bicycle with equal-sized wheels and mechanical gearing was actually invented by H. J. Lawson in 1876, and by the next decade bicycling became a universal craze.[1]

June 1, St. George, Utah

FEW Americans excited so much universal curiosity and outrage as did Brigham Young, who this day celebrated his seventy-fifth birthday among some of his devoted disciples. Early in the morning a band and choir serenaded him at his house. Later the bewhiskered, piercing-eyed patriarch gathered together several of his wives and crossed the plaza of this newly built settlement to attend services in the handsome sandstone tabernacle, services at which hymns to the Mormon God were interspersed with paeans to the living messiah. Returning home, Brigham Young was greeted by a group of young ladies dressed in white, "who sang a touching song, composed for the occasion, and suiting action to the word, strewed flowers from the gate to the house for him to walk on."[1]

If the Mormon leader did not rest content with the admiration of his womenfolk, he could reflect upon a lifetime of mingled triumphs and vexations. Currently he was involved in a divorce suit and other litigation of a political nature. These scandals and his whole career as a pioneer and a polygamist were being well canvassed in the press back East in this golden age of inquiring journalism.

The Mormon religion was divinely revealed to Joseph Smith in the 1830s. After the assassination of this native American prophet in Illinois, 5,000 of his followers under the direction of Brigham

Young had made their heroic trek across the American wilderness and created a thriving group of settlements around Great Salt Lake. By 1870 the Church of the Latter-Day Saints had 171 branches and 87,838 members concentrated in the Utah region. St. George, 350 miles south of Salt Lake City, was one of the most recent colonies, created by thirty families who joined the "United Order of Enoch" and pooled their worldly goods, at the instigation of Brigham Young's words to them: "There will be no poor, no rich, or rather all will be rich."[2] Such communistic arrangements really bespoke an earlier Utah, whose farms, mines, and stores were now very much in the hands of capitalists, large and small, Mormon and "gentile." Brigham Young himself was a millionaire business operator, having only recently retired from such enterprises as the Zion's Cooperative Mercantile Institution, which paid 15 percent, and the Deseret National Bank. Besides the modest cottage at St. George, which he favored for this birthday celebration, Young had a mansion in Provo and was building a thirty-six-room house in downtown Salt Lake City that was known as Amalia's Palace.

It had proved impossible to create a Mormon utopia isolated from the rest of the United States. After actual military hostilities in the 1850s, federally appointed governors, judges, and marshals administered Utah as a territory. The Mormons' detestation of outsiders did not prevent the main line of the transcontinental railroad from crossing their lands, although they did succeed in detouring it north of their capital (the historic linking of the Union Pacific and Central Pacific took place in 1869 at Promontory Point, Utah). In the course of his running battles with Washington, Young had once labeled President Grant and Congress a bunch of "liars, thieves, whoremongers, drunkards, and gamblers,"[3] but in 1874, as governor, he had graciously escorted the President from the railroad junction at Ogden to Salt Lake City.

The Mormon practice of polygamy was, of course, the cause of all the trouble. Dom Pedro, making a stopover in Salt Lake City in the spring of 1876, said jocularly that he had come to see Brigham Young's seraglio, but he also wondered aloud seriously: "I don't see why the Yankees permit polygamy in the center of the United States."[4] Plural marriage for only the Mormon elders had been the original idea of the martyred Joseph Smith, who was completely a victim of his own animal passions, in the view of even

Mormon historians. Polygamy for the masses was Young's special contribution to Mormon theology, motivated by the shrewd calculation that the faithful needed a distinctive custom to keep them together.

In the course of his life Brigham Young himself had as many as seventy wives, a score of whom were living in 1876. Constantly pestered by reporters and others on the subject of the number of his wives, he once confided suddenly: "I don't know myself! I never refuse to marry any respectable woman who asks me, and it is often the case that I am separated from a woman at the marriage altar, never to see her again, to know her. My children I keep track of, however. I have fifty-seven now living and have lost three."[5] Calling himself "a great lover of women" in the sense that he liked "to see them happy, to see them well fed and well clothed," Young denied that he was subject to lust or even needful of female companionship. He took women to save them, he claimed, citing the case of his first wife, who was "the poorest girl I could find in the town."[6] His enemies, on the other hand, insisted that Young was a lecherous, tyrannical womanizer and spoke of his "queens." As for the women of all types and ages who "sealed" themselves to the Mormon leader, many did it voluntarily, some on parental orders, their motives involving spiritual or material security.

The source of added notoriety and new distress for Brigham Young in his seventy-fifth year was Ann Eliza Webb, wife number fifty or so, who had the effrontery to sue him for divorce, demand substantial alimony, and publicize her disenchantment with marriage and Mormonism. She had married Young in 1868, being forty years younger than her husband. According to Ann Eliza, Brigham became infatuated with her during a visit to the farm of her parents, to whom he made promises of a fine house and a generous allowance for her, and despite her "crying and moaning," she was forced into the union, which turned out to be a nightmare of cruelty and neglect. Young's version was that he was "importuned" by the senior Webbs to save their divorced daughter from going astray and that he made the mistake of allying himself with a silly, inconsiderate creature who turned out to be a slut as well.[7] In 1875 a court awarded Ann Eliza Webb $500-a-month alimony, but not the quarter million cash that she asked for. Young spent a week in jail rather than pay, and the case dragged on for many months, until a judge annulled the marriage and made the husband pay only court costs. The scandal of Ann Eliza's prosecution of Young would probably be "fatal to the system" of Mormonism because it made him look "ridiculous" and robbed him of his "halo of sanctity," in the observation of John Leng, a Scot traveler of 1876.[8]

The Eastern press gave much coverage to Young's being recently acquitted in a murder case and also to charges by a man that he had killed several persons on Young's express orders. Then in 1875 occurred another sensational court case, involving not Young but a former trusted lieutenant, who was convicted and later executed for perpetrating the horrendous massacre of Indians at Mountain Meadows. The condemned man accused Young of having "sacrificed me in a dastardly and treacherous manner" but abjured his sons "to leave vengeance to God."[9] With so many enemies at large, it is small wonder that Young traveled to and from St. George in the summer of 1876 with a guard of seventy-five men. "He went fully armed and protected like some European monarch in danger of assault from disaffected subjects."[10] Yet late in July he was observed by a Centennial traveler from California serenely sitting in the Opera House of Salt Lake City with two of his wives "fanning him assiduously."[11]

Brigham Young lived just past his seventy-sixth birthday. His death moved the New York *Times* to rate him as a "cruel, bloody, vindictive" dictator but one with "abilities of a superior order.[12] The Mormon press dwelled on the unrivaled pioneering achievement and benevolent actions of their departed leader, whom scandals pursued to the grave. Brigham Young, Jr., proved to be anything but a worthy successor, having been released from an English jail only after a lavish expenditure of Mormon missionary funds. Five of the elder Young's daughters accused the church officials of defrauding them of more than half of their father's $2,500,000 estate. As for Brigham Young's cherished polygamy, a Mormon president in 1890 decided that it was an ideal but suspended its practice. Utah was duly rewarded by admission to the Union as a state in 1896.

June 3, New York

SATURDAY was always a pleasant day for Herman Melville since as a federal employee he did not have to work. Today he was further elated by the notice of the publication of his first major work in a decade, a long, philosophic narrative in verse called *Clarel: A Poem and Pilgrimage in the Holy Land.* The book was the fruit of a trip he had made to the Middle East twenty years before.

There were reviews of the book at least, but all were unfavorable. The *Tribune* on June 16 conceded "a vein of earnestness" but otherwise dismissed it as a "mixture of skill and awkwardness, thought and aimless fancy, plan shattered by whim, and melody broken by discords." According to the *World* on June 26, "a work of art it is not in any sense or measure." The *Times* on July 10 declared that "it should have been written in prose." The most revealing review of all appeared in *Lippincott's Magazine* in September: "If Mr. Melville has written anything since the three captivating books *Omoo, Typee,* and *Mardi,* which were the delight of our early youth, we do not know of it."[1] The second of the books mentioned was Melville's first published work of thirty years previously. The reviewer had apparently missed Melville's masterpiece of 1851, *Moby Dick,* which at the time aroused more puzzlement and abuse than awe. As long as Melville wrote adventure stories, he was popular, but when he became metaphysical and psychological, he lost his audience.

Melville, who would be fifty-seven this year, was even more forgotten than Walt Whitman. He now lived very modestly in a yellow brick house at 104 East Twenty-sixth Street with his wife, Elizabeth, who was the daughter of a Massachusetts chief justice. Once Melville's parents had prospered in the Hudson Valley, and the author himself had owned a farm outside Pittsfield, where he mingled with Nathaniel Hawthorne and his set. He had twice traveled abroad.

Weekdays, the square-bearded, grave-looking, heavyset New Yorker left his house on Twenty-sixth Street and walked unnoticed to Madison Square, then down Fifth Avenue, and finally across Fourteenth Street with its newly elegant shops. The New York Customs House was at 507 West Street on the Gansevoort Street Pier, the latter ironically the surname of Melville's uncle, who died this year, having given his nephew the $1,200 needed to publish *Clarel*. As an assistant customs inspector Melville was "a pariah among outcasts, impecunious bankers, broken-down sports . . . political non-descripts, non-entities."[2] Twice, in 1873 and this summer, the politicians of the notorious Customs House Ring tried to have Melville dismissed. As a friend wrote in his defense, the "proud, shy, sensitively honorable" writer was "surrounded by venality," but "he puts it all quietly aside; gently declining offers of money for special services; quietly returning money which has been thrust into his pockets behind his back; avoiding offense alike to the corrupting merchants and their clerks and runners who thought that all men can be bought."[3] In the spring Melville and 282 other inspectors did receive a wage reduction from $4 to $3.60 a day from Treasury officials who apparently felt that reform begins at the bottom. On October 1 the old wage rate was restored.

Life this year for Melville had some bright spots. In mid-August he spent two weeks' vacation with his wife and two daughters in the White Mountains. On his return he wrote: "Lizzie and the girls are jolly. . . . I myself am ever hilarious."[4] Melville's convivial side had returned after the earlier months when he was in a "frightfully nervous state" proofreading *Clarel*, the book having "undermined all our happiness," according to a letter of his wife.[5] On October 11 Melville visited the Centennial Exhibition, which he described to a cousin as a "sort of tremendous Vanity Fair."[6] At the end of the year there was a welcome letter from Stanwix, one of his two sons, who wanted $60 to go from San Francisco to the Black Hills.

Melville lived another twenty-five years. In time, family bequests left him much more comfortably off, and his talent surfaced again brilliantly in his short novel *Billy Budd* of 1891.

If Melville was ignored in 1876, who were the authors considered safe, smart, or popular? Relative to the first category of safe or respectable, one indication was which writers were approached by the Centennial Commission. First of all, they made a gesture to the South by enlisting Sidney Lanier, thirty-four, who did write his cantata "The Centennial Meditation of Columbia" and thereafter remained a genuine but unrewarded poetic talent. For the matching Centennial Hymn the choice fell on Pennsylvania's Bayard Taylor, fifty-one, a facile romanticist past his prime and so bitter about it as to characterize 1876 as the "blackest period" of American literature. Henry Wadsworth Longfellow, almost seventy, was the beloved household poet asked to write the Centennial Ode, but he declined, as did James Russell Lowell, Oliver Wendell Holmes and William Cullen Bryant, the three ranging in age from fifty-seven to eighty-two. Finally, the fifty-year-old John Greenleaf Whittier met the "emergency."[7]

Which writers were considered most promising by the intellectual community was suggested by the contents of the *Atlantic Monthly.* The June issue was particularly rich, containing Mark Twain's "Carnival of Crime" and the opening chapter of Henry James' *The American,* as well as a piece by William Dean Howells, Whittier's "Hymn," an article on railroads by Charles Francis Adams, Jr., and an article on Buddha by Felix Adler. Earlier in the year the magazine had a poem, "Boston," by Ralph Waldo Emerson, seventy-three. The poem was motivated by the Centennial, and the great transcendentalist managed to go to Philadelphia and be "dazzled and astounded" by the exhibition.[8] At other times the magazine had works by Charles Dudley Warner on his travels in the Middle East and poems by Helen Hunt Jackson and James Russell Lowell.

As for the most popular writers, Melville would have been sickened by this year's absolute best-seller, *Helen's Babies* by John Habberton. This saccharine book, now relegated to the juvenile fiction shelves, consisted in considerable measure of baby talk. Three women authors were consistently at the top of the lists. Helen Hunt Jackson was at the peak of her career as a sentimental, formula-type novelist. Louisa May Alcott, of *Little Women* fame, published a work called *Silver Pitchers* this season. Likewise, Harriet Beecher Stowe was exploiting an earlier reputation and fighting old battles. In terms of sales, no one approached the success of Horatio Alger, Jr., with his novels for boys.

June 9, Boston

THE keeper of the Bunker Hill Monument was aroused at six o'clock in the morning by the ringing of a bearlike man with a foreign accent wearing a rumpled Prince Albert coat and a slouch hat. When the visitor was asked for the 50 cents' admission fee, he frowned, and, instead of searching for change, he secured the sum from his cabdriver. Some hours later a new arrival at the monument excitedly pointed out to the guard the first signature in the daybook, "Dom Pedro, Emperor of Brazil." The keeper was less than impressed, rejoining with annoyance: "Emperor! That's a dodge. That fellow was only a scapegrace, without a cent in his pockets."[1]

Dom Pedro had arrived in Boston the night before and subsequently found it to be his favorite American city. Since sharing the honors with President Grant at the opening of the Philadelphia Exhibition, the Brazilian ruler had crisscrossed much of the country. He had gone north to peruse art galleries in Baltimore and to watch naval maneuvers at Annapolis. He had traveled west again by train to Cincinnati, Louisville, and St. Louis, taking in such sights as a slaughterhouse, the Mammoth Cave, and an insane asylum. He went down the Mississippi River on a steamer. In New Orleans for once he did not succeed in avoiding the crush of an official reception before he checked in at the St. Charles Hotel, but as usual, he found a variety of places to inspect privately in the Louisianan seaport, whose old-world, unhurried atmosphere did not altogether please him. And he had the usual disconcerting queries about things like race relations and control of yellow fever, which were problems shared by his own country.

At the beginning of June Dom Pedro was back in Washington. He had opportunity to observe that Mount Vernon was neglected, which it was, and he subscribed to a fund for the Washington Monument, which was not finished in time for the Centennial because of congressional parsimony. Then the Brazilian ruler was off to that must for tourists in 1876, Niagara Falls, where he, but not the empress, donned oilskins for the tour beneath the waters of the torrent. From western New York the royal party entered Canada for a brief stay, which included a boat ride through the Thousand Islands and a dawn visit to the meat markets of Montreal. On his way southeast to Boston, Dom Pedro saw the mills at Lowell, but he had no comments on the strikes in progress or the unemployment problem, which then were not concerns in his own realm.

On the same day he provoked the watchman at the Bunker Hill Monument, Dom Pedro did the most extensive sightseeing imaginable through the hub city of New England. He went from the downtown monuments such as Faneuil Hall and the Statehouse out to the Charlestown Navy Yard, where he was shown about by the commandant, Captain Alfred Thayer Mahan, who was within two months to lose his job and gain his calling. His imperial majesty took the horsecar back to Boston and found time to inspect the city prison, to watch a demonstration by the municipal fire engines and fireboat, and to take notes on a newly invented system of railroad signals.

Everywhere Dom Pedro traveled he paid the keenest heed to educational institutions, and he observed that Boston's public schools at all levels were the finest of the fine in the United States. He visited the just-founded women's college at Wellesley, and he was particularly impressed with the laboratory equipment at the Harvard Medical School. Massachusetts General Hospital also claimed hours of his interest. When asked to speak before the State Medical Society, he demurred with the words "I am not a medical but a social physician."[2] One particularly fateful visit was to the Boston City School for the Deaf, where he made the acquaintance of one of the teachers, Alexander Graham Bell, and asked him to communicate his therapeutic methods to his Brazilian counterparts.

With Boston's cultural celebrities Dom Pedro did not so much make acquaintances as renew them. He was very moved to see again the wife of the late Professor Louis Agassiz, the great paleontologist who had visited Brazil years before. Through Mrs. Agassiz a reception was arranged at the Radical Club so that the emperor could talk with the poet Whittier, whom he had both translated and corresponded with. The exuberant Brazilian managed to give the starchy New Englander an enthusiastic embrace upon parting. Another satisfying time for Dom Pedro was dinner in Cambridge with an even more revered poet, Henry Wadsworth Longfellow, who afterward wrote in his *Journal* that he found Dom Pedro a "genial, hearty, noble person," who traveled about unceremoniously like a "modern Haroun-al-Raschid."[3]

Leaving Boston's schools and scholars with some reluctance, Dom Pedro still had a long catalogue of experiences in the United States before him. He showed up at the races at Saratoga, New York, and he also tasted the "season" at Newport, Rhode Island, where the historian George Bancroft entertained him. He saw more colleges, notably Vassar and Yale, more prisons, notably Sing Sing, and more factories, notably the Bethlehem Steel Works with its relatively new Bessemer furnaces. He made return visits to New York City and Philadelphia, this time going daily to the exhibition as a private tourist, extraordinary only in his thoroughness and tirelessness. No matter how early he arrived, not matter how studied his disguise, he was always recognized by the crowds, an inconvenience for him, but the inevitable tribute to one who may well have been the most familiar and beloved foreign guest this country has ever known.

When Dom Pedro and his empress finally sailed for Europe in mid-July, he had finished a tour of more than 9,000 miles, which, as the press noted, served for a far better acquaintanceship with the country than possessed by most of our own public servants. Thirteen years later, when the monarchy of Pedro II was overthrown in favor of a republic in Brazil, people in the United States who remembered the "Yankee Emperor" were more puzzled than elated.

Many times during Dom Pedro's visit the press found occasion to contrast his earnestness with the frivolity of Britain's Prince of Wales, whose tour of India during early 1876 was represented as consisting mainly in dancing and pigsticking. The hurt, of course, was that the future Edward VII refused to grace the Centennial Exhibition (one editor, distressed by the low attendance figures at Fairmount Park, went so far as to propose enticing Queen Victoria herself to visit this country by hastily erecting a statue of her late husband, Prince Albert).

June 11, Washington

NO politician in America had quite the knack for stealing the headlines that James G. Blaine did. This Sunday, just three days before the Republican convention in Cincinnati, the Maine congressman collapsed on the steps of the Congregational Church and was carried home unconscious. The hostile press might be shrilly satiric, as with BLAINE FEIGNS FAINT, but the sympathy vote was at Blaine's bedside.[1]

Blaine's seizure followed two weeks of other sensational stories involving him. The publication of the first of the "Mulligan Letters" in the *Sun* on May 27 served to confirm the worst suspicions about Blaine's involvement in corrupt railroad dealings. His supporter Garfield wrote shortly afterward: "I greatly fear this letter will lose Blaine the nomination."[2] Mulligan himself was on the witness stand before a House investigating committee on May 31, and the country was treated to the startling testimony that Blaine had gone to Mulligan and on his hands and knees begged him not to ruin him, his wife, and six children by speaking out and that he had promised him a consulship in return for silence. It transpired that Mulligan relented so far as to let Blaine see the incriminating letters and that the Maine congressman took them and refused to return them. Blaine also refused to let the House committee examine the letters when ordered to do so on Friday, June 2.

Blaine used the weekend to plan strategy. Not only his candidacy for the presidency but his very seat in the House could be forfeit. On Monday, June 5, he rose to make one of the most controversial speeches of the year. Always the actor, he brandished the Mulligan Letters in his hand and read carefully selected excerpts from them. He accused the committee chairman of having withheld exculpatory evidence. He reached the crescendo of his eloquence when he said, "I invite the confidence of forty-four million of my fellow countrymen." Obviously relieved, Garfield wrote in his journal: "I have never witnessed so dramatic a scene since I have been in the House. It may give Blaine the nomination."[3] Less impressed was the Democratic committee chairman who muttered to a colleague, "your friend Blaine is the God-damnedest scoundrel in America."[4] Henry Adams wrote Lodge: "Poor Blaine squeals louder than all the other pigs. Schenck, Colfax, Belknap were all nothing to him. Beecher alone can match him. I think Blaine's speech of Monday matches for impudence and far exceeds in insolence anything that Beecher ever did."[5] Historians seeking some event analogous to Blaine's performance may have found it in Nixon's "Checkers Speech" of 1952.

Blaine's speech left too many unanswered questions to still his critics. His fainting at church the following Sunday, however, did effectively postpone further congressional investigation until after the Republican convention.

Friends of Blaine genuinely feared for his life, many of them at this moment gathering in Cincinnati. Hayes put in his diary, rather hypocritically in view of other events, "my eyes are almost blinded with tears as I write."[6] Garfield was bitter: "if he dies of this, it will be the work of political assassination, as really as though he'd been stabbed." The Ohio congressman went to Blaine's house in Washington and took charge of his affairs, sending off wires to Blaine's manager at the convention. On Tuesday, June 13, Garfield reported Blaine "still unconscious though I think he knows a great deal of what is said to him." At 8 P.M., just when his associates were about to send off a pessimistic report, Blaine roused himself and sent off "a connected and beautiful dispatch. . . . The cloud is lifted and he is himself again."[7] Later the great stage manager persuaded Secretary Fish to ride with him in a carriage through the streets of Washington, showing that he had recovered and that, perhaps, he had the blessing of the administration.

June 14, San Francisco

THE most bizarre municipal ordinances of the year came out of San Francisco. On this day, for example, the mayor with a straight face signed into law an authorization for the sheriff to cut the hair of all prisoners in the county jail to within one inch of their scalps. Known as the Queue Law, it had no other aim than to harass the city's growing Chinese population.

The fifth largest city in the country, San Francisco for several decades had been a teeming seaport and more recently the terminus of the transcontinental railroad. In size it was twenty times larger than Los Angeles. The great earthquake was yet thirty years away. San Francisco's Palace Hotel was regarded as one of the most elegant in the country. In 1873 appeared the familiar cable cars which transported people between such diverse sections as the mansion-studded Nob Hill and the flagrantly vice-ridden Barbary Coast. The city boasted several theaters, two opera houses, and eating establishments of all nationalities, attesting to its cosmopolitan nature and spirit. Chinatown was already a picturesque attraction for tourists, but in 1876 for most white San Franciscans the Oriental enclave was the object of hysterical hatred and eventually massive violence.

The gold rush of '49, which rapidly populated California with

Easterners, also brought the first influx of Chinese to the coast. The passage from Hong Kong cost $50, and shipowners and labor contractors conspired to bring over great numbers of "coolies" under conditions which recalled the horrors of the slave trade in blacks. There were 25,000 Chinese on the Pacific coast in 1852; 50,000 by 1867; and 100,000 by 1875. In 1876, 22,000 more entered the United States. The railroad construction boom accounted for the spurt in immigration: nine-tenths of the track-layers were Chinese, unsung heroes of American progress.

The panic of '73 had been slow to produce a bad unemployment situation in California, until the cessation of railroad building drove thousands of Chinese laborers into the cities. A few prospered as grocers, laundrymen, restaurateurs, and gardeners, but the mass of coolies came to compete for the same unskilled jobs as the whites. The press began to picture as a composite of evil the low-subsistence level of the Orientals, their living packed several to a room, their forgoing wives and children, their strange customs and religion, and their association with opium dens and such.

The problem of the "Mongolians," according to contemporary usage, had engaged Californian legislators for several years. The main obstacle to all their efforts was a federal treaty, the Burlingame Treaty of 1868 with the Celestial Empire, which opened China to American businessmen and in return provided that Chinese immigration to this country would not be restricted, nor Chinese immigrants discriminated against in any way. On April 3, 1876, the state assembly appropriated $5,000 for a new lobbying attempt in Washington to secure the abrogation of the treaty, and on the same day the State Senate set up an investigative committee, which duly recommended the total exclusion of the Chinese from the country.

Tried before and voided, the Queue Law that San Francisco's mayor signed on June 14 was the perversely logical consequence of other anti-Chinese ordinances. For example, the city supervisors solemnly decreed that it was illegal to walk on the sidewalks with a stick across one's shoulders from which were suspended bundles or baskets. In case this did not suffice to thwart Chinatown's laundrymen, the supervisors followed it up with an incredible tax statute providing that owners of laundries using one horse for deliveries pay $2 a quarter, those with two horses pay $4, and those with no horses pay $15. Then came a state law levying harsh money penalties on those who let out and those who rented rooms in the city containing less than 500 cubic feet per lodger. Hundreds of Chinese were jailed under these ordinances since they refused to pay the fines. The overcrowding of the county jail was the rationale for the Queue Law. For whites a free haircut from the sheriff was one thing; for the Chinese the loss of their long pigtails meant social disgrace. It took three years for the new law to be declared unreasonable and unconstitutional.[1]

California's Chinese had few defenders, notably a handful of philanthropists who found themselves in an unseemly alliance with exploiters of coolie labor. Both major parties in 1876 took stands in favor of Chinese exclusion. Organized labor in the East was likewise antagonistic, especially after a Massachusetts industrialist brought in a few score Chinese as strikebreakers.

Actually, the Chinese question was primarily a labor problem. Sienkiewicz sensed this fact, reporting that the Chinese would work for one dollar when others wanted two and that therefore, "in the conflict between labor and capital, the Chinese have tipped the scales decisively in favor of capital."[2] David Phillips, author of *Letters from California for 1876,* despised Mexican-Americans as "poor, lazy, vicious, and drunken," but he had nothing but admiration for the Chinese by contrast: "the Chinaman's only sin is he will work . . . he is neat, clean, sober, and patient, always submissive, peaceable, and quiet."[3]

In 1877 the Chinese "menace" spawned a grass-roots reaction in California in the form of the Workingmen's Trade and Labor Union of San Francisco led by a newfound young demagogue named Denis Kearney, who previously had shown nothing but contempt for trade unionism. The intemperate Kearney and his xenophobic mobs used the job issue to justify massacre of San Francisco's Chinese in the "Sand-lot Riots" of that year. Kearney cowed respectable citizens by threatening to turn Nob Hill mansions into worker dormitories, and his party become strong enough to make and unmake elected officials and eventually to rewrite the state constitution. In five years' time the anti-Chinese lobby secured a new treaty with the Chinese Empire which empowered the United States to regulate, limit, and suspend Chinese immigration, but not to prohibit it altogether.

June 14, Valley of the Rosebud

FOR the Sioux the season was the Moon When the Chokecherries Are Ripe. "You could hardly count the tepees" of the great Indian camp which stretched for three miles in this isolated valley in eastern Montana.[1] Near the center of the encampment was a circular arbor of pine boughs with a center pole supporting a buffalo image and other ceremonial regalia. Here for eighteen hours the venerated medicine man and chief Sitting Bull had been performing a sun dance or ghost dance, grunting and crooning as he repeatedly lacerated his naked arms and chest, his eyes glazed and sore as he stared into the blazing sun. At last the dancer began hallucinating and then fainted. When Sitting Bull came to from his trance, he related the vision he had sought so strenuously. He saw hundreds of blue-coated soldiers falling head first into the Sioux camp. A voice told him, "I give you these because they have no ears." So it was to be, his listeners were assured, that victory would be theirs over the white man who would no longer negotiate.[2]

For as long as anyone could remember the Sioux had held a two-week summer conference of all the tribes. The hundreds of lodges were traditionally set up near Bear Butte in the sacred Black Hills. A great circular tent with eighteen-foot roof poles was where the chiefs met to discuss and settle affairs, while elsewhere the men, women, and children engaged in wrestling, racing, singing, and dancing to the drums. Because of the Indians' preoccupation with this annual gathering, Custer and the surveyors had been able to push unmolested into the Black Hills in 1874. Now Bear Butte was in shouting distance of the roaring miners' camp at Deadwood Gulch.

Even if the grand assembly this year had to be in the valley 200 miles west of the Black Hills, the call had gone out, and, after Sitting Bull's extraordinary vision, a final summons was sent to the men still with the Indian agencies in western Dakota and Nebraska. Hundreds more slipped away, but this fact was not reported by the Indian agents for venal reasons relating to their receiving governmental largess proportionate to their reported body counts.

The Indian encampment actually had to be moved frequently to provide fresh pasture for the livestock, and the day after the sun dance the whole horde trekked across the Wolf Mountains to a new location on the west bank of the Little Bighorn River. Back at the earlier campsite the Sioux had left pictures drawn in the sand and rows of painted rocks showing soldiers tumbling down with their hats falling off.

The preeminence Sitting Bull had won as a leader was unusual among the Indians, who rarely extended their loyalty beyond their clan and even in battle were not attuned to taking orders. Every chief in conference was supposedly equal, but now it was conceded that Sitting Bull was "above all the others."[3] His great achievement in 1876 was to unite with his Hunkpapa Sioux not only their kinsmen Sioux like the Oglala but also many Cheyenne and Arapaho.

The only son of Chief Jumping Bull had been born in the Black Hills in the late 1830s and suffered his father to call him the Slow One until he was fourteen and bested an enemy in a fight with coupsticks (for the Sioux landing a blow on a foe at close range was a most important achievement even in a battle with bullets or arrows). With the more prestigious name Sitting Bull, he spent his early years fighting other Indians like the Crow, upon whom he took vengeance for killing his father. The white man was no concern of Sitting Bull until the very end of the Civil War, when he got into a fracas with a general at Fort Rice, Missouri. In subsequent years he emerged as the most belligerent and uncompromising of the nontreaty Indians.[4]

Sitting Bull's name at least was familiar to newspaper readers long before 1876. Occasionally he might be referred to by journalists with heavy-handed humor by such titles as "Slightly Recumbant Gentleman Cow,"[5] but usually he rated terms like "monstrous villain."[6] Little was reported about him personally, and Custer told his Chicago interviewers on February 13 that actually there were physically two Sitting Bulls, a good one and a bad one. Frank Grouard, a pony express rider captured by Indians who was saved by Sitting Bull and lived with him for three years after 1869, could have dispelled some misapprehensions with his later description of the leader: "His name was a 'tipi word' for all that was generous and great. The bucks admired him, the squaws respected him highly, and the children loved him. He would have proved a mighty power among our politicians—a great vote-getter with the people." A missionary woman who met Sitting Bull allowed that the unhandsome but muscular, imperious, and well-spoken Indian was something of a lady-killer; he had "some indefinable power."[7]

Not a battle commander or primarily a political chieftain, Sitting Bull was truly a medicine man, a fakir. His visions were his justification, and he sat out battles communing with the gods. By his logic when Red Cloud and the other treaty Indians went off to Washington and reported back the evidences of the white man's power, theirs were only fantasies induced by white man's medicine. Yet the dreamer and conjurer could be quick-thinking, cunning, and energetic when he had to take responsibility for the daily fate of his people.

Another prominent leader in the Indian camp on the Little Bighorn was Crazy Horse, of the Oglala Sioux, also born in the Black Hills, where as a youth he had a self-induced hallucination from which he gained his name. Lithe, of medium height, Crazy Horse had such a light complexion that he was taken for a white captive among the Indians. For years his father by the same name had nursed hatreds against the despoilers of the Indian lands, and Crazy Horse had also learned first hand of degradation and fraud at Fort Laramie. He was the young chieftain who led the decoy maneuver in 1866 that brought about the massacre of Lieutenant Fetterman and his entire command. Now he was Sitting Bull's loyal subordinate, the best tactician, and the field commander of the Sioux.[8]

The camp of Sitting Bull and Crazy Horse held possibly the largest number of Indians that had ever assembled in one place in North America. Six tribal circles were laid out: the Hunkpapa in accordance with their very name were at the head or upstream end; the Sans Arc, Miniconjou, Oglala, and Brule were ranged below them; and the Cheyenne, "fiercest of all frontier cavalry," occupied the north position.[9] With women and children, there were, perhaps, 10,000 people in 1,500 or more lodges. One rule-of-thumb calculation was 3 warriors per lodge, so that the fighting men numbered around 4,500.

The news that cavalry were approaching from the south on June 16 brought half the Sioux warriors back into the Valley of the Rosebud. General Crook had left Fort Fetterman on May 29 and again marched up the old Bozeman Trail with a force of more than 1,000 men. At 8:30 A.M. June 17 Crook's scouts encountered the Indians, and an all-day battle began in very broken terrain. The cavalry officers were amazed at the combativeness and staying power of their enemy. Crazy Horse's leading what was an organized battle charge at one point was unprecedented in memory. Crook made the mistake of sending part of his command to strike at a nonexistent village, and they were able to rejoin the others only as a result of the steady performance under fire of the Crow and Shoshone auxiliaries. In the end, the Indians left Crook in possession of the battlefield, causing him to claim victory, but the next day he retreated southward to his base camp and did not move his force again for a month, despite urgent pleas from Washington.[10]

Known to the Sioux as the "Battle Where the Girl Saved Her Brother," the Battle of the Rosebud was fully reported in newspapers back East. Unfortunately, news of it could not reach General Terry's joint force now less than 100 miles away to the north in the wilderness. The engagement with equal numbers on a side was realistically General Crook's second defeat in 1876. Crook's assertion that the 25,000 rounds his men fired had killed twice as many Indians as the ten soldiers lost provoked the *Herald* to estimate that it was costing the government $1,000,000 for each Sioux warrior dispatched.

Crazy Horse withdrew his warriors to the great encampment on the Little Bighorn. A week later the Sioux were at first caught by surprise when they were assaulted from another direction. In the recollection of Low Dog: "I heard the alarm, but I did not believe it. I did not think any white man would attack us, so strong as we were."[11]

June 15, Chicago

THE woman on trial, looking pale and drawn and dressed in luxurious widow's weeds, was Mrs. Abraham Lincoln. The hearing in the Cook County Court was brief. The jury found quickly and unanimously that Mrs. Lincoln had been "restored to reason" and thereby reversed a decision of a year previously that she was insane enough to be confined.

Mary Todd Lincoln had endured every possible heartbreak as wife and mother. She had lost two of her sons before her husband's assassination in 1865 destroyed almost all her happiness. Then her favorite son, Tad, had died in 1871. The very next year she was forced to involve herself in newspaper controversy and legal wranglings occasioned by the most scurrilous biography of her husband yet to be published. It was alleged that the martyred President had been illegitimate, that he had not been a Christian, that he had never loved anyone but Ann Rutledge, and that his marriage with Mary Todd had been a nightmare.

The widow's restless wanderings since leaving the White House had brought her to Florida in the spring of 1875. She was suffering increasingly from delusions of persecution, causing her to leave her gaslight on all night and to shun restaurants for fear of being poisoned. Her most bizarre fantasy, later revealed in court, was that an Indian was causing her headaches by pulling wires through her eyes in an effort to remove the bones from her face.

When Mrs. Lincoln had an indelible hallucination that her remaining son, Robert, was desperately ill, she packed up hastily and took the train to Chicago, where she checked in at the Grand Pacific Hotel. Robert Lincoln, a successful lawyer and in sturdy good health, found his mother in her room in a state of complete distraction, raving that Chicago was going to burn to the ground, this four years after the Great Fire. To his dismay he discovered that she had $57,000 in securities hidden in her petticoats. Some time later she tried to leave her room half dressed and had to be physically restrained by her son and the hotel staff, at whom she screamed, "You are going to murder me!"[1]

Mrs. Lincoln began going on shopping sprees. She confided to friends about her being followed and playing hide-and-seek with spies among the clothes racks of stores. Actually, she was being followed—by Pinkerton men hired by the son. On her last grand venture into a Chicago department store on May 19, 1875, she bought $600 worth of lace curtains, $1,150 of jewelry, and $200 of toiletries. When she opened the door of her room to let in the delivery man with these purchases, she was also confronted with the hotel manager and Leonard Swett, a lawyer and close political associate of her husband, who gently informed her that she was under arrest, charged with insanity.

That same afternoon she was hustled off to her first trial, which was a mockery, since the jury and her defense lawyer were already there, handpicked by Robert Lincoln. Seventeen witnesses, including doctors, hotel maids, and store clerks, testified against her, and she was pronounced incompetent in short order. Robert succeeded in his aim to be appointed "conservator" of her estate. In the court's Lunatic Record it was noted by her name: "Does not manifest homicidal or suicidal tendencies." This proved to be a false finding, for that very evening, eluding her guardians, Mrs. Lincoln sought out at various pharmacies a lethal dose of camphor and laudanum. Aware of her situation, all the druggists refused her, until one finally sold her a harmless potion.

The next morning she was taken to the Bellevue Nursing and Rest Home in Batavia, Illinois. Its director later informed the press that she was under a minimum of restraint, that her difficulty was "a general mental feebleness," and that there was no encouragement that she would ever get well.[2] Yet within a few months family pressures got her released to live at her sister's house in Springfield, the very home where Lincoln had courted and wed her. She lived quietly at the Ninian Edwardses' for the next nine months.

Mrs. Lincoln's case was reopened June 15, 1876, because public sympathy had swung to her side and because her family, including Robert, wished to end the stigma of it all. This time Swett testified on her behalf, and Ninian Edwards told the court that recently Mrs. Lincoln had more than lived within her budget. The upshot of the finding of sanity was, of course, that Robert ceased to be her conservator.[3]

Four days later the mother sent the son a chilling letter with no salutation except "Robert T. Lincoln" and signed "Mrs. A. Lincoln." She wrote:

> Do not fail to send me without *the least* delay, *all* my paintings, Moses in the bullrushes included—also the fruit picture, which hung in your dining room—my silver set with large silver waiter presented me by New York friends, my silver tête-à-tête set, also other articles your wife appropriated. . . . Send me my laces, my diamonds, my jewelry. . . . I am now in constant receipt of letters from my friends denouncing you in the bitterest terms, six letters from prominent, *respectable,* Chicago people such as you do not associate with. . . . Two prominent clergymen . . . think it advisable to offer up prayers for you in Church, on account of your wickedness against me and High Heaven. . . . Send me all that I have written for, you have tried your game of robbery long enough. . . . You have injured yourself, not me, by your wicked conduct.[4]

For Mrs. Lincoln vindication was not altogether sweet. She confided to her sister:

> I cannot endure to meet my former friends, Lizzie; they will never cease to regard me as a lunatic. . . . If I should say the moon is made of green cheese they would heartily and smilingly agree with me. I love you but I cannot stay. I would be much less unhappy in the midst of strangers.[5]

Accordingly, she sailed for France in the fall, receiving there great marks of respect. She largely ceased her eccentricities, but she refused to correspond with Robert, who at this moment may have thought he had his other parent safely in the grave, only to be sadly mistaken.

June 16, Cincinnati

WHOOPING and dancing were also part of the tribal ritual known as the Republican National Convention, otherwise a meeting of well-clothed and well-fed politicians, apprehensive for their futures but not desperate. The balloting for president began this morning, and on the first roll call, with 379 needed to win, the vote stood:

Blaine (representative from Maine)	285
Morton (senator from Indiana)	124
Bristow (secretary of the treasury)	113
Conkling (senator from New York)	99
Hayes (governor of Ohio)	61
Hantranft (governor of Pennsylvania)	58
Others	14

Blaine, the front-runner since January, had failed for the time being, and back-room plotters, unknown to him, were emboldened to plan and pursue the victory of another.[1]

All the previous week the thousands of delegates, alternates, dignitaries, and ward heelers had been streaming into Cincinnati, "Queen City" of the Ohio and the eighth largest metropolis in the country. It was the sixth Republican convention, and the first "open" one since 1860 (Lincoln for his second term and Grant for both terms were virtually unopposed). The New England representation included such literary luminaries as James Russell Lowell and Richard Henry Dana, "reformers" and avid supporters of Secretary of the Treasury Bristow, whose pictures and banners seemed to predominate around the streets of the city. One of the busiest headquarters was that of the Blaine supporters, and there and everywhere people were agog with rumors about the leading candidate's fainting fit the previous Sunday. Senator Conkling's delegates arrived aboard a special train and paraded with their brass band through the city, wearing yellow silk hats and carrying a huge sign: ROSCOW CONKLING'S NOMINATION ASSURES THE 35 ELECTORAL VOTES OF NEW YORK. A spectator told a reporter that it was "a mystery to him where the Custom House got bail for all those fellows."[2] A slight excitement occurred when one of the hotels refused admission to black delegates, but the other hotels took them in. Led by Senator Blanche K. Bruce and would-be Senator Pinckney B. S. Pinchback, the black Southerners talked it up for Senator Morton. Everywhere the most active buttonholers, however, were local Ohioans working in the interests of Governor Hayes, who kept in touch with the situation from the executive mansion in Columbus.

Many of the delegates were not pledged to any candidate, like the traveling minister James F. Clarke, who had just finished a few days' visit to the Philadelphia Centennial—a "veritable Parliament of Man," where people from five continents spoke the "one tongue of useful labor." "I go again to Cincinnati," Clarke wrote a friend, "and I shall try to get a good man this time."[3]

The convention began Wednesday morning with a monster parade and then drifted through the opening formalities without incident until it came time for the adoption of the party platform. Amid curses and derision, the one New York delegate not pledged to Conkling insisted on reading the address adopted by the Republican liberals on May 15. Unmoved, the convention eventually approved a statement in the platform offering President Grant "the hearty gratitude" of the country.[4]

Another stir was caused by the well-spoken suffragist Sara Spencer, who demanded the right to address the delegates and then berated them for the discrepancy between their boast of giving the country universal suffrage and the disenfranchisement of

10,000,000 women. Her eloquence was rewarded only with a vague pledge in the platform to give "respectful consideration" to "additional" women's rights.[5]

Otherwise, the platform contained nothing in it that a history student might see as prefiguring the political and social advances due in the next century. Predictably, the Republicans were for a high tariff and a sound currency. Predictably, having said that they "sincerely deprecate all sectional feeling," they identified their Democratic opponents as the party of the menacingly "united South" and "unrepentent rebellion." Among the eighteen planks they found room for one on the danger of "Mongolian" labor and one on the need "to extirpate in the territories that relic of barbarism, polygamy."[6]

The roll call of the states for nominations for president was delayed until 3 P.M. Thursday, when the early summer's heat in Exposition Hall was at its worst. The naming of the various candidates provoked no unusual demonstrations until Maine was called and that state passed to Illinois, bringing to the rostrum the famous orator Robert Ingersoll, who was going to speak for Blaine. Ingersoll did not disappoint his audience, giving the most memorable speech of his career and the most memorable speech at any political convention until Bryan's "Cross of Gold" sensation twenty years later. Blaine's whole career as a waver of the "bloody shirt" was evoked when Ingersoll said he was "a man who preserved in Congress what our soldiers won on the field." Blaine's recent difficulties were turned to advantage when the orator wound up with the words "Like an armed warrior, like a plumed knight, James Gordon Blaine marched down the halls of the American Congress and threw his shining lance full and fair against the brazen foreheads of the defamers of his country and maligners of his honor."[7] The "plumed knight" phrase worked the audience into a frenzy, and observers agreed that if a vote for a candidate had been taken then and there, Blaine would have swept the convention. The session was adjourned, however, since the delegates had been sitting for several hours without interruption and, more important, the gas lighting in the hall was found to be unsafe. Later the Blaine forces declared sabotage.

The first ballot on Friday morning found Blaine within 100 votes of the needed 379; his major opponents, Morton, Bristow, and Conkling, each had around 100 votes; and the favorite son governors Hantranft and Hayes were in the 60 range, the Pennsylvanian having only his own state's votes, the Ohioan having his bloc of 44 plus some others. Blaine gained 13 votes on the second ballot, taken immediately afterward, and then fell back slightly on the next three. Bristow reached a peak of 126 on the fourth ballot. A decisive vote was the fifth ballot, when Michigan shifted to Hayes, who gained 36 votes while all the others slipped. On the sixth North Carolina changed its vote, and Blaine reached 308, but Hayes gained 9 more. A recess was then called from the rostrum, but through a mix-up Alabama had already started the seventh roll call, switching its votes to Blaine, as did other Southern states. More important, however, Indiana withdrew its support of Morton, Kentucky gave up Bristow, New York abandoned Conkling, and Governor Hayes wound up with 381 votes to Blaine's 351. Historians have subsequently picked apart this fast-breaking drama and discovered a well-orchestrated plot by Hayes' managers, including the offer of a Supreme Court position and other offices to Blaine's various opponents.[8]

Since New York's switch had nominated Hayes, besides its having 35 electoral votes, that state won the right to have the vice presidential candidate. Again the party regulars were slightly discomfited. Instead of letting Boss Conkling name his man, the convention turned to New York Congressman William A. Wheeler, the very man Hayes had not heard of at the time of his January letter to his wife. Once Conkling had tried to enlist Wheeler into his Custom House gang, only to get the reply "Mr. Conkling, there is nothing in the gift of the state which will compensate me for the forfeit of my own self-respect."[9]

THE REPUBLICAN PARTY HAS ALMOST MIRACULOUSLY ESCAPED DESTRUCTION headlined the New York *Tribune* in response to the Hayes-Wheeler ticket.[10] Only the extreme reformers and extreme antireformers were dissatisfied. From Boston Henry Adams wrote off to his English friend that Hayes was "a third-rate nonentity whose only recommendation is that he is obnoxious to no one." He would vote for a Democrat.[11] Senator Conkling sulked throughout the subsequent campaign, making only one speech.

The Republicans displayed a remarkable unity as a party in the aftermath of the convention. President Grant kept his preferences to himself and wired Cincinnati: "Governor Hayes is a good selection and will make a strong candidate."[12] Blaine promised Hayes his active support. The "plumed knight" from Maine could afford to be a good loser. Grant could hardly wait to accept Bristow's resignation after the convention and named a Maine senator to be secretary of the treasury: in turn, the Maine legislature designated Blaine the new senator, ending the House investigation of his railroad stock manipulations and furthering a career that would see him secretary of state and a presidential candidate in 1884 who missed by only 1,149 votes in New York State.

Hayes-Wheeler was "an invincible combination," according to the New York *Times*.[13] The main problem, which publicity men and other Republicans set out to remedy, was that two more colorless public figures were hard to find.

June 19, Philadelphia

THE ebullient little French composer Jacques Offenbach received the same acclaim here he had won in New York. On arrival at the Continental Hotel he was greeted by a band playing tunes from *Orfée*. In the evening his first concert took place at the Alhambra, renamed Offenbach Garden for the occasion, and six subsequent nights of his operettas proved to be box-office and critical triumphs.

Ordinarily interested in everything, the loquacious Offenbach had surprisingly little to say about the Centennial Exhibition, which was fully completed when he visited it. Perhaps, his acquaintance with similar expositions on the Continent made him an indifferent or guardedly tactful visitor. He did feel strongly about the Sunday closing of the fairgrounds, commenting that the workers were deprived of an opportunity to educate or amuse themselves and had no other recourse on the Sabbath but a "tête-à-tête with a bottle of whiskey." The Sunday closing of bars also struck him as wrong and paradoxical in a country which had an "abundance of liberties."[1] While on the subject of liberty, Offenbach addressed himself with unusual heat to the discrimination practiced against blacks: "The Negroes have been emancipated. What a beautiful, pompous reform that was! . . . Cars, streetcars, and other public vehicles are forbidden to them; they are not admitted to the theatre under any pretext; they are admitted to the restaurants only if they are serving there."[2]

Offenbach was at his most puckish and flattering when he discussed American women. "It seems to me," he wrote, "that when Lafayette came to fight for the freedom of America he had only women in view, for they alone are really free in free America." As a European he was surprised that young women went into restaurants alone. As a Parisian connoisseur he declared that "there probably exist no more seductive women in the world than the Americans," seductive in their coquetry, in their physical beauty, and in their "truly elegant" clothes. By contrast, American men, in Offenbach's view, dressed frightfully, wearing clothes to his concerts that he would not wear in the country (and they all had bulging revolvers).[3]

For all the hauteur, humor, and hyperbole in his ordinary comments as tourist, Offenbach had important things to say in 1876 in his professional capacity as an artist after considering what this country had to offer. His general conclusion was that while America had "triumphed" materially in terms of conquering the wilderness with railroads and industry, it had "neglected all those things that charm the mind," it had missed "the glory which the arts alone are capable of giving a nation," and consequently it lacked a "soul." He made such specific criticisms as that the theater in America lives "from day to day" and depended heavily on foreign artists, an observation made also by the Polish journalist Sienkiewicz. Likewise, music, painting, and sculpture suffered from want of native talents.

The Frenchman was not pessimistic about America's prospects in the arts in view of its gifted people and its rich people. His prescription was for "private initiative" here to do what had been done by European governments, in the way of establishing museums, art schools, and "especially a conservatory." Above all, "do not spare money."[4]

Offenbach did not see much of the United States besides Philadelphia and New York. On one occasion in some small city he apparently conducted an orchestra that was so bad he would identify the place only as X. He made a brief excursion to Niagara Falls and was disappointed that the only Indians he saw were dingy peddlers who sold souvenirs that probably came from a Paris fire sale. Back in New York to give a final concert for the benefit of the musicians union, July 7, Offenbach was as usual immodestly delighted that the advertisements were in "letters as tall as I am and four times wider."[5] The sparkling, genial Frenchman once again sailed on the *Canada* on July 8. During the voyage he began work on *Les Contes d'Hoffmann,* his one memorable grand opera, which was first performed in 1881, a few months after his death.

June 19, Princeton

"THE American *Republic* will in my opinion never celebrate another Centennial. At least under its present Constitution and laws. Universal suffrage is at the foundation of every evil in this country."[1] The author of this dire prediction was not some embittered New England tory or Southern colonel, but Woodrow Wilson, just about to finish his freshman year at Princeton, not a little groggy from end-of-term worries but essentially groping for a political philosophy in a very political year.

After getting up at 5 A.M. this Monday, Wilson studied his geometry to 7:45, took an hour off for breakfast, and then went back to his theorems and angles to 1 P.M., when he had "dinner." The geometry examination lasted from 1:30 to 5, and he turned in "a very fair paper," although he answered only eight out of fourteen questions "owing to the short time allowed." He got out just a little too late to attend chapel. After supper he took a walk and went over to the hall where the American Whig Society had its rooms. There he caught up on the newspapers, having confessed in his diary some time before that he was "profoundly ignorant of all that was going on in the world."[2]

An article entitled "The American Republic" in the *International Review* provoked him with its optimistic predictions about the country's "future advance and greatness." Just "the old, old story," he wrote, and then added his forecast that there would be no bicentennial. That evening he signed off his diary with the usual "I cannot be too thankful for all God's mercies to me" and then added still two more lines to the effect that he had paid his bills and "on the 26th I leave for home!"[3]

Wilson's unpatriotic feelings about the Centennial included the thought that "America conquered England in an unequal struggle and this year she glories over it. How much happier she would be now if she had England's form of government instead of the miserable delusion of a republic." At times he apparently argued along these lines with his debating-club friends, taking the position that the English form of government was superior to any. This in part was probably a carryover from the monarchical fantasies of his boyhood. Yet it is paradoxical that Wilson went from such disillusion with the system to become the great spokesman of "the New Democracy." Like Mark Twain, who was also having his black thoughts about 1876, Wilson was a perfectionist as well as something of an elitist. What blinded him to everything else at this time was the pervasive corruption in the government.

Wilson, again like Mark Twain, had to cope with his Southern heritage. The Civil War and Reconstruction, which he had seen firsthand, he probably blamed on universal male suffrage. He described one of his Princeton professors as a "jackass" for his opinions on "the Southern question."[4] Significantly, his diary makes no mention of the blacks.

Hayes' nomination by the Republicans came as a "great surprise" to Wilson and gave him hopes that such a "complete unknown" could be easily defeated by the other party. If not a democrat, Wilson was very much a Democrat, and for this something of an oddity among Princetonians. "I do most sincerely hope that the Democrats will nominate a good and prominent man like Tilden," he wrote with enthusiasm. Then, he fell back into cynicism, adding, "The Democrats will be very likely to abuse power if they get it, however. Men are greedy fellows as a rule."[5]

Whatever intellectual snobbery found expression in Wilson's reflections was not matched by any aristocratic pretensions, for the simple fact was that he was in very modest financial circumstances as a student. Perhaps on June 19 he was still upset by a letter two days before from his father "reproving me for my extravagance." Dutifully calling the scolding "thoroughly merited,"[6] Wilson also left the historian records of his income and expenses that hardly suggest riotous living on his part. From time to time his father sent him drafts on a New York bank, usually $50 a month. From this he paid $10 a week for room and board, and his tuition for the second term came to $21.50. He made several book purchases like Rawlinson's *Ancient History* at $2.25 and a pocket dictionary at 75 cents. There was precious little left for such items over the entire spring as an umbrella ($4), a cane (75 cents), singing lessons ($1), mending of pants (25 cents) haircut (20 cents), one trip to New York ($3), church collection (10 cents), and baseball games ($2).

Getting home on June 26 cost him $27.90, since he had to take a train to Baltimore and ships to Norfolk, Virginia, and Wilmington, North Carolina. Wilson's summer vacation seemed as desultory and lonely as many of his college days had been. At home he played "mystery" with his father, a nice name for the more sinful-sounding billiards, and he helped his mother lay carpets. His mother wanted him to "make some visits," but he demurred: "The girls hereabouts are as far as I have seen them so uninteresting. . . . I would much rather stay home and read."[7] As at Princeton, he confined himself largely to the English classics. Once he became disturbed that there were "some very improper passages in Othello" and that all Shakespeare could not be discussed in the drawing room with his family.[8] He made a resolve to avoid novels since "most novels do more harm than good. They have a tendency to make me gloomy."[9] Yet a few days later he admitted to having finished an 1876 potboiler called *Flesh and Spirit*.

Other vacation activities of Wilson included starting a scrapbook of uplifting magazine illustrations, such as "Marie Antoinette going to her execution." He sent a letter to the local newspaper about the "shamefully negligent" upkeep of the city streets, giving the North high marks over the South in this one regard. Under his father's prodding, perhaps, he wrote several articles for religious magazines, such as one called "Work-day Religion" which berated Sunday-only Christians.

"I wish my vacation were only beginning," Wilson decided August 31, four days before its end.[10] On his way back to Princeton he spent two days at the Philadelphia Centennial Exhibition. The historian would not learn much from the collegian's few comments: "What an immense amount of brain work one sees in such a place as Machinery Hall. . . . In the Art Building we found some beautiful sculpture and painting, though most of it was rather second rate in my judgment."[11] So Wilson returned to his sophomore year.

June 20, Anaheim Landing, California

WITH a menagerie that included a dog, a tame badger, and a young eagle with an injured wing, the Polish journalist-immigrant Henryk Sienkiewicz settled down in this fishing village fifteen miles from Los Angeles and awaited his fellow commune members from the old country. The place consisted of "six huts, a tavern, and that's all." Living in quarters next to the barroom, Sienkiewicz wrote more in the next few months in Southern California than he had in as many years in Warsaw. He was helped with his English by two "señorita" friends.[1]

Just five days after his arrival in New York in March, Sienkiewicz had boarded the transcontinental railroad, fully conscious that he would be the first Pole to describe such a trip. He made a detour to admire the "antediluvian barbarity" of Niagara Falls, he saw "beauty" in growing Detroit, and he marveled at Chicago as a city "built by giants for giants," its perpendicularity and rectangularity a forecast of twentieth-century living. Crossing Iowa, Sienkiewicz began to see frontier towns and found the train increasingly packed with "rough types" going to the Black Hills, undaunted that the Sioux were on the warpath.[2]

According to Sienkiewicz, "a traveller literally does not see a single tree" between Omaha and San Francisco, a distance he compared to that between Warsaw and Madrid.[3] After the prairie gave way to the mountains, he saw scenes "from which Doré must have got his 'landscapes of the inferno.'" An incredible phenomenon of this era, which he described, was that the transcontinental railroad had to run through miles on end of snow sheds—that is, man-made wooden tunnels. Heavy snows kept Sienkiewicz from making a side trip to Mormon Salt Lake City, and on March 13 at the little station of Toano in Utah the train was snowbound for five days. The passengers simply turned to the enjoyment of eating and singing together in their Pullman and organized games, revolver contests for the men, walking on the rails for the women. They were rescued by a whole train of locomotives with a giant plow, an event which brought out the poetical in Sienkiewicz. "They approached with clanging bells, roaring whistles, spraying sparks from their smokestacks, and belching clouds of smoke . . . with this uproar celebrating their triumph."[4]

The somewhat discouraged traveler awoke one morning to find

his train descending into California—"a beautiful, fragrant pine forest . . . rose-colored rays of sunrise . . . a warm spring breeze . . . clear blue skies . . . song of birds . . . flowers glistening in the morning dew." Soon they crossed the "gold-bearing" river at Sacramento, and finally Sienkiewicz saw San Francisco "dimly through the ocean mist."[5]

After exploring much of California, the advance man decided on settling at Anaheim because nearby was a thriving community of German colonists, who not only afforded an example of prosperity but spoke a language familiar to Sienkiewicz and his friends (the Pole later realized the wrongness of the Germans' stubbornly clinging to their own culture, to the point of slapping their children for talking English—and this in an area where Mexicans predominated). Four months after Sienkiewicz's arrival on June 20, Count Chlapowski and his wife, Madame Modjeska, reached Anaheim, bringing with them two huge cases of medicines and surgicals and an arsenal of rifles, revolvers, and brass knuckles.

Even more than Sienkiewicz's encouraging letters, sheer romanticism had brought the Poles to Anaheim. Madame Modjeska later wrote in her memoirs:

> Oh, but to cook under the sapphire-blue sky in the land of freedom! What joy! To bleach linen at the brook like the maidens of Homer's "Iliad"! After the day of toil, to play the guitar and sing by moonlight, to recite poems, or to listen to the mocking bird! And listening to our songs would be charming Indian maidens, our neighbors, making wreaths of luxuriant wild flowers for us! And in exchange we should give them trinkets for their handsome brown necks and wrists! And, oh, we should be so far away from everyday gossip and malice, nearer to God, and better.[6]

The Anaheim commune was, of course, not the first or the last attempt at creating little utopias in this country. For example, the press in 1876 still devoted occasional space to the famous Oneida colony in New York, which had its ups and downs for three decades before being disbanded in 1879. The great number and variety of similar experiments in America was attested by the appearance in 1875 of Charles Nordhoff's thick classic tome *Communist Societies*.

The brave new world at Anaheim lasted but a few months. Lacking the most elementary farm skills, the Polish intellectuals were no match for the caprices of nature or the depredations of their neighbors. Homesickness and wrangling took over, but lack of a "shadow of income" did the most to burst "our cherished bubble."[7]

Alarmed that her husband was being ruined financially, Madame Modjeska went off to San Francisco to learn English and resume her acting career. A year later her debut in a Shakespearean drama at the Opera House was reviewed by Sienkiewicz for *Gazeta Polska*. His description of her as "the world's most famous actress" went too far, but one must not miss the fact, as does Sienkiewicz's biographer, that Madame Modjeska soon became the absolute toast of the New York stage.[8]

As for Sienkiewicz, he had clearly fallen in love with his patron's wife, but Count Chlapowski succeeded in keeping him at a distance. The young Pole, now tanned, healthy, and self-confident, resumed his infatuation with the California wilds. Rubbing shoulders with bartenders, squatters in mountain cabins, and Mexican guides, Sienkiewicz shot rattlesnakes and grizzlies, broke mustangs, and coped with bowie knives and lynch law, all of which he described for his Warsaw readers. "I am so happy here," he wrote, "that if I were blessed with eternal life, I should not wish to spend it anywhere else."[9]

In the course of his wanderings, Sienkiewicz's views of America changed from the offhand disparagement evident in his first letters to studied enthusiasm. "American democracy," he declared, "approaches the nearest to that ideal society for which we have striven through the ages." This was not so much for reasons of political theory or institutions as for social factors like "the respect for any kind of labor in America," the educational system's promotion of skills rather than intellectual exclusiveness, and the "lack of any marked disparity of manners."[10] He was speaking as the class-conscious Pole when he marveled that American waiters talked to guests as equals. As for American manners, he now decided that "boorishness" was "straightforwardness," concluding, "I have come to realize that, although Americans may behave with too little ceremony, Europeans mince about with too much affectation."[11]

In view of the wave of Polish immigration to this country about to swell in the 1880s, Sienkiewicz's second thoughts on poverty here may also have been influential. He described a "pauper" in California as a farmer having a comfortable house, three meals a day with wine, and "everything but $100 cash."[12] After visiting the mining boomtown at Virginia City, he informed his editor that "the most prolific writer in Poland does not earn as much as any Irishman here who carries out rubbish."[13]

Sienkiewicz's message to his fellow Polish immigrants was not altogether unrealistic. He noted that the 20,000 Poles already in the country were concentrated in ghettos in cities like Chicago and Milwaukee, unable or unwilling to take advantage of the liberal homesteading policies of the government. Yet he reported that Polish Jews were the first to open stores in frontier towns, and he had nothing but praise for the general tolerance shown foreigners. His confident prediction was that Polish settlers here would be completely assimilated.

Ultimately Sienkiewicz's personal decision was to seek his career not in California but in his homeland. After savoring Madame Modjeska's triumphs on the East Coast, he returned to Europe, sojourning at first in France and Italy, because of the Russo-Turkish War in progress and the possibility of his being drafted. Back in Warsaw, he eventually emerged as the foremost Polish writer of the time. His American experiences were the basis of several short stories, and his great novelistic trilogy of Polish history also embodied character types learned here, as well as a new love of nature and a new optimism. For English-sepaking readers, Sienkiewicz is best known for his novel of Roman-Christian times, *Quo Vadis?*

June 25, Valley of the Little Bighorn

THE troops of his command hidden behind a ridge, Colonel Custer ascended the promontory called the crow's nest and stared searchingly down into the valley beyond. He was jauntily dressed in a light-colored flannel shirt, buckskin trousers, long boots, and a white broad-brimmed hat. His binoculars revealed only wisps of smoke in the blue-gray haze, but he knew many Indians had recently traveled in that direction. When he descended, he listened expressionlessly to the advice of his chief white scout, Mitch Bouyer: "Get your outfit out of his country as fast as your played out horses can carry you."[1] An Indian scout seconded him with the words "If we go in there we will never come out."[2] Custer gave his orders, and the 7th Cavalry rode over the divide almost exactly at noon. The deployment of a whole regiment was a rare sight in the Indian Wars.

General Terry with the combined Montana and Dakata columns had left the junction of the Yellowstone River with the Powder River on June 16 and proceeded westward. At the mouth of the Rosebud he was rejoined by a scouting expedition under Major Marcus Reno that had been sent out to the south. Reno reported sighting a village of 380 lodges, and Custer was furious that Reno had not assaulted it. It is now known that Reno's furthest reconnaissance on June 17 had carried him within forty miles of where General Crook was battling Crazy Horse, and it was "one of the minor miracles of Western history" that the Sioux were not attacked that day from two directions.[3]

At a last council of war on June 21 General Terry, Colonel Gibbon, and Lieutenant Colonel Custer worked out a plan whereby Custer and the 7th would go on a five-day scout up the Rosebud, then cross over to the Little Bighorn, and, returning northward, effect a junction on June 27 with Terry's cavalry and Gibbon's slower infantry coming upstream on the Bighorn River. The oral and written orders issued by General Terry at this time were later subjected to different interpretations, but clearly it was expected that the two forces would be out of communication with each other, and it was assumed that the only real problem was to keep the Indians from scattering and escaping. A lesser worry was that General Crook would catch them first. That night some of the younger officers had a last poker party on the steamer *Far West*.

Under low gray skies Custer's 7th Cavalry marched out of the camp on June 22 as massed trumpets played "Boots and Saddles." Their leader had disdained Terry's offer of a company of the 2nd Cavalry, just as he had refused to take along Gatling guns, saying that they were too cumbersome, perhaps feeling that their use in battle would make him lose face among the Indians. (This primitive machine gun, consisting of ten barrels turned by a crank, fired 350 rounds a minute, but it often jammed.) On the first night away some of his men deserted, heading for the gold settlements of the Black Hills. The 585 soldiers of the 7th included many raw recruits, as well as untrained horses. Most of the 31 officers had been with the regiment for nine years, and they included seven West Pointers and also a few foreign adventurers, like one who had served in the French Foreign Legion and on the Papal Guard. About a dozen officers were absent from the expedition, the nominal commander back at headquarters on recruiting duty, one of the most experienced Indian fighters serving as aide to General Hawley at the Philadelphia Centennial Exhibition. Custer's roistering younger brother Captain Tom Custer and his brother-in-law Lieutenant Calhoun were with him, and also along as civilians were another brother, Boston, a nephew, and the newspaper correspondent Mark Kellogg. Among the Crow scouts with Custer was one named Paints-Half-His-Face-Yellow. The column's 170 pack mules carried hard bread, coffee, bacon, 124 rounds of ammunition per soldier, and extra salt, for Custer apparently foresaw the possibility of their being gone more than five days and having to eat the animals. Just before Custer rode away that day, Colonel Gibbon jestingly called to him to leave a few Indians for the rest of them, but he made no reply.

On the second day's progress along the pleasant Rosebud the column passed the remains of a large Indian camp one half mile in diameter, but this was misinterpreted as evidence of successive encampments. Some of the scouts remarked the signs of an unusual number of wickiups, or detached structures, near where the lodges had stood; Custer's officers decided these were doghouses rather than what they actually were, shelters for extra warriors.

Early on Saturday the twenty-fourth the command passed the site of Sitting Bull's sun dance, and, after marching more than thirty miles that day, they made camp in a valley that lay twenty-two miles east of the Little Bighorn (and eighteen miles north of where Crook had fought a week before). After the scouts reported that the Indians had recently crossed the divide between the rivers, Custer decided to follow after them rather than continue upstream two more days until General Terry got into position as per his orders.

That evening some of the men sang, while a group of officers talked of the Democratic convention due to meet in three days. According to a fragment of a notebook found, Kellogg got "into a real sweat as do some others." One fear voiced was that the Democrats in power would cut back the strength of the Army. Custer may have been thinking politics, too, and considering how much time it would take after a victory for a scout, or scouts, or even himself to reach the nearest telegraph station and send on the news to St. Louis before the nominations started.[4]

The exhausted men of the 7th began their night march at 11 P.M. and kept together only by banging their drinking cups as they stumbled up ravines in the pitch darkness. The next morning at the top of the divide Custer rejected advice that they rest in concealment twenty-four hours or even retreat, and so at noon they started downcountry. The sight of a few Indians in the distance caused an officer to shout: "Thirty days furlough to the man who gets the first scalp."[5]

With the exact strength and location of the Sioux still unknown, Custer made the fateful decision to divide his force. Was this another precaution to prevent the Indians from escaping, or even now did he wish to avoid sharing a victory? Captain Benteen was sent off to the left with 125 men on what he considered a futile "valley hunt." Major Marcus Reno's battalion continued on straight ahead and down toward the river bottom, while Custer himself turned away in a northerly direction and was soon out of sight among some bluffs. At 3:30 P.M. he sent his last message via a lieutenant: "Benteen—come on—big village—bring packs."[6]

The Sioux were aware that "Longhair" Custer was in the vicinity of their encampment, but the appearance of Reno's 112 bluecoats at the river edge near the Hunkpapa lodges took them by surprise. The alarm was given by women digging wild turnips and boys in swimming. One chief, hurrying to the council lodge, later said that "the soldiers charged so quickly we could not talk." Chief Gall, an adopted son of Sitting Bull, led the counterattack after learning that all his family had perished in the first shooting. "It made my heart bad," Gall recalled. "After that I killed all my enemies with a hatchet."[7]

Encountering increasing resistance, with two of his men carried into the enemy village by bolting horses, Reno ordered his men to dismount and went on the defensive. Five minutes' more advance by his detachment, according to one officer there and also some Indian witnesses, would have caused the Indians to break up their encampment; such a charge would have resulted in complete butchery, according to others. In any case, Reno soon found his command surrounded and in an easily infiltratable position among the cottonwood groves of the river bottom. The major now had his men remount, and they retreated in a condition of near panic until they reached a new defensive position on a high ridge behind them. One-third of his men and officers had been lost. An officer thought to shoot Reno, and later he was accused of

[172]

being drunk as well as cowardly, both debatable charges. The important consequence of his action was to release several hundred Indians for action against Custer.

Shortly after Reno's men reached the high timber, they were joined by Captain Benteen's battalion. Many of the Indians had mysteriously moved off downstream, and some of the soldiers present said they heard concentrated gunfire to the northwest. Benteen decided to wait for the packtrain with its ammunition to reach them, this occurring at about 6 P.M. Later Benteen himself joined some officers who were independently making reconnaissances in Custer's presumed direction, and after he saw the extent of the Indian village for the first time, he decided to retreat slightly and dig in at a stronger position, later known as Reno's Hill. While criticisms have been leveled at his immobilizing seven-tenths of the regiment within earshot of a battle in progress, Benteen argued that he saved his combined force from complete annihilation.

Later in the evening of the twenty-fifth numerous Indians, many with fresh scalps on their belts, began to attack Reno Hill. They killed eighteen and wounded fory-six troopers by nightfall, riding in on their painted and feathered horses, slinging themselves by the jaw ropes down behind, and firing past the animals' manes or under their bellies. Then the Sioux returned to the village to celebrate. During the lull Reno was overheard to remark to Benteen, "I wonder where the Murat of the American Army is by this time." An officer, who had other grudges, reported that Reno was quaking with fear as he took cover and "would have pulled the hole in after him."[8] A new onslaught by the Sioux began at 3 A.M.—not a mass charge but several hundred firing at the cavalrymen from the myriad sniping positions the broken terrain afforded. Even more Indians stood about observing from a distance. In the afternoon of the twenty-sixth, just as water and ammunition were giving out, the Reno-Benteen command watched numbly and later cheered as the Indians left off the attack and began to break up the encampment.

As for what happened to Custer late on the twenty-fifth, there is no way of knowing except from a kind of archaeology and from the reports of the sole survivors of his part of the battle—namely, the Sioux, whose reminiscences were to be distorted by either boastfulness or fear of punishment. Presumably, he saw the big fight Reno was involved in at the river bottom but continued along the bluffs northward, always intent on preventing an enemy escape. His exact route has been disputed ever since. It is debated whether his five companies reached a ford opposite the center of the Sioux camp, whether they even crossed it, and whether they dismounted when a charge would have scattered the enemy. Later Custer's force moved even farther downstream and away from the rest of his regiment. Was this already a retreat? Was there panic? Were there four or five last stands? In any event, Custer and about seventy-five remaining men were eventually surrounded on a ridge and fought a final action there, which, lasting anywhere from fifteen minutes to one hour, was probably over by 5 P.M., when all were killed. Many of the dead troopers were found with jammed carbines. "I have been in many fights but I have never seen such brave men" was Brave Wolf's epitaph, of some later comfort to the Army.[9]

No one knows whether Custer himself was the last to fall. Many Indians claimed the honor of killing the famed colonel. One of the most recent and convincing claims is that of White Bull, a twenty-six-year-old nephew of Sitting Bull, who already had two scalps, three slayings, seven coups, nineteen battles, and forty-five stolen horses to his credit. White Bull related only in 1932 that he had killed Custer in a hand-to-hand encounter without knowing who he was; his leading the Indian contingent at an official celebration of the fiftieth anniversary of the massacre is, perhaps, proof that the Sioux accepted his claim.[10] Today few people have not been exposed to the joke about Custer's last words: "Where did all the blankety-blank Indians come from?" Current Sioux humor is more sardonic, attributing to the white commander the final order "Take no prisoners."[11]

The Hunkpapa Chief Gall led the movement northward against Custer after the Indians were released from the action with Reno. Meanwhile, Crazy Horse and the Oglala circled behind the village and closed on Custer's ridge from the other direction. The Sioux swept in "like a hurricane . . . like bees swarming out of a hive."[12] The smoke and dust were so thick in the area of the last stand that Indians shot each other by mistake. Some used bows and arrows.

"The blood of the people was hot and their hearts bad and they take no prisoners that day."[13] The majority of dead troopers were found scalped but not mutilated, contrary to sensational newspaper accounts, which included a report that Chief Rain-in-the-Face ate the heart of Captain Tom Custer, against whom he had a personal grudge.

So many individuals appeared in the years after 1876 claiming to be the sole survivor of the massacre that one historian has speculated that Custer must have been leading a whole brigade.[14] Another contemporary Sioux joke is that a cavalryman escaped by painting himself like an Indian and upon discovery said, "Better red than dead."[15] An officer's horse named Comanche was actually found alive at the battlefield and became a popular sideshow exhibit. Those who died with Custer numbered 215, and with Reno's losses the toll rose to 265, of whom 16 were officers, 7 civilians, and 3 Indian scouts. The Indians suffered casualties anywhere from 30 to 300.

Many ifs crop up concerning Custer's last stand in the vast historical literature on the subject, probably more extensive than that for any other American battle. What if he had brought along the 2nd Cavalry unit or the Gatling guns? What if he had not divided his forces? What if Reno had stormed on into the village? What if Reno and Benteen had ridden to the sound of the guns? In General Sheridan's postmortem of 1877 he declared that if Custer had rejoined the others, he "could have held his own, at least, and possibly defeated the Indians."[16] Most likely all the ifs are misleading and dubious; the Indians were so strong, so determined, and so ably led as to make defeat inevitable and to make even a successful retreat unlikely.

Considerable but not complete agreement exists that Custer himself was primarily to blame for the disaster. General Sherman's assessment was too blindly military when he declared Custer "could do nothing but attack when he found himself in the presence of the Indians."[17] In fact, Custer violated seemingly elementary precepts of warfare by departing from Terry's plan, by not knowing his enemies' strength, by starting a battle with worn-out men and horses, by committing his force piecemeal, and by not keeping the units in communication. While his aggressiveness might be explained as confidence in "Custer's luck," one cannot ignore such other possible motivations as glory seeking, spiting President Grant, and political ambition. In fairness, some blame must be assigned elsewhere, particularly to General Crook, somewhat to General Terry, and ultimately to the chain of command ending in the White House. Nor should one lose sight of the circumstance that "in large part the generals lost the war because the Indians won it."[18]

The Custer massacre, actually the second wipeout in ten years, was the Indians' greatest victory. It was also a "last despairing and futile gesture against a fate the red man could not hope to escape."[19]

June 25, Philadelphia

THE same day, nearly the same hour, 2,000 miles away from Custer and Sitting Bull, a less famous but very fateful encounter took place, that of Emperor Dom Pedro and Alexander Graham Bell at the Centennial Exhibition. The inventor had been given a small table to demonstrate his telephone amid the exhibits of the Massachusetts Department of Education, owing largely to the fact that his backer, Gardiner Hubbard, was a Centennial commissioner from that state. Few people paid any attention to Bell's device, and he would not even have been here this Sunday but for a lark. Friday his sweetheart, Mabel Hubbard, had cajoled him into accompanying her on the train to Philadelphia, and Bell jumped aboard at the last minute, without a ticket.

Dom Pedro, having presided at the grand opening of the fair in May, had been disappointed on his return to Fairmount Park the next day to find many of the exhibits uncompleted, and accordingly, he went about his travels elsewhere, returning to Philadelphia in late June determined to explore the exhibition from top to bottom as a private tourist. He did, however, lend his august presence to a Sabbath-day tour of the mechanical exhibits by the prize committee. The group included Elisha Gray, of all people, Joseph Henry, the famed director of the Smithsonian Institution, and Sir William Thomson (later Lord Kelvin), a valued visitor from Britain as one of the world's outstanding physicists.

By 7 P.M. the committee members were limp from the heat and fatigued from seeing countless contrivances and listening to garrulous inventors. They were about to leave after reaching Bell at his table when the Brazilian ruler recognized his acquaintance of a few weeks before and with typical geniality said, "How do you do, Mr. Bell. And how are the deaf mutes in Boston?"[1] Bell had a chance to explain that he would be forced to return to his teaching in Boston before the committee came again to his display. Dom Pedro insisted on staying for a demonstration. The tall, thin young man with his bushy black beard and intense eyes then recited *Hamlet* into one instrument while the dignitaries listened on another across the room. "My God, it talks" was supposed to have been Dom Pedro's impulsive reaction, well-publicized words now questioned by historians.[2] He did rush over to congratulate the inventor "at a very-un-emperor-like gait," Bell's words.[3] More important, perhaps, Sir William Thomson exclaimed, "It does speak. This is the most important thing I have seen in America."[4] Elisha Gray also deigned to listen on his rival's instrument and caused cheers when he absently repeated what he'd heard: "Aye, there's the rub." The telephone thereafter was one of the sensations of the Centennial.[5]

June 28, St. Louis

AS the Democratic National Convention moved into its second day, most observers were aware, first, that the party itself was unusually confident of its chances of victory in November and, second, that everyone expected Governor Tilden of New York to be its nominee. After the disunited and dispirited Democratic performances in 1868 and 1872, the midterm "tidal wave" victory in 1874, plus the continuing exposure of the Grant administration scandals, convinced the party faithful that they would gain the White House for the first time since the Civil War.

To hold a major party convention in a city west of the Mississippi was a novelty. The fact was that St. Louis was no longer a frontier town, but the fourth largest metropolis in the country, its many railroad lines, commercial houses, and factories serving the great agricultural heartland. The choice of the convention site reflected the delicate balance among the Northern, Southern, and Western factions of the Democratic Party. The diverse types that made up this political conglomeration were eminently caricaturable, and *Harper's Weekly* responded with a cartoon of a trainload full of delegates: a Tammany Indian waving his tomahawk; a priest representing the Catholic immigrant Irish; an ex-Confederate robed as a Ku Klux Klan member; a bloated, overdressed banker suggestive of such *déclassé* mavericks as millionaire August Belmont, who was elected convention chairman; and the "rag doll baby" used by Nast and others as symbolic of the soft-money Westerners.[1]

Although the New York delegation arrived at St. Louis pledged to Tilden, Tammany Hall set up its own headquarters in the Lindell Hotel, of recent Whiskey Ring notoriety, and proceeded to placard the city with posters declaring that Tilden could not carry New York City and would thus lose the state and its vital electoral votes. "Honest John" Kelly, who had succeeded Boss Tweed in power, became so berserkly anti-Tilden that he refused to shake Belmont's hand, snubbed other key personages, and shouted insults and obscenities wherever he went. Although many out-of-state delegates were responsive to charges that Tilden was the tool of the railroad interests, the bullying and quarrelsomeness of Kelly's toughs cost him more support than he gained, a fact exploited by Tilden's astute managers.

Delegates from the South gathered at the Southern Hotel, appropriately, and also clinked their bourbons on a steamboat moored in the river nearby. The press noted the comparative absence among them of old diehard Kentucky colonel types and the presence of younger, practical politicians serenely confident that they held the balance of power and would gain influence in party and government for the first time since secession. According to the governor of Virginia, Southern strategy in St. Louis was one of "masterly inactivity."[2] While a Deep South nominee was out of the question, the South would not lose, in the view of the Columbia, South Carolina, *Daily Register,* and the Democrats could not "gravely err" if the candidate were Tilden, Hancock, Bayard, Hendricks, or one of several others.[3]

The band alternately played "Dixie" and "Yankee Doodle" during the opening day on June 27. Five thousand people took their seats in the Merchants Exchange Building amid stifling heat, and the session was called to order by August Schell at noon. The sixteen-year-old William Jennings Bryan, who would be the party's silver-voiced standard-bearer twenty years hence, gained admission by climbing in through a window. In the organizational proceedings Tilden men dominated.

[178]

Tilden's supporters also had their way in resolving the most controversial issue of the party platform, that of hard money vs. soft money. The inflationists did succeed in presenting a minority report on the floor of the convention calling for total repeal of the Resumption Act of 1875. The acrimonious debate that followed revealed the complete divergency of Eastern city and Western rural interests. The sweating, shouting delegates had to be reminded that the press was reporting it all. The crucial moment occurred when a Tilden manager forcefully argued that the party could not win without New York State and that New York would not stomach the minority position, which was then meekly voted down 515 to 219. The platform plank adopted, while denouncing Republican "financial imbecility and immorality," was so tortuously conservative as to state that the only thing wrong with the resumption clause was that it was a "hindrance" to a "speedy return to specie payments."[4]

Like the Republicans, the Democrats underwent a brief soul-searching on the question of women's rights. Over raucous protests, Phoebe Cousins, younger and sexier than her counterpart, Sara Spencer, at the earlier convention, was permitted to make an address and present a concrete right-to-vote plank. In this "Centennial leap year," she told them, "it is in order not only to receive proposals from fair women but to accept them."[5] The platform, however, did not even pay lip service to her cause.

While the Democratic platform also failed to anticipate history, it had a ring to it that the Republicans lacked in its stress on the need for change. The booming voice of Lieutenant Governor W. D. Dorsheimer of New York stirred the delegates to mounting cheers as he litanized over and over again with the words "Reform is necessary." If reform in taxation and reform in tariffs were routine demands, reform in the civil service was matched by a hard-hitting condemnation of the spoils system. Dorsheimer also read a telling review of past Republican scandals to an appreciative audience, ticking off the sins of a former vice president, a speaker, three senators, five House chairmen, and four Cabinet officers.[6]

The balloting for president on June 28 was little more than a gesture to the idea of an open convention and the presence of favorite son candidates. Delaware nominated Senator Bayard, a commanding figure with the handicap of being Southern. Illinois put up Governor Hendricks of Indiana, and the soft-money delegates went wild, their hysteria matched by their sense of futility. Tilden's nomination caused the stormiest demonstration, marred only by Honest John Kelly's again trying to speak against him and trading curses with those who prevented him. Ohio was virtually isolated in its support of Governor Allen, and Pennsylvania's Hancock faced widespread odium against another general in the White House. On the first roll call the vote was:

Tilden	401½
Hendricks	140½
Hancock	75
Allen	54
Bayard	33

Under the two-thirds rule customary at Democratic conventions, the winner needed 492 votes. Missouri started the train of Southern switches to Tilden, who at the end of the second ballot was within 12 votes of victory. More changes of heart were called out by delegation chairmen, suddenly Pennsylvania moved that the nomination be made unanimous, and it was all over.[7]

The party professionals were quick to heal rifts, and they wed hard-money Tilden to soft-money Hendricks the next day. Hendricks had made known his aversion to accepting the second place, but Tammany's Kelly joined the Tilden men in persuading him that his running as vice president would make the strongest ticket. The Democrats, even more than their rivals, entered the 1876 contest a united party.

The day of his triumph in St. Louis Tilden spent secluded at the executive mansion in Albany preparing his defense in a business lawsuit. A special telegraph line had been rigged to the state capital, but the governor relied on messenger boys to bring periodic reports of the convention. During the crucial part of the balloting Tilden was out taking a carriage ride. Later, when he was having tea with his sister, an aide brought in the wire TILDEN NOMINATED ON THE SECOND BALLOT. With the studied nonchalance that would be part of his undoing as a presidential candidate, Tilden said only, "Is that so?"[8]

June 30, Shanghai

THE formal opening of the first railroad in China brought great satisfaction to its chief promoter, American Vice-Consul Oliver B. Bradford. Invitations were sent out to the "ladies and gentlemen of the settlements" to join the members of the board of directors for the historic occasion, and 164 people turned out, the men in top hats and the women with parasols gaily taking their places in the six spotlessly new carriages. The train made the four-mile run from Shanghai to a local depot in seventeen minutes. Afterward everyone enjoyed cake and champagne. Only two things were amiss: no permission had been given by the Chinese government for the railroad to be built, and no Chinese were aboard for the first ride. The second oversight was clumsily corrected on the return trip to Shanghai, when curious natives were treated to a free ride in the luggage cars. Their "laughter and shouts of delight prevailed in all directions," according to the patronizing account of the *North China Daily News*.[1]

This episode in American-Chinese relations was not unlike the confrontation of white man and red man in the Black Hills: the bringers of civilization masked their greed with high purposes; the receivers of civilization did not really want it but were too weak militarily to resist it altogether and too weak morally to reject its temptations. American traders had made themselves welcome to Canton and other Chinese ports in the eighteenth century, and by the 1840s the era of clipper ships competing in runs to the Orient was in full swing. When Westerners failed to ingratiate themselves into China, they shot their way in, the British being the chief culprits and the First Opium War of 1839 being the most notorious such armed intervention. The United States, which was not backward in asserting itself in a similar manner, sent its warships to shell the barrier forts of Canton in 1856 and landed marines to safeguard American business interests. Ten years later the American Navy took action against Chinese pirates to protect our share of the opium trade, although it was paltry compared to the British, who in the two decades after 1875 forced the Chinese to consume an average of 82,000 chests yearly. The United States had a greater stake in the Shanghai Steamship Company, which, according to our consul, had "almost a monopoly" of the "very large and daily increasing trade on the Yangtse River." From the

1860s it was a frequent practice to station a gunboat or two at Shanghai and occasionally to send one up the river to show the flag—that is, to demonstrate we would "redress any wrongs which they, the Chinese, may inflict upon our people."[2]

Ever since British interests had built a very profitable railroad from Tokyo to Yokohama in Japan in 1872, United States Vice-Consul Bradford had been fascinated with the possibilities of a similar line from the thriving city of Shanghai to Woosung, the deeper water port twelve miles away, where the foreign ships actually anchored. Three obstacles stood in the way of his dream: the Chinese-American Treaty of 1868 specifically forbidding such enterprises; the general policy of the Chinese government reserving to itself the construction of public works; and the absence of Americans willing to put up the large amount of capital required. Bradford succeeded by ignoring the treaty, hoaxing the Chinese authorities, and allowing British money to control the Woosung Road Company.

The Bradford-sponsored company at first pretended that it was building a "horse road" from Shanghai to Woosung, all the while it was constructing a carefully graded right-of-way, bridging creeks and filling in ravines. Hundreds of Chinese were pleased to get construction jobs, but local people also protested the obstruction of roads and waterways. When the company started laying rails, the authorities looked the other way, and somehow Bradford secured permission to import British-built locomotives and cars. A trial run on March 16 brought a crisis.

Bradford's devious designs were strongly backed by the American Consul George F. Seward, son of Lincoln's expansionist secretary of state, who wrote:

> I sympathize most keenly with the promoters. They are striving to confer a benefit upon China. . . . They believe they have a right to build a road over ground which they have bought and paid for. The leading motive of the promotors of the enterprise is to exhibit to the Chinese a railroad in practical operation and thus to hasten the moment for a general introduction of railroads into the empire.[3]

Here was the usual muddle of thinking about property rights, the march of progress, and doing a favor to backward nations.

One clear note in the hesitant, responsibility-dodging reaction of Chinese bureaucrats to the Woosung Railroad was a message to Bradford on March 29 calling the undertaking "a direct insult to the government." The official in question went on to say that if China allowed foreigners to build transportation facilities on its soil "all the nations under the sun would laugh at her."[4]

Bradford's claim that he had permission to build a "suitable road" served to keep the situation in abeyance for a while, until Peking could be consulted. After the Woosung Railroad started operations on June 30, both the central and local authorities appeared to acquiesce in the fait accompli. Later in the year, however, a Chinese was run over by a train, a mob stormed the facilities, and the government put an end to the whole thing by having the rails torn up and all the equipment shipped off to Formosa. One result of the incident was to delay the building of any more railroads in China for several years. Another consequence was Bradford's recall from his post, after he was charged not only with heavy-handed diplomacy but also with lighthearted relationships with Chinese women.

The events of 1876, in a sense, mark the shift from the purely commercial penetration of China by Americans to efforts to invest there, seemingly a classic case of the new imperialism. In this vein, for example, Seward protested to Secretary Fish in February that "the disposition of the government to exclude foreigners from mining still exists."[5] Yet imperialism as a generally recognized term and acknowledged policy was still a couple of decades away, and Americans were not committed until the early twentieth century to the spectacle of a permanent South China Patrol, marines guarding fortified enclaves in Peking and Shanghai, and foreigners collecting all the Chinese customs receipts. Seward could write Fish that same February that it was "pitiable to see this empire borrowing from foreign merchants paltry sums of 1, 2, or 3 millions of dollars, specifically pledging for the repayment of such loans this or that branch of her revenue."[6] President Grant, a year out of office and a visitor to China, could speak of his hope that the "brave, intelligent, frugal, and industrious" Chinese with a little more mechanical progress could "throw off" the treaties which "now cripple and humiliate them."[7]

One illustration that American policy in China was still in the age of innocence was a circular sent to U.S. consuls in March, 1876, telling them that their main problem was not American businessmen but American missionaries. It was more difficult to protect the missionaries than the merchants because they were not concentrated in ports but were often scattered about in remote provinces. Moreover, missionaries were more prone to arouse antagonisms because "with them zeal is a duty and the conservative disposition which grows up when property is at stake is wanting."[8] Typical of frequent embarrassing incidents was a riot in Wuchang in April. A mob of Chinese women invaded a mission chapel and dispensary in search of two children they believed were kidnapped. The report of the American on the spot explained that there was widespread popular belief that foreigners used the eyes of Chinese children to make medicine. The incident ended peacefully. In 1876 there were about 130 American missionaries in China.

From the Chinese point of view the most worrisome problem in relations at this time was not the grievances of Americans in China but the discrimination against Chinese in America. By coincidence on June 29, the day before the opening of the ill-fated Woosung Railroad, the Peking government officially protested to the United States regarding the ill treatment of its nationals in California "at the hands of the low classes of Irish."[9]

July 1, West Point

"ONLY one year more! My friends, my enemies center their hopes on me." Henry O. Flipper proudly but self-consciously entered his fourth year at the United States Military Academy, the first black cadet to get that far in the institution. "The country begins to be agitated by the approaching graduation of young Flipper," editorialized a newspaper in the South, the region which tended to regard the Atlanta cadet's progress as another humiliation. The Northern press had much praise for Flipper's "pluck," but the *Times* pessimistically predicted that he would be "slaughtered in one way or another," as all his black predecessors had been.[1]

The summer of 1876 had many excitements for Flipper, who, like Woodrow Wilson, kept a diary during this period. On June 14 General Sherman delivered the graduation address for the fourth-year men. On June 16 the cadets were turned out for a dress parade for the ubiquitous Dom Pedro (that Flipper lacked the diffidence of most American students about using foreign languages is indicated by his imaginative entry for that day: "Dom Pedro, emperador de la Brasil, estaba recibiado para un 'review' a las cuatro horas y quaranta y cinco minutas. El embarcó por la ciudad de Nueva York immediatemente").[2]

For ten days around the Fourth of July the corps of cadets were at the Philadelphia Centennial, 300 of them occupying a tent camp west of Machinery Hall. Their guard mountings and parades in their tailored gray jackets and spotless white trousers drew many spectators. One newspaper expressed amazement that the West Pointers were perforce "their own chambermaids." Free like the other cadets to go sightseeing much of the time, Flipper was accosted in the United States Building by an outspoken stranger who told him, "You are quite an exhibition in yourself. No one was expecting to see a colored cadet."[3]

Soon afterward Flipper and the corps were in their annual summer encampment near West Point, and here occurred one of the crucial moments of the young black's career. On the night of July 12 he was lying in his tent studying the stars when he overheard a cadet say of him quite loudly, "That nigger don't keep dressed. Some times he's way ahead of the line. He swings his arms, and does other things not half as well as the other devils, and yet he's not skinned for it" (Flipper in an approving lexicon of West Point jargon explained that "devils" were fellows, "skinned" was reprimanded).[4] The problem, Flipper realized, was that the next day he would be senior officer of the guard, according to rotation, while his fellow white fourth classman would be junior officer. The actual guard mounting came off without Flipper making any blunders and with better than usual discipline, he noted with satisfaction, although there were self-conscious smirks and blushes from Southern cadets when they tossed their rifles to him for inspection. As for his junior officer, Flipper apparently won his esteem and general approval by telling him that he did not need to ask for orders formally unless he chose and could simply go about his routinely prescribed duties.

By tactfulness, by not intruding himself, Flipper managed to survive nearly universal hostility of his fellow West Pointers. Of his four black predecessors who had broken under the strain, the most celebrated was James W. Smith of South Carolina, a graduate of Howard University appointed to the academy in 1870. Flipper had a confusion of feelings about Smith, calling him "pugnacious," all the while sympathetically describing the nightmares he endured—the slop bucket thrown on his bed, the incident when he was assaulted in his quarters by a Southerner who objected to his eating before him at dinner, and the humiliation visited on a group of balck relatives and friends who visited him during a prom. After official reprimands for lying and for courting publicity in the newspapers, Smith was dismissed for failing natural and experimental philosophy. The President and the Radical Republican administration were conscience-stricken about the situation. When it was rumored that Flipper would resign, too, after Smith's departure, he was advised to stick it out by the commandant, for whom, together with all the faculty, Flipper had nothing but praise. Smith's place at the academy went to another black. Arriving in the fall of 1876, he was soon involved in an incident where he was struck in the face by a Southerner who claimed he had sneered at him and who was suspended six months for his act.[5]

Flipper's own appointment to West Point reflected both the politics of Reconstruction and his own special upbringing. Although his parents were slaves at the time he was born near Atlanta in 1856, his father, a skilled shoemaker, enjoyed considerable freedom and, after the Civil War, considerable prosperity. The son was tutored and schooled from an early age, eventually attending Atlanta University, run by the American Missionary Association. In his reminiscences Flipper generously attributed his success at West Point to "the early mental and moral training I received at the hands of those philanthropic men and women" who came South to "educate and elevate" the blacks and faced social ostracism and worse for their trouble.[6] "Ordinary ambition" decided Flipper to try for West Point, and he secured the vacancy there belonging to the Fifth Congressional District of Georgia because its member was a Republican.[7] He also had to pass examinations in arithmetic, grammar, descriptive geography, and United States history and to provide himself with a regulation wardrobe and $5-a-week expense money. On his arrival on May 20, 1873, at the West Point landing he was jeered.

If Flipper and his predecessors had been blacker in complexion, there might have been even more difficulty. Described as "coffee-colored," he was an imposing six feet two and 175 pounds, but he preferred to think that other attributes than his physique kept him out of trouble. He was bright, even studious, and clearly more intelligent than Smith, although he ranked only in the middle of his class of about eighty.

Virtually complete social isolation was Flipper's lot during his entire career at West Point. His fellow plebes, some of them friendly at first, learned to call him "nigger" and stopped borrowing books and discussing recitations. The faculty, the barber, the clerk, and others showed no prejudice. The cadet expressed sad amazement at the power of "bullies" to influence the other cadets and related the case of an upperclassman sharing guard duty with him who confided that he wished him success, that he called him names behind his back for sake of appearances, and that he feared being "cut" worse than Flipper if he did otherwise.[8] While at the Point, Flipper kept his hurts to himself, but the press discussed his predicament occasionally and railed against the institution as a "hotbed of disloyalty and snobbery." Many visitors to the academy for proms and other events were equally guilty of making Flipper uncomfortable by staring and pointing at him. One exception was the daughter of General Schenck, then still minister to England, who told him that she hoped he graduated at the head of his class.

Flipper rationalized his circumstances to his satisfaction. He felt that West Point, the hazing system and all, had "unparalleled success" in turning out "officers and gentlemen." True gentlemen, and even "mimic" gentlemen, treated him politely.[9] As for a few "uncouth and rough types"—elsewhere referred to as "poor white trash"—Flipper declared: "In ordinary civil life I should consider such people beneath me in the social scale and consequently give them wide berth."[10] He relished learning that one of his particular tormentors had sold newspapers as a boy and that his mother still scrubbed floors in a bank. He consoled himself with his personal "victory over prejudice." In conclusion, he prescribed a course of conduct for members of his race that would find little support a hundred years later: "We must force others to treat us as we wish, by giving them such an example of meekness and good conduct as will at last shame them into a like treatment of us. This is the safer and surer method of revenge."[11]

Flipper did graduate and was the only cadet to arouse cheers and applause at the ceremony on June 14, 1877. Senator Blaine sent for him and offered to be "an intermediary in Congress to help you out of your difficulties."[12] Two hundred blacks gave him a reception in New York City, at which he appeared in his new blue cavalry uniform and its helmet with yellow horsehair plumes. He was also lionized on his return home to Atlanta. Some Southern newspapers relented enough about his success to suggest that he admit blacks were treated better in the South than in the North, to which he retorted in print that he had never been invited to a Southerner's home or introduced to one's wife.

Second Lieutenant Henry Flipper was assigned to the black 10th Cavalry at Fort Sill and served there without incident. Henry Ward Beecher suggested in a magazine article that he could "be made more useful than as a target for Indian bullets" by the government's having him teach engineering at a black college so as to train bridge and railroad builders for emerging Africa.[13] The Liberia Exodus Association had something of the same idea when they wanted to make him generalissimo of a Liberian army that would aid the "development of a grand African nationality that can command the respect of the nations."[14]

July 4, various places

"THE Founders of Honey have no Names—"[1] This one line, in a note accompanying flowers being sent to a friend, was Emily Dickinson's quiet, provocative reflection on a day when her New England neighbors and Americans throughout the country and also those abroad gave themselves over to a frenzy of patriotic celebrations in honor of a century of national independence. Amherst, Massachusetts, where the poet lived as a recluse, had its special reasons to be festive, for it was also the centennial of the founding of the town. The day began with a parade—men self-consciously dressed in uniforms of colonial times, proudly bemedaled Civil War veterans, the colorful fire company, and a train of youngsters with firecrackers. All the speeches in the town square were heartily applauded, and everyone turned out for the picnic by the riverside, everyone but Emily Dickinson presumably. The weather was sunny and hot, and the picnic was an entirely pleasant affair by a neighbor's account, although "to feed two thousand people when one thousand were expected is beyond the power of man." Later the citizens of Amherst gathered on the lawn of the house of a minister who provided both a band concert and ice cream.[2]

Charleston, South Carolina, like Amherst, had its own local event to celebrate—the defense of Fort Moultrie. The white citizens turned the ceremonies into a demonstration for states' rights, while only the blacks in the downtown city paid formal honor to the events which united the nation. Richmond, however, flew the Virginian and the United States flags together over the Jefferson-designed Capitol for the first time since 1860. Blatant political partisanship triumphed in Lawrenceburg, Kentucky, and a Tilden-Hendricks banner floated over the dome of the County Courthouse.[3] Woodrow Wilson in Wilmington, North Carolina, repeated in his diary his gloomy prediction that the nation would never celebrate another centennial as a republic.

Philadelphia was the natural focus of national rejoicing. On Monday evening, July 3, tens of thousands of people followed a torchlight parade to the square before Independence Hall. At midnight they waited in expectant silence for the ringing of the Liberty Bell thirteen times, and then the human and mechanical pandemonium of New Year's Eve was repeated. Sunrise was greeted by the firing of salutes by the navy yard and by the American and foreign warships in the harbor.

Official ceremonies began at 10 A.M. in Independence Square, where a grandstand with awnings had been erected for such honored guests as Dom Pedro, Prince Oscar of Sweden, Lieutenant General Saigo of Japan, Governor Hayes, and Generals Sherman and Sheridan. President Grant did not come since he was spent physically from receiving hundreds of summer visitors to the White House. His absence was widely condemned in the press, one newspaper deciding that he was "not a gentleman," another speaking of the "finishing stroke to the sum of his offenses."[4] The president pro tem of the Senate, Senator Thomas Ferry, read Grant's speech for him. A chorus sang Oliver Wendell Holmes' Independence Day Hymn, and then the mayor of Philadelphia took the rostrum to display the original manuscript of the Declaration of Independence and to introduce Richard Henry Lee, grandson of the man who proposed the original resolution in 1776, who proceeded to read it. This was one of several gestures of conciliation toward the South that day.

While Bayard Taylor was reading his "noble ode," a women's

rights demonstration briefly upset the decorum of the planned ceremonies. Having been denied any place in the official program or even seats on the grandstand, the leadership of the suffragists decided on a deliberate intrusion. Five of them, armed with press passes, suddenly appeared in the main aisle, pushed their way toward Senator Ferry, and thrust into his hands a new Declaration of Independence embodying their demands. They then scattered through the crowd, handing out copies of their document, which Susan B. Anthony read aloud from the musicians' stand, as Taylor was trying to speak. It was only a flurry but an effective one.[5]

Women were not the only disaffected group that demonstrated vociferously on this most heralded of Fourth of Julys. Chicago was the scene of a labor parade featuring trade union contingents, military marching units of the German Vorwärts Turnverein, a float with a woman wearing a red liberty cap, and the usual brass bands. At a rally speakers talked of the "greater revolutions" yet to come and of the end of the "rule of the capitalists." A socialist was inspired to give the workers too a new Declaration of Independence, promising them "life, liberty, and the full benefit of their labor."[6]

The voices of the would-be revolutionaries were but a whisper in the babble of confident, conventional holiday rhetoric about liberty and free enterprise, exemplified best, perhaps, in a speech given by Henry Ward Beecher in Peekskill, New York. For a score of years having enjoyed both comfortable fame as preacher of the Plymouth Church of Brooklyn, and an annual income of $45,000, Beecher suffered no moral doubts about himself or his country. With utter smugness he reassured his respectable upstate audience that:

> The laborer ought to be ashamed of himself . . . who in twenty years does not own the ground on which his house stands, and that too, an unmortgaged house, who has not in that house provided carpets for the rooms, who has not his China plates, who has not his chromos, who has not some picture or portrait hanging on the walls, who has not some books nestling on the shelf. . . .[7]

That Beecher was not completely out of touch with reality was evidenced by his allusions to the scandals of the Grant administration, but even these could be subsumed to his purpose.

> Men in public or private life are corrupt here and there, but let me say to you, no corruption in government would be half so bad as to have the seeds of unbelief in public administration sown in the minds of the young.[8]

At least some of his listeners must have weighed these words against the lingering sensations of Beecher's trial for adultery the year before.

Across the country the Fourth of July celebrations progressed with the changing time zones. Denver, Colorado, where statehood was in prospect a month hence, had its special local enthusiasm for Centennial Day. Small but fast-growing Los Angeles put on an extravaganza. In its parade marched the Opera House orchestra, the Los Angeles Rifleros, forty-two veterans of the Mexican War, and a colorful contingent of forty-niners. One float contributed by the French Benevolent Society was graced by three ladies representing Liberty, America, and France. Other floats had lavishly begowned women representing each of the thirteen original colonies and the twenty-five later states.[9]

The country's national day was also marked abroad with noise and pomp. At Buenos Aires, for example, the USS *Frolic* in the harbor fired a twenty-one-gun salute at noon, and then the legation was thrown open at 2 P.M. to receive the Argentine president, his Cabinet, members of the legislature, and the diplomatic corps, while 5,000 people and two brass bands celebrated in the street outside. Foreign heads of state sent messages of congratulation, those from the more autocratic European monarchies giving the most wry satisfaction to official Washington. Kaiser Wilhelm noted the "development without parallel" of the American republic, and Czar Alexander remarked our "immense progress." Austria-Hungary's not-quite-yet-venerable Franz Josef telegraphed President Grant, addressing him as "Highly Esteemed and Much Beloved Friend," and the American in reply said it was "peculiarly gratifying" to get the "accolade of the sovereign of one of the most ancient, renowned, and powerful nations of the Eastern Hemisphere."[10]

One foreigner, the irrepressible French composer-conductor Jacques Offenbach, was mostly appalled at the Fourth of July activities he witnessed in this country for the sheer excesses of violence involved. In his chronicle he methodically listed the case of a nineteen-year-old girl walking on Eighth Avenue and burned to death by firecrackers thrown at her, forty-nine persons injured during the day, mostly children and mostly from pistol shots fired by "some unknown person," four murders in Washington and knife fights at Mount Vernon, the result of drunkenness. Some boys in Philadelphia set off some old cannon and burned down a whole block of the city, making hundreds homeless and causing losses of $250,000. "As for me," Offenbach concluded," I admit that these disasters make me appreciate our detestable European governments that come right out and forbid such liberties as endanger the lives of citizens."[11]

To the unintentional mayhem of this Centennial Fourth may be added what was probably the most bizarre suicide of this or, perhaps, any era. A young man of means and good reputation named Frederick A. Jeffery took his life in a room in Chicago's Palmer House, leaving a note saying that his act was motivated by no particular reason other than to confer distinction on the city of Chicago. The coroner's jury that investigated the grisly scene made this report:

> We the jury find that said Frederick A. Jeffery . . . came to his death on the 5th day of July 1876 by cutting his throat with a razor, shooting himself with a pistol through the heart, taking an overdose of hydrate of chloral, and finally hanging himself with a rope around his neck with the intention of committing suicide.

They concluded that the victim was "in a state of insanity," almost an understatement in view of additional circumstances of the case. Jeffery confided in his note: "I am going to put a mirror before me just to see if I will be frightened. I think it more likely that I shall laugh; but as I want to enjoy it all, I'll put the glass up anyhow." Incredibly, he was partially thwarted in his weird plans: a slow torch failed to set afire either his alcohol-saturated clothes or the cords suspending him over a bathtub full of boiling water.[12]

July 6, New York

THE dispatch came over the telegraph wire to the *Herald* in the early hours of the morning: "Bismarck, Dakota Territory, July 5,

1876—General Custer attacked the Indians June 25, and he with every officer and man in five companies were killed." It was the first accurate report of the disaster. Friendly Indians on Wyoming ranches knew days before but were not telling much. The *Daily Herald* in Helena, Montana, where all the businesses were closed for the Fourth of July, managed to open its office that day to publish a garbled account of a "massacre" by a white scout, Muggins Taylor. This bulletin, relayed to Salt Lake City, took more than a day to reach the East. General Sherman in Washington and General Sheridan in Chicago promptly gave interviews in which they said all such rumors of catastrophe were unthinkable.[1]

General Terry, Custer's immediate superior, was campaigning and out of contact with Washington. His 2nd Cavalry and Gibbon's infantry had reached the mouth of the Bighorn on June 23. Their march did not bring them to the junction of the Little Bighorn until late June 25. The smoke up the valley made Terry uneasy, but he did not believe scouts who talked of the Sioux "who covered all the plain."[2] The next day the column was in contact with the Indian's rear guard, and there might have been a fight if they had happened to advance 500 yards farther. Not until early June 27 did General Terry reach the site of the abandoned Sioux village and find the grisly remains on Custer Ridge, after which he relieved the beleaguered force on Reno Hill. A company was sent upriver to reconnoiter, but the Indians, short of ammunition, had completely scattered into the Bighorn Mountains. Having buried the dead, Terry's command returned to the Yellowstone and put the wounded on board the steamer *Far West*, which set off downriver to civilization.

The *Far West* steamed into Bismarck at 11 P.M. on July 5. The tragic news it brought was soon on the wires thanks to the energy and efficiency of Colonel Clement A. Lounsberry, editor of the Bismarck *Herald* and employer of Mark Kellogg, the reporter who died in the massacre. Lounsberry simply set up headquarters in the Western Union office, alternately writing and interviewing survivors. After twenty-four hours he had filed 50,000 words on fourteen columns at the unheard-of cost of $3,000, but he gave the parent newspaper, Bennett's *Herald*, the greatest scoop so far in newspaper history.[3]

The news of the Custer disaster, coming just a few days after the triumphant celebrations of the Centennial, sent the nation into the kind of shock it had only known eleven years before at the time of Lincoln's assassination. Buildings were draped in mourning. The newspapers editorialized on the theme of how a nation of 40,000,000 could be humiliated by a handful of savages. They printed every bit of fact and fancy about the battle itself and the current situation on the frontier. They usually tried to make a brave thing of it. The St. Louis *Post-Dispatch*, for example, had a descriptive headline: THE BLUE COATS STAND UP AND MEET DEATH WITH A GRIM SMILE.[4] The poet Whitman similarly reacted to the event as a "trumpet note for heroes" and, within twenty-four hours of receiving the news in Camden, sent off a piece with that line called "A Death Song for Custer" to Whitelaw Reid of the *Tribune*. He received his asking price of $10 for it when it was published on July 10.[5] Not everyone read heroism into the event. Woodrow Wilson in his diary for July 7 wrote: "Heard of the slaughter of General Custer's force by the Indians. . . . He thought, I suppose, that he would make a name for himself."[6]

The defeat on the frontier temporarily silenced the economy-minded, antimilitarist bloc in the House of Representatives. On July 22 Congress voted funds for two forts on the Yellowstone and bowed to Sherman's demand that the Indians in the agencies be put under military control, a measure that meant treating them virtually like prisoners of war. Three weeks later Congress authorized the enlistment of 2,500 additional cavalrymen.

The quick and the dead associated with Custer's last stand received their due. National sympathy went out to Mrs. Custer as she made her sad journey home from Fort Abraham Lincoln. She fainted at the sight of the Custer homestead in Monroe, Michigan.[7] Afterward she set about in a series of books to establish that Custer was the perfect Indian fighter, and for half a century Elizabeth Custer largely succeeded in inhibiting her husband's colleagues and scholars alike from telling the truth. Had Custer lived, he undoubtedly would have been court-martialed for disobedience. Major Reno, suffering less from official inquiries than tacit condemnation by his peers, was driven to drink and out of the Army.

Americans' reactions to the Battle of the Little Bighorn reflected the mixture of stupidity and intelligence, apathy and concern, barbarism and altruism that characterized Indian policy all along. It was not uncommon to read in newspaper humor columns in 1876 such remarks as that the only good Indians were those standing in front of cigar stores. Anger and a desire for revenge were widespread. The wife of an Army post surgeon in Idaho, for example, wrote bitterly to a friend: "Did you ever hear anything more terrible than the massacre of poor Custer and his command. . . . Don't let anyone talk of peace until the Indians are taught a lesson and, if not exterminated, so weakened they will never molest and butcher again."[8]

Foreigners could be more objective than Americans about the situation on the frontier. The English-born New York grocer John Lewis in his letter to a friend said:

> I suppose you have read in the papers . . . of the massacre of some of our troops by the Indians under "Sitting Bull." That's what its called when our troops suffer. The fact is the Indians are systematically swindled . . . if Uncle Sam would only hang or shoot a few agents and Traders, the continued warfare with the Red Skins could be prevented.[9]

The Polish journalist Sienkiewicz, observing prospectors going to the Black Hills on the coast-to-coast train, wrote sympathetically of the Indians even before Custer: "Civilization is wiping them off the face of the earth, inexorably and brutally." After the news he noted that the whites "likewise scalp their prisoners."[10]

The best people in the American intellectual community were not fooled by the Custers and the policies that made them possible. Helen Hunt Jackson spent part of 1876 traveling in the West. Five years later she shocked the nation with her observations on the Indians in a volume entitled *A Century of Dishonor*. The very July of the news of the massacre the *Nation* published two articles by the distinguished anthropologist Lewis Morgan, including one called "The Hue and Cry Against the Indians," in which he argued that the Sioux were acting only in self-defense and that Washington's mishandling of their affairs was a national disgrace. An honorary member of the Iroquois for four decades, Morgan the following year published his major work, *Ancient Society: Or Research in the Line of Human Progress from Savagery Through Barbarism to Civilization*. Morgan's theory of social evolution in this book greatly influenced Marx and Engels.[11]

Over a century the Custer story has developed a huge bibliography ranging from Elizabeth Custer's adulation to an article by Dr. Karl Menninger, "A Psychiatrist Looks at Custer." The battlefield on the Little Bighorn is now a national monument. While the grave markers and general tenor of the place make it primarily a memorial to the 7th Cavalry, the Park Service also offers such items as a favorable biography of Crazy Horse and a print entitled "Sitting Bull's Vision." The iconography of Custer's last stand is also so considerable as to have merited a couple of books. Painters are entitled to their fantasies, even if no white man lived to describe the scene. Contrary to Whitman in his poem, Frederic Remington in some of his canvases, and Hollywood in many movies, the sophisticated today can be sure of two things: "Longhair" Custer went into this particular battle almost crew-cut, and neither he nor any of the cavalrymen had sabers, since these had been left behind at the base.

July 8, Hamburg, South Carolina

A pitched battle in this dumpy little river town caused the deaths of eight blacks and three whites. The shoot-out might have remained just a local tragedy except that the Republican governor sought to make political capital out of it, and the story might have remained buried in the national press, preoccupied as it was with the Custer disaster, had Republican newspapers not chosen to play it up as the "Hamburg Massacre." In the resulting backlash South Carolina white Democrats were emboldened to capture the state government, and in turn this revolution helped determine not only the outcome of the 1876 national election but also the course of race relations in the South for a century.[1]

On the afternoon of July 4 two South Carolinian whites, Thomas Butler and Henry Grafton, were riding home through Hamburg, an all-black settlement which lay on the Savannah River across a bridge from prosperous Augusta, Georgia. Their carriage's way was blocked by a company of black militia standing at parade rest. Insults were traded between the hotheaded young gentlemen and the militiamen's captain, Doc Adams, a white hater whose lieutenant had been openly advocating that the blacks should drive the whites from the state altogether. Eventually Butler and his friend succeeded in driving off, but the next day they returned to demand an investigation, applying to a black magistrate named Prince Rivers, who happened to be an enemy of

Adams. At the hearing Adams became so angry that Rivers cited him for contempt of court, but he postponed further action until 4 P.M. on Saturday, July 8, because of the hostile stance of Adams' men.

Young Butler sought out the aid of his uncle, General Matthew Galbraith Butler, a leading South Carolina Democrat who was actively engaged in trying to unseat the Reconstruction government and restore white rule in the state. Butler's plantation near Hamburg had been destroyed during the Civil War, presumably by local blacks. No account of the Hamburg Massacre would deny that General Butler was the single commanding figure at the scene. His defenders said he patiently sought to avoid bloodshed; his detractors see him as deliberately provoking it. The first local newspaper accounts written in the heat of the moment were probably more accurate than later dispatches which tried to put Butler and the whites in a better light.

General Butler arrived in Hamburg the afternoon of the eighth and entered into negotiations via Magistrate Rivers with Captain Adams, who refused to appear for a formal hearing because of the numbers of whites who were beginning to gather menacingly in the town. At one point, alluding to Hamburg's reputation as a haven for criminals, Butler browbeat Rivers with words to the effect that "this sort of thing had gone on long enough and it was about time that it was put a stop to." He told him that the blacks "must give up their arms at once" and that he would guarantee their safety and the protection of the town during the coming night. When Adams would not even offer an apology, General Butler "rode over to Augusta and told several young men that he might need their services in Hamburg during the afternoon." Forthwith "a large number of young men hastily procured arms and ammunition and hastened to the scene," forming a "large crowd" at the bridge by 7 P.M. These developments were not so casual as they were made to sound, for the fact was that for some time rifle clubs of whites had been drilling in Edgefield County.

After further demands for surrender were rejected by the blacks, "General Butler determined to accomplish by force that which could not be done by peaceable means."[2] Adams' militiamen had barricaded themselves in their armory, a large old two-story brick structure. According to the first account, they "defied the Whites" and "the latter surrounded the house and at half past 7 o'clock opened fire on it," their fusilade being "returned."[3] The slightly later version was that the blacks "defied Rivers and his posse" and "general firing opened on both sides."[4] Bloodthirsty yelling accompanied the shooting, which went on for two hours. At about 8 P.M. a twenty-three-year-old white named T. Mackey Merriweather, who was sniping from an abutment of the bridge, was hit in the head by a shot from the windows and killed instantly (the later dispatch claimed that two blacks crept up through the river reeds and gunned him down from the back). When Merriweather's body was brought back into Augusta, the whites were driven to an even greater frenzy and now dragged a piece of artillery over the river. They fired three or four rounds of canister, lighting up the area with the cannon flashes, but doing little damage to the building. The blacks stopped firing, however, and took to the cellars. Later the militia lieutenant "was caught while trying to escape. After he was arrested, he was shot in the back by an unknown party. . . . This action was condemned in the severest terms by everyone including General Butler."[5]

At the height of the evening all Hamburg was a "battlefield," and in Augusta everyone was in the streets, "anxious to learn the latest news from the front."[6] When the shooting stopped around 10 or 11 P.M., the whites across the river made a search of the town and found it almost deserted, except for a few blacks hiding under floors. Twenty-nine blacks were taken into custody. The on-the-scene reporter was going to conclude his dispatch with the information that the prisoners were being kept under guard so that they could be turned over to the civil authorities the next day, but he was forced to add the following:

> Since writing this we learn that seven of the prisoners were taken out and killed. At about two o'clock or a little before, the roll was called of the prisoners and those who were considered the disturbing element in the county were carried to a cornfield near the river and turned loose. As they ran they were fired upon and killed.[7]

The men guarding the prisoners had deliberately determined "to kill the ringleaders." After the intervention of "some gentlemen from Augusta" the other captives were released.[8]

The Hamburg Massacre was yet another chapter in the grim drama of Reconstruction in South Carolina. Historians are divided, of course, in assigning blame for the degradation and near paralysis of the state government after the Civil War. One fact is indisputable: blacks outnumbered whites in the population by about four to three. Before the decade ending in 1876 and for nearly a century afterward the blacks were disenfranchised. During the Reconstruction decade the Republican Party controlled the state by means of soliciting black votes and barring ex-Confederates from the political process right down to jury duty. The rule of carpetbaggers and scalawags was also enforced by martial law and federal troops.

The best-known single pictorial illustration of the Reconstruction era shows the South Carolina legislature in the hands of a black majority, the gaudily dressed members sitting with feet on desks, smoking cigars, laughing, and carrying on shamelessly amid a debris of peanut shells and whiskey bottles. This scene was matched in actuality by the legislators' corruption and fiscal irresponsibility, to the point that white taxpayers were often forced to hand over half the income of their properties to tax collectors or in many cases forfeit the properties themselves. The state debt multiplied many times. One of the worst of the white corruptionists, "Honest John" Patterson, actually boasted in 1873 that "there are five years more of good stealing in South Carolina."[9]

There was another side of the coin. Recent research has indicated that black legislators were man for man no less qualified or upright than their white counterparts. Their concern for education and other welfare measures for the ex-slaves was commendable. In view of the Tweed Ring in New York or the corruption of the Grant administration, it was a distortion to single out South Carolina as peculiarly misgoverned. Nonetheless, white South Carolinians were up in arms, literally, and incidents like the Hamburg Massacre were inevitable.

The Republican governor, Daniel H. Chamberlain, reacted sharply to the news from Hamburg. The investigators sent from Columbia accepted the militia captain Doc Adams' version of events. On August 1 a coroner's jury handed down indictments for murder against fifty South Carolinians and thirty Georgians. Chamberlain also appealed directly to President Grant, even going to Washington in person. His report on Hamburg published on July 20 described it as a simple case of white Democrats oppressing black Republicans. He urged the administration to "exert itself vigorously to repress violence . . . during the present political campaign."[10]

Although a carpetbagger, Chamberlain until now had been

something of a hero to white South Carolinians as well as to the blacks who voted him into office in 1874. Massachusetts-born and a Yale graduate, he was more scholarly than demagogic. The cultivated, reserved Yankee had bought a plantation in South Carolina and came to sympathize with his fellow property owners. As governor he daringly refused to appoint known grafters to office, he vetoed unsound appropriation bills, and he tried to disarm the rampaging black militia in Edgefield County.

The Grant administration received Chamberlain's appeals with mixed feelings. For one thing, available troops were needed for fighting the Sioux. Because of the Custer disaster, all but 2,800 officers and men had been taken from the states of the Old Confederacy. Moreover, Grant and his Republican advisers were aware of a growing national disenchantment with Reconstruction, a feeling that all the federal interference in the South had created more problems than it solved. Nonetheless, for partisan reasons Grant had to back the Republican governor. In a message of July 26 he described Hamburg as "cruel, bloodthirsty, wanton, unprovoked, and uncalled for." The President at this time expressed his hope that Chamberlain and the good citizens of South Carolina could handle the situation themselves.[11] On August 15 Grant's secretary of war, J. Donald Cameron, sent firm instructions to General Sherman:

> You are to hold all the available force under your command not now engaged in subduing the savages on the Western frontier in readiness to be used upon the call or request of proper legal authorities for protecting all citizens without distinction of race, color, or political opinion in the exercize of the right to vote.[12]

Rather than help Governor Chamberlain and the Republicans, however, this show of force backfired on him, and he lost the governorship to the Democrats. The whites indicted for the Hamburg Massacre were never brought to trial because public opinion mattered more than the troops.

July 12, Washington

NEITHER racial violence nor Indian troubles nor political corruption nor massive unemployment could stay Anthony Comstock from his self-appointed crusade against sexual vice. Under his prodding Congress took time this day to pass a strengthened anti-obscenity law, which became popularly known as the Comstock Law.

The mail-order type of vice Comstock was concerned with was the province of the House Postal Committee, which held hearings earlier in the year to receive the crusader's dramatic testimony.

> Mr. Comstock had with him for exhibition a large lot of the worst specimens of pictures and appliances for the induction and cultivation of vicious practices that could be imagined by the basest mind. The committee put on its spectacles and investigated them with fear and trembling; as well it might, for really the ingenuity displayed in efforts to demoralize the youth of this country surpass credulity.[1]

After Congress dutifully legislated against such things, Comstock became a special agent without pay in the Post Office Department, and no one showed greater zeal in providing the police and prosecutors with evidence in the way of dirty pictures and phallic equipment. Three out of four persons accused were found guilty at the trials in which Comstock served as an expert witness.

Comstock made himself guardian of the nation's morals for forty years. His chief worry was young boys. His definition of vice extended beyond pornography to such practices of reading dime novels and participating in candy-wrapper giveaway offers. Eventually, Comstock's effort "to impose on the nation the moral standards of his own rural Connecticut" was contested by people who saw him as a threat to legitimate literature, art, and entertainment.[2]

Prudery was quite universal in 1876, and serious discussion of sex almost nonexistent. When the *Herald* ventured to run an article on kissing during the summer, the *Labor Standard* promptly condemned it as "disgusting."[3]

July 14, Columbus

FROM his office in the executive mansion Governor Rutherford B. Hayes released to the press his letter of acceptance of the

Republican nomination for president. In four well-composed paragraphs he generally endorsed his party's platform but also broke new ground. Hailed at the time as an effective campaign document, Hayes' words were restudied and had a decided impact on events when the outcome of the November election was disputed.[1]

Contrary to twentieth-century practice, the letter of acceptance was the only campaigning Hayes was to do in 1876. The custom then was for candidates to be lofty and refrain from partisan speech making, whistle-stop appearances, gladhanding party workers, baby kissing, and so forth. The governor remained in Columbus, where he received visitors and exchanged messages with his supporters. The voters at large were expected to size him up through newspaper reports and also through a campaign biography of him rushed to completion that summer by no less a literary light than William Dean Howells. Any writer would face insurmountable difficulty investing Hayes with any glamor, for the fact was that he was simply a substantial citizen and family man with a creditable record in the war and successes as a vote getter. He was considered scrupulously honest by everyone, a positive, if uncolorful, attribute in the Grant era. That no one had ever pinned a nickname on Hayes was a telling characteristic of him and probably an asset, in view of the many wished on his opponent.[2]

Eight years younger than Tilden, Hayes was born in Ohio in 1822. His boyhood in small towns was not marked by any redeemingly lovable adventures, nor was his educational career at a Connecticut prep school, Kenyon College, and Harvard Law School. During the Civil War he advanced from major to major general, being wounded five times, once severely at the Battle of Antietam. Elected to Congress while still in the service, he later won the governorship of his state three times against strong opponents. Objectively, Hayes was slightly inferior to Tilden in sheer intellect and political experience.

The campaign pictures of Hayes that voters saw in illustrated magazines in 1876 showed a handsome man with a broad forehead, regular features, sandy-grayish hair, and a restrained beard and mustache. He had a good figure, keeping in shape by daily boxing sessions. No more of an orator than Tilden, the Ohioan was not so standoffish as the New Yorker. Hayes did not possess his opponent's several millions, but he was very comfortably off, having inherited half a million dollars' worth of land, stocks, and businesses from two uncles.

The Republican candidate was the father of seven sons and one daughter. His wife, Lucy Webb Hayes, was a pretty, graceful woman with brown hair and sparkling brown eyes. While well educated and not generally straitlaced, Mrs. Hayes had stronger religious convictions than her husband and was fanatical about abstinence from alcohol. *She* earned a nickname, Lemonade Lucy and was also the butt of a famous quip by a New York politician to the effect that at her parties "water flowed like champagne."

Hayes himself did not want to be committed on the subject of alcohol politically, telling Howells, who was then composing the campaign biography, not to mention his membership in the Sons of Temperance.[3] This attitude suggested that Hayes was becoming concerned and excited about his campaign prospects, a change from the diffidence he had shown all through the spring. Nonetheless, he remained a reticent figure in the summer of 1876 and was the despair of newspaper reporters seeking interviews.

Before issuing his letter of acceptance, Hayes had solicited the opinions of various Republicans, listening especially to the reformers. Carl Schurz, whose ready endorsement of Hayes had shocked and disgusted liberals like the Adamses, was quick to offer advice. In a letter of June 21 he warned that the Republicans would lose the election if they ran on their record and advocated that Hayes make civil service reform the main issue in a "campaign worthy of this centennial year."[4] Accordingly, in his July 12 message, Hayes vigorously denounced the spoils system as a "temptation to dishonesty" and promised "strict regard for the public welfare solely in appointments." He also went beyond the party platform in his one-term declaration:

> believing that the restoration of the civil service to the system established by Washington and followed by the early presidents can be best accomplished by an Executive who is under no temptation to use the patronage of his office to promote his own reelection, I desire to perform what I regard as a duty in now stating my inflexible purpose, if elected, not to be a candidate for a second term.[5]

This commitment of Hayes caused Grant some annoyance, the President sensing a criticism of himself in it.

The treatment of the South was another vital issue dealt with in Hayes' letter, which by coincidence was dated the same day as the Hamburg Massacre. While echoing the traditional Republican position about the "protection of all citizens in the free enjoyment of their constitutional rights," Hayes also responded to the desire of many Northerners to be done with Reconstruction and, in so doing, gained himself crucial friends in the South. "What the South most needs is peace," he wrote, adding phrases about the need to bring it "honest and capable local government" and to attract "labor and capital." Recently Hayes had exchanged letters with an old college friend from Texas, a former slaveholder and secessionist, who wrote: "Rud . . . are we done with the Negro? . . . Are you not satisfied by this time that he is not fit to govern himself?" The revealing reply was: The Whites of the South *must* do as we do, *forget to drive and learn to lead* the ignorant masses around them." To another correspondent Hayes admitted: "I doubt the ultra measures relating to the South." One is forced to conclude that Hayes "had tentatively accepted the Southern position,"[6] and this was the important political fact of the year.

That Hayes was willing to stand aside in the unequal contest of Southern whites and blacks did not mean that he was willing to let the South control the Washington government. "Our main issue must be: *It is not safe* to allow the Rebellion to come into power," Hayes announced in a letter of August 5. Another time he advised Senator Blaine to emphasize the issue of "rebel rule," since "it leads people away from 'hard times' which is our deadliest foe."[7] In thus discovering the "bloody shirt," Hayes was also changing his original posture that civil service reform was the key issue.

Not campaigning himself, Hayes had the active services of men like Blaine, who spoke for the general Republican cause many times. Vice presidential candidate Wheeler did not leave New York, pleading physical disability, and contented himself with the slogan in his letter of acceptance calling for "good government, good will, and good money."[8] Senator Morton, Representative Garfield, and Carl Schurz were the party's heavy artillery. The Republicans also commanded the talents of a disproportionate number of leading intellectuals, notably Whittier, Bryant, Mark Twain, and Howells. Two prominent Confederate generals, John Singleton Mosby and James Longstreet, lent their unexpected support.[9]

Hayes' campaign had begun a month before Tilden's. By early summer an active national headquarters had been organized in New York City's elegant and capacious Fifth Avenue Hotel by party chairman Zachariah Chandler, Grant's secretary of the interior. An energetic man, practical, without a jot of Hayes' idealism, Chandler successfully raised more campaign money than the opposition. While businessmen since the recession of 1873 were less generous than usual with contributions, federal jobholders gave to the party treasury freely if not always voluntarily. After all, Chandler was aware, there were 40,000 postmasters alone. Another major concern at the Fifth Avenue Hotel was the organization of Boys-in-Blue Clubs to drum up enthusiasm among Union veterans.[10] The party chairman was willing to write off support from the South, except the three states that still had Republican governments, proving himself to be as perspicacious as he was unscrupulous.

July 15, Philadelphia

THE International Workingmen's Association, known to history as Karl Marx's First International, at its height was credited by its enemies with almost unlimited power. Its plottings supposedly brought about the bloody Paris Commune of 1871 and caused the great Chicago fire of the same year. Its alleged millions of supporters, drawn from the lowest classes and desperately anti-everything, gave nightmares to European statesmen and drove hostile monarchs into each other's arms. In the United States the International was additionally feared for its identification with sexual revolution. This day the General Council of the International held a crucial, closed-doors meeting. The ten delegates present declared the organization dissolved. Their somber session was one of the least noticed in the press of the hundreds of groups that chose to convene in Philadelphia during the Centennial summer.

America had its socialists since the 1840s, when the Fourierists attracted notice for their utopian theories and experimental communities. The Communist Club of New York, established in 1857, was the first small group here dedicated to the "scientific" socialism of Karl Marx. Its leading spirit was Friedrich Sorge, who, like Carl Schurz, was a transatlantic exile from the German Revolutions of 1848. He settled in West Hoboken and earned a living as a music teacher. A "man of education and deep discrimination," retiring and modest, with a neat beard and thin spectacles, he looked more like a diplomat than a revolutionist. Yet his way of fixing a person with searching eyes and his indefatigability as propagandist and organizer were remembered by a whole generation of radicals.[1]

Sorge and his group were consequential enough to be admitted to the National Labor Union and in 1869 to be recognized as American Section No. 1 of the IWA, which Marx had founded in London five years previously. By 1871 there were eight sections with 203 members subordinated to a Central Committee of the North American Federation.

When a native American section, No. 12, was brought into the federation, Sorge and the foreign-born internationalists were initially gratified only to find themselves overwhelmed with scandal and threatened with loss of control. The Americans, ostensibly inheritors of the Fourierist tradition, turned out to be the followers of the notorious sisters Victoria Woodhull and Tennessee Claflin, "the most seductive pair of reformers this country has ever known." From obscure origins in Ohio and early careers as palm readers and spirit healers, the Claflin sisters somehow made their way to a glittering place in New York society. They attracted great attention as "lady stockbrokers," being encouraged and given business tips by Commodore Vanderbilt, who was one recipient of Victoria's favors. They began publishing *Woodhull and Claflin's Weekly*, which became a sensational success after running an exposure of the adultery of Henry Ward Beecher, who may once have been another conquest of Victoria's. The masthead motto of this journal was "Progress! Free thought! Untrammeled Lives!" and the Claflins were not idle poseurs at radicalism, demonstrating this when they editorially glorified the Paris Commune and tried to capture the women's suffrage movement in the name of "freedom of sexual relations," meaning, actually, not so much license as legal emancipation.[2]

Sorge and his German-speaking colleagues were bourgeois in their life-styles and were shocked by the antics of the Claflin sisters, especially after Section 12 and twelve other sections held a convention in Philadelphia in July, 1872, and launched a campaign for Woodhull as president of the United States on an equal rights platform which offered sex and socialism in equal doses.

Section 1 and twenty-two others denounced political action and appealed to the parent organization in Europe (a practice that was the curse of American communists vis-à-vis Moscow in the 1920s). The Hague Congress of 1872 duly voted to expel No. 12 and associated sections, which went their merry way, having forever branded the International in the minds of many Americans with the terms "Paris Commune" and "free love."

The Hague Congress was one of the most crucial in the history of the IWA for other reasons than its slapping down Victoria Woodhull. It was the final, decisive confrontation of the Marxists and the Bakuninists, the ones favoring mass organization, deliberate preparation for revolution, and the dictatorship of the proletariat afterward, the others with romantic ideas of terrorism, spontaneous insurrection, and anarchism afterward. The Bakuninists lost and were expelled, but the several national federations supporting them promptly set up an "anti-authoritarian" movement rival to Marx's General Council. In their refusal to buckle down to a central authority, the supporters of Woodhull and Bakunin were significantly alike, but anarchism as a general doctrine did not gain a foothold in America until the 1880s. At the time of his death this very July, 1876, Bakunin was contemplating coming to this country.[3]

Although he had ostensibly won, Marx was still so alarmed at the prospect of the Bakuninists taking over the International that in 1872 he made the momentous decision to move the General Council to New York City and "into the hands of the trustworthy Sorge."[4] Marx had some positive hope that the rapid industrialization of the United States would make it a powerful new base for socialism.

New York's receiving the General Council was at once an "empty honor," in view of the deterioration of the European movement, and a "gift" that prolonged the life of the North American Federation. Secretary Sorge did his best to revitalize the organization but found his main task to be the dreary one of expelling the dissenting sections abroad. Briefly, the cause seemed to prosper in the United States with the German sections joining to launch a solid daily newspaper, the *Arbeiter Zeitung*. Later factional disputes drove Sorge and Section No. 1 to purge several American sections. When the depression of 1873 struck, the International did little except to organize relief for its German members in New York, and this inactivity prompted militants to organize rival socialist parties. By late 1874 "the organization of the International was weakened to such a degree that it practically ceased to exist."[5]

Sorge was tired of his thankless task and was preparing himself for his eventual role of Marxist theoretical writer above factions. In 1876 he published his best work, *Socialism and the Worker*. The antagonist of Woodhull was careful to point out that socialism was "not directed against morality and the family, but against prostitutionism in all its phases." He was even at pains not to alarm millionaire capitalists, saying that socialists "consider personal property an accomplished fact, so much so that they consider stealing a crime." His idea was in the future to stop the exploitation that made possible great fortunes.[6]

In early 1876 the General Council had sent out circulars declaring that it was unable to continue functioning. Also, it notified such European sections as it could contact of a congress to be held at Philadelphia, but only the German Social Democrats authorized a delegate to act in their name. The ten men who met at Germania Hall at Seventeenth and Poplar streets on July 15 claimed to speak for nineteen American sections representing 635 members. The congress took only a few hours to finish its business, accepting in silence and with unanimity a resolution of self-destruction. No reporters were present, but the group methodically provided for the publication of their proceedings, including a declaration that was both frank and optimistic:

> The International is dead! The bourgeoisie of all countries will again cry out, with scorn and joy, and with trumpet blasts will announce the resolutions of the Conference as documentary proof of the defeat of the international labor movement. Let not the shrieking of our enemies divert us from our purpose. We have given up the International in the light of the political situation in Europe; but in recompense we see the advanced workers of the entire civilized world acknowledging and defending its principles. . . . The comrades of America pledge themselves to guard and foster the aims of the International until conditions are more congenial for bringing together the workers of all countries in common action. The cry will then resound again and louder: Workingmen of all countries, unite![7]

The following day the same ten men, joined by three others, met again as the third congress of the North American Federation. The treasurer reported a balance of $76. After lively exchanges in the way of self-criticism this congress elected Sorge as one of its delegates to a unity convention of all American socialists scheduled for July 20, and then the federation also dissolved itself.

In their postmortems American Marxists admitted that they had erred in trying to translate German conditions to this country and in being out of contact with the masses. (Marx's collaborator, Engels, later accused them of using their theories as "a credo and not a guide to action. Added to which they learn no English on principle."[8]) Yet their influence on later developments was far from negligible. The "no politics" dogma of the American Federation of Labor until recent times had its origin in the attitude of American Marxists toward middle-class reform parties during the period of Sorge's leadership. Samuel Gompers himself, the guiding light of the AFL, admitted his debt to the "philosophers" of the International—"a strikingly unusual group of brainy men"— with whose circle in New York he was closely associated throughout 1876.[9]

The demise of the First International in Philadelphia was followed by the emergence of united, nation-oriented socialist parties in various countries, instantly in the case of the United States, later, say, in France and Britain. These parties in turn sponsored a Second International, which held the first of a series of brilliant congresses in Paris in 1889 and lasted down to World War I.

Ironically, just when Sorge and his colleagues were committing organizational suicide, a flicker of grass-roots internationalism occurred in the form of a delegation of French workers coming here to help celebrate the "glorious centennial of a sister Republic." France was at first edgy about having a group of its proletariat stirred up anew by contacts with American workers, but the government ended up aiding the delegation financially after a Paris police investigative dossier of April 24 assured it that even the American Internationalist was "less phrase-monger, less striker and revolutionary, and much more industrious than the European."[10] In the United States the press initially expressed alarm at the prospects of "terroristic Communards" reaching our shores, but later it contented itself with fanning fears in the American labor movement that the French were coming to look for jobs.

The hundred-odd Frenchmen arrived in New York Harbor on July 6 aboard the *Canada.* An opening contretemps occurred

[209]

when they drove away with derisive shouts an official welcoming steamer as representing only bourgeoisie and greeted with cheers a rowboat claiming to be a workers' reception committee. Later the delegation paraded to a labor hall on Prince Street, where they had an "elegant collation," and the next day, after sightseeing, they banqueted and danced at Bellevue Gardens.[11] Their hosts were primarily New York's socialists, for the city trade unions, leaders and rank and file both, did in fact snub them.

In Philadelphia the labor movement acted less antagonistically toward them, although investigators were sent to check up on what the Frenchmen did in their hotels at night. The visitors set about studying the Centennial with great thoroughness, and they also submitted to whoever would take them thirty-four questions about labor conditions in America. The French were particularly distressed to learn of yellow-dog contracts, whereby American workers pledged themselves not to unionize. Upon departure, their general conclusion was that capitalism was as much the master here as in Europe.[12]

July 18, Cleveland

IF the First International failed in making a revolution because so few paid it any attention, John D. Rockefeller succeeded in making himself a multimillionaire also because so few paid him any attention. He deliberately wrapped his magnificently piratical oil business dealings in obscurity, and in this period he so cleverly avoided any show of wealth or power that he was virtually unknown outside the Midwest. The sheer brutality and ruthlessness involved in creating America's first industrial monopoly are suggested in a few extant letters. On this date, for example, Rockefeller's newfound henchman C. N. Camden wrote Cleveland headquarters relative to the small refiners of West Virginia: "We will either get them or starve them." On August 23 Rockefeller himself described his losing competitors in the Pittsburgh area as "a whole crew of broken down oilmen" who were out to "pension themselves upon us." He even used the word "debris" to characterize what were, in fact, scores of ruined businesses and hundreds of broken lives.[1]

One aspect of the story of Rockefeller's rise that he and his family would have liked to suppress was the fact that his father was a self-styled doctor who was almost never at home in Rockford, New York, because he was out on the road peddling snake-oil-type cures for cancer. After a minimum of schooling, the tall, thin, taciturn, and self-righteous son went off to Cleveland to work as a clerk in a brokerage house and soon prospered in business for himself. In 1860, the year after Drake's first oil well, Rockefeller was sent by a consortium to investigate the money-making potentials of the burgeoning oilfields. His advice was to steer clear of oil production and go into oil refining, advice he took himself. The very newness of the oil industry lent itself to monopoly, and Rockefeller's single-minded determination to gain control of it appeared an irresistible force. Rockefeller positively disliked competition as "waste" and "lack of order." The first step in his well-calculated scheme was to promise to deliver to the Lake Shore Railroad so much oil daily in return for a preferential shipment rate, done through rebates or kickbacks. This dirty trick quickly reduced the number of Cleveland's refineries from thirty to ten. The next year, 1870, when Rockefeller was just thirty-one, he organized Standard Oil of New Jersey with a capital of $1,000,000. Far more potent and more mysterious was the South Improvement Company of two years later, which had as its aim the buying of the largest refinery in every oil city and using it to wreck or win over the competition.

The secret preferential railroad rate was just one of Rockefeller's predatory maneuvers. He broke the resistance of the independent refineries in Pittsburgh by an underhanded deal with the chief barrelmaker in the area, the man to whom he wrote about "debris" in August. Sometimes he secretly bought into the ownership of competing companies and gained control; this was the case with C. N. Camden, who had the good sense to become a Rockefeller troubleshooter and made a fortune doing so. Once all of Rockefeller's outraged rivals in an area bestirred themselves to organize a giant rival company, only to find that it was owned by Standard Oil. In the year 1876 alone Rockefeller bought or leased forty other companies. From Cleveland he moved in on Philadelphia, Pittsburgh, New York, and West Virginia. By 1878 he controlled 95 percent of all oil refineries and pipelines.[2]

Such a juggernaut did not go wholly unnoticed, of course. Rockefeller was burned in effigy in oil towns, and mass meetings of oil producers vowed countermeasures. The Pennsylvania legislature at one point revoked the charter of the South Improvement Company, but the indictments drawn up against Rockefeller and his associates were inexplicably withdrawn. In March, 1876, the shady goings-on in the oilfields were brought to the attention of the national Congress when a Representative from Pittsburgh introduced a bill "to regulate commerce and prohibit unjust discrimination by Common Carriers."[3] This effort to strike down Rockefeller's rebates was also doomed to oblivion. Few doubted then or later that Rockefeller had bought up enough congressmen to keep the bill from being considered. As yet there simply was no public demand for antitrust legislation.

John D. Rockefeller did not come to New York City until 1881, and even then he bought a modest place at 4 West Fifty-fourth Street. Only William H. Vanderbilt of the New York Central seemed to know who he was, telling reporters, "The Rockefeller crowd are mighty smart men. I guess if you ever had to deal with them you would find *that* out."[4] The pity was that everyone had to buy Rockefeller oil, but so few "had to deal with them."

To many Clevelanders in 1876 Rockefeller was remarkable only for the devotion he showed to teaching Sunday school. The faith that he was doing God's will apparently also enabled him to cripple a competitor or suborn a legislator without remorse. Twenty years later, when Rockefeller retired from business, he was worth $200,000,000 and four times that in another fourteen years after the automobile brought the oil industry far past the era of kerosene lamps.

One of the few men to rival Rockefeller in the size of his fortune was Henry Ford, who as a youngster in 1876 received the inspiration that determined his career. In his own words:

> I was twelve when I saw my first engine-driven vehicle. I had seen plenty of threshing-machine engines being hauled by horses, but this one had a chain connecting it to the rear wheels. The engineer stopped to let us pass with our horses, and I was off the wagon and talking to him before my father knew what I was up to. It was that engine which took me into automotive transportation. From the moment I saw it, my great interest was to make a machine that would travel the roads.[5]

Ford, of course, did not invent the automobile, but he made his first car the year Rockefeller retired and started a real revolution in 1908, when he began mass-producing the Model T.

July 18, War Bonnet Creek

BUFFALO BILL killed Cheyenne Chieftain Yellow Hand in a small skirmish in Wyoming, and many Americans heaved a sigh of relief that Custer was being avenged. Militarily, the action was part of a fumbling strategy, but theatrically, it built up imperishable legends.

Buffalo Bill had signed up as a scout with the 5th Cavalry at Fort Laramie in early June. The regiment, commanded by the baby-faced but tough new Colonel Wesley Merritt, had moved westward as part of the general closing in on the Sioux, and on July 10 at Sage Creek received the incredible news of the Custer massacre. At the same time Merritt got urgent orders from General Crook to rush him supplies and reinforcements, but he was distracted by the will-o'-the-wisp of intercepting a large party of Cheyenne reportedly leaving their reservation in Nebraska to join the hostiles. Circling the Red Cloud Agency, Merritt made a forced march of eighty miles to achieve a confrontation at War Bonnet Creek.

Contact with the Cheyenne having been made on July 7, Buffalo Bill was part of a scouting party the next day that sighted a group of warriors on the point of attacking Merritt's supply train. This group headed off the wild charge of the Indians, and in the course of the fighting Buffalo Bill shot the minor leader Yellow Hand from his horse, then killed him with a knife thrust to the heart, and in five seconds neatly scalped him. Within weeks the Eastern press was dramatizing the encounter as a lengthy, hand-to-hand duel between two inveterate enemies, like something out of the Trojan War.[1]

When the full force of Merritt's cavalry was brought into play on July 8, the Indians retreated, and the "Battle of War Bonnet Creek" ended with practically no casualties. The Indians were chased back to their reservation, and Merritt's regiment was delayed from joining General Crook at Goose Creek until August 23. The encounter made the career of the thirty-year-old Buffalo Bill, who sent off Yellow Hand's scalp and weapons first to be exhibited in his hometown, Rochester, New York, and then to be shown in cigar stores all over the country. Actually, William F. Cody already had genuinely impressive credentials as a frontier hero. As a boy of twelve he had shot his first Indian. He served as pony express rider and as a shotgun guard on stagecoaches; he fought in the Union Army in the Western campaign; and he had won his nickname as a hunter and supplier of meat to the crews of the Kansas Pacific, killing 4,280 buffalo in seventeen months, by his own boast. As early as 1872, when he was serving as a scout for Custer, he lent his name to a series of lurid and successful dime novels, and he found it to his fancy in the slack winter months to tour as an actor in cowboy and Indian dramas, playing Chicago and points east.

Eventually, Buffalo Bill turned everything to his great profit by organizing his Wild West Show, which for the rest of the century enthralled audiences of ordinary people in the United States as well as the crowned heads of Europe. One favorite stage extravaganza of his was an enactment of Custer's last stand following a near-miss rescue attempt by himself. Putting Sitting Bull himself into the act was even better. When Cody died in 1917, four states claimed the body of the hero, and Colorado safeguarded its right of possession only by sinking his coffin in an impenetrable tomb blasted out of the solid granite of Lookout Mountain near Denver.[2]

With Buffalo Bill a myth in his own lifetime, the mystique of the frontier was obviously well established long before Hollywood. For every movie involving stagecoaches, rustlers, and shoot-outs there was an equivalent dime novel in the 1870s. And reality itself was accommodating in 1876, if one sought a dramatic or romantic story.

The "hanging judge," for example, was Isaac Parker, who was appointed to the bench in Fort Smith, Arkansas, by President Grant in May, 1875, and in the course of the next two decades sentenced 172 men to the gallows. In defense of Parker, it must be noted that one in three of the hundreds of deputies he commissioned were killed in the line of action. Only half of the judge's victims were ever executed.[3]

The "kissing bandit" of the pulps was Billy the Kid. In actuality, William H. Bonney was a homicidal maniac born on New York's Lower East Side who had stabbed a man to death by the time he was thirteen. Seeking his fortune out West, he killed his first three Indians to steal their horses, and later he did in a soldier. Seventeen in 1876, he had a certain notoriety as a robber, cattle rustler, and quick-tempered gunman. His fictional reputation as a gallant lover of the women who crossed his path was belied by his gangly 135 pounds, his buckteeth, and his dull-witted look. Billy the Kid was dead at twenty-two, after he had been hunted down for shooting a sheriff and two prison guards.[4]

Many sociological facts about the frontier were also surprisingly at variance with the legends. The idea that the winning of the West was strictly a native American achievement is contradicted by the amount of European money invested in the frontier states, close to $100,000,000 yearly in the two decades after 1876.[5]

While most people are aware that barbed wire was a decisive technological factor in bringing settled agriculture to the West, few appreciate how relatively recently it was put into use. A number of almanacs assign the year 1876 to the invention, but 1873 is more accurate. Several varieties of barbed wire were exhibited at the Philadelphia Centennial. Until it was widely manufactured and strung, the era of the great cattle drives continued. In 1876, 322,000 steers were moved north on the trail from San Antonio, the town's fourth greatest annual drive.[6]

One impression of the West that was abruptly dispelled ten years before the end of the century was that the frontier would be with us indefinitely. Half the country's area was wilderness in 1876, the frontier running southward down through the western edges of Minnesota, Iowa, Missouri, Arkansas, and Louisiana with advanced wedges into Nebraska, Kansas, and Texas. Another frontier faced eastward from the Pacific coast and mountain states. Many people questioned whether the huge area in between, which was largely brownish in its vegetation in contrast with the green areas already settled, would ever support a considerable population. The Army, whose geodetic survey was a tremendous scientific accomplishment in this period, issued several reports in 1876 reassuring people that there was still good land left, and the railroads for their own reasons were quick to second the Army's optimism. By 1890 a frontier line no longer existed, just isolated pockets—the startling discovery of the historian Frederick Jackson Turner, who was a Wisconsin schoolboy the year of the Centennial.[7]

July 20, Philadelphia

"THE month of July 1876 shall be memorable in our history as the date upon which the thoughtful and earnest and well-disposed workingmen of America met in Philadelphia and united for their common interests." So said the *Socialist*.[1] Actually, only seven men met, and they might better be described as intellectuals rather than workingmen. No cowboys and Indians could divert such persons, nor did they even visit the Centennial Exhibition. Their mission was to bring together the warring socialist factions, and they ostensibly did so.

The site was the same as for the meetings earlier in the month—Germania Hall. Only two of the participants were the same, Friedrich Sorge and another representative of the ex-International and the 635 American members it claimed. Peter J. McGuire was the most prominent of the three delegates for the Social Democratic Party, which boasted 1,500 members. The Illinois Labor Party with 593 members and the Cincinnati Workingmen's Union with 250 had one delegate apiece. A "credentials committee" denied votes to the Liberal League of Philadelphia and other groups as not being socialist.[2]

Just as American leftists in 1976 are accused of undue preoccupation with foreign models—Stalin, Mao, Castro—so in 1876 socialists were called un-American imitators of the French commune or the German Social Democrats. Two rival German theorists, Marx and Ferdinand Lassalle, were actually the touchstones of the socialists' debate in the 1870s. The two differed on whether or not the time was ripe for political action. Each viewpoint was backed by important sections of the German Social Democratic Party, which in 1875 compromised between them in the celebrated Gotha Program, an example of unity for American socialists.[3]

Marxist Internationalists were the first socialists to establish a foothold in America in the 1860s, years of economic growth and the flourishing of trade unions. The followers of Lassalle did not appear here in strength until after the panic of 1873, illustrating the general principle that "if the Marxists enjoyed the fruits of prosperity, it was the Lassalleans whose views were to prevail during periods of depression."[4] One Lassallean group was the Labor Party of Illinois, organized in January, 1874, to combat the immediate problem of unemployment by running candidates pledged to state ownership of railroads and state aid to cooperatives. Another larger Lassallean group was the Social Democratic Party of North America, which held a convention in New York in 1874 and put political action as the first order of business. By early 1876 Peter McGuire, the firebrand of the Social Democrats, was confidently telling a Connecticut audience, "We intend to commence at the bottom and build up. We must carry the towns first, the States next, and the presidential election last."[5]

Weakened as the International was by 1876, its American members held tenaciously to their belief in unions before politics. In 1875 the German-speaking Marxists were heartened by the adherence to their organization of the United Workers of America, a small group of primarily Irish workers headed by the dynamic J. P. McDonnell, who, after a career as a Fenian revolutionary, had served as Marx's secretary in London.

Indications that rank-and-file socialists were disgusted with the theoretical bickerings of their leaders led to discussion of unity in 1875. The factions were brought closer by a desire to present a common front at the Pittsburgh Labor Conference in April, 1876, and the rebuff of the socialists there served to show that disunited they were no match for such movements as Greenbackism.

The "Congress" of seven men that met in Germania Hall on July 15 deliberated with all the formality of a great parliament. The chairmanship was rotated among them. Th first sharp debate was over a new name for the movement. The Marxists argued passionately for keeping "international" as symbolic of the past and also of the multinational character of the laboring class in America. Moreover, they wanted international connections to prevent the possibility of cheap foreign labor being brought into this country. The Social Democrats saw no need for international affiliations. They wanted the word "socialist" in the name, but the others countered that the term scared off native Americans. The name finally adopted was Workingmen's Party of the United States. Four days of such wranglings produced also a party platform and constitution. Then "speeches were made congratulating the delegates on the success of their work."[6]

The general principles of the new party, taken from the statutes of the International, explicitly looked to the "abolition of all class rule."[7] Further:

> We demand that all the means of labor (land, machinery, rail-
> roads, telegraphs, canals, etc.) become the common property of
> the whole people, for the purpose of abolishing the wages system
> and substituting in its place cooperative production with a just
> distribution of its rewards.

No mention was made of revolution, but it was in the delegates'
minds. As the party's chief editor defined it later in the year, "a
forcible and bloody overthrow of capitalism" would be avoided
only if the state came under the control of "all the sufferers armed
with scientific remedies." In the way of immediate measures, the
platform was taken from earlier demands of the Social Democrats, including the eight-hour day, labor statistics, no use of prison labor, no labor by children under fourteen, free education at
all levels, abolition of conspiracy laws, and government ownership
of transport and communications.

The socialists did not endorse women's rights any more than
the major parties did. They acted by their own logic, avowing that
"the emancipation of women will be accomplished with the emancipation of men, and the so-called women's rights question will be
solved with the labor question."

The Marxists scored an unequivocal success in the platform's
declaration that the party "will not enter in a political campaign
before being strong enough to exercise a perceptible influence."
The Social Democrats bitterly opposed this formulation and probably would have stormed out of the meeting if McGuire had not
been able to push through an additional declaration that the party
executive might permit local campaigns under very favorable circumstances. The tense vote on this amendment was four to three,
the Marxists being opposed. Then one delegate switched his support to allow a further clarification definitely on Marxist lines.
The economic struggle was "in first place" for the party, which
should avoid a political movement, for such attracts "an enormous
amount of small reformers and quacks." The party specifically
and workers in general "were earnestly invited . . . to turn their
backs on the ballot box" so as "to save themselves from bitter disappointment" and to allow them to concentrate on economic organization, which "is frequently destroyed and always injured by a
hasty political movement."

The new party gained control of the resources and periodicals
of the former factions. The *Socialist* became the *Labor Standard,*

and J. P. McDonnell of the United Workers was rewarded with its editorship of the latter, replacing a Social Democrat. His was the dominant voice in the movement for a brief while. Gompers remembered him as a "striking figure," tall, with clean-cut features, "wonderful eyes," and an abundance of curly red hair.[8] It was also Gompers' recollection that the primary objective of the New York Marxists, with whom he was associated at that time, was gaining control of the *Socialist*, so as "to secure a going concern and to retard Socialistic [political] activity."[9]

"If a settlement was reached at Philadelphia, an understanding was not," particularly on the matter of politics.[10] The outward unity achieved was considered so fragile that the original plan to hold a referendum among the entire socialist membership was dropped, provoking angry readers' letters to the *Labor Standard* about the "mystery" of the proceedings and the "undemocratic reticence" of the leadership.

The tactical question was soon out in the open when McGuire announced plans of the New Haven section of the party to run candidates for local offices, including two state legislative seats. On the basis of his assurances of "real prospects of success," the Chicago Executive Committee gave its "reluctant" assent, warning that a bad precedent might be set and that a "ridiculous failure" would do more harm than good. Sorge protested the assent in an "extremely personal and offensive communication."[11]

The approach of the November, 1876, election was generally greeted with negativism by the *Labor Standard*, which editorialized at one point: "Workmen, don your rags and go to the polls next Tuesday to record your votes for those who trample on you and despise you."[12] As for the New Haven efforts of McGuire, he at least was pleased by the result. His cigarmaker candidate for assembly won 640 votes when Peter Cooper got only 565 in the state. The 5,000 leaflets distributed during the campaign had a great educational effect and cost only $41.02, according to McGuire, who crowed that "a breach has been made in the enemy walls."[13]

The New Haven vote excited political activists in the party, and in 1877 local tickets were run in Cincinnati, Milwaukee, and Chicago to the displeasure of *Labor Standard*. Votes running into the thousands and a handful of socialist aldermen and other officials elected further encouraged the Lassallean element, who held a surprise convention in Newark in late 1877, with the Marxists largely absent, and changed the name of the party to the Socialist Labor Party. McDonnell left the editorship of *Labor Standard* in disgust, and Sorge retired from the fray, too. In the early 1880s the appearance of the anarchists brought more divisions to the movement, and a really cohesive Socialist Party would have to wait until 1901. Meanwhile, many of the leaders of 1876 turned toward what the latter called "pure and simple trade unionism" and beginning in 1877 did succeed in revitalizing the labor movement. Ironically, McGuire also came around to this position.

Thus, the high hopes of socialists in July, 1876, were followed by the "visionless routinism" of the trade union movement and the "sectarian caprices of the Socialist Labor Party."[14] In vain, a reader had written the *Labor Standard* in August: "in the name of common sense let us fight against the system that is crushing us and not against each other. The capitalists are watching us."[15] Endemic factionalism among socialists was one explanation of the indifference of the masses to the movement then as now. A more fundamental cause was the "get rich quick mentality in all segments of American society," which particularly baffled the socialist-minded immigrants. The Greenback program of the "capitalism of the many against the capitalism of the few"[16] had a greater appeal than would be admitted by the seven men at the Philadelphia congress, whose fault was lack of realism, not lack of vision.

July 21, Saratoga, New York

FOR decades this Northern watering spot had been the most fashionable resort in the country, and it still was a far more lively and comfortable place to be in midsummer than sweltering Philadelphia. All sorts of groups gravitated here. Tilden and Hendricks would soon come to hold crucial strategy talks. The clergy favored Saratoga, despite the drinking and gambling, and the Society for the Advancement of the Social Sciences would hold its learned sessions in no other place. Today began regatta weekend, the most colorful and gala of the season, with rowing clubs from all over the East competing on the lake. Carriage prices shot up to

$30 for a day, but hundreds of people arrived in farm wagons to picnic and view the races and watch society.

College students were here in force, and some came to organize—not a protest, however, but rather the Intercollegiate Association of Amateur Athletes of America. The IC4A, as it came to be known, was the first major organization concerned with campus sports. Rowing was its chief interest, and Cornell won the regatta this year, in part because Yale and Harvard withdrew because they considered sixteen crews racing at once unwieldy. Field and track events, which hitherto had been sort of an appetizer to the regatta at Saratoga, now emerged as the main concern of the IC4A, and it sponsored ten events, including a 100-yard dash, a 120-yard hurdles, a mile run, a three-mile run, and a seven-mile walk. Princeton won with four firsts in 1876, and colleges began from this date to establish and beat records. Football, a popular activity left outside the purview of the IC4A, would get its own association in the fall. The fourteen forming the new group were the cream of Eastern men's colleges: Amherst, Bowdoin, Brown, CCNY, Columbia, Cornell, Dartmouth, Harvard, Princeton, Trinity, Union, Wesleyan, Williams, and Yale.[1]

The collegians in Saratoga wearing their boaters, blazers, and white ducks were scarcely noticeable in the throng of the more or less fashionable and wealthy, which included Western bonanza kings, disgraced Tweed politicians, Southern carpetbaggers with dim futures, generals, patent-medicine doctors, dowagers with marriageable daughters, and female eccentrics with white-fringed fans in tribute to Peter Cooper's beard. The richest ladies came with fifteen "Saratoga trunks" so as to be able to change clothes five times a day, but hundreds did with less as they lounged about the grand piazzas of the innumerable hotels or rode up and down Main Street in their landaus or shays. The largest of the hotels was the late A. T. Stewart's Grand Union with its brass spittoons, elegant murals, and French cuisine. Booker T. Washington had been one of the black waiters here before becoming a teacher in rural Virginia.

On the outskirts of the town were the places where people "took the waters," three glasses of mineral water, for example, before sitting down to a lavish breakfast. High Rock was the popular spring that required a good drive before lunchtime. Moon's Lake House was the favored place to visit in the afternoon, to view the lake, to watch the fish in artificial pools, and to partake of the novelty "Saratoga chips"—that is, french fries cut especially thin and iced thoroughly before cooking.[2]

The Saratoga racetrack was the first great course built in the United States. It was the creation of John Morrissey, undefeated prizefighter when he retired in 1858, sometimes powerful New York state senator, and owner of the daring Chateau de Chance. Offenbach singled out the tall, well-proportioned, "gentlemanly" Morrissey with his flattened nose as one of the celebrities of his visit to America.[3]

Saratoga no longer thrilled the second-generation rich and the fastidious. James Gordon Bennett called it "a cradle of fashion and intrigue, rendezvous of lackeys and jockeys." Henry James sneered that it was a "shoddy community of boasters."[4]

Newport, Rhode Island, was becoming the citadel of true millionaires and New England Brahmins alike. Bennett had a grand estate there, as did August Belmont. Less palatial residences were enjoyed by such members of the intelligentsia as Thomas Higginson and Helen Hunt Jackson. George Bancroft, who had just completed a revised, six-volume Centennial edition of his classic *History of the United States,* had a place called Rosecliffe where he grew 500 varieties of roses.[5]

President Grant was still satisfied with a resort as old as Saratoga. This summer, as before, he settled down to shirt-sleeved comfort in a Long Branch, New Jersey, beach house. Many politicians and just ordinary citizens made the pilgrimage to Long Branch to greet the Grants on their front porch. The President invited Governor Hayes to pay a visit, but his party's presidential nominee gave a sick son as an excuse for not coming and thus avoided being personally identified with Grantism in any way.

July 26, Cincinnati

FIVE hundred unemployed men were milling about Fountain Square at 8 A.M. Suddenly, an individual named J. Brown got up on a soapbox and shouted, "I am a workingman, and you all know what we want. *We want bread or blood!* What I say I mean! That's all I have to say." The crowd applauded and then became restless when no one else came forward. Someone said, "Is there no working-man here who can make a speech and tell us how we can be saved from starvation?" A socialist named Gustav Luebkirt consented to address the assemblage, which had tripled in numbers. He spoke of the evils of capitalism and invited his listeners to join his party that they might "educate themselves by organization so as to become powerful enough to enforce their demands." When there were cries for a march on City Hall, Luebkirt warned that policement were "ready to shoot them in cold blood." While the revolution was "near," he assured them, "the time is not at hand to strike a blow against the authorities. We must do that at the ballot box on election day."

Later the crowd heard the Independent Party's vice presidential candidate, Samuel F. Cary, who outlined his plans for getting more greenbacks into the hands of the workers. A voice interrupted him, saying, "We have none. We want work. Then we will get them." Cary warned insistently against violence. Eventually, a few hundred of the crowd formed a line of march to City Hall, where they found the gates barred to them by heavily armed police. They sent in a message, "We want work or bread," and said they would return on Friday. The mayor did eventually receive a delegation and told them that he, the City Council, and all officials were powerless to help them.[1]

What happened in Cincinnati was repeated in cities all over the country.[2] In New York, for example, as many as 50,000 at one time marched in unemployment demonstrations during August. Actual rioting was almost unheard of, since the majority of workers were law-abiding. They wanted jobs rather than handouts; the work ethic as yet had little competition from the welfare ethic. The financial panaceas of the Greenbackers held little appeal for most of them. Nor were the socialists prepared to offer immediate redress. The unions were altogether out of the picture when it came to taking responsibility for the jobless. Finally, the authorities merely passed the buck, disclaiming any duty or competence to intervene in the workings of free enterprise. This ignorance and apathy about the recession proceeded from the Grant administration on down. Rare was the local official who took it upon himself to provide jobs in public works.

Unlike 1976, when any newspaper reader can find out within one-tenth of a percent what the current rate of unemployment is, a hundred years ago no one kept statistics regarding what was a relatively new phenomenon. It is simply a guess whether the jobless totaled 400,000, as conservative newspapers of the day suggested, or 4,000,000, as radical historians now suggest. If the latter figure was true, the percentage rate of unemployment was worse than in the Great Depression of the 1930s. In any case, the human dimensions of the problem were readily ascertainable from contemporary accounts. The San Francisco press, for example, reported hundreds of people living off the city garbage dump. The Cincinnati *Enquirer* told of vagrants seeking to be sent to the workhouse, quoting the following exchange between judge and prisoner:

> Do you wish to be sent up?
> I ain't particular.
> Have you looked for work?
> Yes, sir.
> Where did you come from?
> New York.
> How did you come here?
> Walked.
> Well, you can go up for four months.[3]

In Manhattan about 90,000 homeless workers, 40 percent women, became known as revolvers, for during the winter months they put up for a day or two at each of the city police stations.

Much of the press was callous to the point of viciousness about the plight of the jobless. The *Nation* condemned New York's revolvers for their lack of "reliance on one's own resources" and the police stations for the "thoroughly communistic" practice of sheltering them.[4] The armies of "tramps" evident on roads all over the country were objects of fear more than compassion. The *Commercial Advertiser* of Cincinnati advised its readers: "A great deal of the current crime is attributed to tramps . . . these wanderers would rather steal than beg, but prefer begging to work. Legislation is needed that will compel them to work and *work hard* for their daily bread."[5] That editor apparently forgot that the real problem was that there *was* no work. The Evansville (Illinois) *Courier* was more careful when it took up the question "The Poor and How to Aid Them":

> We do not mean that the times are prosperous or that the people have all the work they could do, but we do mean that there is

not a man in this city who is willing to labor that could not earn enough to supply himself and his family with food. Twenty-five cents a day will keep a family of five from hunger. It won't supply the husband with his three glasses of beer and his half dozen pipes of tobacco besides. . . . A strong man can live and grow fat on ten cents a day.[6]

A millionaire, of course, earning 6 percent on his capital, would be living on $160 a day. Of the many similarities between 1876 and 1976, the greatest is the failure of the free enterprise system to provide work for millions of people, all the while the system's proponents mouth nonsense about the laziness and thriftlessness of the masses.

August 1, Denver

THE telegraph relayed the news that President Grant had signed the proclamation making Colorado the thirty-eighth state. The territory's voters had ratified the state constitution on July 1 just in time to make the Fourth of July celebrations especially festive in this capital city, which was something of an oasis on the Kansas Pacific Railroad, roughly 500 miles away from Kansas City in one direction and from Salt Lake City in the other. Now once again shooting and toasts and parades and speeches commemorated the onset of the "Centennial State."[1]

Colorado had sought statehood for a decade. The matter acquired some urgency in Washington only when the House of Representatives was about to be lost to Republican control. The would-be state was potentially Republican, and on the crowded last day of the Forty-third Congress in March, 1875, a majority pushed through the enabling act. The territory's lobbyist, a Democrat, had persuaded some of his fellow party members not to block the measure. In a sense, Colorado's three electoral votes determined the outcome of the national election in 1876.

Colorado's population was less than 40,000 in 1870, but it almost quintupled by 1880. Much of the state's 100,000 square miles had just been surveyed geologically in a major federal project completed in 1876, a reminder that dedicated professionals, as well as corruptionists, came out of Washington. People could now read of Colorado's more than fifty mountain peaks over 14,000 feet and also of its Penitente sect among the Mexicans who practiced crucifixion.

No more states were allowed to join the Union until 1889, the centennial of the Constitution, when North Dakota, South Dakota, Montana, and Washington were admitted. The next year brought in Wyoming and Idaho, the scenes of 1876's Indian battles. Mormon Utah was kept out until 1896. The map of the continental United States was completed in 1912 after the admission of Oklahoma, New Mexico, and Arizona.

August 2, Deadwood, Dakota Territory

WILD BILL HICKOK was shot dead while playing draw poker at a saloon in this brawling mining town, which had been built from scratch during the previous year or so in the midst of the Sioux's sacred Black Hills. Reputedly, Deadwood had one church and a hundred bars. The famed gunfighter had had a winning streak in the same saloon the previous afternoon. Arriving late today, he did not get to sit again with his back to the wall, as he preferred, and a local good-for-nothing, James McCall, crept up behind him and shot him in the head. The celebrated "Deadman's Hand" he held at the moment consisted of the aces of spades and clubs, the eights of spades and clubs, and the queen of diamonds.

Like Buffalo Bill, Wild Bill Hickok was already something of a hero to Eastern newspaper readers. His real name was James Butler Hickok, and he had the same sort of rugged upbringing and drifter job record as his friend Cody. He gained the reputation of being the fastest gunslinger around, and he did several stints as marshal of towns needing law and order, such as Abilene, Texas, which paid him $150 a month and a quarter of the fines he collected. At times he served as a scout for Custer, who praised him in print as "one of the most perfect types of physical manhood I ever saw." Buffalo Bill tried to get him into the theater circuit, but

Hickok proved too unsophisticated, to say nothing of his winging a few fellow actors by accident. In the summer of 1876 the thirty-nine-year-old gunfighter was newly married, slightly down in his luck, and aware of his failing eyesight and coordination. By chance, he was with Buffalo Bill at the time of the news of Custer, but he did not sign up with the Army, continuing on as a leader of a party of prospectors to Deadwood, where he hoped to make a profitable gold claim before retiring.

The newspapers at first informed the public that the man who shot Hickok had grimly pursued him to Deadwood to avenge the killing of his brother. Later they speculated that local gambling interests wanted to rid themselves of a potential reforming marshal. Actually, McCall was a psychotic barfly who sought the fame of shooting down the number one trigger man. An impromptu barroom court tried McCall and let him off, but justice eventually caught up with Hickok's too boastful murderer in the person of a United States marshal.

The two-penny press and dime novels also created legends about Hickok's supposed girlfriend Calamity Jane. The twenty-four-year-old Martha Jane Canary was the daughter of a man who decided to make his bedmate in a whorehouse an honest woman. Under frontier conditions, Calamity Jane took to wearing men's clothes at an early age, and she won acceptance as a rough-talking, hard-as-nails mule driver. She also served as an Army scout and might have been with Custer except for the fact she was ill at the time. A contemporary diary indicates that she was thrown in with Hickok on his journey to Deadwood, but there is no evidence of a romance à la Gary Cooper and Jean Arthur. Later Calamity Jane made up the story for her autobiography that she had tried to revenge herself on McCall with a meat cleaver, but she was just pandering to what the public wanted to hear. By the turn of the century, when the old woman was a wayward eccentric in the most pathetic circumstances, she would lend herself to any fanciful press stories about her love for Hickok, the child she bore him, and her bereavement that August 2. The lovable tomboy was duly buried next to the straight shooter.[1]

August 4, Albany

SAMUEL J. TILDEN finally issued his statement of acceptance of the Democratic nomination for president, pleading the press of official business as governor as the reason for his delay. Like Hayes, he was not going to travel and make speeches during the campaign. Some Republicans credited Tilden, as the master politician, with deliberately holding up his declaration so as to keep public attention focused on him. Others accused him of simple evasiveness in the face of widely divergent views within his party.

Tilden was, indeed, capable of supreme evasiveness, as he demonstrated right after his nomination when he received a group of curious and excited reporters in the garden of the executive mansion. One asked him how he would get along with his running mate Hendricks, and the governor imperturbably turned to a rose bush and murmured, "A week ago that was covered with flowers. How quickly they fade." When another sought his reaction to the party platform, Tilden cut a flower and handed it to him with a smiling "Will you have a rose?"[1] Some time later Tilden treated William C. Whitney to the same maddening reticence during a visit by a delegation of Democratic leaders to Tilden's mansion in Yonkers. Taking Whitney aside and leading him up into a tower, with the seeming intention of imparting confidences, Tilden whispered only the words "You can see Staten Island from here." Whitney was "so infuriated that he felt like pushing the old gentleman down the stairs."[2]

Tilden's prolonged silence led to rumors that there was an irreconcilable split between him and vice presidential candidate Hendricks on the currency question and that one or the other might step down. Since the June conventions, the Democratic House of Representatives had voted to repeal the Resumption Act; they thus went against their party platform, but this action could be interpreted as merely a sop to the Western inflationists, since the Republican Senate was certain to block the measure. The news that Tilden and Hendricks were meeting in Saratoga, New York, on July 28 suddenly dominated the headlines, but after dinner and a long drive with the Indianan, Tilden left without issuing any press release. Talk of discord increased. Only after another meeting in Saratoga a week later did Tilden announce that he and Hendricks had reconciled their views, which were to be made public in separate letters.

Tilden's letter, dated July 31 and released on August 4, was a wordy document three times as long as the party platform. Without ringing phrases, it read like a lawyer's brief and raised little enthusiasm. He made a great point of his forty years of public service.[3]

On the currency issue Tilden went on at length to blame the Republicans for the depression and high taxes, then spoke of the need for economizing and a sound currency, and finally called for resumption of specie payments by "gradual and safe processes." It was the hard-money position essential to carry the Eastern states and keep the confidence of Wall Street. Later, with the straight face he was so capable of, Tilden said he was only concerned that "the mechanics, the servant girls, and laboring men should not be robbed of their earnings."[4] Hendricks' statement did not exactly contradict Tilden's, but it left him free to return to the West and preach soft-money doctrines. The Democrats had decided to have it both ways, as their opponents found to their frustration.

Relative to civil service reform, Tilden did not go so far as Hayes in denouncing the spoils system, and he did not make a personal one-term commitment. Tilden verbally straddled the Southern issue, just as Hayes had. He pledged himself to "protect all citizens . . . in every political and personal right," but he was also concerned about the "systematic and insupportable misgovernment imposed on the States of the South," which he claimed was partially to blame for "the distress in business."

The candidate knew that he could count on the votes of the nearly solid South. In addition to this sectional group, he expected to be supported by other political, racial, and economic groups already within the Democratic Party—Tammany Hall, the Irish, and many laboring men, for examples. There were fewer celebrities to campaign for Tilden than for his opponent; among those who did were Grant's rival, Union General George Brenton McClellan; the millionaire Cyrus McCormick; the writer James Russell Lowell; and the liberal's favorite, Charles Francis Adams, who left the Republican Party and ran for governor of Massachusetts as a Democrat.[5]

In this more gentlemanly era of politics than today, Tilden had no qualms about selecting Abram S. Hewitt as party chairman and

Edward Cooper as party treasurer, the two being son-in-law and son of Peter Cooper, the Greenback candidate. A highly successful businessman, yet an idealist who quoted Sir Thomas More, Hewitt set up party headquarters in Everett House, a more modest address than Chandler's Fifth Avenue Hotel but no less busy. Actually, Tilden himself played the major role in supervising the campaign. He spent almost all his time now at Gramercy Park rather than in Albany.

The sheer organizational effort of the Democratic Party in 1876 was unprecedented. It reflected Tilden's experience as a New York vote getter who knew the importance not only of precinct-by-precinct activity but also of keeping tabs on each Democratic voter. One first in the campaign, which Hewitt considered decisive, was the *Democratic Campaign Book,* a 750-page compendium of serious propaganda material, mostly relating to Grant administration scandals and designed to give ammunition to Democratic speakers and journals. He also thought to distribute widely an illustrated song and joke book. Called "perhaps the most efficient organization of its kind," headquarters' "Literary Bureau" was the word mill that produced all these books, leaflets, and posters.[6] Republicans might complain that identical editorials in Democratic newspapers were the price of the central effort, but this hardly mattered. Another effective department was the Speakers Bureau, which not only provided orators on demand but kept a huge file of up-to-date timetables to make sure that they kept their appointments.

In his ambition to be president, Tilden drew on his considerable abilities at equivocation as a lawyer, on his unmatched skills as a politician, and finally on his private means as a millionaire. Many rich Democrats refused to give the party money since they thought that Tilden could afford to pay for his own campaign and should do so. Nor did Tilden enjoy the advantage of contributions from thousands of federal jobholders. In the absence of records, historians can only guess at the amounts he spent—perhaps $150,000 of his close friends' money, $100,000 of his own. Hewitt later complained of Tilden's parsimony in a couple of key states, while William C. Whitney was convinced that he spent much more than $100,000. The cartoonist Nast pictured limitless sums coming out of "Uncle Sammy's barrel."[7]

August 4, Elmira, New York

GOVERNOR TILDEN'S protestations left one visitor to his state unmoved, namely, Mark Twain, who within two months would take to the political stump in Connecticut for Hayes. Currently, Twain was staying at his sister-in-law's place at Quarry Farm, above Elmira, where he had the use of a detached octagonal building for a study. There was also a billiards table for diversion when he got tired of writing. "I am tearing along on a new book," he told his confidante Mary Fairbanks this summer Friday.[1] Four days later he wrote Howells more fully and frankly:

> Began another boy's book—more to be at work than anything else. I have written 400 pages on it—therefore, it is very nearly half done. It is Huck Finn's Autobiography. I like it tolerably well, as far as I have got, and may possibly pigeonhole or burn the manuscript when it is done.[2]

By midsummer Twain was fully conscious of the disastrous delays involved in the publication of *Tom Sawyer*. His publisher Bliss, taking advantage of Twain's earlier successes, had extended his commitments too much. Howells' review of *Tom Sawyer*, a "splendid notice," according to Twain, had appeared in the May *Atlantic Monthly,* and Twain had expected to be able to offer books to the public right afterward.[3] Months later the only ones available were editions pirated in Canada—a maddening financial loss.

Twain's complicated position as a director and stockholder in Bliss' firm also led him into difficulties at this time with his fellow writer Bret Harte, an Easterner turned Californian who had won recognition for short stories like "The Luck of Roaring Camp." Younger than Twain but taking a patronizing attitude toward him, Harte had been a frequent guest in Hartford and owed Twain considerable money. With little to go for it other than Twain's earnest sponsorship, Harte's latest novel, *Gabriel Conway,* was also delayed in publication by Bliss, and the writer churlishly blamed his friend. Twain could only reply with the words "ineffable idiocy."[4] At Christmastime Harte's overbearing ways and unguarded wit led to a scene with Twain's wife and a new falling-out.

Tom Sawyer finally appeared on the market in December, but it sold only 24,000 copies in a year, leading to Twain's parting company with Bliss also and to a harrowing career as his own publisher. Eventually, of course, the book became an all-time best-seller.

One aspect of Twain's beloved work of 1876 was pure nostalgia for his own boyhood in Hannibal. *Tom Sawyer* was definitely Western in its setting, "incomparably the best picture of life in that region as yet known to fiction," according to Howells.[5] "It is *not* a boy's book at all," wrote Twain at the time he finished the story. "It is only written for adults."[6] Not all adults at the time approved, for *Tom Sawyer* was a kind of satire on the prevalent Sunday-school morality expected of children. The famous whitewashing scene is just a prelude to his winning a Sunday-school prize by presenting the merit tickets he has bartered away from his friends.

For all its irreverence, *Tom Sawyer* was far from shocking in its language. Twain himself had a Victorian sensibility about profanity or lewdness in print. Nonetheless, the book was banned in the new Denver public library and in the children's reading room of the Brooklyn Library.[7]

Huck Finn, who was a fairly one-dimensional "juvenile pariah" in *Tom Sawyer,* became a much more complex character in the masterpiece by his name, which Mark Twain began in the summer of 1876 and finished eight years and seven books later. The book is an adventure story, but philosophically it can be seen as an attempt to resolve Twain's current confusion and doubt about freedom and restraints, about ignorance and responsibility. Huck on his raft, in a sense, is Mark Twain himself adrift.

The textbooks usually hail Mark Twain the novelist as a realist, as well as a great satirist. On the one hand, he did reject with disgust the sentimental mush and contrived melodramas so popular at this time. On the other hand, Twain was not a muckraking, topical writer of the sort of John De Forrest, whose work of 1875–76, *Playing the Mischief,* dealt with the Credit Mobilier scandal. Although De Forrest was published in the *Atlantic Monthly,* Twain did not seem to appreciate this truly pioneer realist, whose works were too everyday to be popular.[8] Twain was quite respectful of the literary Establishment. In October he toyed with a scheme that not only he and Harte but also Holmes, James, and Lowell join in writing a series of novels with a single plot. To picture Twain as a writer apart, as a complete iconoclast, is mistaken.

August 7, New York

And so, at the age of thirteen, Edward Bok left school, and on Monday, August 6, 1876, he became office boy in the electrician's department of the Western Union Telegraph Company at 6 dollars and 25 cents per week.

And, as such things will fall out in this curiously strange world, it happened that as Edward drew up his chair for the first time to his desk to begin his work on that Monday morning, there had been born in Boston, exactly twelve hours before, a girl-baby who was destined to become his wife. Thus at the earliest possible moment after her birth, Edward Bok started to work for her.[1]

This passage from the highly regarded autobiography *The Americanization of Edward Bok* marked the beginning of the great American success story of a Netherlands-born immigrant whose family was so poor that he had to break off his education in the sixth grade and go to work. The atypical real story was the stuff of the fiction of Horatio Alger, the most widely read writer of the day.

Bok's youthful penchant for collecting the autographs of the illustrious in politics and literature—for example, President Grant and Mark Twain—brought him much advice about improving himself and also employment opportunities. Not long out of night school, he became advertising manager of *Scribner's Magazine* at age twenty-four and soon afterward won the editorship of the *Ladies' Home Journal,* a position he held for thirty years. Innovation was the basis for Bok's genuinely great reputation as a journalist; ahead of his times, he promoted not only women's suffrage but also ecology, pure drugs, and public discussion of venereal disease.

If the admirable thing about Bok was that he went from rags to right causes, the more obvious rags-to-riches story was the only thing that interested Horatio Alger, who in his lifetime served up more than 100 novels of this sort, which together sold some 30,000,000 copies. The year 1876 was a peak time in the career of the forty-two-year-old Alger. In March appeared *Sam's Choice; Or How He Improved It* (part of the *Tattered Tom* series); in June *New York Weekly* began the serialization of *Tony the Tramp* (published in book form as *Tony the Hero*); and in November came out *Shifting for Himself; or Gilbert Greyson's Fortune* (part of the *Brave and Bold* series).[2]

Alger's life story was only minimally a fairy tale. From a small-town Massachusetts family, he attended Harvard and unsuccessfully tried to enlist during the Civil War. His father browbeat him into ordination as a Unitarian minister, but he soon resigned and went to work at New York's Newsboys Lodging House, a kind of YMCA which served to acquaint Alger with the adolescent types found in his books. *Ragged Dick* of 1867 was the first novel following the surefire formula. Alger's brief term of service as tutor to the ten Seligman children revealed him to be quite the opposite personally from the manly types he idealized in print. The unruly young relatives of the great banker discovered that their mentor was a timid, delicate, mild-mannered man who practiced ballet steps in his off hours. Once they succeeded in locking him in a trunk in the attic.[3] In his later years Alger played the *bon vivant* here and abroad.

Returning a wallet found in the street, stopping a runaway horse, or coming to the aid of a cripple served in Alger's stories as the sure path for a youth's meeting a benefactor and rising above his misfortunes to wealth and power. Obviously, Alger was romanticizing on a one-in-a-thousand chance, but this improbability was what millions of people wanted to believe or at least wanted their children to believe. Incidentally, Alger's newsboys were advised in 1876 by Henry Ward Beecher to trust to individual enterprise and to avoid collective bargaining like sin. The point was that thousands of slum children could not even get to be newsboys. One estimate assigned New York City some 40,000 vagrant children at this time. Whiskey was available to kids at a penny a glass.

A man who had a career similar to that of Edward Bok and one who faced up to the side of life that Horatio Alger ignored was Jacob Riis, an immigrant from Denmark who returned to that country in March, 1876, to marry and to bring his bride back with him. As a young newspaperman, Riis explored and exposed the seamiest aspects of New York—the slums and the immigrant ghettos with their derelicts, fallen women, and vagrant children. Like Bok, he became a great public benefactor.

August 15, Columbia, South Carolina

GENERAL WADE HAMPTON was unanimously nominated as candidate for governor by a tumultuous Democratic convention held in this small capital city. Citizens poured out into the streets and hugged each other, as if a new era were on hand, and the day ended with a giant torchlight parade. It was a strange spectacle for Columbia, with its Republican governor and legislature, its racially mixed new society and night life, and its garrison of federal bluecoats. During Reconstruction old Columbia society isolated itself in shuttered houses.

The stately buildings of the university were sorely debilitated; in 1861 the student body had marched off to war en masse; in 1869 the facilities were given over to a school for blacks.[1]

A month and a half previously it appeared certain that the incumbent Republican governor, Daniel H. Chamberlain, would receive the Democratic endorsement, for, although a carpetbagger, he had gained widespread admiration for his bold policies of retrenchment and reform. In fact, Radical Republican leaders in Washington like presidential hopeful Senator Morton had accused Chamberlain of going over to the enemy. It was Chamberlain's determination to prove his Republicanism that led him to react so belligerently to the Hamburg Massacre of July 8 and to call for more federal troops—actions that proved his political ruin.

While many Democratic moderates, including businessmen, aristocrats, and the influential Charleston *News and Courier,* had been Fusionists prepared to back Chamberlain in 1876, there were also the Democratic Straight-Outs who favored no compromise with Republicans, rather their complete overthrow and the restoration of white supremacy. General Butler, of notoriety in the Hamburg events, was of this persuasion, as was General Martin Witherspoon Gary, an elegant bachelor of forty who lived in splendor at Oakly Hall in Edgefield County and was capable of tremendous feats of fiery eloquence and organizational drive.

When sixty citizens in Aiken were arrested in August in connection with the Hamburg Massacre, Gary and Butler turned the event into a "rowdy Democratic jubilee."[2] They even managed to disrupt Governor Chamberlain's opening political rallies by demanding equal time to speak at meetings before black voters.

Gary used the opportunity to castigate Republican rule: "I spoke to him in rude and rough language in order that the rude and rough Negro might understand it. That is what killed the spirit of the Negro, to see the Governor of the State and the chosen leader of their party abused in such measured terms." Chamberlain had to put up with this treatment because Butler massed thousands of mounted red-shirted Straight-Outs around the meetings, and the governor and his supporters had reason to fear for their lives.[3]

Butler and Gary needed a respectable candidate, and they found him in General Wade Hampton, who had been away on vacation during the Hamburg events and who had hitherto been a Fusionist until angered by Chamberlain's and Grant's maneuvers. Often called South Carolina's George Washington, Hampton was an aristocrat of aristocrats, who before the war had lived like a baron on his plantation, Millwood, near Columbia. His other estates in Missisippi produced cotton crops worth $250,000. Six feet tall, powerfully built, with fair hair and blue-gray eyes, Hampton was a magnificent presence. He was a superb equestrian, but his favored sport was killing black bears on foot with a knife—some eighty in his career. Otherwise a man of cultivated tastes, Hampton unambitiously served in the state legislature and then with alacrity embraced the secessionist cause, becoming a dashing cavalry commander. He returned to Millwood in 1865 to find it destroyed, with only the pillars of its portico standing.[4]

A cautious man, Hampton before his nomination wrote to Governor Tilden to seek his opinion whether a person who had been a distinguished Confederate soldier should lead South Carolina's Democrats. He also wrote the Democratic National Committee to ask about his campaigning for the national ticket. No replies were made. Tilden apparently did not want to commit himself, an instance of his fatal lack of leadership. As for Hampton, he made the vital decision: "I am not in the big fight. I am in the fight to save South Carolina."[5]

Hampton was the only candidate the Democrats considered at their August 15 convention, which ended the split between the Fusionists and the Straight-Outs. Even the Charleston *News and Courier* came around. Ironically, but not really accidentally, Hampton's nomination occurred the same day the Grant administration ordered Sherman to hold troops in readiness for the Southern elections.

In Columbia's Confederate Memorial Museum near the university campus are three prominent exhibits dealing with the postwar period: various personal effects of Wade Hampton; a large reproduction of the picture of the Assembly in the hands of black legislators; and a faded red shirt with the motto "August 1876" on it. The Red Shirts were the great and decisive novelty of the Hampton political campaign, which took on aspects of a crusade. Thousands of South Carolinian whites enlisted in the Rifle Clubs or mounted Saber Clubs, and their massed presence was felt at every political gathering in the state, whether in a rural hamlet or a large city, whether a rally of friends or of foes.

Hampton and Gary had opposing views on what use to make of the Red Shirts. The latter frankly favored breaking up opponents' meetings and outright intimidation of black voters so that they would not go to the polls. The wholesale resort to brutality and murder had succeeded in restoring white supremacy to Mississippi in the so-called Revolution of 1875. Hampton, however, rejected the Mississippi solution and stood by the slogan "Force without violence."[6] The Red Shirts were to be deployed only as a menacing presence, circling around Republican rallies, indulging in organized hissing, and occasionally heckling speakers with cries of "liar" or "thief." They were also to be employed to protect blacks who switched to Democratic, both at meetings and even at their homes. Hampton encouraged blacks to enroll in their own Democratic clubs, explaining to his friends that to overcome the four-to-three black majority in population he needed 10,000 black votes. Accordingly, Hampton parades and rallies were pointedly biracial, with reserved sections for the nonwhites. In the final analysis, of course, both Gary's and Hampton's strategies came into play: when persuasion failed, intimidation was often used.[7]

Hampton was probably not being hypocritical when he advocated racial harmony during the fall of 1876, even though the end result of his career was just the opposite. At his opening rally at Abbeville on September 16 he declared that "the only way to bring prosperity in this state is to bring the two races in friendly relations together." He forthrightly espoused equal justice with the words "If there is a white man in this assembly who believes that when I am elected Governor, I will stand between him and the law, or grant to him any privileges and immunities that shall not be granted to the colored man, he is mistaken."[8] As an orator Hampton was neither spectacular nor brilliant, but forcefully plain and soft-spoken.

Meanwhile, the Republicans nominated Chamberlain again. He was on the defensive from the start, refusing joint debates with Hampton. He expected more help from Washington than just the active support of federal patronage holders, arguing that he was the key to South Carolina's giving its vital seven electoral votes to Hayes. In this he was proved wrong. South Carolinians were to split their tickets as they had never done before: some voted for Hayes and Chamberlain, some voted Tilden-Hampton, and, most important, many voted Hayes and Hampton.

August 18, Boston

COMMANDER ALFRED THAYER MAHAN, commandant of the Boston Navy Yard, informed his friend Representative Samuel Ashe of North Carolina that he had just been detached from active service and put on half pay as a result of Congress' drastically reducing the annual appropriation for the fleet. The "wholesale slaughter" of the Navy officer corps Mahan blamed on politics. "This makes my yearly income $1150 after twenty years of service," he wrote in bitterness, refraining from adding that he could not now afford to visit the Philadelphia Centennial Exhibition with his family as planned.[1] One of his fellow officers this year solved his problem of unemployment by joining the 5th Cavalry fighting the Sioux. Mahan just brooded, and his broodings in time transformed him into history's greatest navalist, the author of *The Influence of Sea Power upon History,* and the darling of late-nineteenth-century expansionists and warmongers.

Mahan's plight was symbolic of the fact that the United States Navy had become a laughingstock by 1876, ranking twelfth in strength among the world's fleets, somewhere behind the Netherlands and China. There were fewer than thirty serviceable ships, the largest of which was the *Franklin* of 3,173 tons and 39 guns, currently stationed in the Mediterranean. For reviews the Navy was reduced to bringing out its "alphabet of floating washtubs," including Civil War monitors, the side-wheeler *Pohattan,* and even the ancient frigate *Constitution.* The press treated the Navy as a burlesque, reacting with glee, for example, when one of the country's best warships was sunk in a collision with a coal barge.[2]

The world was well into the age of ironclads, but the last new vessels authorized by Congress in 1872 were built of wood. While most of the country's warships did have steam, sail power was preferred by traditional-minded officers as cleaner and by Congress as more economical. As for armament, whereas breech-loading rifled cannon were standard in other navies, on American warships more than 80 percent of the guns were smoothbore muzzle-loaders. It was not surprising that the Navy Department was terrified of fighting modern Spanish cruisers during Secretary Fish's war scare of January, and it reacted the same way three years later during a minor crisis with Chile.

Just as the huge Army establishment of the time of the Civil War had been whittled down to comic-opera proportions, so too the Navy had been allowed to languish from its great strength when it blockaded the entire Confederacy and defied Britain as well. The basic reasons were the same: parsimony and antimilitarism. The cavalry at least had Indians to fight, but the warships seemingly lacked any mission, and Admiral Porter once confessed he feared to "wake up to find the Navy abolished."[3] America had no overseas colonies and as yet few foreign investments. Nor was there even much merchant marine to protect, the amount of American trade carried in American-registered ships declining drastically to less than 20 percent by 1880.[4] One naval officer whose ship made an extended cruise in the Atlantic reported ruefully that he had sighted only four merchant ships flying the stars and stripes.

Reports of the naval progress of other countries made most American Navy professionals wince with frustration, but a few officers and congressmen also were aware of the advantages of this country's playing a waiting game in a period of rapid obsolescence in naval technology. Let Britain experiment with expensive new warships like the *Inflexible* launched in May, 1876—armored, fast, big-gunned, and hailed as the most powerful warship afloat.

The Navy was also the victim of corrupt politics in the person of the secretary of the navy since 1867, George Robeson, outstanding as a grafter even in this era. To use the later words of a humorist, the only salt water Robeson ever saw was at the bottom of the pork barrel. One of the chief reasons that money was wasted on reconditioning wooden ships was to give jobs to Robeson's friends among the Republican faithful. Moreover, the secretary treated himself liberally to kickbacks, some $320,000 during his tenure in office. His $13,582 cottage near the Grants' at Long Branch was entirely paid for by a firm that got a $500,000 Navy contract. Such scandals naturally led to talk of impeaching Robeson, but Congress resorted only to treating Navy budget requests with contempt.[5]

Mahan's becoming Boston commandant made him acutely aware that the Navy was a "football" for Robeson and local politicians. He told Ashe in early 1876 that he was "very busy . . . writing everyone I could think of that would be likely to feel an interest, or a duty, in seeing justice done in and by the Navy."[6] Mahan's distress, however, did not cause him to abandon his own Republican politics. For one thing, he was a hard-money believer. Pleased with Hayes' nomination ("a better, purer man than Blaine, Conkling, or Morton"), he conceded to Ashe, a Democrat, that Tilden was capable, and "in either event we are likely to get a good president." He wondered in his letters if the Republicans could win in view of the "iniquities of Belknap, Babcock, Blaine, Robeson, and others," but he distrusted the Democrats in power, fearing that they would further reduce the Navy or favor ex-Confederate naval officers.[7]

Mahan's evolution to being the most strident advocate of a big navy was a slow process. He kept apologizing to Ashe with phrases like "I don't want you to think that I want to raise a howl because I am going to be hurt."[8] Within a year he was back on the active list, but another budget crisis of 1880 left him "hanging by the eyelids." He then shifted his position from merely opposing reduction of personnel to demanding expansion of the fleet. Once having looked with indifference at "the ship canal business," Mahan suddenly took a great interest in an American-controlled Panama canal and wrote that such would necessitate "a Navy which will at least equal that of England."[9] After he became president of the Naval War College, newly established in an abandoned poorhouse in Newport, Rhode Island, Mahan developed the grand vision of control of the seas expressed in his celebrated book of 1889. From then on Captain Mahan, later Admiral Mahan, was a one-man lobbyist for many warships, large warships, colonies, bases, and all the other concomitants of imperialism.

After fifteen years of the doldrums the "new Navy" of the United States got under way with a congressional appropriation for four powerful cruisers in 1882. Contrary to Mahan's apprehensions, the Democrats in power continued the expansion during the strong secretaryship of William C. Whitney. The steel industry became the major pressure group for ship construction—an early working out of the military-industrial complex. Later Theodore Roosevelt, due to become a Harvard freshman in 1876, was one of the chief promoters of a big navy, in part because of his reading Mahan.

August 22, New York

THE New York *Times* accused Governor Tilden of filing fraudulent tax returns for 1863. The next day's edition followed up the story with the headline IS MR. TILDEN A PERJURER?, and for several days the newspaper ran parallel columns purportedly showing Tilden's reported and nonreported income. The articles were inspired by material furnished by Republican Chairman Chandler. From now on the election campaign descended from lofty discussion of the issues to partisan nastiness and sensationalism.[1]

The majority of newspapers in the country supported the Republican Party, which was also fortunate in having the best cartoonists and satirists on its side. While a few papers maintained a pretense of objectivity, the influential Chicago *Tribune* and the New York *Times* committed themselves completely to a campaign to wreck Tilden. "The *Times* attacked him with a bitterness explainable by a fear that he was going to be elected."[2] Its managing editor, John C. Reed, had never forgotten his experience in the Confederacy's Libby Prison.

"The income tax charge is doing a great deal of harm," wrote Whitney on September 5.[3] Tilden had hoped to let the matter drop, lacking all the necessary old papers. A month after the original accusation, Hewitt felt impelled to publish a detailed refutation, which was convincing enough to the fair-minded but too late to undo all the bad publicity. Curiously, Hayes became very nervous about his failure to file any tax returns at all in two past years, but his friends dissuaded him from making an open breast of it, and the Democrats did not find out.[4]

At the end of September the Chicago *Times* ran a story accusing Hayes of pocketing $1,000 given to him for safekeeping by a soldier who was serving in his regiment during the Civil War and who was subsequently killed. It was not hard for the Republicans to prove that behind the charge were the soldier's father seeking extortion and Democratic schemers.

Momentarily at least, Hayes was more harmed by the revelation on October 4 that his secretary had accepted the endorsement of the Republican candidate by the American Alliance, the right-wing antiforeign and anti-Catholic group. Hayes simply repudiated their support. Actually, both candidates sought to play on religious discord, but not very openly. The venerable New York politician Horatio Seymour frankly told Tilden to seek the Catholic vote by playing up various statements of Hayes hostile to the Irish.

When Seymour counseled Tilden, he also observed, "The word 'reform' is not popular with the workingmen. To them it means less money and less work."[5] Tilden, of course, did not forgo his image of reformer to seek the labor vote, nor did Hayes appeal to any kind of class conflict. The largely unnoticed socialist press futilely tried to blacken Tilden simply for being a millionaire and to besmirch Hayes for ordering militia sent against the miners of the Tuscarawas Valley.

Generally, the Democrats found little in Hayes' public or private life to attack. The cartoonist Nast once pictured him as an impregnable iceberg against which the Democratic ship was smashing itself. Hayes' backer Schurz was very distressed that Republican officeholders were being systematically assessed for political contributions, writing him a letter about it on September 5, but Hayes was blissfully unaware, or played being so, of what uses Chandler was making of the power of the administration in his behalf. For their part, the Democrats decided to concentrate on the known evils of Grantism rather than the unknown quantity that was Hayesism.

The Republicans were successful in putting the Democrats on the defensive about Tilden. He was, indeed, a big railroad lawyer, and it did not take much imagination or evidence for a partisan copywriter to portray him as a shyster, a swindler, or a profiteer. Moreover, Tilden's personal circumstances lent themselves to a whispering campaign against him. Because he was in ill health, he was rumored to be a drunkard or a syphilitic; because he was involved in a carriage accident the day after his nomination, he was a reckless driver; because he was a bachelor, he was sexually depraved in some manner. To counter comment on Tilden's being

unmarried, his supporters—inspired by the Literary Bureau perhaps—made much of reports that he was on the verge of wedding
an "accomplished and beautiful woman" of distinguished Kentucky lineage.[6] In response to the repeated gossip concerning
Tilden's various marital possibilities, one editor suggested that he
was going to embrace Mormonism.

The most spurious and also the most serious charges Tilden
faced were those linking him as a Democrat to the South and
secession. Republicans exaggerated his having no war record to
his being a slacker to his opposing the Union. Blaine in the Senate
put words in Tilden's mouth to the effect that the Union invaders
of the Confederacy were trespassers and therefore liable for damages, including the losses sustained by slaveholders. The Cincinnati *Commercial* took up this theme and editorially decided that
"the main question is whether the voters of the North want to pay
the bills of the Southern Confederacy."[7] Eventually, Tilden was
forced to take the humiliating step of writing an open letter to
Hewitt on October 24 which contained assurances that "no rebel
debt will be assumed or paid."[8]

One of the most effective Republican propagandists was David
Ross Locke, who created the character Petroleum V. Nasby to sati-
rize the Democrats as the party of the ignorant and greedy Irish.
In 1875 Nasby's purported work *On Inflation* had been Locke's
scathingly funny counter to Greenbackism both within and without the Democratic Party. Late in the 1876 campaign Nasby made
a final fictional exhortation to his fellow Democrats:

> Rally agin hard money in the West. Rally agin soft money in the
> East. Rally agin offishls uv a corrupt administration. . . . Rally
> agin the military power, which prevents us from killing niggers as
> we please. . . . Rally for victory and post-offices. . . . P.S. I for-
> got to say we might as well rally for reform.[9]

The stridency of newspaper charges and the viciousness of rumors did not affect the outward calm and decorum of the two major candidates. Tilden on September 21 visited the Philadelphia
Centennial Exhibition for "New York Day," which attracted the
record attendance to date, 135,000. The governor found so many
well-wishers seeking to shake his hand at the New York pavilion
that he was persuaded to make a speech from the terrace. All he
said were a few good words about the "great state of New York."[10]

A month later Hayes was on hand for "Ohio Day" and likewise in his speech to an enthusiastic crowd he made no mention of his candidacy. A few hours afterward he was refused admission to a Philadelphia building by a guard who did not recognize him.

August 24, Honolulu

THE ship *City of San Francisco,* which slipped into Pearl Harbor on the afternoon tide, brought the welcome news that the United States Senate had approved the Reciprocity Treaty with Hawaii on August 14, and that President Grant had signed it into effect the next day. The treaty, which eliminated tariff barriers between the two countries, meant that Hawaiian sugar could come into the United States duty free. It also contained the important political provision that the kingdom of Hawaii would not "alienate" any of its territory or ports to a foreign power except the United States.[1] America passed another milestone in its hesitant, even reluctant, progress towards empire.

The United States interest in Hawaii began with Boston traders and Nantucket whalers before the turn of the century. To their dismay, an influx of Congregational ministers brought sabbatarianism among other new ways to the islands after 1820. As early as 1851 an American admiral decided that the acquisition of Hawaii was "intimately connected with our commercial and naval supremacy" in the Pacific.[2] Secretary Fish echoed him when he declared that the United States would soon need a "resting spot in midocean between the Pacific Coast and the vast domains of Asia."[3] In 1874 the USS *Tuscarora* landed marines to protect our businessmen. American trade in the Pacific, however, was less than 10 percent of the nation's total. The Senate, suspicious of the expansionist dreams of Fish and Grant, simply would go no further than the Reciprocity Treaty.

The *City of San Francisco* this Thursday also brought to Hawaii Claus Spreckels, a hard-driving California capitalist who owned sugar refineries. He bought up half the islands' sugar crop and made a killing on the mainland under the new dispensation. The next year Spreckels returned to buy land, eventually becoming an unusual example of an American millionaire who made his fortune in overseas land speculation.[4] By the end of the century Hawaiian sugar plantations represented a $33,000,000 industry, and virtually all were in the hands of American-born settlers in the islands. Even some of the Congregational missionaries abandoned their humble livings to become owners of thousands of acres. The chief beneficiaries of the 1876 treaty appeared to be this self-appointed ruling class, not the masses of Hawaiians, whose numbers declined drastically in the face of civilization.[5]

In the decade after the treaty Hawaiian sugar production quintupled. Fully 99 percent of the islands' exports went to the United States, which accounted for about 75 percent of their imports. The Navy gained control of Pearl Harbor by a new treaty of 1884; American businessmen and U.S. marines together overthrew the queen's autocratic government in 1891; and finally full annexation followed the Spanish-American War of 1898.

Samoa was another overseas area which claimed Americans' particular attention in 1876. Again, whalers, merchants, land grabbers, and naval officers were the actors in the piece. The fifty Americans actually living in Samoa began clamoring that the administration send warships, while they intrigued against the native chiefs in the name of "republican" forms of government. In 1872 the American naval commander Richard Meade negotiated a treaty with the Great Chief of Pago Pago giving the United States the exclusive right to establish a naval coaling station in Samoa, but by 1876 the Senate had taken no action on the administration's request for approval.

Undaunted by Congress, the State Department sent Colonel A. B. Steinberger as an observer to Samoa. His abilities won him control of the islands' government and the praise of the missionaries; but his policies alienated the British and German merchants in the area, and he was unceremoniously taken away on a British warship. Far from arousing patriotic indignation, this incident merely provoked the House of Representatives on March 15, 1876, to pass a resolution questioning and, in effect, condemning the administration's meddling in distant islands. Two years later, after the sensational Washington appearance of the Samoan "tattooed prince" La Mamea, the Senate ratified the 1872 treaty, but the newspapers rejoiced that we had not become involved in a protectorate kind of relationship. The United States annexation of Samoa, like that of Hawaii, came in a later age of imperialism.[6]

August 26, Cincinnati

"WHY, I ain't dead," gasped James Murphy. "I ain't dead." The hangman's rope had broken, and the youth came to on the ground, suffering greater mental shock than physical injury. His escape from his fate was but short, however, for the public executioner strung up another rope and did not bungle the second hanging. "The facts in the case as they appeared to the writer were simply that a poor, ignorant passionate boy, with a fair coarse face, had in the heat of drunken anger taken away the life of a fellow being, and paid the penalty of his brief crime by a hundred days of mental torture, and a hideous death." The reporter of this ghastly episode was Lafcadio Hearn. "Gibbeted" was his "most exquisite work of sensation and pure horror."[1] In an era when comfortable citizens liked to be entertained over their breakfasts by shocking stories about the unfortunate, Hearn served them up the most probing and gruesome reports of any writer and also the most honest and literary ones.

Just two years before Hearn had made his reputation with his article "The Tanyard Murder." A worker at a Cincinnati tannery had been set upon by three enemies, beaten nearly unconscious, then prodded with pitchforks into a furnace, and cremated. "Fancy the shrieks for mercy," Hearn wrote, "the mad expostulation, the frightful fight for life, the superhuman struggle for existence—a century of agony crowded into a moment—the shrieks growing feebler—the desperate struggles dying into feeble writhings . . . until the skull exploded and the steaming body burst, and the fiery flue hissed like a hundred snakes."[2] The author called himself "The Ghoul," but fortunately for his sanity his relentless pursuit of horror was firmly grounded in conscience and artistry.

Still in his mid-twenties, Hearn had bitter personal experience with what he once called "the wolf's side of life, the ravening side, the apish side, the ugly facts of the monkey puzzle."[3] The son of an Anglo-Irish surgeon captain and a Greek woman, Hearn gained his exotic name Lafcadio from the Ionian island, Leucadia, where he was born. After both parents disappeared, the boy was raised fitfully by a great-aunt, and he received a partial education at French and English schools. He then knew dire poverty in the slums of London. A windfall enabled him to emigrate to the United States, but after he arrived in Cincinnati in 1869, he once again was forced to sleep in the streets and subsist from odd jobs. Eventually, Hearn was rescued from physical and intellectual starvation by a friendly printer, who taught him the trade and who also exposed him to current literature, Fourierist socialism, and "hosts of fantastic heterodoxies."[4] The seedy young man boldly spent hours in the public library, and finally his writings won him a place on the staff of the Cincinnati *Enquirer*.

Hearn quickly won attention as the imaginative and tireless exposer of the rawest aspects of existence in this Midwestern hog-packing and soapmaking metropolis. His articles revealed the ways of gravediggers, pawnshop dealers, ragpickers, prostitutes, opium addicts, mediums, and temperance fanatics. He produced masterfully realistic descriptions of slaughterhouses and madhouses. Most of his material was simply picturesque, but much was social protest, as when he wrote of the life of seamstresses as "Slow Starvation." Something about Hearn made low-life people confide in him, perhaps, his own quaint appearance. He was a pale, thin, very short person, younger-looking than his age and with a woebegone expression exaggerated by his thick spectacles, which only partially hid one sightless, scarred eye, the result of a schoolboy injury.

The olive-complexioned Irish-Greek was particularly attracted by Cincinnati's waterfront, which contained a large black population. His associations here put Hearn's career in jeopardy, for in the summer of 1875 he insisted on marriage, illegal actually, with his mulatto mistress, Mattie, who had once worked as a maid at his boardinghouse. Local politicians, possibly more aroused by Hearn's reportorial probing than his living with a black, pressured his editor into firing him summarily. Hearn rushed off to throw himself in a canal, a halfhearted gesture, for, as a reporter friend observed, suicide would have appealed to Hearn only if he himself could have written up the story in the same passionate detail as his crime accounts.

The unmistakably gifted writer was promptly hired by Cincinnati's rival daily, the *Commercial*, and he proceeded to win further notoriety with his articles of the year 1876. On January 16, for example, his readers were startled to learn from "Bones" that people made a living from gathering and selling skeletal remains. "What do they grind them up for?" the reporter persisted. " 'Spect they sell em for flour," was the bone picker's reply.[5] "Steeple Climbers" of May 26 revealed that the frail, myopic reporter had let himself be dragged in chains up the spire of the Cathedral of St. Peter by a steeplejack and deposited breathless on the horizontal bar of the cross at top. Hearn's terror and awe were poetically shared with his readers, but not the private satisfaction he had of urinating down on the city which was so demanding of him.

Sensationalism was not Hearn's only stock-in-trade. "Levee Life," which appeared on March 17, was an unforgettable picture, unflattering but unpatronizing, of the daily existence of blacks in the waterfront district. Hearn went to the pains of describing "Sausage Row" house by house. No. 1 was "kept by old Barney Hodke, who has made quite a reputation by keeping a perfectly orderly house in a very disorderly neighborhood." The "American Clothing Store" at No. 2 earned its owner a "fortune by selling cheap clothing to the negro stevedores." Following a saloon, a lodging house, and a barbershop, No. 7 was "a house of ill-fame, kept by a white woman, Mary Pearl, who boards several unfortunate white girls . . . a great resort for colored men." Another saloon at No. 8 was run by Maggie Sperlock, "a very fat and kind hearted old mulatto woman, who is bringing up a half dozen illegitimate children, abandoned by their parents." Hearn ended his "glimpse of roustabout life" with a brilliant summation:

> Their whole existence is one vision of anticipated animal pleasure or of animal misery, of giant toil under the fervid summer sun, of toil under the icy glare of the winter moon; of fiery drinks and drunken dreams; of the madness of music and the intoxication of fantastic dances. . . .[6]

The last, the music and dancing, were something Hearn had an especially appreciative ear and eye for. No northern writer before him had recorded so many songs of the blacks, without softening them in the manner of Stephen Foster.

For the $20 a week Hearn earned as a reporter he put in long hours. He would write up his nightly forays at dawn in the newspaper office deserted by all but the newsboys taking out the morning editions. The intensity of his efforts was indicated by the fact that on August 27, the day after the shocking "Gibbeted" appeared, the paper ran Hearn's most richly romantic piece, "Dolly, An Idyl of the Levee." Here he told the tragic story of a savagely voluptuous but kindly and comparatively respectable black woman who gave herself over entirely to vice so as to pay the $50 court fine of "her man," only to have him desert her for a woman up the river. She wasted away and died from heartbreak, as the musicians downstairs in the saloon played "Big Ball Up Town," while "upstairs the women were chanting to a weirdly sweet air *My Jesus Arose.*"[7] The young writer seemed uniquely capable at this time in perceiving generous emotions among the unfortunate.

Few people knew Cincinnati as intimately as Lafcadio Hearn, but the brief relationship of writer and city at length became one of mutual contempt. His affair with Mattie provoked social ostracism without providing any private content, for she was ignorant, quarrelsome, and wayward. Not without remorse, Hearn simply abandoned her, moving to New Orleans in 1877. In this cosmopolitan atmosphere he not only could take an interest in the Creole subculture but also indulge his wider concerns, which ranged from Asiatic religions and astronomy to modern French and Russian literature. The police reporter of "Gibbeted" was now able to contribute scholarly pieces to magazines like *Harper's* and the *Atlantic*. His restless preoccupation with the exotic determined the rest of Lafcadio Hearn's career: his sojourn as a novelist in French Martinique; his failure to make a go of Philadelphia or New York's Greenwich Village; and finally his triumphant thirteen years in Japan, teaching at the Imperial University, writing prodigiously, and happily married to a Japanese.

August 29, Constantinople

TWO Americans were being cast this year in the singular role of redrawing the map of Europe and starting a major war. One was Consul General Eugene Schuyler, whose report on Ottoman Turk atrocities in Bulgaria was leaked to the London *Daily News* and was published in this morning's editions. The other was the most colorful of newspaper correspondents, J. A. MacGahan, whose simultaneous, on-the-scene dispatches did even more to inflame world opinion against the Ottoman Empire and intensify the existing diplomatic crisis in the Near East.

Schuyler arrived to take up his post as consul general in Constantinople in July, satisfied that a scholar like himself, instead of a general or political hack, had at last been so rewarded.[1] A linguist and one of Yale's first doctors of philosophy, Schuyler had occupied minor diplomatic posts in Russia for a decade. As a Russophile he was more than willing to believe the findings of George Washburn that thousands of Bulgarian Christians had been massacred in retaliation for the killing of 200 Turkish officials. Washburn was director of Robert College, an American missionary enterprise in the Ottoman capital. Britain's pro-Turkish prime minister, Benjamin Disraeli, had recently dismissed the talk about atrocities as "mere coffee house babble."[2] Fearing a cover-up or whitewash of the whole situation, Washburn persuaded Schuyler to join correspondent MacGahan on a firsthand investigation in Bulgaria itself.

Januarius Aloysius MacGahan was a self-educated Ohio farm-boy who became the star reporter for James Gordon Bennett's New York *Herald.* The Irish-American was a handsome, charming, cultivated, and reckless man of six feet three. Among his legendary exploits were his being the only journalist in Montmartre at the very outset of the Paris Commune, his spending ten weeks with the Carlist insurgents in Spain, his sailing on a ship seeking the Northwest Passage, his reporting from Cuba during the *Virginius* affair, and, most exciting of all, his following the Russian Army on its conquests deep into Turkestan despite the efforts of Russians and Turkomans alike to stop him. His recent book about that adventure, *Campaigning on the Oxus,* had failed to mention the *Herald,* and this oversight caused a big row at the newspaper's Fleet Street offices with Bennett himself, who had been drinking heavily. The upshot was that the American went to Constantinople as a correspondent for the British paper the *News.*[3]

MacGahan, accompanied by Schuyler, left for Bulgaria on July 23 and began sending back dispatches in early August telling in a clear and earnest manner of the barbarities he had seen—the burned churches, the ruined farms, and the evidences of torture, killing, and mutilation of people without regard to sex or age. His most horrendous report was from Batak, where he interviewed the survivors of a Turkish massacre that took 5,000 of a population of 7,000. His searing revelations were confirmed in a sober, restrained official report of Consul Schuyler.[4]

The dispatches of MacGahan and Schuyler confirmed Russia in

its determination to come to the aid of its fellow Slavs in Bulgaria, even at the price of war with the Ottoman Empire. More important, their reports were used by Britain's opposition leader William E. Gladstone as the basis for his celebrated pamphlet of September 6 called the *Bulgarian Horrors of the East,* which sold 50,000 copies in five days.[5] Public opinion in Britain swung to support Gladstone in his anti-Turkish position, and Prime Minister Disraeli found himself powerless to defy the Russian war threats. The best he could do was secure a diplomatic congress on Ottoman affairs, the Constantinople Conference.

The crisis in the Near East had few repercussions in the United States. The House of Representatives on May 22 did adopt a resolution expressing its concern for the safety of Americans in the area. Many Americans were privately anti-Turkish, such as Commander Mahan, who wrote in July: "I have an intense desire that the Christians may finally drive the Turks out of Europe—and that if England interferes again to uphold the Crescent that she may get a good thrashing as she will deserve."[6] In the fall the *Sun* rather cold-bloodedly editorialized that "a general European war would undoubtedly greatly stimulate every branch of business and every industry in this country."[7] This newspaper, concerned with the lingering depression, saw hostilities abroad as particularly beneficial to our merchant marine, grain exports, and arms industry. On the other hand, the *Labor Standard* fumed against the "ruling miscreants" of the world seeking more "robbery and murder" and went so far as to urge workers to "Strike the Arsenals."[8]

Eugene Schuyler, writing his sister of events on November 15, reported: "Just now I am getting up a Constitution for Bulgaria. General Ignatief is to present it at the Conference, and, as Russia threatens to fight unless she gets what she wants, I am anxious to make it a good one."[9] The Constantinople Conference failed, and Russia did go to war with Turkey in April, 1877, and Britain stood aside. MacGahan joined the victorious Russian forces as a war correspondent, was twice wounded, and died of typhus in 1878, the year Bulgaria received its autonomy. His body, at the instance of the Ohio legislature, was brought back on an American warship. For many years MacGahan was known as the Liberator in Bulgaria, and a mass was annually said in his honor in the national cathedral. As for Schuyler, the Turkish government demanded his ouster, saying his Bulgarian report had done "more to influence England than any other document of the war."[10] Secretary

Fish agreed that the consul had meddled beyond the call of duty, but he refrained from transferring him until 1878.

American missionaries shared importantly in these events. Robert College, which was founded in 1863 through the benefaction of a sugar and tea millionaire, was called "the nursery of Bulgarian statesmen" by a later ruler of that country.[11] The missionaries in this and other schools sought to teach the natives to save souls through the Gospel, but they often ended up training dedicated nationalist revolutionaries. The Ottoman Empire was the focus of more American missionary effort than anywhere else, as indicated by the yearly 50,000 Bibles translated into Turkish, Armenian, Syrian, Arabic, and Bulgarian. One of some 200 missionaries in the area was Dr. Harry S. West, who died of typhus in 1876 at age forty-nine, having spent seventeen years in a small town in western Turkey, where he preached, taught, and performed some 1,650 eye operations.[12]

By early 1877 the American Navy had concentrated six of its few warships in the Mediterranean. Their mission was to protect "the interests which American citizens have acquired, or rather created, in Turkey and Syria," according to Admiral Worden, who was thinking more of the missionaries than of businessmen. Other Americans envisaged a much greater United States role. The consul in Tripoli, for example, wanted to establish an American naval base at Tobruk, taking advantage of Turkey's difficulties in 1876. Another American diplomat had earlier recommended establishing a station at Bab el Mandeb at the entrance of the Red Sea. Such schemes left Congress unmoved, in contrast with a hundred years later when the presence of the Seventh Fleet in the Middle East is taken for granted.[13]

In the early 1870s American exports to the Ottoman Empire were worth $1,200,000. The exports included $52,000 in liquor and $170,000 in firearms. Americans happily sold the Turkish army 236,000 sabers, 60,000 surplus Enfield rifles, and 50,000,000 cartridges, at the same time as this country sold Turkey's enemy, Russia, Springfield rifles and Smith & Wesson revolvers.

Incredibly, the greatest American export to the Middle East was oil, $890,000 worth. In the words of a consular report, "even the sacred lamps over the Prophet's tomb at Mecca are fed with oil from Pennsylvania."[14]

August 30, New York

AT a mass meeting at Cooper Union, similar to the one he addressed in January, Peter Cooper delivered his standard attack on the degradation of the economy by big government and big business provoking "deafening cheers" by even the admission of the hostile *Herald*. There was something pathetic about this benign, guileless old man going about offering his fatherly lectures when a youthful militant would have seemed more appropriate to the Greenback cause. The press found it humorous that Cooper's party was so short of funds and of organizational sophistication. His campaign had its stirring qualities, such as the fact that hundreds among the poor and distressed and even many young trade unionists listened earnestly on occasions like this and later lined up to shake hands with the one millionaire who seemed to merit their trust.

Cooper's originally conditional acceptance of the Greenback nomination became more firm after both the Republican and Democratic conventions failed to adopt soft-money proposals, yet he ruefully admitted at the end of June that "if I am elected I believe the duties of the office would kill me before the term had half expired." When Cooper's son-in-law Abram Hewitt became Tilden's manager, rumors went about that Cooper would ease the Greenbackers into the Democrats' camp. Cooper even called at Tilden's house to urge him to support the repeal of resumption. Nothing availed, and on July 25 Cooper made his final commitment:

> I have consented with great reluctance to go before the people . . . for the vindication of a great principle that underlies all true Republican or Democratic Institutions—namely, that the interest and happiness of the whole people are superior to the demands or interests of any one class.[1]

The bondholders were the class Cooper had in mind to thwart.

For professional Republican and Democratic politicians, the Greenback movement contained the menace of an unknown quantity. No one expected Cooper to win millions of votes. If, however, he took just a few thousand votes away from the Democrats in New York, it could give Hayes that state's large block of electoral votes and probably the whole election. One of the Green-backer national committeemen predicted that his party would carry enough Midwestern states to deny either Hayes or Tilden a majority of the electoral college, with the denouement that the House of Representatives would choose Cooper as a compromise president. Others speculated that if Cooper won just the state of Indiana, where he appeared to be strongest, the same sort of deadlock and outcome could be expected.

Whatever their prospects, the Greenbackers were in the running and had the advantage of being the first party to begin active campaigning. Eventually, they fielded state tickets in every state north of the Mason-Dixon line except Colorado and Rhode Island, and throughout the country thirty-six congressional candidates were running as Greenbackers. In the Western states particularly, the Independent Party was endorsed by many granges and some small-town newspapers, and people began to turn out for hundreds of picnic basket meetings to hear Greenback orators. In Cooper's home state, New York, the party also ran a full ticket and gained the support of three minor journals.

One of the difficulties that plagued the Greenbackers was lack of money, to the point, for example, that their Indiana convention met in a field because it could not afford to hire a hall. In the bitter reminiscence of a supporter from the labor movement, "Mr. Cooper was expected to 'come down' with a lot of money but he didn't 'come down.' It was found that he was more intent upon circulating documents than giving away his money."[2] His associate Groom had made unauthorized, exaggerated commitments of Cooper's money at Indianapolis, and he subsequently misappropriated money he did get from Cooper for printing materials.

Another big problem for the Greenbackers was their unfortunate decision to give a major place in their campaign to a political charlatan named Marcus Mills Pomeroy. Known as Brick Pomeroy, he had made something of a reputation as a journalist, earning his nickname for a series called *Brickdust Sketches* he did in Wisconsin. As editor of his own newspapers in New York, Chicago, and elsewhere he had attracted notoriety for his polemics against the "bondocracy" and also "Wall Street Jews." Now called upon to be chairman of the National Committee for the Organization of Greenback Clubs, he responded "with his usual vigor and his usual humbuggery" and later claimed to have personally founded 4,000 clubs in a few months.[3] He also decided to establish a national party journal called *The Great Campaign,* which came out in sixteen issues during the summer and fall. Before long the Honest Money League was so aroused by Pomeroy's propaganda that it denounced it as being "communistic, inflationary, and treasonable" and "filled with the most villainous falsehoods and advice to laboring men to get ready for secession and to rob the banks and homes of eastern people."[4] While this description was lurid exaggeration, Pomeroy did go too far often in *The Great Campaign,* once calling the Republicans "political harlots" and another time labeling Tilden "the paid tool of the Jews who control the gold market." Such expressions of anti-Semitism were seized upon by the press to show that the Greenbackers were throwbacks to the Know-Nothings. Finally, Pomeroy resorted to an easily refutable big lie, publishing a purported circular from the chairman of the "Bankers Association" calling for the suppression of democracy and the silencing of critics of the banks. Toward the end of the summer the other Greenback leaders were protesting that the egotistical, quarrelsome Pomeroy was hurting their campaign more than helping it.[5]

Yet another mistake of the Greenbackers was their failure to make a solid appeal to the labor movement and to still critics from the left. Most of their propaganda was addressed to rural districts. The Party did not commit itself to the cause of unionism or even the right to strike. Accordingly, the radical labor press lashed out against the Greenbackers in the cities as small shopkeepers who wanted to be monopolists, "sore-headed capitalists," "place seekers," and "middle class quacks." The *Socialist* referred to Peter Cooper as "that philanthropic advocate of long hours and low wages" and editorialized that the Greenback program was "chimerical." "The disease from which we suffer is not the want of currency, but a planless system of production."[6]

Peter Cooper's showing against Hayes and Tilden in the 1876 election results would not be impressive. According to one historian, "Americans once again proved that a political fight interested them more than the class struggle."[7] But the problem was really that the Greenback campaign was more a single-issue crusade than a genuine call to class struggle.

September 6, Scranton

FUTURE labor leader Terence Powderly finally ended his "search" for the secret organization the Knights of Labor. Two years previously at an antimonopoly convention in Philadelphia he had been befriended by a fellow delegate who invited him to his hotel room and, after locking the door, told him to kneel before him. Powderly protested but later consented to take an oath to a secret order that stood for workingmen's rights. Now this day a shopmate of his at the locomotive works invited him to go to a "labor lecture," and in the evening the two proceeded to a hall. Powderly was "mystified when we were ushered into a small room and told to wait awhile." Then a man came in, "wearing a black gown and mask," and subjected the two to an intense questioning. "He appeared more satisfied with our answers than I was with his appearance, for I had no thought of joining a society of any kind that night." Nonetheless, Powderly forthwith was initiated into Lodge Number 88 of the Noble Order of the Knights of Labor. His friend congratulated him afterward, and only then did Powderly realize that his shopmate was not a fellow candidate but already a member.

At a typical lodge of the Knights, a member had to send a card with his name on it into the meeting room in order to gain admittance. Powderly calculated that this system was responsible for hundreds of workers learning to form their signatures. Inside the meeting room, known as the sanctuary, with its altar and an open Bible, the long and elaborate ceremonial was conducted by the Master Workman, the Worthy Foreman, and the Venerable Sage. Despite their grandiloquent titles, the chief officers never sat on a platform or were in any way elevated above the general membership—an object lesson in democratic equality.

When Powderly was presented for his initiation, he took the oath of secrecy and pledged himself to the defense of labor before the entire membership standing in a circle with hands joined. In the "base of the sanctuary" he then received the instructions of the Worthy Foreman, who delivered a homily about work, including the following words: "In the beginning God ordained that men should labor, not as a curse but as a blessing. . . . By labor is brought forth the fruits of the earth in rich abundance. . . . It is the 'Philosopher's Stone': everything it touches turns to gold." Some time afterward Powderly decided that the reference in this to "gold" offended his principles as a Greenbacker, and he succeeded in having the word changed to "wealth."

The highpoint of the initiation was when he was introduced as a "fitting and worthy person" to the Master Workman, who took him by the hand and then told him of the general principles of the order:

> On behalf of the toiling millions of earth, I welcome you to this Sanctuary dedicated to the service of God by serving humanity. Open and public associations having failed, after a struggle of centuries, to protect or advance the interests of labor, we have lawfully constituted this Assembly. . . . We mean no conflict with legitimate enterprise, no antagonism to necessary capital. . . . We mean to uphold the dignity of labor. . . . Without approving of general strikes among artisans, yet should it become necessary to enjoin an oppressor, we will protect and aid any of our number who thereby do suffer loss. . . .

The Master Workman's carefully chosen words about capital made it plain that the Knights were far from being a socialist group; his bare mention of strikes suggested that they were not a very radical one; his constant invocation of God made them seem positively respectable.

Finally, on this memorable evening for Powderly, he was taken in hand by the "V.S." or Venerable Sage and instructed in the secret procedures of the Knights, the passwords, the special hand grips, and the signs advising of meetings. He learned, for example, that if he saw the symbol 10 148/88 on a fence or other public place, it meant that the next meeting of lodge number 88 would be on October 1 at 8 P.M.[1]

The passion for secrecy on the part of the Knights of Labor was not playacting but necessity. No spy of the boss must ever learn of their objects, methods, membership, or even names. The employers had taken advantage of hard times and unemployment to mount an unprecedented campaign of lockouts, blacklists, and legal prosecution of unions through the revival of state anticonspiracy laws. The Knights were merely the most long-lived of several underground workingmen's organizations that had sprung up after the demise of the fully open National Labor Union; another was the Junior Sons of '76, the sponsor of the abortive Pittsburgh labor conference of April. The fictional Molly Maguires served only to give secrecy a bad name.

One of the first to acknowledge in print the existence of the

Knights was Pinkerton, the victimizer of the Irish miners. He speculated that the Knights were probably an amalgamation of the Molly Maguires and the Commune. In the vicinity of Scranton and Wilkes-Barre, "two thirds of the workmen belong to it." Pinkerton made the further wild assertion that the group's aim was "the destruction of all government by the ballot and, if that should fail, by force."[2] Actually, the Knights were gradualist rather than revolutionary. For all practical purposes, in the late 1870s the Knights *were* organized labor.[3]

Historically, they go back to 1869 when Uriah Smith Stephens persuaded part of the membership of his garment cutters union in Philadelphia to secede and form Assembly No. 1 of a secret order. Stephens, educated to be a Baptist minister, had been forced to take work as a tailor and later taught school. His travels in Europe in the 1860s brought him into contact with Marxists, but he returned to America to pursue his own more utopian dreams of labor solidarity. The Knights made very little progress until 1873, when suddenly more than thirty new local assemblies came into being, and Stephens established over them District Assembly No. 1 in Philadelphia. By 1875 there were enough locals in the Pittsburgh area to warrant the establishment of District Assembly No. 3, led by the well-known editor of the *National Labor Tribune*, John M. Davis.

Unlike labor unions where membership was restricted to those in a single trade, the Knights were open to men of all callings, with some restrictions. In a given assembly, floor sweepers were the equals of skilled craftsmen. Women were not admitted until 1881. A guess, since no central records were kept, was that total membership in the order was about 5,000, concentrated in industrial centers from Massachusetts to Ohio. The Knights recruited with particular success among the locals of old national unions that had collapsed.

Powderly's joining the Scranton assembly this fall was not quite so innocent-minded as he made it appear. He had been a labor militant ever since he had at age twenty seen the charred bodies of 100 men and boys, the victims of a mine disaster. Within a week of his own initiation into the Knights, Powderly persuaded twenty-five of his shopmates to join, and in six weeks they organized their own local assembly with him as Master Workman. "Prior to my admission to the Knights of Labor," Powderly reminisced, "I had a little time for rest and recreation. After September 6, 1876 I knew

Above: The comfortable citizenry turned out on this special Fourth of July for parades, fireworks, and picnics. Orators celebrated a hundred years of civil liberty and material progress. There were 40,000,000 Americans and thirty-eight states (Colorado was admitted in 1876).

CENTENNIAL SELF-SATISFACTION VIES WITH SOCIAL DISTRESS

Below: Since 1873 the country was in the grips of its worst depression to date. The unemployed numbered several millions. Wage cuts, despite high dividends paid stockholders, provoked labor unrest culminating in the violent nationwide railroad strikes of 1877.

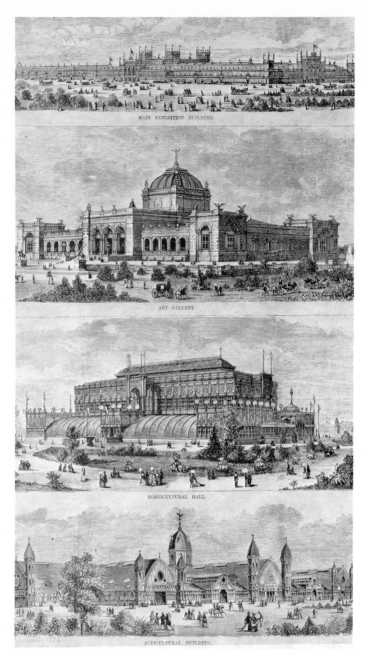

MAIN EXHIBITION BUILDING.

ART GALLERY.

HORTICULTURAL HALL.

AGRICULTURAL BUILDING.

Newark Public Library

PHILADELPHIA'S INTERNATIONAL EXHIBITION ATTRACTS FIVE MILLION VISITORS

The country's first world's fair was not a financial success, but it was the central event in the lives of many Americans. The huge exhibition buildings in Fairmount Park displayed considerable functionality despite their Victorian ornateness.

FAIRGOERS COULD VIEW THE LATEST CORSETS OR THE LATEST CANNON

Current fashions shared attention at the exhibition with new types of machinery. Visitors with an eye to the future could view such novelities as the carpet sweeper, the typewriter, and the telephone.

New York Public Library

The eagerness with which foreign countries sent displays to the Philadelphia fair was taken as a great compliment to the American Republic. Britain exhibited its best artworks; Italy and France offered bric-a-brac; Egypt chose archaeology; and Germany contributed mammoth guns from Krupp, the firm that was well on the way to becoming arms sellers to the world.

New York Public Library

MAJOR POLITICAL FIGURES CONTEND IN A DISPUTED ELECTION

Newark Public Library

New York Public Library

Above left: Incumbent Republican President Grant had third term ambitions, but the scandals of his administration turned the voters' attention to reformers. The painting is by Ulke.

Above right: Ex-Speaker James G. Blaine of Maine dominated the headlines in early 1876, but he did not win the Republican nomination until eight years later. The photograph is by Brady.

Below left: "Dark horse" candidate Rutherford B. Hayes of Ohio became the Republican nominee. He parlayed civil service reform and the end of Reconstruction in the South into winning the presidency.

Below right: Millionaire Governor Samuel J. Tilden of New York won the Democratic nomination. He carried the "Solid South" and enough Northern states to gain a majority of the popular vote, but his indecisiveness cost him the election.

New York Public Library

New York Public Library

THE GREENBACKERS OFFER A COLORFUL THIRD-PARTY ALTERNATIVE

Advocates of a managed paper currency, farmers hurt by low prices, and members of organized labor combined to launch a presidential ticket headed by Peter Cooper, octogenarian industrialist and philanthropist. The Greenbackers' crusading zeal scared the major parties, but Cooper carried no states in the election.

THE INDIAN WARS CULMINATE IN THE CUSTER DISASTER

New York Public Library

New York Public Library

Above Left: The greed of land grabbers, the ineptness of the War Department, and Custer's insane bravado produced the confrontation with the Sioux Indians at the Valley of the Little Bighorn in which Custer's detachment was massacred to the last man. This fanciful lithograph, distributed by a brewery to a quarter million saloons, erred in such details as Custer's having long hair and wielding a saber.

Above Right: In this Indian painting of Custer's Last Stand, the wily tactician Chief Crazy Horse is shown painted with protective hailstone marks. The fallen cavalrymen depicted recall Chief Sitting Bull's hallucinatory vision of victory.

OTHER PROBLEMS GRIP THE NORTH, SOUTH, AND WEST

The cartoon that captured William Marcy Tweed.

In 1876 Nast pictured Tammany's boss as willing to sacrifice lesser rascals to preserve his own power. The drawing was used by officials in Spain to identify and arrest the fugitive Tweed.

Above: "Boss Tweed," who bilked New York City of $7,000,000, made his name a byword of big-city corruption. This cartoon by Nast was used by police in Spain to identify the fugitive politician, who was then brought back on a U. S. warship to face jail and disgrace.

Below left: The James brothers, Jesse and Frank, staged several spectacular robberies throughout the Mississippi Valley in 1876. Their attempt to hold up a Northfield, Minnesota, bank misfired when the outraged citizens fought back and killed several of the gang of desperadoes.

Below right: Violence between whites and blacks dominated the politics of many Southern states, as Reconstruction governments were replaced by white rule. The contested election in South Carolina temporarily resulted in rival Republican and Democratic officials simultaneously trying to run the legislature in Columbia.

**MEN AND WOMEN CONTRIBUTE TO THE
PROGRESS OF THE ARTS AND SCIENCES**

Above left: In Lynn, Massachusetts, Mary Baker Eddy founded a new religion in 1876—Christian Science. Her difficulties in having her works published were matched this year only by her romantic adventures.

Top right: Emily Dickinson, a recluse living in Amherst, made wry comments on the Centennial. Her stature as a poet remained unknown in her lifetime.

Bottom right: Two noncriminal James brothers who were beginning to win acclaim were Henry, author of *The American* and expatriate critic in the Paris of the Impressionist painters, and William, a pioneer in psychology at Harvard.

Below: Alexander Graham Bell was a dedicated teacher at Boston's School for the Deaf (he is sitting upper right). His experiments with speech and electricity led to his patenting the telephone and a series of successful tryouts this year.

no working hour that I did not devote, in whole or part, to the up-building of that Order."[4] Activism for Powderly meant sharing his shanty with others interested in the movement and sleeping in ashpits or railroad cars as he traveled about the state organizing more locals.

In the fall of 1876 Powderly also functioned openly as the president of a Greenback Club, finding no discrepancy in his two roles. Of his 300 followers, he said, perhaps jokingly, that "over two thirds of them just joined the club to sit down somewhere and rest." As for himself, Powderly wrote: "I was so enthusiastic that I began to pity Tilden and Hayes for how bad they'd feel the morning after election to see Peter Cooper swept into the White House by a tremendous majority." Without really expecting a Cabinet post or ambassadorship as his reward, Powderly did have a telegram of congratulation all ready to be sent to the Greenback leader.

Powderly was astonished that Peter Cooper received only three votes in his district, the same district that the majority of the members of his club came from. He sought to find out why:

> It was described to me that it wasn't because of any lack of votes we didn't carry the district, but because being new and inexperienced, we hadn't selected the right kind of counters to sit on the election board . . . it was customary for the board to credit as many votes as might be necessary in that district to the Democratic ticket, it being "naturally Democratic," and that there was no sense in throwing away good votes on weak, foolish, unknown, and unnecessary third parties.

Powderly was further "horrified" to find out that the same thing went on in other districts and was "not confined to one party."

The following year Powderly became so aroused about corrupt politics that he ran for office on a Greenback-Labor ticket. In his speeches he would threaten: "If we find that the ballot boxes have been stuffed as in previous elections and ascertain the identity of the scoundrels who do it, let us hang every one of them." Powderly's reward in 1878 was being elected mayor of Scranton.[5] Although his later career saw him working for the Republican Party and serving as United States commissioner of immigration, Powderly kept a vision of himself as the militant of 1876: "Some of my friends in defending me against assault denied that I was an agitator; they were wrong. I was an agitator . . . against the injustices practiced on working men and women."[6]

As for the Knights of Labor, the rivalry for leadership of District Assemblies 1 and 3, Philadelphia and Pittsburgh, was among the factors prompting it to become a national organization with a central or General Assembly in 1878. Simultaneously, the secrecy of the order was challenged as self-defeating. Local 82 of Brooklyn petitioned that steps be taken "to make the name of the Order public so that workingmen know of its existence."[7] Out in the open, the Knights served mainly as a stepping-stone to the organization of the far more powerful, yet far more exclusive American Federation of Labor in 1886.

September 7, Northfield, Minnesota

THE aroused citizenry of this Minnesota town outfought the notorious James gang in a shoot-out around the First National City Bank. In so doing, they proved that this area was no longer frontier.

Popular fiction of the day tried to romanticize even Jesse James by making him out as a carefree Robin Hood rather than the cold-blooded, calculating robber that he actually was. A case could be made, however, that he had been sorely victimized in his early life. His family in Missouri suffered for their Southern sympathies at the hands of Union men during the early days of the Civil War, and at age fifteen Jesse was provoked to join Quantrill's Raiders, becoming a daring scout and expert marksman. When he surrendered at the end of hostilities, he was treacherously shot and wounded and declared an outlaw. Thereafter, not yet twenty, he made himself leader or at least chief strategist of a band of desperadoes that included his older brother, Frank James, and two cousins of theirs, the Younger brothers. The gang operated over a wide area and specialized in stagecoach holdups, train robberies, and bank thefts, trying one of each in 1876, their peak year.

Their holdup of the Austin-San Antonio mail coach on May 12 followed the familiar Hollywood script. The James boys and one of the Youngers suddenly appeared on an isolated stretch of road, leveled rifles at the driver, on top of the stage, and ordered him to throw down the mailbag. Next, they made the dozen passengers descend, searched them, and took their valuables. A sweet young thing with her entire savings in her satchel protested with such pretty indignation that she was spared. The robbers then sped off with their take of $3000.

Two months later back in Missouri Jesse James rounded up a larger group for a railroad job. This took place on the night of July 7 near Otterville, where the Missouri Pacific line ran through a narrow valley. The eastbound train was forced to stop because of a pile of railroad ties on the tracks and was quickly surrounded by eleven masked men on horseback firing their revolvers. When the bandits found that the safe in the baggage car was locked, they searched the whole train for the express manager, taking purses and jewelry as they stormed through the terrorized passengers. The safe eventually yielded them $17,000. The gang escaped without a trace, except that Jesse James, as was his wont, wrote a half-nasty, half-funny letter to a local newspaper disclaiming responsibility for the robbery.

Another two months, and the James gang was 1,000 miles from the scene of their first crime of the year, looking over banks in southern Minnesota. A new associate persuaded Jesse James that in a peaceful, rural, settled area it would be easier to effect both a holdup and an escape. On the afternoon of September 7, two days before Jesse James' twenty-ninth birthday, the gang leader and two men came trotting into Northfield and casually tied up their mounts near the county seat's one bank. When five other bandits rode in at a gallop firing their guns, the original three took advantage of the confusion to enter the bank with drawn pistols. The chief cashier was clubbed down when he first tried to close the safe and later was shot dead when he went for a revolver in a drawer. Meanwhile, the townspeople, instead of hiding under their beds, grabbed weapons and began firing at the horsemen in the streets. A young man named Wheeler picked off one from a window in a building opposite the bank. The sound of the fray led Jesse James and his men to leave the bank almost empty-handed, but their efforts to outshoot and overawe their assailants were to no avail. After another bandit was killed, the remaining six, all of them wounded, fled the town. By nightfall Wheeler had organized a posse of 400 men to hunt them down. In a later shoot-out in a wooded area where the gang had tried to hide, the forces of law and order killed one and captured three, including both Younger brothers.

The American Bankers Association meeting in October in Centennial Philadelphia passed a resolution of commendation of the heroic conduct of the cashier who lost his life defending the First National's vault. The Younger brothers were put on trial in November, but they received only long prison terms because Minnesota was one of the few states at the time with a law against capital punishment.

The James boys remained at large until 1882, when Jesse was shot in the back by two brothers, members of his gang, who hoped to collect the $10,000 reward for him, "dead or alive," offered by the governor of Missouri. Frank James gave himself up, was twice tried and acquitted, and lived out his long life as a Missouri farmer, unwilling to discuss his past with the ever-curious, ever-amoral press.[1]

The James gang had most of the publicity, but they had no monopoly on robberies. One of the three major express companies, Wells Fargo reported 313 such holdups in the period 1870–1885. Their standard reward of $300 plus one-fifth of the money recovered led to the apprehension of many of the bandits, but Black Bart, who operated in California and habitually sported a linen duster and a sack with eye holes in it over his head, got away with twenty-eight robberies in eight years.[2] Black Bart liked to leave behind bits of doggerel, such as this:

> I've labored long and hard for bread
> For honor and for riches,
> But on my corns too long you've trod
> You fine-haired sons of bitches.[3]

Eventually, he was traced through a San Francisco laundry mark and arrested, at the time sporting diamond studs and a gold watch. Despite it all, Wells Fargo paid handsome dividends to its stockholders year after year.

September 11, London

"WHISTLER dined. Most entertaining with his brilliant description of his successful decorations at Leyland's." This concise entry in the diary of the young English man-about-town Alan S. Cole chronicled the beginning of one of the most innovative and dazzling of the works of the expatriate painter James Abbott McNeill Whistler, his taking in hand a whole dining room and painting over its expensive leather panels with fanciful designs of peacocks. Whistler was at the very height of his notoriety, inwardly suffering but outwardly laughing away the incessant battles with bewildered patrons or outraged critics, and his establishment at No. 2 Lindsey Row was, for the fashionable, the most unpredictably exciting of places to dine.

Lord Redesdale, who lived a few doors away from Whistler and put up with such of the artist's eccentricities as his borrowing furniture for his parties, returned that fall from Scotland and called at the Leyland house at 49 Prince's Gate to see what was going on. The Englishman, providing an appropriately stuffy foil for Whistler's impish conceit, found him atop a ladder in the Peacock Room:

> But what are you doing?
> I am doing the loveliest thing you ever saw.
> But what of the beautiful old Spanish leather? And Leyland? Have you consulted him?
> Why should I? I am doing the most beautiful thing that has ever been done, you know—the most beautiful room.

Other visitors came upon Whistler lying on a hammock suspended from the ceiling doing his designs with a paintbrush affixed to a fishing rod.

The victim or beneficiary of Whistler's inspiration, F. R. Leyland, had bought his mansion at Princes' Gate with the fantasy of living like an old Venetian merchant prince in modern London. He indulged in such extravagances as putting in a whole gilded staircase taken from a razed palace, as well as displaying his fine collection of Italian Renaissance painters and contemporary masters like Millais and the pre-Raphaelites. Whistler's "Princesse du-Pays de la Porcelaine" hung in a place of honor over the mantel in the dining room, but the artist complained to his old friend and patron that the red accents in the carpet and paneling killed the delicate rose and silver tones of his painting. Leyland consented to have the offending portions of the rug cut out and more reluctantly to have the panels toned down. Whistler, however, understood that he had permission to redo everything and set about covering virtually every flat surface in the dining room with gold-on-blue and blue-on-gold peacocks. In the broken surfaces of the heavy, lamp-hung ceiling he was able to execute only designs of peacock eyes and breast feathers, but on the wall opposite his painting he created full figures, including matching ones of a peacock clutching a pile of coins and a peacock showing angry but triumphant disdain. Ordinarily avoiding symbolism in his art, Whistler later explained them as the Rich Peacock and the Poor Peacock, an anticipation of the haggling he expected with his patron. For three months Whistler was up at 6 A.M. to work all day at Princes' Gate and in bed as soon as he got home "so full were my eyes with sleep and peacock feathers."

The progress of the Peacock Room became the talk of London, and newsmen and even royalty found excuses to drop in on Whistler, who thoroughly enjoyed giving interviews and holding receptions. Critics at all levels were nonplussed by what Whistler referred to as a "noble work" of muralistic design unrivaled in his age. As for Leyland, he found himself excluded from his own house and forced to read about parties there in the newspapers. Whistler had originally asked 500 guineas for the redecorating, then 1,000, then 2,000. At one point Leyland was willing to pay the 1,000 if Whistler would just leave, but the painter insisted on finishing, after which he was treated to the studied insult of being paid 1,000 pounds, as if he were a tradesman, rather than receiving the extra shillings merited by artists. Whistler never forgave Leyland, who, for his part, had the grace to leave the masterpiece untouched and even the courage to face the caricature on the wall each time he dined.[1]

A brash but lovable confidence in himself and his works marked most of Whistler's career. Born in 1834 in Lowell, Massachusetts, he spent his early youth in Russia, where his father, a civil engineer, helped build the czar's first railroads. After a brief stint at West Point, dismissed because he was preoccupied with caricature rather than chemistry, Whistler worked for the Geodetic Survey in Washington and imposed on his acquaintance with the Russian minister to use his carriage and spend his money. In 1855 he willfully left for Paris to become a painter and after 1859 lived in London, at first finding favor in the Royal Academy, later resorting to less sanctioned showings of his increasingly unconventional paintings.

Artist critics called his work amateurish and "unfinished." The American was quite ready with the retort that the others' own paintings were "not begun."[2] He was not so concerned with subjects per se as arrangements of colors and tones (his best-known work, "The Artist's Mother" often taken to be kind of sentimental calendar art, was conceived as "an arrangement in black and gray"). Besides doing the Peacock Room, in 1876 Whistler was busy executing and exhibiting a number of works called nocturnes, the most celebrated of which was the "Nocturne in Black and Gold—the Falling Rocket." He also painted a number of portraits in a more or less realistic style, including one of Lord Redesdale. A friend wrote of him that he was "quite madly enthusiastic about his power of painting such full lengths in two sittings or so."[3]

The following year the "Falling Rocket" was to cause the most sensational episode of Whistler's career—his lawsuit against John Ruskin, the most powerful art critic living, whose reaction to Whistler's canvas was the brutally phrased: "I have seen and heard much of cockney impudence before now, but never expected to hear a coxcomb ask two hundred guineas for flinging a pot of paint in the public's face." In turn, Whistler, reading the review at the Arts Club, exploded that he was the victim of "libel." The much publicized courtroom exchanges that ensued included these taunts by the attorney general and the painter's sarcastic rejoinders:

How soon did you knock if off?
I *knocked it off* possibly in a couple of days.
That labor of two days then is that for which you ask two hundred guineas?
No, I ask it for the knowledge of a life time.

Whistler lost the case for all practical purposes, being awarded damages of one farthing and forced to pay his court costs.[4]

Fortunately, Whistler thoroughly enjoyed being the center of controversy and attention, eschewing the role of misunderstood artist and recluse. He dined out frequently and was a sought-after single man at parties. Once at a dinner he was in the presence of Mark Twain for the first time; the two men asked their hostess almost simultaneously who the noisy fellow down the table was. Another time his host started a conversation with the remark "The Prince of Wales says he knows you," to which Whistler replied, "That's his side of the story."[5]

Being the kind of person who could not dine alone, hardly be alone, Whistler was led to run an open house of his own at Lindsey Row, to which flocked earnest young artists and dilettantes, the important and the self-important, buyers and people seeking handouts, conversationalists and social bores, people who wished to see the eccentric celebrity and people who wished to be seen. One man came for an afternoon visit and stayed on for three years as an errand-runner, greeter, table setter, and piano player. An art dealer to whom Whistler owed money found himself impressed into duty along with two students holding candles while the painter worked on a canvas at nighttime. Bailiffs come to serve papers or collect bills ended up serving as waiters because Whistler told them he was entertaining important clients.

Often there were twenty for dinner, which might be an elaborate series of French inspiration. Whistler did such things with care and style, sending out invitations with his butterfly insignia, seeing to the laying out of the silver and the cherished blue and white table settings, and making flower arrangements such as nasturtiums floating in a bowl of goldfish. A "flight of fans" decorated the wall of the dining room, for Whistler was entranced by Oriental motifs, telling Cole in January that art "reached a climax" with the Japanese. One particular novelty in Whistler's entertaining was the late Sunday breakfast. Guests arrived at noon instead of nine, and even then they might hear their host still taking his bath. The meal was usually of American buckwheat cakes and corn, and a person who scorned such fare was never invited back.[6]

It was Whistler's misfortune that people came to see him more than to see his paintings. A diminutive, nervous, excitable person with searching eyes, he loved conversation on serious subjects as well as enjoyed gossip. In the reminiscence of a visitor in the 1870s: "We have listened to him with wonder and delight and have gone away and tried to remember what he said, to find it all fall flat and lifeless without the play of his expressive hands, without the malice or music of his laugh."[7] Young Cole, writing in his diary of successive dinners with "Jimmy" during 1876 might hear

Whistler hold forth on spiritualism or on Napoleon III, Hugo, and the Paris Commune, "with which J. sympathized." Two days before New Year's Whistler read out and discussed Bret Harte's stories.[8] Cole had to admit once that an English companion was "shocked" by the audacity of Whistler's views, but no one ever complained of being bored or of being needlessly offended.

September 12, Brussels

A GATHERING of Europe's most distinguished geographers and travelers listened to King Leopold II outline his dream of finally suppressing the slave trade and of bringing Christian ways to the Congo, the least-known area of Darkest Africa. The meeting in the royal palace resulted in the founding of the International Association for the Exploration and Civilization of Central Africa. The guests should then have realized, as Mark Twain was to realize thirty years later, that the wily Leopold with his reputation of being royalty's most hardheaded businessman was not the disinterested benefactor of the Africans he pretended to be. In time, the king's Congo Free State became the most monstrous case of colonialist exploitation in history. Of what interest was this to the self-absorbed United States of 1876? First, the man standing at Leopold's side at the Brussels meeting and his chief adviser thereafter in the international association was the American Henry S. Sanford, an ex-minister to Belgium. Second, the man who did the most to open up the Congo, for better or worse, was another American, Henry M. Stanley, a name already familiar to newspaper readers.

Stanley ranks with MacGahan was one of the great traveling journalists of the nineteenth century. Of Welsh birth and illegitimate, he was reared in an orphanage until he beat up the director, ran away, and shipped off to the United States as a cabin boy. After serving on both sides in the Civil War, he became a star reporter for the *Herald* and covered Indian campaigns, a British expedition to Ethiopia, and the Spanish Civil War. His greatest exploit came after James Gordon Bennett, Jr., gave him what amounted to a blank check and the terse instruction "Find Livingstone."

Stanley duly set off in 1871 on a safari from Zanzibar flying the American flag and located the British missionary, who had disappeared from public view five years previously. The resulting "Dr. Livingstone, I presume" dispatch was one of Bennett's biggest newspaper scoops: Stanley and Livingstone subsequently conducted joint explorations in Central Africa until the latter's death in 1873.

In 1874 a British newspaper decided to sponsor Stanley in an "Anglo-American Expedition for the Discovery of the Nile and Congo Sources." The *Herald*'s publisher again put up much of the money after sending a wire reading YES. BENNETT. Leaving from Zanzibar again, Stanley penetrated to Lake Victoria, which he circumnavigated, and later to the Lualaba River, which he determined flowed into the Congo rather than into the Nile. He then sailed down the Congo until he reached the Atlantic Ocean in August, 1877, surviving an expedition on which his three white companions and half his bearers perished. All during 1876 the *Herald* published Stanley's exotic dispatches from Africa, which contained accounts of hairsbreadth adventures with wild animals and bloody skirmishes with the natives.[1] While his brutal, aggressive ways shocked some London circles, he provided sheer escapism to American newspaper readers and also an inspiration to evangelists. Stanley's desciptions of "cannibalism and even more unspeakable depravities" of the Africans caused a great upsurge of American missionary activity in this area.

The first person to greet Stanley when he returned in triumph to Europe in 1877 was King Leopold's representative Henry Sanford, who eventually persuaded the journalist to become the mainstay of the Belgian's efforts to develop the Congo. During the next five years Stanley opened up more water routes and negotiated numerous treaties with native chiefs. Strangely, his activities alarmed the celebrated French empire builder Count Savorgnan de Brazza with the notion that Stanley was laying the foundations of a United States empire in Africa. At the end of his career Stanley resumed his British citizenship and received a knighthood. His cocksureness and American ways to the last alienated the stuffy members of the Royal Geographical Society, but try as some did, they could not denigrate his outstanding achievement in pulling all the earlier discoveries and guesses together to create a cohesive map of Central Africa.[2]

Except for Stanley, Americans had a minimum of contact with

Africa in the 1870s. Before the Civil War American merchants predominated in Zanzibar and other ports, the natives seeming to have a preference for American cottons, hatchets, rum, tobacco, and kerosene, but European competition and the decline of our merchant marine brought an end to this trade. The United States Navy sporadically patrolled in African waters and occasionally shot up tribal chiefs who harassed Americans. Three times in the 1870s the Navy intervened in Liberia against local rebels. The West African state was regarded as a kind of American protectorate, at least to the extent of keeping out the British and French. Africa was barely represented at the Philadelphia Centennial. Morocco's bloodthirsty sultan grandly sent over a Moorish villa and native wares to commemorate what happened to be the hundredth anniversary of relations between the two countries.[3]

The khedive of Egypt also contributed a lavish display, which Howells noted. Some thirty American ex-officers, both Union and Confederate, were engaged in modernizing the Egyptian Army, but they were unable to keep it from a disastrous defeat at the hands of the king of Abyssinia in March, 1876.[4]

A postscript to the founding of the Central Africa Association in September, 1876, was provided by Mark Twain in 1905 in an article called "King Leopold's Soliloquy." The Belgian ruler was depicted as alternately gloating of his success and complaining of "these meddlesome American missionaries" who reported the truth of how:

> I have ruled the Congo State not as a trustee . . . but as a sovereign . . . sovereign absolute, irresponsible, above all law . . . seizing and holding the state as my personal property, the whole of its vast revenues as my private "swag"—mine, solely mine— claiming and holding its millions of people as my private property, my serfs, my slaves; their labor mine, with or without wages, the food they raise not their property but mine; the rubber, the ivory, and all the other riches of the land mine—mine solely—and gathered for me by the men, the women, and the little children under compulsion of lash and bullet, fire, starvation, mutilation, and the halter. . . .[5]

All this, in a sense, was the sad consequence of the adventurousness of Henry Stanley and Bennett's drive to sell newspapers.

September 21, Indianapolis

FIFTY thousand veterans of the Grand Army of the Republic held their annual encampment outside this Midwestern capital city. They paraded in their old Union uniforms, they held memorial services, they fired cannon salutes, and they roistered and drank as in past years. They also heard a lot of speeches, all by Republicans and of unusual intensity, nearing hysteria. The choice of Indianapolis for the meeting was no coincidence, for in just three weeks Indiana and Ohio were to have their state elections, and the political strategists considered them the bellwethers of the national contest in November.

The Union Veterans Association of New York City took the initiative in organizing the encampment, with the close cooperation of Zachariah Chandler's Republican National Committee. They sent urgent messages to Boys-in-Blue Clubs across the country, they advertised extensively in the press, and they put up huge posters in railroad stations offering half-fare tickets to induce veterans to make the trip. The Grant administration also cooperated, providing tents, cooking equipment, and other supplies from the Army depot at Jeffersonville.[1]

The numbers of veterans who showed up pleased the organizers. The most famous of them was General Ambrose E. Burnside, whose admirers happily remembered his brief distinction of being overall Union commander and forgot that his record of defeats was longer than his record of victories. Congressman Garfield was also there in his capacity as a former general.

It was yet another general, Joseph Kirkpatrick, who some weeks before had written Hayes with brutal frankness that "a Bloody Shirt campaign and plenty of money and Indiana is safe; a financial campaign and no money and we are beaten."[2] The embarrassing letter, found by accident in the reading room of the Grand Hotel, was published in a local Indianapolis paper and then was taken up by the press all over the country. The advice was taken, nonetheless, by the Republican speakers.

Since Senator Blaine was unfortunately unavailable to be principal speaker, the organizers had to settle for Robert G. Ingersoll. The Illinios lawyer, a veteran, of course, had already that year electrified the Republican convention with his "plumed knight" speech. His reputation for eloquence was now so great that this sultry Thursday afternoon the veterans were on their feet cheering even before he started speaking. Ingersoll relied as much on his wit and choice of material as he did on his delivery and timing. He warmed up his audience with such sallies against the Democrats in general as "That party has never had but two objects— grand and petty larceny." He went on to hit at Tilden personally and achieved roars of laughter with the words "Think of a man surrounded by beautiful women, dimpled cheeks, coral lips, pearly teeth, shining eyes, think of a man throwing them all out for the embrace of the Democratic Party. Such a man does not even know the value of time."

When Ingersoll got to the subject of the Civil War, he became deadly serious and let go full force:

> Every State that seceded from the Union was a Democratic State. . . . Every man that endeavored to tear the old flag from the heaven it enriches was a Democrat. . . . Every man that shot down Union soldiers was a Democrat. . . . The man that assassinated Abraham Lincoln was a Democrat. . . . Every man that raised bloodhounds to pursue human beings was a Democrat. . . . Every man that clutched from shrinking, shuddering, crouching mothers babes from their breasts and sold them into slavery was a Democrat. . . . Every man that tried to spread smallpox and yellow fever in the North . . . was a Democrat. Soldiers . . . every scar, every arm that is missing, every limb that is gone is the souvenir of a Democrat. . . . Shall the solid South, a unified South, unified by assassination and murder, a South solidified by the shotgun—shall the solid South with the aid of a divided North control this great and splendid country?[3]

It was the classic "Bloody Shirt" speech of all time.

Curiously, Ingersoll's reputation was also that of an outspoken atheist, and he was the despair of churchmen. This circumstance did not bother the Republicans, and Locke even contrived to use it to partisan advantage, having Petroleum V. Nasby say of Ingersoll that "when he shakes our faith in the savin of the thief upon the cross, he destroys the only hope the averidge Democrat has of a blessed immortality beyond the grave."[4] Clearly, the Republican Party had a monopoly of oratorical and satirical talent of a scurrilous sort.

September 27, Boston

ONE of 246 freshmen entering Harvard this fall was Theodore Roosevelt, a thin-faced, frail-looking young man of medium height, who was just beginning to sprout some reddish whiskers and to be fastidious about his clothes. The event was recorded in a letter to "Darling Motherling" two days later:

> When I arrived here Wednesday night I found a fire burning in the grate and the room looking just as cozy and comfortable as it could look. The table is almost *too* handsome, and I don't know whether to admire most the curtains, the paper, or the carpet. What would I have done without Bamie. I have placed your photograph on the mantel. . . . Please send on the valise, as soon as possible, with the paper and inkstand, my skates. . . .[1]

His room was on the second floor of a boardinghouse at 16 Winthrop Street on the southwest corner of Holyoke, two blocks from Harvard Square toward the river. The interior decorating had been done by his older sister Anna, "Bamie," whose popularity in Boston social circles was a great asset to him.

Freshman Roosevelt at Harvard had the confidence of having money, and this was the first striking contrast between him and sophomore Woodrow Wilson at Princeton, as revealed in their letters and diaries. The latter was hardly in the position to write to his mother that "I have not yet bought my afternoon coat, being undecided whether to have it a frock or a cutaway."[2] The Roosevelts had been prospering in New York for so many generations that even twenty years before the Civil War Theodore's grandfather had left an estate of nearly $500,000. Theodore Roosevelt, Sr., continued to build the family fortune in a more leisurely way and was active in politics as a Republican of the lofty reformer sort. More than anyone, he had worked to block his state's endorsement of Senator Conkling for president in the spring of 1876.

The Roosevelts had a New York City residence at 6 West Fifty-seventh Street, which boasted a well-equipped gymnasium and also a room set aside as a museum for Theodore Jr.'s growing collection of birds, snakes, and other objects associated with natural science—the delight of the boy, the mission of the environmentalist president. The summer before his going to Harvard, Roosevelt spent at Oyster Bay, the Long Island locality which eventually became the family seat. Here he had his own horse and sailboat. Previously, the Roosevelts had made two very lengthy tours abroad, ranging as far as Aswan on the Nile. Associates of the Roosevelts in this era spoke of them as "rarely gifted," capable of "explosions of fun," but also given to the "unconventional family habit of reading and studying at all hours of the day and night and at any season of the year."

Because of his delicate health, Roosevelt was educated by tutors, one of whom reminisced that "the young man never seemed to know what idleness was." He was described by a woman friend of the family as having high-mindedness almost to the point of priggishness but also an "unquenchable gaiety."[3] On the occasion of his birthday a month after entering Harvard, Roosevelt wrote the following about himself to his mother: "It seems perfectly wonderful, in looking back over my eighteen years of existence, to see how I literally never spent an unhappy day, unless by my own fault."[4]

His father advised in a letter: "Take care of your morals first, your health next, and finally your studies."[5] The son was proud to reply: "I do not find it nearly so hard as I expected not to drink and smoke," adding that most of his friends did not indulge.[6] He wrote to his sister on October 15 of his disdain for his fellow students who sought out the flashier delights of Boston on weekends, but a few months later he confided to her that he had himself gone to the theater, "where thirty-five of our boys had taken seats in a row—and made the most awful fools of themselves." Increasingly his first fall, he enjoyed the social whirl of dances and sleigh rides, again in contrast with Woodrow Wilson's austere style of college life. Two years later, however, he could still avow sententiously, "Thank heaven, I am at least perfectly pure," the occasion of this outburst being the "disgrace to the family" of a cousin's marrying a "French actress"—"the vulgar brute."[7] On the positive side of morals, Roosevelt, who was brought up a Presbyterian like Wilson, taught Sunday school faithfully every week from the very beginning to the end of his career at Harvard. He was called "Teacher Four Eyes" by his mission school class.

Aside from difficulties of vision, Roosevelt's most serious health problems were anemia and chronic asthma. As with Wilson, Roosevelt's frailty condemned him to being just a spectator of organized athletics. More than his counterpart, Roosevelt was determined to build himself up from the measurements he noted in a diary a year previously—chest 34 inches, waist 26 , shoulders 41, forearm 10, height 5 feet 8, and weight 124 pounds.[8] The Harvard gymnasium became for him what the Whig Club was for Wilson. A strapping classmate of Roosevelt's first caught sight of him working out on the parallel bars and remembered thinking, "What a humble-minded chap this must be to be willing to give such a lady-like exhibition in a public place." The two soon became friends. One day skating together, Roosevelt boyishly exclaimed, "Isn't this bully!"—another reminder of the president-to-be.[9]

Roosevelt's studies, which his father rated last in importance, were also well taken in hand. Freshman year he had courses in classical literature, Greek, Latin, German, advanced mathematics, physics, and chemistry His highest grade was 92, his lowest 58; most were just above the 70 considered "honor" grades then. It was all easier than he expected, he admitted to his parents, and in December he told his sister of his astonishment "how few fellows have come here with any idea of getting an education"[10]—something Wilson could just as easily have written. The New Yorker confounded one classmate by his ability to read and concentrate, oblivous to the noisiest horseplay. Another observed that "Roosevelt was always running," when most freshmen were cultivating a languor including a "Harvard drawl."[11]

"Now, look here, Roosevelt. Let me talk. I'm running this course."[12] The professor provoked by the student's brashness may have been the soon-to-be-famous William James. Generally, like Wilson, Roosevelt did not appear to have been moved very deeply by any one of his professors, then or in recollection. He came to Harvard really too late to have known the imaginative historian Henry Adams, and, what was truly surprising, he did not apparently come into contact with Adams' successor, Henry Cabot Lodge, who was to become the mature Roosevelt's closest political associate.

Legend has it that the freshman was so flustered in his first interview with Harvard's head that he blurted out, "Mr. Eliot, this is President Roosevelt."[13] To an undergraduate, Charles Wilson Eliot must have seemed a formidable man, indeed, if also slightly ridiculous. He went about campus without ever acknowledging students, apparently loath to lift his head or look sideways and thereby expose an ugly birthmark covering half his face. Eliot's

[274]

greatness as a liberalizer and builder of Harvard was lost on Roosevelt, but as much could be said of Adams, Lodge, and others who condemned the atmosphere in Cambridge as sterile. Oliver Wendell Holmes was one of the few who were consistently appreciative of Eliot, writing that "our new president had turned the whole university over like a flapjack."[14] In practical terms, this meant that Eliot dared disturb the ingrained custom of the Medical School and order written examinations for doctors. He also abolished perfunctory master's degrees upon payment of a $5 fee and instituted a genuine graduate school of the arts and sciences. All divisions taken into consideration, Eliot recruited for Harvard a faculty better than that of Oxford and Cambridge combined, according to no less an authority than Charles Darwin.

Among the Eliot innovations that Roosevelt merely took for granted were his efforts at establishing elective courses followed by the complete elimination of prescribed courses. The sheer number of course offerings at Harvard was unique: for 821 students there were 291 hours of courses available each week (Yale with 119 and Vassar with 118 were the nearest competitors). Yet years after he graduated, Roosevelt declared that his education at Harvard had been too formalistic. He went so far as to say that he got more out of the periodical *Our Young Folks* "than any of my textbooks."[15]

Possibly, freshman Roosevelt in the fall of 1876 looked down on Harvard's president and faculty out of a sense of snobbishness, for he seemed as much preoccupied with caste as with morals, health, and studies. There were constant complaints in his letters similar to this one to his sister on November 26: "I most sincerely wish I knew something of the antecedents of my friends. On this very account I have avoided being very intimate with the New York fellows."[16] In 1876 about 1 in 5,000 of the population ever received a bachelor's degree. When Roosevelt finished Harvard, his thought was: "I stand nineteenth in the class. . . . Only one gentleman stands ahead of me."[17]

Early in 1876 Roosevelt had written a family friend that he expected to go into business after college. Instead of doing so, he almost immediately entered politics, being elected assemblyman at age twenty-three. Three years later he headed the New York State delegation that unsuccessfully opposed Senator Blaine's nomination for president. In 1886 he ran for mayor of New York but was defeated by Abram S. Hewitt. In the later 1890s, as assistant secretary of the navy, he promoted the imperialist doctrines of Alfred Thayer Mahan, drawing the scathing criticism of Eliot, still president of Harvard. Like Grant, Roosevelt was not content with two terms as president, but on his third try the onetime Harvard freshmen, the snobbish, pragmatic outdoorsman, was defeated by Wilson, the touchy, idealistic scholar.

September 30, Hartford

BESIDES being president of the Philadelphia Centennial Commission, General Joseph Hawley was running again for a congressional seat in Connecticut. One of his campaign mistakes was having the local celebrity Mark Twain preside at the big Republican rally in the state capital.

It was not that Twain was less than a committed Republican, although he had a lingering distaste for politics generally. He wrote Howells that fall: "Don't you worry about Hayes. He is bound to go to the White House as Tilden is to go to the devil when the last trumpet blows."[1] When Howells urged him to speak out publicly, however, Twain was fearful that his wit might be counterproductive, and his instinct was probably right.

Following the inevitable torchlight parade and the band music, Twain opened the meeting by saying that the "literary tribe" usually did not bother with elections but that he was now seriously motivated by the "chance to institute an honest and sensible system of civil service." The humorist soon got carried away, saying:

> Our present civil system, born of General Jackson and the Democratic Party is so idiotic, so contemptible, so grotesque that it would make the very savages of Dahomey jeer and the very Gods of solemnity laugh. We will not hire a blacksmith who never lifted a sledge. We will not hire a schoolteacher who does not know the alphabet. . . . We even require a plumber to know something about his business that he shall at least know which side of a pipe is the inside. But when you come to our civil service we serenely fill great numbers of our minor offices with ignoramuses. We put the vast business of a Custom-House in the hands of a flathead

[276]

who does not know a bill of lading from a transit of Venus, never having heard of either of them before. Under a treasury appointment we put oceans of money and accompanying statistics through the hands and brains of an ignorant villager who never before could wrestle with a two weeks wash bill without getting thrown.[2]

All this provoked storms of laughter, but people were not really sure whether Twain was alluding to Grantism or to the Democrats.

Twain's actual introduction of General Hawley was even funnier and even more equivocal. He presented him as having put on "the most astounding performance of this decade . . . impossible, perhaps, in any other public official in the Nation." He had "taken in as high as $121,000 gate money at the Centennial in a single day and never stole any of it."

Howells chose to praise his friend's speech as "civil reform in a nutshell," and the equally partisan *Times* reported vast applause at its end. The Boston *Transcript*, however, said of Twain that "somebody should have led him off the platform by the ear."[3]

If a person could forget the election, the experience of hearing Twain was one of a lifetime. A veteran reporter once wrote of his giving a lecture: "but it was not a lecture much more than it was a sermon, a story, a panorama, a magic lantern show, a song, or a concert by a brass band. It was disjointed and incoherent. Yet, its very novelty made it pungent, and its supreme absurdity drew the crowd and held it, expectant of what he might say next." The speaker was described as "a thin man of five feet ten, eyes that penetrated like a new gimlet, nasal prow projecting and pendulous, carroty curly hair and mustache, arms continually in the way, expression melancholy." His gestures were complicatedly awkward, and "sometimes he got his arms twisted in a bow knot, but he untied himself during the next anecdote."[4]

Twain's campaign effort for General Hawley was not his worst speaking disaster. That came a year later at a banquet in Boston in honor of Whittier's seventieth birthday. The humorist constructed an elaborate lampoon of Whittier, Longfellow, and Emerson while the venerable trio sat there smiling weakly and people stared at their plates in embarrassment. Even Howells called it a "hideous mistake," the result of some sort of "demonaical possession."[5]

October 4, Philadelphia

LIKE the chemists, the college athletes, and many other groups, the librarians decided that the Centennial year was an appropriate time to organize themselves. Unlike the socialists, they had enough sense not to brave the summer heat of Philadelphia but waited until fall to hold their first professional meeting. The hundred-plus scholars found their deliberations prodded their tasks prescribed for them by a brash twenty-five-year-old, Melvil Dewey, who had just this year published his Dewey Decimal Classification. In collaboration with the aggressive editor of *Publisher's Weekly*, R. R. Bowker, Dewey also contrived to put into the hands of the librarians the first issue of the *Library Journal*, which they gratefully adopted as their official organ thereafter. As his reward for these and other labors, Dewey was able to rent an office in Boston and put a sign on the door "American Library Association, Melvil Dewey Secretary." Below that was lettered "American Metric Bureau, Melvil Dewey Secretary." And still farther down the visitor could read "Spelling Reform Association, Melvil Dewey Secretary."[1]

"Whichever way I turn I see something that sadly needs improvement," Dewey once declared.[2] The son of an upstate New York general storeowner, he was remembered as a youth who saved his nickels so as to buy Webster's unabridged dictionary. At Amherst College he made extra money by teaching shorthand to his fellows. During his junior year in 1873 he "devyzed the Decimal Clasification," the idea coming to him "during a long sermon by President Stearns while I lookt stedfastly at him without hearing a word."[3] The next year, as assistant librarian at Amherst, he was in a position to test his ideas and perfect his celebrated classification. The first edition contained forty-two pages, growing to 1,647 pages a half century later.

American librarians were on the point of professionalizing themselves, Dewey or no.[4] As of 1876 the country had 3,647 libraries with collections more than 300 books. The Library of Congress was the largest with 293,500 volumes. Harvard led the private collections with 228,000. The big problem was cataloguing. Hitherto librarians just numbered each book consecutively as it was put on the shelves, without regard to its content, and often the four conventional sizes were put in separate locations. Dewey's innovation was to assign numbers to the books, not to the shelves. By his system O was assigned General works, 1 Philosophy, 2 Religion, 3 Social Sciences, 4 Philology, and so forth. History, which was 9, would further be broken down into 910 Geography and Travels, 920 Biography, 930 Ancient History, and so forth. His classification, which was ahead of anything currently used in Europe and reflected an American passion for standardization and efficiency, came to be almost universally used in this country within fifty years.

Dewey had a broader view of library science than numbers on books. He put forth the slogan the Library Association later adopted: "The best reading for the largest numbers at the least cost."[5] The idea that stirred him above all was that libraries were not for hoarding books but for getting them into the hands of readers. Availability of books would become a crucial concern of college librarians when President Eliot and his imitators succeeded in making elective courses widespread in higher education. What Dewey and other progressives had to counter this time was the attitude of such traditional custodians as the Harvard librarian who once joyfully boasted that all his books were in place except two in the possession of Professor Agassiz, which he was just then on his way to fetch. The newer library philosophy would be propagated systematically a decade later when Dewey established the first school of library science at Columbia University.

Although the young reformer had unbounded confidence that the adoption of "international metric weits and mezures" and "syentifik speling" would save three years of "skool lyf,"[6] these other enthusiasms of his in 1876 did not fare so well later. Succeeding in chartering the American Metric Bureau in April, "I induced Charles Francis Adams as 1 of the leading Americans to accept the presidensi whyl I as secretari had all the hard work."[7] The United States enters its bicentennial with Dewey's metric dream still unfulfilled. Nor did a convention held in Philadelphia in August and Dewey's subsequent five decades as secretary of the Spelling Reform Association bear much fruit, other than a much contested presidential executive order of Dewey's near contemporary Theodore Roosevelt seeking to reform the spelling of 300 words. Incidentally, Dewey himself changed the spelling of his given name from "Melville" to "Melvil," and he considered rendering his surname as "Dui."

In his later years Dewey turned his energies to the development of the Lake Placid Club in upstate New York, an enterprise which grew from a single house for thirty-two members to 400 buildings sprawled over 10,000 acres, including one for the Forrest Press, which published the Decimal Classification and ran off menus for the dining room with listings of such dishes as "stued pruns." Dewey's original vision was of a club where brains and character were more valued than wealth.

October 9, Boston

BELL'S telephone remained a scientific curiosity whose practical use was doubted by the press until he gave a successful demonstration of outdoor transmission over a private telegraph line strung the two miles between his ship and an East Cambridge factory. He and his assistant, Watson, talked and sang hymns for three hours, and the next day the Boston *Advertiser* printed convincingly alike parallel columns of what each had said and each had heard. Bell called it "the proudest day of my life."[1] Soon afterward he married his sweetheart, Mabel Hubbard, and went off to Europe for a honeymoon, spending the money he had earned in 1876 lecturing before scientific groups.

Meanwhile, Bell's friends and backers met resistance in their efforts to promote the telephone commercially. Finally, they interested the owner of a burglar alarm company, who started off by nailing up instruments in six banks, one being promptly removed by a no-nonsense banker. A crude switchboard was set up in the company's office, and within a year there were several hundred private phones in use. After one newspaperman scooped another by means of a telephoned dispatch, the journalists clamored to use the invention.

Bell's father-in-law provided most of the energy and money for organizing the Bell Telephone Association in which Hubbard, Bell, and his other promoter Thomas Sanders each had a 30 percent share and Watson 10. None of them, however, had much of a hand at business, and they soon offered to sell their whole enterprise to the Western Union Company for $10,000. At the time Western Union was a giant concern with 7,072 offices and 184,000 miles of wire. Its president initially showed indifference, but he changed his mind when the telephone began to compete with his stock tickers. Western Union formed a rival telephone company and brought in Elisha Gray and Thomas Edison as its experts. Edison did invent a better microphone than anything the Bell people had, and this produced legal wranglings. Western Union failed, however, in its suit claiming Gray as the original inventor of the telephone, and it settled out of court, selling its subsidiary to the original company. Later, in 1885, the Bell Telephone Association was consolidated with other companies and emerged as the all-powerful American Telephone and Telegraph Company. By the end of the century this organization had fought 600 lawsuits concerning its patents, winning all but two minor cases.[2]

Literally thousands more inventions had to appear to produce the telephone of today. The ringing signal was itself a later improvement, the original Bell prospectus of 1876 claiming that "any person within normal hearing distance can hear the voice calling through the telephone."[3] A Serbian immigrant contrived the boosting coils that made distance transmission feasible—the 235 miles from New York to Boston in 1884 and, finally, the 3,400 miles to San Francisco in 1915, the year in which the first dial system came into operation. For the transcontinental message Bell and Watson from different coasts repeated the original message of March 10. Bell had long before disassociated himself from telephone operations, giving his stock in the company to his wife as a wedding present and returning to his work with the deaf. Later he built a grand estate in Nova Scotia and lived winters in Washington, where he lent his sponsorship to a wide range of scientific activities.

October 10, Indianapolis

IN a hotly contested, nationally watched governorship race, Democrat "Blue Jeans" Williams defeated Republican Benjamin Harrison by 5,000 votes. The result caused a prominent Democrat to gasp, "Tilden is really to be elected."[1] The Republican leaders hastened to restudy their strategies, and Garfield confided to his journal: "I am clear that his will be the closest presidential election I have ever seen."[2] While all states would hold the voting for president on November 6, the various state elections for local offices were held at widely differing times of the calendar in this era. Vermont was one of the earliest, for example, with its voters going to the polls on September 5 and handing in a solid Republican result as usual. Of more interest was the election in Maine on September 11: here also the Republicans won again, but by a larger margin than in 1874, despite the continuing recession that particularly affected this state. Colorado and West Virginia held elections on October 10; the new Centennial State favored the Republicans, and the Southern border state went all-out for the Democrats, but no one really expected otherwise. The contests in Ohio and especially Indiana were much more crucial, since they were unpredictable and these states had large blocs of electoral votes. As early as August 13 Hayes had written in his diary that Senator Morton predicted "if Indiana is Democratic in October, our chance is not one in ten of success in the country in November."[3]

The Democratic Party in Indiana had lost its popular and able Governor Thomas Hendricks to the vice presidential race. After a series of clashes of factions and personalities, the party's nominating convention finally managed to agree on a new gubernatorial candidate in the person of a little-known nearly seventy-year-old Congressman, James D. Williams, better known as Blue Jeans Williams. Unwittingly, they had brought to the fore one of the most colorful political figures of the year. The man had acquired his nickname, Blue Jeans, because he always wore whole suits made of this material. Williams' sartorial predilections were matched by homespun ways, gawky mannerisms, and a twang. Nonetheless, his oratory was effective, even if digressive and simplistic, and by late summer he was drawing large and appreciative audiences, especially among his peers in the rural areas. "Get yourself chuck full of the subject, knock out the bung, and let nature caper" was his formula for speaking.[4]

Indiana's Republicans were confident at first that they had an unbeatable candidate for governor in Benjamin Harrison, great-grandson of William Henry Harrison, of "Tippecanoe and Tyler too" fame and President for the briefest of terms. Benjamin Harrison offered himself as a successful lawyer, wartime brigadier general, and prosperous citizen. His supporters thought it safe to

[282]

ridicule the contrasts his opponent presented, especially Williams' eccentric appearance and rustic ways. Their efforts backfired: among dirt farmers the elegantly turned-out Republican was easily derided as "kid-gloves Harrison," the smooth-talking lawyer with too much family tree.[5]

The choice between the city-slicker Republican and the hick Democrat seemed clear-cut enough, except that there was a formidable third-party candidate in the race. In Indiana the Greenbackers had a particularly strong organization and following, and their party convention early decided to field a complete slate of nominees for state offices. No one expected them to win outright, but the politicians were concerned how big a vote they would get and at the expense of which major party. Senator Morton decided that they would hurt the Democrats more and, accordingly, gave secret subsidies to Greenback newspapers.

Dispatches in the New York *Herald* almost four weeks before the Indiana election reported that "the state is flooded with orators . . . women and children talk politics day in and day out. The men make everything secondary to the vital issues of the campaign. . . . As is a common expression in the state—'There's hell on the Wabash this summer.' "[6] In an age a half century before radio and television, political rallies not only were the chief means of appealing directly to the voters but also represented one of the main forms of excitement and entertainment in people's lives.

The campaign literature showered on Indiana voters was in the volume of millions, and the speakers who went from station to station numbered in the hundreds. The Republican National Committee spent more money there than in any other state and turned out its leading national figures, like Senator Blaine, to give addresses. Carl Schurz, one of the few Republicans with enough convictions and bravery to advance the hard-money position forthrightly, made dozens of speeches. The Democrats contrived to find a countervoice to Schurz in the rising young newspaperman Joseph Pulitzer, another politically sophisticated immigrant who had special appeal to German-speaking audiences. The Democrats also made full use of vice presidential candidate Hendricks, whose soft-money rhetoric took the arguments away from Greenback orators.

The Greenback effort in Indiana, despite all the enthusiasm of a new cause, was plagued by mishaps, such as the withdrawal from the governorship race of two of its nominees in succession. The very last week the Greenbackers did produce a third candidate to head their ticket, but it was too late for him to make an impact. On the eve of the balloting the bets were on the Democrats. The GAR encampment at Indianapolis and Ingersoll's sensational speech had not produced the hoped-for swing to Harrison.

Blue Jeans Williams' 5,000-vote victory on October 10 occurred despite the fact that simultaneously the Republicans gained five congressional seats in Indiana and most of the state offices. Moreover, it became known that the Greenback candidate had hurt Harrison more than Williams: he attracted twice the vote in normally Republican districts than in normally Democratic ones. The Democrats took the result to mean "victory is in the air."[7] Their confidence would have been overwhelming if they had won Ohio, too, on October 10, but the election there for state offices went Republican by a small margin.

With four weeks to go before the national election, the Republican strategists began desperately rejuggling their electoral vote tallies. Vice presidential candidate Wheeler wrote Hayes on October 16: "New York is to decide the contest. I have no hopes of Indiana in November. Nor of *any* Southern State."[8] His calculation, which was echoed by many newspaper analysts, was simply that the electoral vote total of the expected Republican states in New England and the West would be almost equalized by the total of the Democratic South plus a few states like Indiana, so that the thirty-five votes of New York would become the determining factor. Hayes himself, being pessimistic about New York, developed an alternative hope of victory. He wrote to the Republican National Committee that "we must look after North and South Carolina, Florida, Mississippi, and Louisiana."[9] Two of his targets in this plan to break the "Solid South" were realistically out of the question: North Carolina and Mississippi could not be taken back from the control of recently victorious Democratic white supremacists. The other three states where Reconstruction governments held on precariously with the aid of federal troops were another matter, the key matter.

Generally, Hayes was gloomy about his party's chances, all the while pretending to himself that the country's highest office did not entrance him. He wrote in his diary on October 22:

It would be a calamity to give the Democrats the Government. . . . On personal grounds, I find many reasons for thinking defeat a blessing. . . . The huge registration in New York City looks sinister. It seems to look to our defeat in that state.

Another danger is imminent. A contested result. . . . Bloodshed and civil war must be avoided if possible.

This prognosis of a disputed election with the potential of a new resort to arms was not overdramatizing, but rather again Hayes chanced onto an astute prognosis. A week later Hayes once more confided his pessimism to his diary: "With the possibilities of fraud and violence—fraud, North, violence, South—the chances are that we shall lose the election."[10]

October 10, Amherst, Massachusetts

"DROVE back to Ashfield by way of Amherst. . . . Called on Emily Dickinson—Lovely day." That was all Helen Hunt Jackson put in her diary about seeing her childhood friend, who, for her part, described the visit as a matter of "moments." It was an encounter of two complete opposites: the one woman, elegant, sophisticated, well traveled, confident, hailed as the most popular female writer of the day; the other, plain, guileless, reclusive, diffident, accorded only by posterity the status of America's greatest female poet, if not simply greatest poet.

The autumn meeting of the two in the Dickinsons' sturdy brick house in the center of the quiet college town was actually tense and unsatisfying, for Mrs. Jackson was impelled to write and apologize to her friend a week later:

> I feel as if I had been very importunate that day in speaking to you as I did—accusing you of living away from sun light—and told you that you looked ill, which is a mortal piece of ill-being, at all times, but truly you seemed so white and moth-like. Your hand felt like such a wisp in mine that you frightened me. I felt like a great ox, talking to a white moth, and begging you to come and eat grass with me to see if it could turn itself into beef. How stupid—

In another note the same day, however, Mrs. Jackson returned to the matter of their dissension: "You say you find great pleasure in reading my verse. Let someone else somewhere whom you do not know have the same pleasure in reading yours."[1] Almost alone among Emily Dickinson's contemporaries, Helen Hunt Jackson had the privilege of reading her work and had the insight to recognize her true stature. Earlier in the year, in a letter dated Colorado Springs, March 20, the successful author had written the reluctant one of her desire to become reacquainted and of her admiration.

> I have a little manuscript volume with a few of your verses in it—and I read them often. You are a great poet—and it is a wrong to the day that you live in that you will not sing aloud. When you are what men call dead, you will be sorry that you were so stingy.[2]

In September of the year Mrs. Jackson had published another of her bestselling novels, *Mercy Philbrick's Choice.*

Her authorship of this story set in Amherst had to be surmised by reviewers since the work was unsigned, and speculation also arose about their being a second person's hand in the work. A faculty wife, writing her son abroad to tell him that the Jackson book was "stupid," added that "some pretend to say Emily Dickinson helped her."[3] Actually, there was no question of collaboration between the two women, but Mrs. Jackson had been very insistent when she saw Emily Dickinson that she contribute something to the series she was currently publishing.

Failing to convince Mrs. Jackson that she was "unwilling" and "incapable," Emily Dickinson wrote for advice to Thomas W. Higginson in Boston: "She is so sweetly noble, I would regret to estrange her, and if you would be willing to give me a note saying you disapproved it and thought me unfit, she would believe you." Higginson was one of the foremost essayists and reviewers of the day, having gained a reputation before the Civil War as a radical abolitionist. His reply on October 22 to Emily Dickinson was the assessment that "stories . . . would not seem to me to be in your line."[4]

It was to Higginson that Emily Dickinson had first turned back in 1862, sending him a small selection of her verses with the query whether they "breathed." In his puzzled reply he expressed some reservations about her metrical originalities but asked to see more poems. The abiding relationship between Higginson and Emily Dickinson did not result in the publication of any of her poems. In fact, in her lifetime only seven of her verses ever appeared in print—anonymously. She deliberately chose obscurity, and Higginson, although fascinated, remained noncommittal about her work. He also kept his distance, confessing after one visit to Amherst, "I never was with anyone who drained my nerve power so much. Without touching her, she drew from me. I am glad not to live near her."[5]

The most ineffable and the most self-effacing of American poets was born in 1830 in the homestead built by her grandfather. She was the daughter of Edward Dickinson, a distinguished lawyer and treasurer of Amherst College until just before his death in 1874. Her father's service as congressman took her to Washington for one year, schooling took her to Mount Holyoke Female Seminary and the need for eye operations took her twice to Boston—the only ventures of Emily Dickinson beyond Amherst in her entire lifetime. In 1876 she was sharing the homestead with her invalided mother and her sister, Lavinia, while next door lived her brother, Austin, and his wife, Susan.

"I . . . am small, like the wren; and my hair is bold, like the chestnut burr; and my eyes, like the sherry in the glass that the guest leaves," Emily Dickinson wrote in self-description.[6] Slender, quick-moving, with composed, plain features, she pursued the whim of dressing in white. Increasingly in the later years she avoided people, becoming a mysterious presence that visitors felt was hovering about upstairs or in another room. The much whispered-about recluse was surprised one summer day in her garden by a young boy who was tearing about looking for his playmates. His recollection may even have been of the summer of 1876, which was so hot and rainless that the poet remarked it in a letter.

> As I passed the corner of the house, Miss Emily called me. She was standing on a rug spread for her in the grass, busy with the potted plants that were all about her . . . a beautiful woman dressed in white, with soft, fiery brown eyes and a mass of auburn hair. Her voice I can never forget—clear, low-toned, sweet. She talked to me of her flowers, of those she loved best, of her fear lest the bad weather harm them; then cutting a few choice buds, she bade me take them, with her love, to my mother. . . . To have seen "Miss Emily" was an event, and I ran home with a feeling of great importance to carry her message.[7]

Even two cousins coming to the house in July, 1876, experienced her remoteness: "Oh, there's Emily, now we can get a good look at her . . . she banged the gate, and presto—she was gone." She sent them a note and flowers for their trouble.[8]

Another time she was called upon by an old family friend, Samuel Bowles, the crusty liberal editor of the Springfield *Republican*. When sending up his card produced no response, Bowles went to the foot of the stairs and shouted, "Emily, you wretch! No more of this nonsense. I have travelled all the way from Springfield to see you. Come down at once." To her sister's "utter astonishment," she did appear and was never "more brilliant or more fascinating in conversation than she was that day."[9]

Emily Dickinson did read the Springfield *Republican*. From it and from the Amherst newspaper emerge a picture of mundanely exciting local events in 1876, events that find little or no reflection in the poet's memorabilia, every scrap of which has been collected and published. A firebug burned down three buildings in the town. The Reverend Mr. Lothrop was accused of beating his wife and daughter, and the ensuing chronicle involved the intervention of Austin Dickinson, a horse whipping, Amherst students' pelting the minister's house with rotten eggs, a trial, and an excommunication. The death of President William A. Stearns of the College in early June did draw the response of a four-line poem and flowers from Emily Dickinson to his wife. The Fourth of July, celebrated with such fervor nationally and with special local reference by Amherst, elicited from her only the enigmatic fragment in a note to Mrs. James S. Cooper already quoted: "The Founders of Honey Have no Names." Her brother, Austin, visited the Centennial Exhibition in the fall; seen there by neighbors "in an apparent daze," he returned to Amherst very sick with malarial fever, the result of his being "such a self-indulgent visitor in Philadelphia," according to a letter from Bowles to Austin's wife.[10] All the patriotic celebrations and effusions of the year produced at best a wry reaction in the poet. In another note to Mrs. Cooper some time at the beginning of the next year she wrote:

"My Country 'tis of thee," has always meant the woods—to me—
Sweet Land of Liberty, I trust is your own—[11]

Her house and garden were Emily Dickinson's sufficient world in 1876. She found enjoyment in her sister's new cat, who had "the color of Bramwell Brontë's hair" and was called the "minute hand" because he caught a mouse every hour.[12] The gift of flowers from a child cousin inspired her to reply with a delightful poem:

> You must have skillful hands—to make such sweet
> Carnations. Perhaps your Doll taught you.
> I know that Dolls are sometimes wise. Robins are my Dolls.
> I am glad that you love the Blossoms so well.
> I hope you love Birds too.
> It is economical. It saves going to Heaven.

Her devotion to the young also found expression in her consenting to subscribe "for all time" and to contribute to a neighborhood playroom newspaper, "The Fortnightly Bumble Bee," its title being her invention as well.[13]

During the year she corresponded sporadically with Higginson in Boston. In January she had sent her "Master" five poems, including one with the vaguest political overtones.

> The Heart is the Capital of the Mind—
> The Mind is a single State—
> The Heart and the Mind together make
> A single Continent
>
> One—is the Population—
> Numerous enough—
> This ecstatic Nation
> Seek—it is in yourself.[14]

The news that Higginson's wife was sick caused her to pen him an affectionate note in August. In their exchange of letters regarding Mrs. Jackson in October, Higginson invited Emily Dickinson to visit him and his wife in Newport and sent his picture.

Once Emily Dickinson confided to Higginson her idea of poetics: "If I feel physically if the top of my head were taken off that is poetry."[15] Her intensity and exaltation ran counter to the taste of her era, which was an age of sentimentality that often fell into pompousness and occasionally was uplifted by some lingering transcendentalism. Her almost 2,000 poems were terse lyrical outbursts, the longest being fifty lines. Also, she was too bold in her experimentation with meters, rhymes, capitalization, and punctuation. Language in itself fascinated her. In content, she ranged from the cosmic to the comic, never the commonplace. Unlike her too easily successful friend Helen Hunt Jackson, she never pandered to popular demand. As for Higginson, he did not understand; at the end of the year he rather churlishly referred to his devoted correspondent in a letter to another as "my partially cracked poetess in Amherst."[16]

The neighboring children appreciated her at least. Some young visitors this or another winter began singing around the piano, and the sound of their voices coaxed Emily Dickinson downstairs. "As she stood before us in the vague light of the library we were chiefly aware of a pair of great, dark eyes set in a small, pale, delicately chiseled face, and a little body, quaint, simple as a child, and wholly unaffected."[17]

October 11, Kirkwood, New Jersey

WHILE Emily Dickinson was unknown because of her diffidence, Walt Whitman was unappreciated by the public because of his outspokenness.

Of record, the two incomparable poets were unaware of each other, but one can almost imagine Emily Dickinson writing this instead of Whitman: "wandering most all day (well clad and shod for it is cool weather) about the banks, trees, grass, etc., by the very beautiful secluded druidic creek."[1] Whitman was staying at the old farmstead of the Staffords in southern New Jersey and was regaining his health rapidly. Going with his friend Harry and other young men to the swimming hole, sometimes by moonlight, was a particular delight of the nearly sixty-year-old writer—call it lust or zest, as you will. He spent nine days with the large Stafford family, which he found relaxing company, possibly to get away from the importunities of the person he wrote the letter to, Anne Gilchrist.

Mrs. Gilchrist had made good her warning of the spring and arrived from London on September 10. She rented a house in Philadelphia, and Whitman came over from Camden frequently, taking a loving interest in her children. By December he was forward enough to ask her in a letter to install a wood stove in the room he customarily occupied in her house. The poet resisted, however, her obvious determination to make herself Mrs. Whitman, and fortunately for her she had letters of introduction to Philadelphia society.

Whitman now was frequently absent from his brother's house. When some nieces were in town, he went with them to the opera at the Philadelphia Academy and also to the Centennial Exhibition. Although only one letter mentions a visit to the exhibition, without comment, it is likely that the chum of horsecar drivers and ferrymen rode over to Fairmount Park many times and that he thoroughly delighted in all its hurly-burly.

Whitman's literary activity fell off after the effort of publishing the Centennial edition. He did see his new poem on Custer in print in July, but material he sent to *Scribner's* in December was rejected by its editor, Josiah Holland, the most complacently moralistic of Establishment Americans. Holland's own book of 1876 called *Every-day Topics* has been characterized as having "a secure place among the unread masterworks of the self-satisfied and didactic" and also as betraying its period "eloquently" by "not giving a true picture of it."[2] A few years later Whitman explained his publishing difficulties in part as owing to the fact that American magazines were "in the hands of old fogies like Holland or fops like Howells."[3]

Socially, Whitman was rejuvenated this fall by the companionship of a number of young men, who, while not his intellectual equals, were neither fops nor fogies but just honest, plainspoken friends to a fascinating and kindly old man. Overt homosexuality in their relationships is suggested in some of the poet's letters. In the case of the eighteen-year-old Harry Stafford, Whitman referred to him to a potential host as "my nephew" with whom he liked to "share the same room together and the same bed."[4] Addressing Stafford himself, Whitman wrote that he longed for him to "sit down in my lap." To "my loving boy" Peter Doyle he expressed a desire to "put my arm around you and hug you up close, and give you a good buss—often."[5] Doyle was not a selfish recipient of Whitman's affection apparently, for the poet wrote him in December that he had gone "down to see a poor young man, an oysterman, Jim Davis, very low with consumption" and "took him some stewed chicken for his dinner."[6] Jealousies did seem to account for a letter this winter that Whitman sent Edward Cattell, a twenty-six-year-old farmhand he had met at the Staffords in the summer. Whitman advised his new friend not to call on him anymore at the Staffords, and then he also crossed out the suggestion that he come by Mrs. Gilchrist's. A letter of Cattell to his "old man" has appealing directness for all its illiteracy: "would love to See you once moor for it seems an age Since i last met with you down at the pond and a lovely time we had of it. . . . I love you Walt and know that my love is returned to."[7] On December 20, 1876, Whitman sent $35 to a jeweler he knew and asked him for "as good a *gold watch* . . . middling showy and best inside as you can give me for that sum. I want it for a Christmas present for a young man."[8] It is not known whether Stafford or Cattell was the recipient.

October 16, Pottsville, Pennsylvania

NINETEEN prisoners chained together were brought into the county courtroom to be sentenced for various crimes associated in the public mind with the Molly Maguires. The degrading spectacle, given extensive coverage in the press, was a reminder that interlocking trials had been going on all year in the coal region, thanks to the efforts of Franklin B. Gowen, the capitalist, and of James McParlan, the Pinkerton informer, both of whom were hailed as heroes at the time, in contrast with history's later judgment. The nineteen were sentenced to prison terms ranging from one to fourteen years. Much worse retribution against the Irish miners was yet to come.

The successful convictions in the Jones case beginning in Mauch Chunk on January 18, in the Yost case beginning in Pottsville on May 4, and in the Sanger-Uren case beginning there on June 27, all encouraged railroad-coal boss Gowen to institute a wholesale prosecution of purported Molly Maguires and to charge them with crimes going back as far as 1862. That year in the coal region was marked by open resistance to the wartime draft, including insults to the flag and rioting, and now, fourteen years later, the prosecution trotted out a general in full uniform to prove that the Molly Maguires were not only criminal but unpatriotic.

Jack Kehoe, once militant miner and currently a politician and officer in the Ancient Order of Hibernians, was made out as the archvillain in the 1862 events and also in the Thomas case trial, which began on August 8, 1876, and involved nine men charged with assault and battery during an incident in June, 1875. McParlan testified that the conspirators told him of their intention to murder Thomas beforehand and confessed to him when he brought a bottle of whiskey to their meeting after the crime. He was too sick at the time, he said, to stop them, as well as fearful for his own life. His facile explanations provoked the defense to declare that McParlan "was always first to advise and counsel outrages, see to their execution, and never in the slightest manner adopted any means for the prevention of same. In this way he became the main instrument for the commission of all this crime."[1] The prosecution countered by putting Gowen himself on the stand, and he made an impassioned appeal. "Has there been a murder in the past ten years that these prisoners do not know about?" he asked the jury, and then he told them that the crowds around the courtroom refrained from violence against Kehoe and the others only because they expected a guilty verdict.[2] Obediently, the jury took only twenty minutes to condemn each of the nine accused.

Kehoe was put on trial for the third time in Pottsville on January 9, 1877, charged with the murder of a man in 1862. The defense produced ample evidence that he was not at the scene of the assault, but he was convicted anyhow on the strength of his having said to the victim, "You, son of a bitch! I will kill you before long because you are robbing me and robbing the men by your docking." (A foreman docked miners' earnings for having slate mixed in with the coal they dug.)[3]

"Pennsylvania's Day with the Rope" took place on June 21, 1877, when six men were hanged as Molly Maguires in Pottsville and four at Mauch Chunk. In the former place a carnival atmosphere prevailed, with businesses suspended and the saloons closed. Troops patrolled the streets since the governor believed rumors that an attempt would be made to rescue the condemned. Women and children were in the dense crowd that watched Boyle and McGehan mount the scaffold first, the latter carrying a brass crucifix in his hand and sniffing nonchalantly at red and white roses in his lapel. Boyle said, "Goodbye, old fellow. We'll die like men."[4] To the end the victims affirmed their innocence or said nothing, except Kelly, who confessed complicity in the murder of

Jones. In a statement of Carroll released afterward, he avowed, "I have never heard anyone say they wanted murder committed, only Kerrigan [the informer]."[5] Seven more men were executed in the course of 1877, and two later, including Jack Kehoe.

JUSTICE HAS TRIUMPHED, the headline in the Philadelphia *Times,* was the typical press reaction to the June, 1877, hangings. New York's *Irish World,* however, firmly insisted that the Molly Maguires were a "myth," a "bugbear invented by the Coal Ring," and they had no more reality than "hob-goblins."[6] This viewpoint found virtually no echo among the many sensational histories of the violence in the coalfields published in the decades after 1876, and to this day respectable historians write books and chapters titled "Molly Maguires" as if the organization was just as identifiable as the Ku Klux Klan or the Oglala Sioux. Since about 1900 other scholars have built up a better case that the Molly Maguires did not exist as such, that they were a figment of Gowen and his predecessors among coal businessmen, and that also they are an imperishable popular legend. There simply is no convincing written or oral evidence that men considered themselves Molly Maguires and behaved as such.

To deny the existence of the Molly Maguires is not to deny that specific murders and criminal conspiracies took place. Some of the men tried in 1876 and executed in 1877 were probably guilty. Some were undoubtedly victims of a gigantic frame-up made possible by the hysteria of the time. Almost every purported Molly Maguire arrested in 1876 was convicted of something. Later, when the public felt assured that a fearful conspiracy had been wiped out, courts tried suspects as individuals and required stricter evidence of specific wrongdoing.

Retrospect makes clear the antilabor aspect of the persecution of Mollies. Not satisfied with breaking the miners' union, Gowen set about preventing any resurgence of it by linking labor agitators with the crime wave, and he told his stockholders in 1877 he was prepared to do the same thing again. He and his supporters also inflamed public opinion with preposterous charges that the coal miners were under the influence of socialists from the Paris Commune and the International. Underneath all the rhetoric about the Mollies' trying to destroy capitalism was the simple fact that "the miners were guilty of wanting a union."[7] Furthermore, current scholarship is beginning to document that more terrorism and violence was directed against the coal miners than committed by them.

Gowen's shooting himself in a hotel room in 1889 has been interpreted as motivated by guilt about his wicked role in 1876. More likely, it was a result of his failures as a businessman, which included twice being ousted as president of the Philadelphia and Reading Company.

Another critical aspect of the Pennsylvania trials concerns the role of Pinkerton agents in general and McParlan's behavior in particular. One historian has avowed that the reliance on a private detective agency for the investigation, as well as on private police for the arrests and private lawyers for the prosecution, with the state providing "only the courtroom and the hangmen," was "one of the most extraordinary surrenders of sovereignty in American history."[8] The judges at the time were not greatly worried about possible abuses of justice by the Pinkerton informer. One ruled that he was "not an accessory," for "although he may have encouraged and counselled parties who were about to commit a crime," he fully intended that they should be discovered and punished."[9] A radical interpretation of the activities of men like McParlan that can be neither proved nor disproved goes as follows:

> The Pinkerton agents did not confine themselves to a spy service which often extended to the invention of uncommitted crime, nor even to the activities of an agent provocateur. When they could discover nothing and invention would not serve, they actually committed crime and charged it to the miners.[10]

The factual coincidence did exist that the years of the renewed crime wave in the coal areas were the years of Pinkerton activity. Specifically, McParlan, who claimed knowledge of all the activities of the Molly Maguires, never did anything to have anyone caught in the act.

Whatever the intentions of Gowen, McParlan, the courts, and most of the press in prosecuting the Irish coal miners of Pennsylvania, one consequence of their actions was of lasting importance—namely, the discrediting of the labor movement in general in many people's minds. Terence Powderly, for example, trying in 1877 to gain recruits for the Knights of Labor, was frequently branded a Molly Maguire, provoking him to write: "I am sick of that term being slung at us."[11] The *National Labor Tribune* cravenly suggested that organized labor publicly condemn the Molly Maguires so as to escape guilt by association. Only the socialist press had the courage to talk of a frame-up of workers in 1876 and to organize street protests in New York and Chicago the next year in honor of the "martyrs" of Mauch Chunk and Pottsville.

October 17, Cainhoy, South Carolina

THE level of violence mounted in the South Carolina election campaign. A new massacre took place at this village near Charleston, reachable by water. The Democratic Party chartered a boat, hired a band, and proposed to have a picnic combined with a debate. Both whites and blacks promised to leave their arms behind. An altercation led to a group of blacks taking up rifles and firing into the crowd. More than a dozen whites were killed or wounded.

Republican Governor Chamberlain chose to publicize the Cainhoy Massacre as violence by Democrats rather than against them. Many of his opponents suspected that he might have provoked the incident so as to be able to proclaim martial law and prevent the November election. His ally, "Honest John" Patterson, was crudely optimistic: "That Cainhoy Massacre was a Godsend to us. We could not have carried Charleston County without it."[1]

The state had been convulsed with various disorders since late summer. In Combahee "rice riots" occurred, arising from a wage dispute and causing black workers and scabs to go at each other with clubs and knives. The governor, with the approval of the Democrats, intervened with troops to protect the interests of the white plantation owners. The incident provoked New York's *Socialist* to editorialize that party differences were really meaningless whenever property was threatened.

The Chamberlain-Hampton political contest was sufficiently real to bring turmoil to the whole of downtown Charleston on September 7. After a black Democratic club held its first meeting for Hampton and Tilden, its members were set upon by a mob of black Republicans who considered the others traitors. The men eventually had to take refuge in the Citadel, where there were federal troops. Thereafter the rioters stoned houses, stopped horsecars, and beat up isolated individuals. Order was restored some hours later by the Carolina Rifle Battalion, whose commander wisely refrained from ordering his excited but disciplined men to shoot, thus avoiding a bloody outcome that would have been sensationalized in the Northern press.[2]

Ten days later the so-called Three Days War broke out in Ellenton and spread to several counties. Again, blacks and Republicans had reacted hostilely to the sudden upsurge of political activity by whites and Democrats. The impetus for wholesale violence was the arrest of two blacks for the robbery and abuse of a white family. The rumor of a lynching drove thousands of blacks to begin a virtual guerrilla warfare from the forests and swamps, while a posse of 200 whites, Red Shirts supporting Wade Hampton, added their share to the carnage, which mounted to close to twenty dead, mostly blacks. Only the arrival of a company of federal infantry prevented further slaughter.[3]

The Three Days War led Governor Chamberlain to make the ineffective gesture of ordering the dispersal of the Red Shirts. The Cainhoy Massacre of October 17 produced a peremptory demand for the same thing from Washington. The evening of that very day President Grant gave the rifle clubs three days to disband. To enforce the order, the Secretary of War commanded the sending of all available troops to South Carolina. Twenty-two additional companies of infantry and artillery arrived in major towns around the state. Some commanders of units from as far away as Boston were so jittery as to bring in their men carrying loaded arms.[4]

A directive of September 4 from the attorney general empowered local marshals, Republicans, of course, to command federal troops as they saw fit. On October 19 at Aiken a United States marshal marched a squad into the middle of a Democratic meeting being addressed by Wade Hampton himself and placed eleven men under arrest for "conspiracy." If this was a deliberate effort to provoke a new riot, it failed, for Hampton with the greatest self-control urged submission by his followers.[5]

Increasingly confident of victory, Hampton rejected advice that he withdraw altogether from the gubernatorial race as a protest against intimidation by federal troops. The Red Shirts did not disband but grew in numbers. With as many as 2,000 of his picturesque followers in attendance—banners flying, bands playing, women tearfully offering provisions, children shouting—Hampton's progress through the state took on the aspect of a "medieval crusade."[6] The culmination was the most gigantic rally ever held in Charleston, with whites in predominance but enough blacks to justify Hampton's hopes.

The Northern press showed awareness that the belated application of armed intervention was backfiring. In the view of the New York *Sun*, "this attempt to overawe the vote of South Carolina by Grant's soldiers will react against the party in whose behalf it is made."[7]

October 23, Red Cloud Agency

GENERAL CROOK, whose battle record this year was inglorious, watched with satisfaction as the 4th Cavalry smartly surrounded the camps of the agency Indians here and then marched in to search the tepees and roust out their occupants. All weapons were confiscated, including hunting rifles, and the herd of ponies was taken away, some to be given to the Army's Pawnee scouts, some to be sold in exchange for cows. The Sioux braves were further humiliated by being driven on foot to a new camp under the guns of an Army post. About the same time, in the northern agencies, General Terry and the 7th Cavalry supervised the disarming and dismounting of the Indians there. In this way the obedient Indians suffered for the sins of the hostile ones, and another white man's treaty was proved worthless.[1]

On August 15 Congress had stipulated in its annual Indian appropriation bill that no supplies were to be given the peaceful Sioux until they had formally given over the Black Hills and the "unceded territory" to the United States. This demand was explained to the chiefs at a conference with a Washington delegation headed by a George Manypenny, with a Bishop Whipple doing the talking. Unlike the situation during the similar negotiations the year before, there were no militant young Sioux leaders on hand to protest the sellout. These were, indeed, far away with the hostiles under Sitting Bull and Crazy Horse. Their absence and their recalcitrance were given as excuses to break the 1868 treaty provision that the lands could not be ceded except by an affirmative vote of three-quarters of the adult male Sioux. In vain,

Chief Spotted Tail argued that his agency Indians had not taken up arms and that even the warriors who fought Custer were the attacked rather than the attackers. Told by the bishop that the Great Father insisted that the Indians also move to a new reservation on the Missouri, Chief Red Cloud declared that he did not want to go because "there were a great many bad men there and bad whiskey." Another chief pointed out that the government had broken its promises and moved the Indians five times, adding sardonically, "I think you had better put the Indians on wheels and you can run them about wherever you wish."[2] In the end, Spotted Tail and Red Cloud signed away their birthright, having been alternately cajoled, bamboozled, and threatened.

October 27, Boston

WITH ten days to go before the election, the major parties outdid themselves with rallies and parades. Harvard students this evening had their own flippant version, marching through downtown Boston and back to Cambridge with torches and illuminated transparencies. One of their banners read HONESTY IN POLITICS AND CRIBS IN EXAMINATIONS. Another called for HARD MONEY AND SOFT ELECTIVES. Still another proposed FREE TRADE, FREE PRESS, AND FREE BEER. For many of them it was evident that at least the beer was flowing freely that night.

Legend says that Theodore Roosevelt, just one month arrived in Cambridge, was a vociferous participant in the demonstration. Back at Harvard Yard his continued shouting provoked a pro-Tilden upperclassman to yell out from his window, "Shut up, you freshman," and throw a potato at him. The student body was overwhelmingly for Hayes, sincerely equating reform with the Republican Party. Additionally, their elitism made them scoff at the Democrats as the party of the ignorant, whether Southern ignorant or immigrant ignorant. The banner for "Free Trade" happened to reflect Roosevelt's youthful liberalism on this issue, which would embarrass him when he became a high-tariff Republican later in life.[1]

November 7, nationwide

NEARLY 8,500,000 Americans went to the polls, exceeding the 1872 election total by 2,000,000. Both major parties predicted victory in what was the hardest fought and most exciting contest since the 1860 election of Lincoln. Clear, cool weather favored the voters in the West, but even persistent rain over the whole East Coast did not discourage a big turnout. When the final tally of the popular vote was made, Democrat Samuel J. Tilden had won 4,300,590 votes to Republican Rutherford B. Hayes' 4,036,298.

Tilden had carried New York City and Brooklyn by 70,000 votes and New York State by 32,000, giving him its bloc of 35 electoral votes. He had also won in three other doubtful states in the North—New Jersey, Connecticut, and Indiana. Their combined votes with New York and the sure Southern states put him at 184 electoral votes, with 185 needed to be elected president. The results were in doubt in three Southern states and Oregon, with a total of 20 electoral votes. Almost everyone considered it impossible that Tilden would not carry at least one of them.[1]

The voting in disputed South Carolina, Florida, and Louisiana was marred by charges of fraud and intimidation on the part of both Republicans and Democrats, but there were no actual shootings such as had occurred in the weeks before. The South had no monopoly on preelection violence: the press reported many incidents of brawls in the North and even a killing in Kingston, New York, when rival clubs clashed in the streets. Troops were stationed at the polls only in the three Reconstruction states and at the last moment in Petersburg, Virginia, causing the Richmond *Daily Dispatch* to run screaming headlines about a new "invasion" by the North and "bayonet rule."[2] There was no interference by the military with the normal balloting process. Under existing law, soldiers could not themselves vote, producing the anomaly in Wyoming that the wives and domestics of the Indian fighters went to the polls, but not the officers and enlisted men. Wyoming was the only state where there was woman suffrage.

The third parties had not seriously cut into the strength of the major parties. The Prohibitionists' Reverend Green Clay Smith garnered fewer than 13,000 votes in nine states. The Independents' Peter Cooper won 100,000, mostly in Western states. The "pitiful showing" of the Greenbackers actually had its explanations and compensations. As Terence Powderly observed in Scranton, the polling officials often simply did not register the third-party votes. The official tallies of 10 votes in Philadelphia for Cooper, 93 in Pittsburgh, and 21 in Cincinnati were ridiculously low in these cities with working-class populations both numerous and militant. While the small vote may have momentarily hurt morale and caused some radical journals to fold, the Greenbackers were far from finished. In fact, they went on to poll more than 1,000,000 votes in the congressional elections of 1878 and win twenty-four seats in the House—another suggestion that their vote was deliberately and drastically undercounted in the close presidential contest of 1876. Whatever his party's showing on November 7, Peter Cooper himself retained his political principles and also his equanimity, inviting the apparent winners Tilden and Hendricks to dinner at his New York mansion.

In a "curiously oblique" way the Greenbackers did determine the eventual outcome between Hayes and Tilden. The third party helped to elect a new senator in Illinois, David Davis, who then resigned as Supreme Court justice and thus removed himself from membership on the bipartisan commission that settled the electoral count. If Davis had remained in Washington, his vote almost certainly would have given the presidency to the man other than the one who was eventually inaugurated.[3]

On election day Governor Tilden was more smiling and outgoing than usual. Dressed in a black suit with a red carnation in his lapel, he left his Gramercy Park house at noon to go to Democratic headquarters at Everett House, stayed until 4 P.M., and returned again after dinner. Crowds stood outside in the rain, cheering as the good news came in from New York's two neighboring states. Around midnight, when he was assured of the New York result, Tilden went home again, the word "landslide" among those ringing in his ears.

Governor Hayes did not make public appearances election day. The morning after, he sat down and wrote a resigned letter to his son Ruddy, who was a student at Cornell University: "It would have been a great gratification to try to establish civil service reform, not to mention the good work for the South. It is decreed otherwise, and I bow cheerfully to the result."[4] As late as three days after the voting Hayes made the entry in his diary: "The election has resulted in the defeat of the Republicans after a very close contest." His supporter James A. Garfield was less philosophical about it all, writing bitterly that "we were defeated by the combined power of rebellion, Catholicism, and whiskey" (his phrase interestingly prefigures a Republican's costly slip in the 1884 election about "rum, Romanism, and rebellion"). "If we had carried the House," he added, "it is almost certain I should have been elected Speaker, but of course that has gone down in the general wreck."[5]

The press was nearly unanimous in conceding Tilden's victory. The Republican New York *Tribune* early on November 8 had a page one story and editorial accepting defeat. The more independent *Herald* rhapsodized: AVE! CENTENNIAL SAM! COMPLETE DEMOCRATIC VICTORY. Other papers were openly distressed. The Chicago *Tribune* ran the headlines: LOST. THE COUNTRY GIVEN OVER TO DEMOCRATIC GREED AND PLUNDER. TILDEN, TAMMANY, AND THE SOLID SOUTH ARE TO RULE THE NATION. It editorialized sorrowfully: "The true cause of the terrible defeat we have experienced was 'Grantism.'"[6] On the other hand, Melville Stone's fledgling Chicago *Daily News* announced simply that "Tilden has won by a considerable majority of the electoral vote"[7]

November 7, Springfield, Illinois

A MAN has a going counterfeiting operation, but it would be even more profitable if he could have the services of the best criminal engraver around, who happpens to be up for ten years in the penitentiary. How does he get him out? One scheme would be to steal the remains of the martyred national hero Abraham Lincoln and use them to ransom the counterfeiter. When is a good time to pull this off? What better moment than election night, when everyone is preoccupied with the voting?

The mastermind of this real, if bizarre, plot was James B. Kineally, who himself had done time in the state prison at Joliet for passing bad fifties in Peoria. Wiser for his experience, he went to St. Louis, until recently home of the Whiskey Ring, and organized a very sophisticated counterfeiting ring that included several engravers, a gang that distributed the bad money wholesale, and dozens of common criminals who passed the bills retail.

As early as June, 1876, the Springfield chief of police got wind of a grave-robbery-type plot and had warned John C. Powers, custodian of the Lincoln Monument at Oak Ridge Cemetery and, not surprisingly, later the author of a confused narrative called a *History of an Attempt to Steal the Body of Abraham Lincoln*. Kineally had apparently enlisted the services of a gang of sixteen desperadoes who had bought a saloon in Springfield and intended to pull off the crime the night before Fourth of July. One of the gang, however, was drunkenly indiscreet in a brothel, and the police broke up the gang, from whom Kineally turned in disgust.

Lincoln's son Robert, who had already this year gone through the trauma of his mother's insanity case, was also privy to a spate of rumors involving his father's tomb. It became difficult to tell how many people were involved in how many plots.

By November 4 the Secret Service was firmly cognizant that there would be an attempt on November 7: the new gang working for Kineally would break into the tomb, take the Lincoln coffin to a hiding place in the dunes of Lake Michigan, and then demand $200,000 cash and the release of the imprisoned engraver Ben Boyd. Secret Service Captain P. D. Tyrell knew all this because he had an informer, named Louis C. Swigles, in the inner circles of the gang. Moreover, Tyrell was determined not to nip the crime in the bud but to let it lead him to the mastermind. Accordingly, when some of the criminals journeyed to Springfield in the evening of November 6, Tyrell and two Pinkerton men were on the same train with them. Swigles and another of the gang cased the tomb during the day of November 7, but custodian Powers had been instructed not to alarm them in any way.

When the grave robbers arrived at the imposing granite monument late in the night of November 7, Tyrell, Powers, and several detectives were hiding inside. The men of the law, in stocking feet and showing no lights, listened as two men, John Hopkins and Terence Mullins, sawed through the lock of the room containing the sarcophagi of Lincoln and his sons, lifted the marble lid off the President's tomb, and ripped open the cedar coffin containing the lead casket. When, however, Tyrell finally decided to burst in on them, gun and torch in hand, the criminals had disappeared. Tyrell ran up to the terrace of the monument and exchanged shots with two figures lurking in the gloom. They turned out to be his own men. Fortunately, all the shots missed, but unfortunately, the criminals had fled the scene entirely.

Hopkins and Mullins made their escape in the wagon intended for their ghoulish cargo, and a farmer later remembered giving them breakfast. Ten days later they showed up at the Hub, a Chicago saloon owned by a man named Hughes. Here they ran into Swigles again and unsuspectingly compared notes about their escapade with the informer. Swigles tipped off Tyrell, who had the men arrested on November 19. When it developed that the state of Illinois had neglected to put a law against stealing bodies on the statute books, Hopkins and Mullins were tried and convicted of attempted robbery of a casket costing $75, and they were sent up for a year of hard labor. The bar owner Hughes turned out to be a partner of Kineally, whom he had visited in St. Louis, and the law finally caught up with the master plotter.[1]

November 8, New York

TO try to steal the dead president was macabre; to try to steal the current election was outrageous. The two plots were almost simultaneous. The ghouls failed, but the Republicans ultimately succeeded.

William E. Chandler, a former general and a political force in New Hampshire, returned from the theater around midnight to find Republican headquarters in the Fifth Avenue Hotel deserted except for a clerk or two. Party chairman Zachariah Chandler, no relation, had retired to his room with a bottle of whiskey, as resigned to Tilden's victory as were the departed party faithful. Studying the election returns, the newcomer was struck by the indefiniteness of the results in South Carolina, Florida, and Louisiana. Together with another late arrival, Chester A. Arthur, collector of the Port of New York, Chandler made some rapid calculations of electoral votes, and they then sent out, over Zachariah Chandler's signature, wires to the Republican officials of these three remaining Reconstruction states: "With your state sure for Hayes, he is elected. Hold your state."[1]

The New York *Times* extra published at 6:30 A.M. was virtually alone in headlining that the election outcome was "uncertain." When Zachariah Chandler got up that Wednesday morning, he saw a later edition of the same newspaper claiming that Hayes had won 185 to 184. In the meantime Democratic Chairman Hewitt had made the grave tactical slip of sending inquiries to the *Times* about the results in the three Southern states and thereby alerted editor John C. Reid to the Democrat's uncertainty. Soon Reid and Chandler were conferring in the Fifth Avenue Hotel, and the two conspiracies converged, so to speak.[2] At 10:30 P.M. Chandler blithely announced to the press the dream as an accomplished truth: "The election of Hayes is assured by a majority of one."[3]

During the afternoon William Chandler was dispatched by his namesake to Tallahassee, Florida to put pressure on the Republican Board of Canvassers there, and other Republican agents were sent to dragoon officials in Columbia and New Orleans. Belatedly, the Democrats too were to detail observers to the Southern capitals, but their opponents had the inside track.

The *Times* and Chandler did not waver in their assurance of victory ever after. Curiously, the titular head of the Republican Party, the man they considered president-elect, was oblivious to their plottings, for Hayes kept insisting in public and private that Tilden had won. Not until Friday, November 10, did he reverse himself and tell reporters, "I think we have undoubtedly been elected. That's the way it looks to me now."[4]

When the Democrats became conscious that a concerted effort was being made to steal the election from them, Hewitt submitted a public address for Tilden to make, stating the Democrats' view of the facts of the case and encouraging the country to protest the attempted fraud. Tilden, however, rejected the call for actual protest meetings as an invitation to violence, he procrastinated about delivering the rest of the message, and in the end he did nothing of substance. The week after the election his deadpan face and stylishly dressed figure were often in evidence in New York City, as he received delegations, greeted dinner guests at Gramercy Park, and rode horseback in Central Park. He was all confidence and reasonableness when he talked to the press: "They have given me a pretty good popular majority. . . . The fiery zealots of the Republican Party may attempt to count me out, but I don't think the better class of Republicans will permit it."[5]

With the election remaining in dispute day after day, the press could write of nothing else, business fell off, and partisan rancors dominated all social intercourse. Princeton sophomore Woodrow Wilson's diary provided an interesting barometer of the atmo-

[305]

sphere of rumor, hope, and fear. Election day for him ended with
the satisfying news that Tilden is "doubtless our next president."
Wednesday, after contrary bulletins appeared, campus Republicans and Democrats held rival bonfires, and he went to bed "tired
out with shouting and excitement." Thursday was a "day of suspense." For November 10 he wrote:

> Still another day of the most harrowing suspense about the size
> of the election. Conflicting reports pour in from all parts of the
> country. This evening's papers have given Tilden 184 of a neces-
> sary 185 electoral votes and make him pretty sure of Florida,
> which will give him 188 votes in the electoral college. The election
> is close beyond all precedent. Recitations in Greek history, De-
> mosthenes, De Corona, and Horace. Did little reading today ex-
> cept a little in Shakespeare's King Lear. Oh for some decision one
> way or another in the election! The suspense is almost insupport-
> able when I feel all the time that so much is at stake—the salvation
> of the country depends upon the success of the Democratic cause.
> The popular vote for Tilden overwhelming but the electoral vote
> very close. Surely this shows some wanting of good working in our
> institutions! Spent this evening most pleasantly in Whig Hall and
> in forgetfulness of the election returns and other disturbing ques-
> tions. Thank God for health and strength.

Two more days of "tiresome suspense," and then on the thir-
teenth Wilson wrote prematurely "Hurrah for Tilden."[6] How
much turmoil the young Southern Democrat was going through
was made evident in an anxious letter from his mother on November 15: "Tommy dear, don't talk about knocking anyone
down. . . . Such people are beneath your notice."[7] A friend of
Wilson's from Columbia, South Carolina, in a letter of November
23 also alluded to "your nearly getting into some scrapes with
some of the fanatics." In a perceptive analysis of the particular situation in South Carolina, this correspondent wrote: "I might tell
you of some of the disgraceful frauds that have been enacted and
some that will be enacted." Although sure that the "entire Democratic ticket has been fairly elected," he expected that the gubernatorial vote would be counted for Hampton, the electoral vote for
Hayes.[8]

A fistfight for Wilson was one thing, a civil war for the country
was another, and President Grant took measures to reassure the
electorate. On November 11 he granted an interview to reporters

in the executive office and calmly informed them over his cigar that "everything depends on a fair count."[9] He revealed that he was sending impartial "visiting statesmen" to the disputed states and had alerted the War Department to guard against fraud and violence. Grant's position was a very difficult one: as President he tried to be impartial; as a Republican he wanted Hayes to win; and as an ambitious man he could not ignore the prospect of solving the impasse by staying on in the White House for the third term he and even more his wife dreamed of. Actually, events were not in Grant's control or Hayes' or Tilden's but were manipulated by lesser politicians and interests.

November 10, Philadelphia

"I NOW declare the International Exhibition of 1876 closed," said President Grant, in the briefest of speeches, and he made a signal with his hand that told distant technicians to turn off the great Corliss engine in Machinery Hall. In the same plaza where the opening ceremonies had taken place in May, the assemblage now joined the choir in the singing of "America." It was a dreary day, cold and wet, and the sudden absence of the familiar hum of the machinery produced a feeling of wistful sadness.[1] The President's leaving Washington and his poker-faced performance of his duty in Fairmount Park had a somewhat reassuring effect on the nation three days after the exciting and disturbing election.

General Hawley and others made long speeches at the closing ceremonies extolling the success of the Centennial. The chief director hid his personal hurt that he had lost his congressional seat in the course of the Democratic sweep of Connecticut. Also, largely concealed until the official report of the Centennial Commission was published were certain disappointments and recriminations about the whole enterprise.

In the matter of attendence, the directors had hoped to tally more than 10,000,000 paid admissions but got only 8,000,000 with almost 2,000,000 freeloaders recorded. The railroads were blamed for not lowering fares sooner and more, and the press for publicizing the difficulties of opening on time. The absence of

Southerners was a sore point. The daily average in May had been a mere 19,000 visitors, rising to only 24,000 in July because of the excessive heat in Philadelphia. The somewhat desperate management succeeded in pushing the average to 82,000 in September and 90,000 in October, largely by promoting special days like Italian Day or the state days, particularly for the populous ones near Philadelphia. Admissions brought in $3,800,000 and the concessions $290,000. Meeting costs and having to pay back the federal government's $1,500,000 left the stockholders with a net loss.[2]

The financial difficulties of the Centennial Exhibition were rather gleefully reported in the labor press in its continued resentment of the Sunday closings which so effectively discriminated against wage earners. During the summer General Hawley had relaxed the sabbatarian rule on one occasion to allow him to show Prince Oscar of Sweden around, and the *Socialist* was quick to sneer at the "select American toadies ready to lick the dust from the royal feet."[3] According to reports in this publication, factories and shops were shut down weekdays and even for whole weeks during the summer, but this circumstance, far from encouraging workers to go to Philadelphia, meant that they were expected "to glorify the Centennial on empty stomachs and empty purses."[4] The Steinway piano company was accused of cutting wages 25 percent in order to pay for a workers' excursion to Fairmount Park and of actually making money by charging their families and friends to ride on the special train.

Steinway and Company figured in another criticism of the running of the exhibition—namely, that official awards for various products and brands were handed out almost indiscriminately and in such numbers as to make them meaningless. *Harper's Weekly* reported that Steinway, Weber, and Decker were each running large advertisements claiming to make the best pianos because of awards given. All this may explain why in our day liquor bottles, condiments, and the like are festooned with so many medals from so many world's fairs.

Contemporary critics and historians evaluated Philadelphia's achievement in 1876 according to their lights. If a William James found it "trashy," so another writer could speak of it as "gaudy, vulgar, high-spirited" and a "great cultural barbecue."[5] While William Dean Howells expressed his disappointment that much of the architecture was "unrepresentative," some people sniffed at the seemingly uniform Gothic extravaganzas and the compulsion to put decorative motifs even on machinery. The Centennial was supposed to sum up an age, and it did so, representing both the good and the bad, the pretentious and the genuine, the groping in the arts and the surehandedness in the machines. It gave Americans a big history lesson and occasionally opened up a view of the future. As a spectacle it was undoubtedly a success; for many people who had never seen sidewalks, to say nothing of South Americans, it was the central event of their lifetimes.[6]

November 23, New York

THE city desk reporters were out in full force when the USS *Franklin* docked at the navy yard. On board was William M. Tweed, once the all-powerful boss of New York, now a prisoner. The figure who at length came down the gangway was almost unfamiliar. Still a hulk of a man, Tweed had lost 60 of his 280 pounds, and his ruddy-faced content had given way to a haggard, distracted look. Instead of a neat frock coat and the inevitable diamond stickpin, he was wearing a black alpaca jacket, a collarless shirt, and checked pants, the nondescript outfit of a common wandering sailor, which, indeed, had been his recent lot. Tweed stumbled and fell when he reached the bottom of the gangway. Recovering his poise, the once-booming-voiced man quietly replied to reporters' questions and expressed a friendly curiosity in such recent political developments as the disputed contest between Tilden and Hayes. Then he was led away once again to the Ludlow Street jail to answer for having looted the city treasury of $6,500,000.

Tweed was rather uncommunicative about his whereabouts just after his escape from the two wardens at his own mansion the previous December 14. One theory was that he took an evening train to Cos Cob to hide out with a woman friend. A telegraph operator recognized the fugitive, did not report him, and was later rewarded handsomely, so the story goes. A more likely place for him to go underground was Weehawken, New Jersey, which had the advantage of access to New York Harbor. Tweed lay low all winter, even after the news that the jury had found against him on

March 8. Not until May 29, after making arrangements with a schooner captain and reportedly paying him $60,000, did Tweed leave the area, sailing out of the Lower Bay bound for St. Augustine, Florida. There a few days later he met up with his son-in-law, and the two of them then took a fishing boat to Santiago, Cuba. The Spanish authorities on the island, still wary of American adventurers, clapped Tweed in prison. After several weeks he secured his release, having made a few bribes and obtained the intervention of the American consul, who, incredibly, was not suspicious of him.[1]

On July 27 Tweed sailed from Santiago on the bark *Carmen* destined for Spain. The fifty-three-year-old man shipped as an ordinary seaman, and when he was apprehended by the Spanish police at Vigo Bay, he was found scrubbing decks. The circumstances of his arrest are full of ironies. The American minister in Madrid had been notified that Tweed was on his way, but this official had no picture of the fugitive to give to the local authorities. A Spanish friend of his happened to subscribe to *Harper's Weekly* and provided him with a cartoon by Thomas Nast, Tweed's nemesis. The cartoon, entitled "Tweed-le-dee and Tweed-le-dum," showed the boss in convict stripes collaring two small figures. Since Nast made a practice of drawing close facial likenesses rather than caricatures, Tweed was entirely recognizable. The caption and message of the drawing were obscure even to Americans, but the Spanish police simply concluded from it that Tweed was a kidnapper.[2] At Vigo Tweed was kept in prison until the arrival of the *Franklin*, once Farragut's flagship. Actually, Spain had no extradition treaty with the United States, but after the war scare of the beginning of the year, the government of King Alfonso XII was only too happy to be accommodating.

On board the *Franklin* Tweed was treated as well as a first-class transatlantic passenger. He had a cabin next to the captain's, he took mess with the officers, and he played cribbage in the wardroom. According to an officer:

> His behaviour was always that of a perfect gentleman. He was always glad to see any of us when we called on him. . . . He did not smoke, nor did he drink, either wine or spirits, unless when unwell. Most of the time he spent in reading, and when urged by the Captain, on the Surgeon's recommendation, to take an airing on

the deck, he availed himself of the privilege only once. Perhaps, he felt it humiliating to walk on deck with an officer of the guard.

By Tweed's own admission later, he avoided going on deck because he was feeling suicidal.[3]

Even before Tweed's ungraceful landing on American soil on November 23, the Democratic press began to speculate that the Republican administration had made haste to repatriate him for the purpose of using his testimony to discredit the Democratic Party. President Grant flatly denied such an intention in an interview. Nast, however, found Tweed's reappearance the inspiration for a number of below-the-belt political cartoons. In one he pictured Tweed as a determinedly emerging jack-in-the-box while Tilden sat unconcernedly on the lid. In another, Nast had Tilden actually embracing the convict Tweed as both men thumbed their noses at the public.[4]

Politics was less on Tweed's mind than survival. This time his stay at the Ludlow Street jail was confining, although he did secure the warden's own rooms, for a fee, and the services of a black valet. At first he spent hours on end sitting at a window and calling out the names of passersby, using the phenomenal memory for faces that had been part of his stock-in-trade as a politician. Increasingly despondent, the boss at length decided to confess all, and on December 5 he so advised the former head of the bar association: "I am an old man, greatly broken in health, and cut down in spirits and can no longer bear my burden, and to mitigate the prospects of hopeless imprisonment, which must speedily terminate my life, I should, it seems to me, make any sacrifice or effort." Tweed was suffering from heart trouble as well as diabetes and bronchitis.[5]

The use or misuse of Tweed's written confession is still a matter of some mystery. According to Tweed himself, Attorney General C.S. Fairchild agreed to release him in exchange for this confession, his promise to appear as the state's witness in any case requested, and his surrender of all real and personal property. Fairchild, however, returned Tweed's confession to him, claiming that there was a "fatal variance" between it and what Tweed orally told city official William C. Whitney.[6] Historians speculate that Fairchild did not really want Tweed's full testimony aired for the great damage it would do the reputations of hundreds of both city and upstate politicians. Tilden himself, still governor and a close friend of Fairchild's father, was one who may have feared exposure and was in a position to order a cover-up. When the completely broken-down William M. Tweed died in jail on April 12, 1878, his last words were: "I hope that Tilden and Fairchild are satisfied now."[7]

The city of New York recovered less than $1,000,000 of the huge sums that had been funneled into private pockets. Some of Tweed's more fortunate colleagues lived out their days in luxury abroad. One of them on his deathbed did make restitution of a few hundred thousand, alleging that his brother had stolen it. William C. Whitney, who made his early reputation as an unusually honest and efficient corporation counsel for the city, pleaded in vain for the use of Tweed's testimony in order to get back the taxpayers' money, as in the specific case, for example, of $1,000,000 spent on water meters that were completely unusable. On May 28, 1876, he did win one bizarre case that evoked all the bad memories of the Tweed Ring: the widow of the architect of the County Courthouse sued the city for $150,000 more than the $84,000 her husband had already received as a fee of 3 percent, unsuccessfully claiming that the actual cost of more than $8,000,000 should be taken into consideration rather than the estimated cost of under $3,000,000.[8]

November 23, Springfield, Massachusetts

REPRESENTATIVES of Columbia, Harvard, Princeton, Rutgers, and Yale held a gentlemanly but turbulent meeting at Massasoit House and agreed to new rules for football, making the game more on the order of rugby than soccer. They also founded the Intercollegiate Football Association, another Centennial year achievement in organized sports along with the National League in baseball of February and the Intercollegiate Amateur Athletes of July.[1]

Football as a campus sport was widespread enough by midcentury but usually so riotously rowdy as to be banned officially by most colleges. The first intercollegiate game between Rutgers and Princeton in 1869 was played according to "Princeton rules" with twenty-four men on a side and a round rubber ball. It was basically a kicking game, running with the ball was not allowed, and winning for Rutgers meant getting six goals between two posts and under a crossbar. At Harvard, however, the game evolved differently under modified rules of the English Rugby Union, which stressed ball carrying and tackling and called for an oval ball. Yale played Harvard under the latter's rules in 1875 and became converted to the new game, as did two Princeton players who attended. The Springfield meeting ensued, and all five of the big Eastern colleges agreed to the Rugby-type rules and also decided to play in the fall rather than the spring. Yale held itself somewhat aloof from the association for a while, until it succeeded in getting the others to reduce the players to eleven men. The size of the field was shortened from 140 yards to 110 yards only in 1880. Many other modern conventions developed but slowly, like tackling below rather than above the waist and the ten yards-four downs requirement.

November 28, Columbia, South Carolina

AT midnight General Thomas Ruger's troops occupied the statehouse. A command post was set up in the rotunda, sentinels were posted at the doors, and arms were stacked around the statue of George Washington. With both Republicans and Democrats claiming to have won the state election on November 6, Chamberlain and Hampton intended to set up rival executive governments with rival legislatures as well. South Carolinians were streaming into the capital city to lend support to their opposing champions, and the possibilities of new bloody riots in this violence-rent state were very real. Two days later President Grant interrupted his Thanksgiving holiday to preside over an emergency Cabinet meeting on the situation.

As for South Carolina's prized seven electoral votes, the determination was to be made by the Republican-controlled State

Board of Canvassers. They eventually found that the Republican elector with the most votes had a 964-vote edge and that even the Republican with the least had a 230-vote edge over the Democrat with the most votes. While many Tilden supporters were content to complain of fraud and intimidation at the polls, two New York politicos took the more direct course of simply bribing the board to give Tilden a majority of their votes. Such a deal was struck in mid-November involving the exchange of $80,000 in a Baltimore hotel room, but Tilden and his treasurer got wind of it and called it off. On November 22 Hayes was certified the winner of South Carolina's electoral votes.[1]

With South Carolinians far more concerned with the state outcome than the national, Governor Chamberlain and his reporters resolved to entrench themselves legally as soon as possible. On the day the troops occupied the Statehouse, the Republicans organized the State Senate on the basis of their uncontested 18 to 13 majority, and they also convened a State Assembly on the basis of sixty Republican legislators, fifty-four of whom were black. These chose a speaker, white, and a clerk, black. Meanwhile, sixty-four Democratic assemblymen met in caucus and then marched on the Statehouse to assert their claim to being a majority. The doorkeepers at the Assembly chamber barred admission to nine of the Democrats from Edgefield and Laurens counties on the ground that they had been elected by "violence, intimidation, and fraud." The rest of the Democrats refused to accept this, withdrew from the Statehouse, and at 7 P.M. met at Carolina Hall to constitute themselves as the legal Assembly and to elect officers.[2]

Two days later the Democrats succeeded in occupying the Assembly chamber, arriving at 11 A.M. When the Republicans came in at noon, there was a shouting match, following which the rival legislatures held forth on opposite sides of the same room. The Democratic speaker occupied the speaker's chair, the Republican speaker the clerk's. Later, when crowds outside the Statehouse threatened to intervene, General Hampton took charge of the scene, told his supporters to return home, and later ordered the Democratic assemblymen to convene again at Carolina House. The Democrats were soon buoyed by the desertion to their side of two black Republicans.

In desperation, the Republican assembly declared Governor Chamberlain the winner of the election by 3,433 votes, and the Massachusetts-born executive was formally inaugurated a second

[314]

time on December 7. This almost furtive ceremony in the State-house and his brief speech were over before the people of Columbia were aware of what was happening.

Less than a week later the Democratic Assembly certified Wade Hampton the victor by 1,134 votes, and on December 14, although refused admission to the Statehouse, he was inaugurated governor before a biracial throng in front of Carolina Hall. In the course of his long, confident address, Hampton turned to the blacks in the audience and said, "We owe much of our success to these colored voters, who were brave enough to rise above the prejudices of race and honest enough to throw off the shackles of party in their determination to save the State."[3] Hampton issued orders from the executive office he set up in Democratic head-quarters and kept his assemblymen in session. One of their first acts was to choose a United States senator, to take his seat in Washington once the imbroglio in Columbia had been resolved. Their choice was General Butler, the controversial figure involved in the Hamburg Massacre on July 8.

On April 10, 1877, a captain led the last detachment of blue-coats out of the Statehouse in Columbia past curious but quiet by-standers, and the troops retired to their barracks. Both Governors Chamberlain and Hampton had gone to Washington in late March to present their cases to the new President, who, in effect, sided with Hampton after his assurance that blacks would be guaranteed equal rights. The Democrat returned to the capital to claim the executive offices in the Statehouse the day after the troops were withdrawn. It was the end of Reconstruction. "The reign of the carpetbagger was over," wrote Claude Bowers accurately enough at the very close of his 1929 work *The Tragic Era*.[4] This historian, however, was utterly insensitive to the subsequent fate of the blacks when he concluded: "South Carolinians resumed the possession of their government and the direction of their destiny."

In front of the handsome old Statehouse in Columbia now stands the luxuriously modern Wade Hampton Hotel, whose bar and restaurant are a natural meeting place for today's legislators. In the area between the buildings arises a gigantic equestrian statue of Wade Hampton that dwarfs the nearby monument to George Washington, an instance, perhaps, where 1876 looms larger than 1776.

December 1, Columbus, Ohio

ANOTHER important scene in the drama of the Republican effort to steal the election was a three-hour meeting between Governor Hayes and Colonel William H. Roberts, editor of the New Orleans *Times* and a self-appointed spokesman for Southern conservatives. Referring to the upcoming electoral dispute in Congress, Roberts told the would-be president that "if we felt that you were friendly to us, we would not make that desperate personal fight to keep you out that we certainly will make if you are not friendly." The Southerner brought up the case of Governor Hampton of South Carolina, describing him as determined to put an end to carpetbagger rule but yet desirous of keeping racial peace. Hayes conceded that the Reconstruction governments had failed and that honorable white leaders like Hampton were the best hope for the South. The two men agreed that Hayes' letter of acceptance of the Republican nomination of July 14 provided a basis for Southerners to support him as president.[1]

The fact of the Hayes-Roberts interview was reported in the press, and Colonel Roberts subsequently talked openly about it. Northern Democrats immediately raised a furor about the possible treachery of the Southerners, and likewise the Republican Radicals wondered if Hayes intended to betray the administration policies in the South. Hayes himself refused to discuss his plans with reporters, saying that it would be improper until he assumed office.

The rumors of some sort of deal became daily fare in the newspapers all during December. Some stories were far from the mark, such as ones of secret negotiations between Hayes' managers and such respected Southern leaders as Senator B. H. Hill of Georgia and Senator L. Q. C. Lamar of Mississippi. Yet there was fire underneath all the smoke. Hayes did have a number of visitors from the South to Columbus during the Christmas season, men like Thomas J. Mackay, a former carpetbagger who switched his support to Hampton and who now brought a message from that governor.

One of the key Republican strategists was James A. Garfield, who in early December had been easily defeated for the speakership of the House by Democrat Samuel Jackson Randall. From the point of view of his own ambition, Garfield could dream of some bargain with Southern Democrats to secure their votes for him for the speakership in the future. On December 13 Garfield gingerly put his views to his fellow Ohioan Hayes: "Let me say I don't think anybody should be the custodian of your policy . . . but it would be a great help if, in some discreet way, those Southern men who are dissatisfied with Tilden and his more violent followers could know that the South was going to be treated with kind consideration by you."[2] "Kind consideration" for the South meant among other things pulling out the federal troops. A Cabinet position or two for Southerners would also be appreciated, as Garfield learned during the course of his own soundings of Southern congressional leaders at Christmastime meetings.

Another facet in the picture of a Hayes-South deal was the matter of the Texas and Pacific Railroad, a line controlled by Tom Scott, who was also the president of the Pennsylvania Railroad. The extension of this line from western Texas to California was envisaged as a major means of reviving the whole Southern economy, which had remained stagnant since the Civil War. Since the Crédit Mobilier scandal, however, both political parties had gone on record against federal subsidization of actual railroad construction (as against land grants). Involved in the railroad scheming were a number of men: the chief lobbyist Scott; General H. V. Boynton, Washington correspondent of the Cincinnati *Daily Gazette;* and William H. Smith of the Western Associated Press and one of Hayes' closest advisers. Of great historical interest is a letter from Boynton to Smith of December 20 in which he proposed Hayes' support of the railroad in return for "thirty or thirty six votes" of Southern congressman to assure Hayes' winning the election. Boynton argued that it was "fair that the South should have a road at the hands of the government as the North has received aid for one." Such a line would also be good for competition's sake, for controlling the Indians, and for reaching out toward the "richest mineral regions of Mexico." The go-between concluded: "If such arguments and views commend themselves to Governor Hayes and Tom Scott and the prominent representatives of the States I have named *know* this, Scott with his whole force would come here and get those votes in spite of all human power and all the howlings which blusterers North and South would put up."[3] Rarely does history afford such clear-cut documentation of the brutal intervention of big business in politics. Both Garfield and Hayes met with Smith, the letter's recipient, and must have known of the proposal at this time. Unquestionably, some sort of understanding was reached between the Republicans and certain Southerners in late 1876 that would secure Hayes' election and a new Southern policy simultaneously. What was surprising was that an astute newspaper reader at the time could accurately put together most of the pieces of the plot from current press speculation.[4]

December 5, Washington

"MISTAKES have been made, as all can see and I admit": this was President Grant's strikingly candid declaration in his eighth and last annual message to the Congress.[1] His recapitulation of the accomplishments of his administration would be greeted with some derision by many of his contemporaries and by most historians, but few would fault his personal honesty.

Grant had difficulty preparing his final message because "so many other exciting matters preoccupy my time," as he wrote his brother-in-law. He expressed a hope that he would be "brief but to the point." Later he complained that he had not had "one single half hour without interruption" or "four hours all told" and that he had left out things because he could not be "sure I was right."[2] The resulting ten-page document was remarkably forthright. Mark Twain was to say of Grant that he was the last chief executive to speak and write with "clarity of statement, directness, simplicity, unpretentiousness, manifest truthfulness . . . and soldierly avoidance of flowery speech."[3]

Right off in the second paragraph of his message, Grant faced his accusers, saying, "It was my fortune, or misfortune, to be called to the office of Chief Executive without any previous political training." His inexperience led him to make "errors of judgment, but not of intent." Grant then further excused himself by saying that his assistants were "in nearly every case selected without a personal acquaintance with the appointee, but upon recommendations of the representatives chosen directly by the people."[4] It was all a fair beginning to explaining why his was the most scandal-ridden administration in the country's history. Grant might le-

[318]

gitimately also have blamed the times in general for producing the Whiskey, Indian, and Navy rings. Yet one is left with the nagging question why such a limited man was so presumptuous as to let the country's affairs be thrust upon him.

There was much talk in late 1876 of impeaching Grant, but no one could really come up with specific accusations, and Congress was more concerned with the disputed election. Either Tilden or Hayes in office promised relief from the current regime. The mood of all Democrats and many Republicans was summed up in poems like the following:

> Gone am de days
> When Grant was young and gay
> Gone am his friends
> From de Old White House away
> Gone am de thieves
> All their heads are bending low
> And now I hear de people calling
> Go, Grant, go.[5]

Grant's own final evaluation of his administration was positive. He pointed with pride to such things as the Philadelphia Exhibition and Colorado statehood. "Taxes have been reduced within the last seven years nearly $300,000,000 and the national debt has been reduced in the same time over $435,000,000." He noted that in the current year he had expended only about $2,000,000 of $5,000,000 appropriated by Congress for "river and harbor improvements," which traditionally involved "pork barrel" extravagances. Such impoundment of appropriations was not practiced by other presidents until Franklin Roosevelt and Nixon.[6] Grant admitted to a deficit of $4,000,000 in the Post Office Department, an indication that public finances in 1876 were not altogether different from 1976.

There was no mention in the message of the fact that millions were still unemployed. His administration's inaction regarding the plight of the poor has been excused on grounds that few people in this era regarded providing work or welfare as a governmental responsibility, and in any case, the government lacked statistics. Yet Grant did take credit and did have the statistics involving the change in our balance of trade from $130,000,000 against the United States in 1869 to $120,000,000 in our favor in 1876. The administration had some classes' welfare at heart.

[319]

The outgoing President reported with satisfaction that "the relations of the United States with foreign powers continue on a friendly footing."[7] The Hawaii Treaty was held up as a great gain, as well as successful negotiations with Britain over the Canadian border.

One of the most surprising things in Grant's swan-song report was his devoting two pages near the end to his effort to annex Santo Domingo in 1869, blocked by Congress. He asserted that if his view had prevailed, "the country would be in a more prosperous condition today, both politically and morally." Trade with Santo Domingo would have revitalized the merchant marine, and most important, the island would have provided employment for "several millions of people." Annexation would have solved the Negro problem, because many, if not most, of the blacks could have escaped the "great oppression and cruelty" visited on them in the South by settling there, and moreover, the blacks remaining in the country would have been in a position to "demand" their "rights at home on pains of finding them elsewhere."[8]

Another unexpected aspect of the presidential message was his frankness about the Indians. He bluntly declared that the hostilities in 1876 "have grown out of the avarice of the white man, who has violated our treaty stipulations in his search for gold." Answering his own question why did not the government remove the trespassers from the Black Hills, Grant allowed that such an attempt would have resulted in "the desertion of the bulk of the troops that might be sent there to remove them."[9] These startling admissions still concealed the fact that the White House plotted the war with the Soux.

At the close of his official farewell Grant declared tht "it is not probable that public affairs will ever again receive attention from me further than as a citizen of the Republic, always taking a deep interest in the honor, integrity, and prosperity of the whole land."[10] Privately, he was sad to be leaving the comforts of office. He wrote his brother-in-law tht he hoped his mother would make a final visit to him as president. "If she would like to come during the holidays we could make room by sending one of the boys out o' nights. The children will be at home all during the week, possibly the last time we will have them all at home together."[11] The admission that the White House was not big enough to hold all the Grants was interesting.

Back on May 22 Grant had announced his plans for an extensive world tour after he left office. The Grants and one son duly sailed in the spring of 1877, and their progress through Europe, alternately triumphant and homey, included meetings with Queen Victoria, King Leopold II, King Alfonso XII, Czar Alexander II, and Pope Leo XIII. They also traveled in Africa, the Orient, and parts of Mexico and the West Indies, returning to the United States only in September, 1880.

Grant never gave up his dream of a third term. At the 1880 Republican convention he received 304 votes on the first ballot, and it was a full thirty-five ballots later before Senators Sherman and Blaine gave up and switched the nomination to Garfield. At the end of his career Grant was involved in a disastrous business venture. As usual, the ex-President trusted the wrong people. He subsequently paid his debts by writing his *Personal Memoirs,* heroically working on them despite cancer of the throat until four days before his death in 1885.

December 5, Brooklyn

WITH five minutes to go before the end of the first act of the play *The Two Orphans,* smoke and fire appeared center stage in the Brooklyn Theater. A piece of scenery, a tree limb, had broken loose from its fastenings, fallen into the border candles, and caught fire. Before panic could seize the audience, some of the cast stepped forward to urge calm. Then, unfortunately, someone lowered the main curtain, which burst into flames and spread the conflagration. People now stampeded for the doors. Most of the orchestra seat holders were able to make their way out of the main exit on Washington Street, but not so those in the gallery, which had only one staircase and that with a sharp turn in it. Some of those trapped upstairs jumped from the windows, suffering severe injuries. Hundreds of others piled up on each other and died from suffocation and smoke inhalation.

Two of the cast perished in the fire, and the total death toll was 292, far exceeding the worst such calamity previously, a fire in the Richmond Theater in 1811 which killed 61. After the Brooklyn Theater tragedy many of the remains were so charred as to defy identification as man, woman, child, or animal. Four days later a mass burial was held at the Greenwood Cemetery for approximately 103 people—unclaimed dead.

Needless to say, the newspapers led the public outcry for better safety precautions in places of public entertainment. The radical press was especially incensed that most of the victims of the holocaust were the less affluent gallery seat occupants. Changes did come, but theater attendance was markedly off for several years.[1]

By the weirdest of historical coincidences, the same day as the Brooklyn Theater disaster occurred the first cremation of a dead person to be performed in the United States. The Baron De Palm, a sixty-seven-year-old German, had insisted on this funeral arrangement for himself.

December 6, Washington

THE electoral college met. Actually no such body sat, but what happened was that the electors in each of the thirty-eight state capitals sent their votes to the clerk of the Senate to be counted. Usually a routine procedure, the tabulation spelled intensifying crisis this year when 184 votes were cast for Tilden, 165 for Hayes, and 20 were contested. The three Southern states submitted rival sets of returns, and so did Oregon, where the Democrats, feeling desperate, decided to make an issue of the fact that one of the Republican electors also held the job of assistant postmaster and was thereby disqualified.

The drama of the electoral count had begun on November 16, when the returning board of Louisiana first met behind closed, guarded doors. All four of its members were Republicans, appointed by the carpetbagger governor; three of them had been involved in corrupt dealings in the past; all four would be indicted for fraudulent actions within a year. Democratic observers were allowed to attend the opening sessions of the board, and they resigned themselves to seeing their claimed plurality of the vote cut from 20,000 to 7,000. Later the board sat secretly and threw out the votes of additional whole Democratic precincts, alleging fraud or intimidation. The entire procedure seemed guaranteed to cheat Tilden of his victory.

Incredibly, the Louisiana returning board members then sent out secret messages to Tilden's managers that their decision could be swayed by a substantial bribe. Their original asking price was $1,000,000, but they came down to $20,000. Tilden and Hewitt had to stop some of their associates from going along with the scheme, just as they did in the case of South Carolina. Hewitt long after asserted without evidence that the Louisiana board was bribed anyhow—by the other party.[1]

The same kind of disgraceful farce was enacted in Florida. Here the returning board had two Republicans and one Democrat, but the majority of two, openly before observers and later in secret, went about manipulating the county returns until they came up with the desired result—24,337 for Hayes and 24,292 for Tilden. A general sent as an observer by President Grant concluded that the Democrats should have won, but his pleas went unheeded.[2]

In the midst of the nation's uneasiness about the vote counting came the news of an interview between Hewitt and Grant on December 3 at which the President was asked what he would do if there were a deadlock. Grant was more than frank with the Democratic chairman, expressing his belief that Tilden should get Louisiana and that, even if the Louisiana vote was altogether thrown out, as had happened in 1872, and neither candidate had the 185 electoral votes needed, the election would be decided by the Democratic House of Representatives. These remarks were made in confidence, but Hewitt unwittingly revealed to reporters Grant's doubts about Hayes' victory.[3] Republicans were momentarily stunned, and a few newspapers, claiming that Grant must have been drunk, started calling him his "Inebriated Excellency."[4]

Grant had not foreseen what actually happened on December 6 when four states submitted two sets of returns. Now it was for not only the Democratic House but also the Republican Senate to determine which votes were valid and, first of all, to devise some procedure for reaching agreement between the two bodies of Congress.

With so much fraud and harassment perpetrated against the voters in the three Southern states by both parties, it is impossible for historians to say with final accuracy what the true results were, even though some have taken the trouble to examine the records in minute detail. The consensus of best guesses was that Tilden clearly won in Florida, he probably won in Louisiana, and he lost in South Carolina. All he needed was one of them. As for the Democratic claim to Oregon, it rested only on a legalism.

December 17, St. Louis

"THE South is in no mood for armed conflict," declared General Joseph Shelby in a sensational interview with reporters in which he revealed that he had turned down proposals from unnamed men to command an army of Democratic volunteers that would march on Washington and force the inauguration of Tilden as president. Shelby, who had never capitulated in 1865 and briefly left the country to fight for Emperor Maximilian in Mexico, was a spokesman for Southern conservatives, the men who were even then groping for an accommodation with Hayes and the Republicans. The ex-Confederate blamed Northern Democrats for all the talk of a new civil war.[1]

The word "civil war" was on most people's lips in December, 1876; but not many hearts were set on it, and few hands took it up seriously. Jefferson Davis, unamnestied, ignored a letter from a friend talking of "putting Tilden in *by force* if necessary."[2] In faraway France Mrs. Lincoln wrote on December 15 that the election impasse "overshadows everything" and that "we can only pray that no civil war will occur, to blight our prosperous land."[3] Blue Jeans Williams, newly designated governor of Indiana, said armed conflict was an "inevitable consequence" if the Republicans tried to inaugurate Hayes.[4] Garfield on December 18 asserted that "if we were to go by the talk of the Democrats we should come to the conclusion they really mean war."[5]

Colonel "Marse Henry" Watterson of the Louisville *Courier-Journal* was the Democrat who most insistently talked of a march on Washington by 100,000 or more, but he had in mind "peaceful citizens."[6] Other newspapers printed every conceivable rumor of mysterious groups plotting armed descents on the capital, of minutemen for Tilden organizing from New York to Kansas, and of the Democratic Veteran Soldiers Associations in various localities serving as recruiting centers (shades of the Ancient Order of Hibernians and the Molly Maguires). A few hotspurs strutted on village greens, and cranks threatened in letters to the editor; but that was the extent of real action. Given the passions aroused by the disputed election, it was surprising that there was no violence.

Official Washington took heed of the rumors of civil war without betraying undue alarm. In late November several companies of artillery were moved into the capital, and engineers began inspecting the city's defenses, unused for eleven years. The Navy stationed the warship *Wyoming* in the Potomac where it could guard the bridges approaching the city from both north and south.[7] All these developments were reported in the press which also printed false speculations such as that the Secret Service had contingency plans to seize all the Democratic members of Congress.

It was not Grant and his troops, however, that deprived the Democrats of their election mandate but rather the spirit of compromise and above all Tilden's pitiful indecisiveness. When the Forty-fourth Congress met for its final session in early December, the Democratic caucus was all defiance about opposing any inauguration of Hayes, and the newly elected Speaker Randall could write privately that "all that is needed is a little nerve,"[8] but in the end they surrendered to legalisms concealing fraud.

Tilden simply lacked the courage of his conviction that he had been fairly elected. At the outset, when the first evidence was coming in that the Republicans were stealing the election, he rejected Hewitt's proposal to call protest meetings as inflammatory. Later, when he became aware of the "Tilden or blood" sentiment of some of his supporters, he issued on November 25 a public rebuke to "hotheads" and canceled a Democratic victory parade scheduled to be held in Washington on November 29. Even after the farce of the returning boards in the three Southern states, Tilden remained outwardly unworried and unhurried. Hewitt became increasingly alarmed and impatient, but his chief rejected his suggestion that he appeal privately to Hayes' sense of fairness or that he make a dramatic public protest outlining the facts and figures in his favor. In rejecting the course of arousing popular sentiment, Tilden appeared to put a blind trust in the workings of the law.[9]

Tilden's hesitation encouraged certain Republicans to be bold

[325]

and certain Democrats to look for salvation elsewhere. Admittedly, in 1876 politics were still too decentralized for the titular party leader to dictate policy from on high. Just as Governor Hayes did not, could not, orchestrate the plottings on his behalf, Tilden was limited in his capacity to mobilize local and congressional leaders in a counteraction. What is remarkable is that he did nothing. Even after an Ohio congressman warned him of a deal, Tilden did nothing. Even after a Washington editor told him "the railroad men in Congress have sold you out," Tilden remained passive.[10]

By refusing to assert his rights, Tilden, indeed, averted the possibility of a new civil war. His inaction also averted the more likely prospect of a peaceful change of the parties in power. He condemned himself to being nothing more than a corporation lawyer and Albany politician.

December 18, Redwater Creek

IT fell to the obscure Lieutenant Frank Baldwin and his small battalion of mounted infantry to defeat the mighty Sitting Bull, defeat only in the sense of capturing his village of 122 lodges near this stream in northern Montana and scattering the band of hostiles into the mountains. Aside from a sharp skirmish on December 7, there were no pitched battles, and Sitting Bull still remained at large, when the lieutenant returned to Captain Nelson Miles' base camp December 23, having marched 716 miles in a month. Captain Miles, with never more than 500 men in his force, had been chasing the Indian chief back and forth across Montana since October, and he could claim greater success in fighting the Sioux on their own terms than any other officer. Destitution in the bitter cold, however, was what really defeated the Indians.

While Generals Crook and Terry were futilely campaigning with their unwieldy armies, Captain Miles was at the junction of the Yellowstone and the Tongue, building Fort Keogh. He fought off an attempt by several hundred Indians to block his supply trains in mid-October and then marched swiftly against their encampments. Soon he was in contact with the forces of Sitting Bull himself, and at Cedar Creek the two leaders held two conferences at shouting distance between honor guards of cavalrymen and Sioux. Miles, who from this time was dubbed Bear-coat for the clothing he wore, demanded that the hostiles leave the Black Hills and turn themselves in at the agencies. Sitting Bull refused, replying that God had made him an Indian and not an agency Indian. A two-day running battle followed, during which Miles effectively stood off all Indian charges by using hollow square tactics and artillery. The Sioux then fled over the Yellowstone, abandoning tons of supplies.

Later Miles put his troops in winter clothing and kept them on the move. He showed the effectiveness of infantry, who became known as "walk-a-heaps," for dogging the hostiles and preventing their concentration.[1] More than any of his counterparts, Miles solved the desperate difficulties of supply, and he developed a spy system to inform him of the enemy's capabilities such as Custer never dreamed of. Frustrated by having senior officers over him, Miles could tell headquarters with great justification, "if you give me this command and half the troops in it I will end the Sioux War once and forever in four months."[2]

Crazy Horse was the first hostile chief driven to seek peace, but talks were broken off after Miles' Crow scouts treacherously attacked the Indian's envoys on December 16. At the turn of the year Miles led his troops against Crazy Horse's camp on the Upper Tongue, taking along two cannon disguised as supply wagons. On Janury 7 he fought the Battle of Wolf Mountain against several hundred fiercely attacking Sioux and Cheyenne, and although there were few casualties because of a blizzard, it was a decisive demonstration that the soldiers, properly led, could not be defeated. Indians numbering in the thousands began turning themselves in at the agencies in the early spring, and on May 6 Crazy Horse himself with 889 Oglala surrendered to General Crook at Camp Robinson. The great Indian tactician was killed there in a scuffle in September. Ironically, the Indian police officer probably responsible for his murder was Little Big Man, the chief who had breathed defiance at the 1868 treaty negotiations. By now constant military harassment had eliminated all Indian resistance on the American Great Plains, but after Crazy Horse's death thousands again left the agencies to join Sitting Bull, who was still under arms in Canada.

Sitting Bull had moved across the border into the country "of the Great Mother" early in 1877. Even the *Times* wondered by now whether he was a fugitive from justice or injustice. The people under his direction numbered 4,000, his own Hunkpapa plus refugees from Crazy Horse and even remnants of Chief Joseph's battered Nez Percé from Idaho. The fact that they did not clash with the Canadians was cited then and later as proof of the wrongness of the Indian policies of the United States. The 300 men of the four-year-old Royal Canadian Mounted Police "treated the Sioux firmly, fairly, and above all consistently and in return they were accorded not only obedience but respect bordering on reverence."[3] The Canadians' task was made much easier by the circumstance that the Sioux occupied lands not wanted by anyone else and, in fact, unsuitable for supporting the Sioux either. Facing famine, the Sioux leader in the fall opened negotiations with the United States about their return to this country, but he ended up spitting in Captain Miles' face. This energetic commander was intent on pursuing the Sioux wherever he could find them, but General Sherman and others wisely took precautions to avoid an international incident. In 1879, seeking food and forage across the border, Sitting Bull fought one last battle with Miles before finally giving himself up at Fort Buford in 1881 along with a sorry band of 145 men, 67 women, and 73 children. "I wish it to be remembered," he said, "that I was the last man of my tribe to surrender my rifle."[4]

Less than a decade after Custer's last stand the Northern Pacific Railroad was completed, and General Sherman could come and declare that "prosperous farms and cattle ranches exist where ten years ago no man could venture."[5] Sitting Bull was carefully watched on his reservation, when he was not on tour with Buffalo Bill, and he lived until 1890, at which time rumors of his organizing a new ghost dance led to his attempted arrest and shooting. Two weeks later the renewal of Indian unrest provoked the Battle of Wounded Knee, in which 200 Indians and 60 soldiers were killed. As they mowed down women and children with Hotchkiss guns, some of the new generation of the 7th Cavalry were heard to shout, "There's another blast for Custer."[6]

December 22, Washington

SENATOR FERRY, president pro tem of the Senate, designated four Republicans and three Democrats to sit on a committee to resolve the election impasse. The day before Speaker Randall had set up a similar House committee of four Democrats and three Republicans. Both houses of Congress were acting to implement a resolution of December 7 calling for the establishment of an electoral "tribunal whose authority none can question and whose decision all will accept." This final Friday before the legislators adjourned for the holidays the House passed still another precautionary resolution reaffirming the Twenty-second Joint Rule, which gave both houses equal power over the vote counting.

The evidence of the spirit of compromise by men of both parties enabled President Grant to reassure the nation on Christmas Eve that he did not anticipate violence because of the election dispute. Denying any intention of himself interfering in the resolution of the impasse, he delcared that he was "anxious for the coming of the fourth of March when he would gladly give way to his successor."[1] Meanwhile, Hayes and Tilden were each confidently planning their Cabinets. The country was getting used to the protracted uncertainty. One advertiser turned the situation to humor, running a picture of "our next president smoking Marburg Bros. Seal Tobacco" with the figure's head completely enveloped in smoke.[2]

When Congress reconvened after the holidays, the two committees acted swiftly to set up an Electoral Commission, duly constituted of senators, representatives, and Supreme Court justices so as to have seven Republican members, seven Democrats, and one independent.

The compromise turned entirely on the fact of the independent, Justice David Davis, having the deciding vote. By a strange twist of history, on the very day of his designation, Davis was elected senator by the Illinois state legislature. Illinois Democrats were either unaware or indifferent to the national problem, and the Illinois Greenbackers, whose vote put Davis in, had thus a final voice in the 1876 election. Since Davis would not serve on the Electoral Commission, his place fell to another justice, a Republican, there being no other independents.

The Electoral Commission went through all the motions of fair-

[329]

ly evaluating the rival returns from the three Southern states and Oregon, taking 13,000 pages of testimony in the process, but on all important matters the vote was a strictly partisan 8 to 7. Florida was counted for Hayes February 10, and later the others. Informed of his defeat by excited reporters, Tilden with his maddening vagueness declared he was not surprised and changed the subject to a new horse he had bought. The Democratic candidate began to busy himself with plans to tour Europe.

Tilden's unwillingness to protest the unfairness of the Electoral Commission did not prevent other Democrats from expressing their outrage. Talk of war revived. Hewitt led an unsuccessful effort to delay everything beyond March 4 by questioning the returns of Vermont, Wisconsin, and other hitherto-uncontested states. Although a firm Tilden believer, Speaker Randall consistently made rulings which prevented filibusters. Not until March 2 was Senator Ferry able to announce to a joint session that Hayes had officially won, 185 to 184. Typical of the reaction of many Democrats to the news was the headline in the Cincinnati *Enquirer*: THE MASTER FRAUD OF THE CENTURY IS CONSUMMATED.[3] In vain, on the last day of the Congress, House Democrats passed a resolution, 146 to 82, that Tilden was "duly elected President of the United States."[4]

Hayes rode to Washington in a special train provided him by Tom Scott of the Pennsylvania Railroad, and the Grants gave a state dinner for him on March 3, the last time liquor was served at the White House for four years. Since March 4 fell on a Sunday, Grant took the precaution of having Hayes secretly take the oath of office that evening. Inauguration day, March 5, was cold and bleak. Three regiments of troops and Republican marching clubs chanting, "Seven Can't Beat Eight," escorted Hayes to his public swearing-in.[5]

If Hayes lacked nicknames in 1876, he acquired them quickly on becoming President, among them His Fraudulency and Granny Hayes. Three men prominent in the negotiations with the Southern Democrats sat in his Cabinet, and the immediate removal of all federal troops from the South indicated what the "Compromise of 1877" was all about. Not all the promises were kept: the Southern Democrats did not support Garfield for speaker; the Republicans did not subsidize the Texas and Pacific Railroad. As late as 1878 the Democrats were still moving to question the "Fraudulent Election," but the *Tribune* that year shifted people's attention to the "Crime of 1876," publishing the cipher telegrams sent by Tilden's managers concerning bribes to the Southern returning boards. Discredited, Tilden retired from politics and died ten years after he was cheated of the presidency.

Politically, the year 1876 opened with the word "reform" in the air and ended with cries of "fraud." The will of the majority who voted for Tilden was cynically thwarted by the Republican bosses and their allies. The blacks in the South were the particular victims of this political expediency, which brought about the return of lily-white rule, Hayes' good intentions notwithstanding.[6] The masses of the underprivileged—the poor and unemployed of both races—were also defrauded of the real concern the government should have shown them instead of diverting their attention to the legal wranglings and warlike posturings of the major parties. The disputed election of 1876, even though resolved without armed conflict, was a sad thing for the Centennial Republic.

December 29, Ashtabula, Ohio

THE Lake Shore Road's Pacific Express sped westward through the darkness of a nighttime blizzard, its human cargo huddling around the stoves in each of the seven passenger cars, which were joined to four baggage cars and two locomotives. Having almost gained the far side of the iron truss bridge across Ohio's Ashtabula River, the engineer in the lead locomotive heard a cracking sound, felt the track buckling, and gunned his engine, which tore loose from its coupling and reached safety. He watched helplessly as the eleven-year-old bridge slowly collapsed from one end to the other and the rest of the train crashed car by car into the ravine seventy feet below. Many of those who survived the horrendous plunge were subsequently burned to death when the wooden cars caught fire. The official death toll was seventy persons, its being impossible to identify the remains of many of the victims.[1]

A few days after the worst train disaster to date in the United States the chief civil engineer of the Lake Shore Line shot himself, and five years later the financier who had built the bridge on the cheap was driven by public outrage to a like suicide. Railroad magnate Commodore Vanderbilt, who this year's end lay in his New York mansion a few weeks away from his death, was spared the news of the tragedy by his physicians. For the reflective, the Ashtabula wreck was a reminder that the railroads symbolized most of what was right and most of what was wrong with the nation: on the one hand, marvels of technical achievements and economic progress, and, on the other, fraud and injustice.

Almost all European travelers here in 1876 remarked American railroads as a kind of miracle of efficiency and comfort. France's Offenbach could not say enough good things about the Pullman's swivel seats, the cold water on tap, the WC in every car, and the provision of books and magazines. He called the Pullmans "cradles on wheels."[2] The so-called silver palace cars were George Pullman's creation back in the 1860s but were still enough of a luxurious novelty to be featured at the Philadelphia Centennial. One millionaire spent $38,000 for a specially lavish private Pullman in 1876. One thing that particularly fascinated the foreigners was the conversion of the parlor cars to sleepers at night by the flip of a few levers. The fact that the upper and lower berths on each side were shielded only by curtains suggested to both Offenbach and Sienkiewicz all sorts of possible sexual escapades, which they admitted did not occur in America but would under the same circumstances in Europe. The relatively few dining cars also evoked wonderment and praise, the Frenchman Jules Leclerq rating it a "sublime experience" when he dined crossing the Rockies in 1876.[3]

Americans took pride that their railroad system exceeded that of any other country. From 2,818 miles in 1840 it grew to 30,626 in 1860 and then to 76,808 in 1876. The capitalization of all the nation's lines was $4.5 billion, on which in 1876, $94,000,000 was paid in interest on bonds and $94,000,000 in dividends on stocks.[4] Virtually all the great fortunes of the day, except the Rockefellers, had been made in this one industry, which was dominant over all others in size and was the "taking-off" sector that triggered the entire American Industrial Revolution since the 1840s.

Technically, American railroads still had a long way to go. The roadbeds were good by European standards, but the transition had not yet fully been made from iron to steel rails, and it was a lack of steel bridges and cars that lay at the bottom of the Ashtabula disaster. Yet speed and efficiency were becoming bywords of the American system. The run from New York to Chicago took only thirty-six hours. On June 1, 1876, a theatrical producer sponsored a Lightning Train from New York to San Francisco, which was spurred on by cooperating officials and cheering crowds at each stop to make the cross-country journey in eighty-three hours and thirty-nine minutes.[5] The Philadephia Exhibition was another indication of what the railroads could do: on its busiest day Gowen's Philadelphia and Reading Railroad carried 185,000 passengers in 370 trains to the fair.

American railroads were just beginning to present problems of monopoly. In the early decades there were hundreds of different companies—Elmira, New York, was served by twelve lines—with such results as ruinous rate wars and frequent business failures. One ludicrous example of cutthroat competition occurred early in 1876 in New Jersey where one line crossing another at right angles parked a locomotive at the junction so as to block the other's operations. The trend toward consolidation began with Vanderbilt's New York Central, which united ten separate companies. The Commodore went even further in 1873, when he sponsored a conference at Saratoga of the Central, Pennsylvania, and Erie systems for the purposes of mutual rate-fixing. Such collusion among the railroad magnates as yet provoked no outcry from the public or Congress. The man who made himself the leading expert on railroad politics was Massachusetts sometime Democratic candidate for governor Charles Francis Adams, and in a series of articles in the *Atlantic Monthly* he put his stamp of approval on combination rather than competition. The danger with railroads was not monopoly, by Adams' lights, but governmental regulation and the Brotherhood of Locomotive Engineers, which he described as a "public menace."[6]

If governmental control over the railroads was unthinkable to all but a few radicals, the railroads' control over the government, in the sense of their being pampered and fraud-ridden, did cause wider concern. In the period 1850–1871 the railroads received 200,000,000 acres of free land from Congress, an area the size of France, and the local benefactions they got amounted to as much as a quarter of the area of some particularly generous states. The corporations would receive by 1890 three or four times as much acreage as awarded to 377,000 families under the Homestead Act. In its eagerness to encourage railroads, the government was bilked in other ways: the infamous Crédit Mobilier charged the

Union Pacific, and indirectly the public, $94,000,000 for trackage that cost $44,000,000 to lay. As a senator sadly pointed out regarding the transcontinental railroad: "Every step in that mighty enterprise has been taken by fraud."[7] For making greed and corruption seemingly the norm in 1876, the railroads bear the largest responsibility.

The railroads also set the standards for monstrously unfair labor practices. Despite the depression, net earnings of the railroads in 1876 were slightly higher than in 1873, as a result of trimming expenses, mostly wages. The Boston and Maine, for example, cut the wages of all employees ten percent in 1876 but managed to pay its usual 6 percent dividend and to have a surplus at the end of the year as well. The next year this line raised the salaries of its president and other officials but refused an increase of 10 cents to sixty-seven members of the Brotherhood of Locomotive Engineers, currently earning $6.70 a day. The union took courage from the fact that their counterpart in Canada had forced the railroads to capitulate in a wage dispute the very same date as the Ashtabula train disaster. The upshot was the great nationwide railroad strike of 1877, which saw more violence and counterviolence than any previous labor struggle.[8]

To financial corruption and labor injustice, two other things could be added to the catalogue of the woes wished on the country by the railroad expansionists. The Indian problem was sorely aggravated by the building of the Northern Pacific. The Southern problem too, specifically the sellout of the blacks after the disputed election by the "Compromise of 1877," was in part a function of railroad politics. The distorted values that permitted the train to crash through the Ashtabula Bridge two days from the close of 1876 were symptomatic of much else.

December 30, Lynn, Massachusetts

"DR. SPOFFORD, won't you exercise reason and let me live or will you *kill me*?" wrote Mary Baker Glover in bitter reproach to her onetime favorite. "*Turn your thoughts* wholly away from me . . . read *Science and Health* p 193." She went on in her letter to deny that Dr. Eddy had come between them. In the future, she said, she would rely wholly on God and would "never again trust a man."[1]

Later that day Dr. Eddy called on his teacher at 8 Broad Street and made her a proposal of marriage, which she turned down. She changed her mind the next day after a dream during the night, which she later described to a student:

> She seemed to be standing on one side of a beautiful field of wheat. As she was rejoicing in its promise, dark swinish forms seemed to move underneath it, their uprooting instincts were destroying thought. She could not cross the field as she intended. Terror and abhorrence chained her to the spot. Then, on the other side of the field she saw Gilbert Eddy's manly form. "Come on, Mary," he said. "I will help you."

It was Eddy who was sent to Spofford on December 31 to give him a note from Mrs. Glover saying she had changed her "views in regard to marrying" and asking him to engage a Unitarian clergyman.[2]

In a very private ceremony Mrs. Glover became Mary Baker Eddy on New Year's Day. A few weeks later some of her students held a surprise party for the Eddys at which the couple was given presents and toasted in lemonade. Others of her following were hostile, however, resenting Eddy's sudden ascendancy in the affairs of their "mother."

At age fifty-five Mary Baker Eddy was in the prime of her life. In the recollection of a young friend of one of her students, "she was a very attractive woman with a lovely face and a very good figure."[3] She made a point of being beautifully dressed. Her great spiritual energies had been fully engaged in the year 1876, during which she received Alcott and other visitors, founded the Christian Science Association, supervised the sales of her book, and wrote several magazine articles, including one on women's rights that was sharply critical of Victoria Woodhull's extravagances. In the fall she found time to visit the Philadelphia Centennial before it closed, returned "gushing about it," and wrote an appropriate piece for the Lynn *Transcript*.[4] Also during the year, she had several nervous breakdowns, and this health problem led her to the realization that she needed someone to lean on. She at first resisted her desire to have a man around the house as weakness on her part, but she finally yielded to Gilbert Eddy's promise that he would take care of details and free her for her larger mission.

Gilbert Eddy was content to wait on his wife. In the words of an adulatory biography, "he forsook all to follow in this line of light."[5] Before marriage he had been "a spinsterish type bachelor" who did his own housework and made his own clothes.[6] Now this short, stocky, self-effacing, and slightly fussy man took over the running of 8 Broad Street. Mrs. Eddy came to praise her husband's obedience, and she probably found relief in his very simplicity in contrast with the flaming souls she so often had to deal with.

Mrs. Eddy's marriage turned several of her students against her. George Barry sued her for $2,700, which he claimed was the value of five years' service he had given her. The man with the greatest grievances, however, was Daniel Spofford, whom she had led on mightily in 1876 and then jilted for Dr. Eddy. As late as October 1 she had written Spofford: "My joy at having one student after these dozen years of struggle, toil, and defeat, you at present cannot understand but will know at a future time when the whole labor is left to you."[7] Spofford evidently expected to share her life as well as her work, for earlier in the year he had instituted divorce proceedings against his wife, charging her with repeated infidelity. In November, however, the case was decided against him. With the coming of the New Year Spofford was left with nothing except a lot of unsold copies of *Science and Health.*

Spofford's troubles with Mrs. Eddy were just beginning. In the spring of 1877 she briefly fled from Lynn and wrote him that he and others were "killing her" by calling on her mentally. After Spofford sold her remaining books, she expelled him from the Christian Science Association for "immorality." Later she accused him of mesmerism, developing the doctrine of "malicious animal magnetism" to explain how he could hex her without being physically present. To prevent his evil thoughts from getting through to her, she persuaded twelve of her disciples to sit up for two-hour shifts at her house and give forth countervibrations. Nor did she consider Spofford the only one of her enemies trying to crush her: her publisher Kennedy preceded him, and her latest favorite student, Arens, came after. Mrs. Eddy claimed she could tell which of her enemies from afar was trying to get through and attack her at any given time.[8]

These goings-on became a sensation in the newspapers in 1878, when it was announced that Dr. Spofford was found murdered and that Dr. Eddy and Arens were being held for committing the crime. Spofford had disappeared, and his friends jumped to conclusions. His supposed corpse in the morgue, however, turned out to be that of another man, and then Spofford himself showed up again in Boston alive and well. This scandal had barely died down when a saloon keeper came forward and swore Eddy and Arens had offered him $500 to kill Spofford and that he had hoped to collect by just getting Spofford out of town. Eddy and Arens were arrested again, with bail set at $3,000 each, but this case too was dropped when contrary evidence was brought out. Afterward Mary Baker Eddy announced that all the accusations had no other aim than "to injure the reputation of metaphysical practice."[9]

"I feel like a tired and wounded soldier of the cross . . . but my wounds are enlivening my soldiers, I do believe," Mrs. Glover wrote Spofford on October 22, 1876, before her remarriage and all the bitterness.[10] Her prayer that she receive more wounds and also the strength to bear them was answered. She moved to Boston in 1882, the year Dr. Eddy died, and there founded the mother church of Christian Science. The list of her incredibly many accomplishments ends in 1908, when at eighty-seven she brought into being the successful daily newspaper the *Christian Science Monitor* and set for all time its standard of being free from gossip and negative news. In 1928, eighteen years after her death, there were 2,370 churches and societies in her image.

Mrs. Eddy's works were apparently not known in 1876 to that other celebrated New Englander of the time Mark Twain. By the turn of the century, however, he was moved to write a scathing spoof of the new "mariology," as he called it.

December 31, New York

JAMES GORDON BENNETT, JR., got drunk. So did many other people this New Year's Eve, but they were not so newsworthy as the spoiled brat owner of the *Herald*. Moreover, for Bennett it was the most fateful drunk of his career, leading him to do something at his fiancee's house the next day "which cannot be told politely," to use the words of an inhibited biographer.[1]

The senior James Gordon Bennett had become one of the most influential American newspaper publishers, after starting the New York *Herald* with $500 and announcing his intention "not to instruct but to startle." He was responsible for many innovations: the first Wall Street financial article, the first European correspondents, and the first account of a society romance-murder. Once he was horsewhipped by an offended reader, one distinction the son may have wished to avoid. Bennett, Jr., who took over the *Herald* in 1872 at age thirty, was also a great journalist in his own right. Second-generation wealth, however, enabled him to be the most outrageous playboy of the day, a kind of "Regency type blood" who "never stifled an impulse."[2] Not content, for example, to be reputed the introducer of polo to America or even the sport's most reckless player, Bennett obeyed his urge to ride his polo pony into Newport's venerated Reading Room and earned social ostracism for his action. In New York he indulged such caprices as riding a bicycle around his block at night while a butler stood outside the mansion holding a tray with a snifter of brandy on it for the sportsman to quaff after each round.

Bennett's self-indulgence spilled over occasionally into his profession. Really drunk, he would start off editorials "To hell with the Pope." More sober and with an eye to selling newspapers, he was capable of things like the great wild animal hoax of November, 1874, when the *Herald* headlined a straight story that all the beasts in the zoo had escaped, terrorizing the city, killing forty-nine persons, and compelling the governor to take up tiger shooting. Other extravagant stunts of Bennett's were truly exciting journalism, especially his promotion of the exploits of Stanley and MacGahan. In 1876 he was still at the top of his trade with his scoops involving Custer and the disputed election.

To the great relief of prim society, Bennett seemed about to settle down at last and marry. So many of his previous escapades with women had required the intervention of expensive lawyers. Now he was properly engaged to a young woman from Maryland named Caroline May, whom he had entertained at his Newport estate the past summer. The May parents had a New York town house at 44 West Nineteenth Street, and, like many people of their class, they held an at-home New Year's Day, at which Bennett presented himself quite the worse off for the night before.

Bennett's progress into a party was normally one of slapping men on their backs, making risqué jokes to the women, and grabbing drinks whenever a waiter chanced by. Today he staggered about for a long time before reaching the center of the festivities. Suddenly feeling a call of nature, he would not or could not contain himself and proceeded to commit "a breach of the most primitive good manners"—that is, he simply unbuttoned and let fly into the fireplace. Some say he urinated into the piano, but in any case all was confusion with the women fainting and screaming and with the men stunned momentarily before they surrounded Bennett and hustled him off.[3]

Bennett's subsequent failure to apologize for his performance suggested that he accepted with equanimity the breaking off of the engagement by Caroline May. The publisher dared to show up at the Union League Club on January 3 and was pleased to find no particular hostility shown him. Leaving later to go to the *Herald* offices, he was confronted by Caroline's twenty-six-year-old brother Fred May armed with a massive cowhide whip. Before Bennett had a chance to remember whether this was the grim brother who had killed a man in a duel in Virginia or the fun-loving brother who had ridden a horse three flights up the stairs of a Baltimore hotel, he was vigorously assaulted and bloodied. The two men wrestled in the snow for a while before the Union Leaguers stopped watching from the windows and sent out servants to break it up. A few days later the two fought a formal duel with pistols, the last such recorded in the United States. Both missed. Thereafter Bennett left for Europe and for the rest of his life supervised his newspapers from abroad.

Bibliography

ADAMS, JAMES TRUSLOW. *The Adams Family.* Boston: Little, Brown, and Co., 1930.

ADLER, JACOB. *Claus Spreckels, the Sugar King of Hawaii.* Honolulu: University of Hawaii Press, 1966.

ALLEN, GAY W. *William James: A Biography.* New York: Viking, 1967.

Appleton's Annual Cyclopedia and Register of Important Events of the Year: 1876. New York: D. Appleton and Co., 1877.

ASBURY, HERBERT. *The Gangs of New York.* New York: Alfred A. Knopf, 1927.

ASHE, SAMUEL A'COURT. *Papers* (Alfred Thayer Mahan Letters). Flowers Collection, William Perkins Library, Duke University.

AURAND, HARRY W. *From the Molly Maguires to the United Mine Workers.* Philadelphia: Temple University Press, 1973.

BARNARD, HARRY. *Rutherford B. Hayes and His America.* Indianapolis: Bobbs-Merrill, 1954.

BARTLETT, RUHL J. *The Record of American Diplomacy.* New York: Alfred A. Knopf, 1952.

BEASLEY, NORMAN. *Mary Baker Eddy.* New York: Duell, Sloan, and Pearce, 1963.

BELL, DANIEL. *Marxian Socialism in the United States.* Princeton: Princeton University Press, 1967.

BEMIS, SAMUEL F., ed. *The American Secretaries of State and Their Diplomacy.* New York: Cooper Square Publications, Inc., 1963.

———— *A Diplomatic History of the United States.* New York: Henry Holt and Co., 1950.

BENNETT, NORMAN R., ed. *Stanley's Despatches to the New York Herald 1871–1872, 1874–1877.* Boston: Boston University Press, 1970.

BERGAMINI, JOHN D. *The Spanish Bourbons: The History of a Tenacious Dynasty.* New York: G. P. Putnam's Sons, 1974.

BERNSTEIN, SAMUEL. *The First International in America.* New York: Augustus M. Kelley, 1962.

BIMBA, ANTHONY. *The History of the American Working Class.* New York: International Publishers, 1927.

BIRMINGHAM, STEPHEN. *Our Crowd: The Great Jewish Families of New York.* New York: Harper and Row, 1967.

BOK, EDWARD. *The Americanization of Edward Bok.* New York: Charles Scribner's Sons, 1923.

BOWERS, CLAUDE G. *The Tragic Era: The Revolution after Lincoln.* Cambridge. The Riverside Press, 1929.

BRAUNTHAL, JULIUS. *History of the International, 1864–1914.* London: Thomas Nelson and Sons, 1966.

BROEHL, WAYNE G., JR. *The Molly Maguires.* Cambridge: Harvard University Press, 1964.

BROWN, DEE. *Bury My Heart at Wounded Knee.* New York: Holt, 1970.

_____ *The Year of the Century: 1876.* New York: Charles Scribner's Sons, 1966.

BRUCE, ROBERT V. *Alexander Graham Bell and the Conquest of Solitude.* Boston: Little, Brown, and Co., 1973.

_____ *1877: Year of Violence.* Indianapolis: Bobbs-Merrill, 1959.

BULLARD, F. L. *Famous War Correspondents.* Boston: Little, Brown, and Co., 1914.

BURTON, JEAN. *Lydia Pinkham Is Her Name.* New York: Farrar, Straus, 1949.

CALLOW, ALEXANDER B., JR. *The Tweed Ring.* New York: Oxford University Press, 1966.

CARMAN, HARRY J., et al., eds. *The Path I Trod: The Autobiography of Terence V. Powderly.* New York: Columbia University Press, 1940.

CARRUTH, GORTON, and associates. *The Encyclopedia of American Facts and Dates,* 5th ed. New York: Crowell, 1970.

CATER, HAROLD D. *Henry Adams and His Friends.* New York: Octagon Books, 1970.

CHADWICK, F. E. *The Relations of the United States and Spain.* New York: Charles Scribner's and Sons, 1909.

CLENDENEN, CLARENCE, et al. *Americans in Africa, 1865–1900.* Palo Alto: Stanford University Press, 1966.

COLEMAN, J. WALTER. *The Molly Maguire Riots: Industrial Conflict in the Pennsylvania Coal Region.* Richmond, Virginia: Garrett and Massie, 1936.

COMMONS, JOHN R., et al. *History of Labor in the United States,* vol. 2. New York: Macmillan, 1918.

CRAMER, JESSE GRANT. *Letters of Ulysses S. Grant,* New York: Putnam, 1912.

CROFFUT, WILLIAM A. *An American Procession, 1855–1914.* Boston: Little, Brown and Co., 1931.

CURTI, MERLE. *American Philanthropy Abroad: A History.* New Brunswick: Rutgers University Press, 1963.

———— *Peace or War, the American Struggle, 1636–1936.* New York: William Norton, 1936.

CURTIS, GEORGE W., ed. *The Correspondence of John L. Motley,* vol II. New York: Harper and Bros., 1889.

DAKEN, EDWIN. *Mrs. Eddy, the Biography of a Virginal Mind.* New York: Scribner, 1929.

DAMON, ALLAN L. "Impoundment." *American Heritage,* vol. XXV, no. 1 (December, 1973), pp. 22–23, 89–91.

DANA, RICHARD HENRY. *Hospitable England in the Seventies: The Diary of a Young American, 1875–1876.* Boston: Houghton Mifflin Co., 1921.

DANIEL, ROBERT L. *American Philanthropy in the Near East, 1820–1960.* Athens: Ohio University Press, 1970.

DAWE, GROSVENOR. *Melvil Dewey, Seer, Inspirer, Doer.* Melvil Dewey Biografy, Lake Placid Club, Essex County, New York, 1932.

DE CAMP, L. SPRAGUE. *The Heroic Age of American Invention.* Garden City, New York: Doubleday and Co., 1961.

DELORIA, VINE. *Custer Died for Your Sins: An Indian Manifesto.* New York: Macmillan, 1969.

DEMOCRATIC PARTY. *The Campaign Textbook.* New York: 1876.

DENNETT, TYLER. *Americans in East Asia.* New York: Macmillan, 1922.

DIAMOND, SIGMUND, ed. *The Nation Transformed.* New York: George Braziller, 1963.

DRAPER, THEODORE. *The Roots of American Communism.* New York: Viking Press, 1957.

DULLES, FOSTER RHEA. *Labor in America: A History.* New York: Thomas Crowell, 1949.

EDDY, MARY BAKER. *Retrospection and Introspection.* Norwood, Massachusetts: The Plimpton Press, 1891.

EDMOND, WILLIAM, and WILLIAM E. CURTIS. *Letters and Journals.* Hartford: The Case, Lockwood, and Brainard Co., 1926.

ENCYCLOPAEDIA BRITANNICA, INC. *The Annals of America,* vol. 10, 1866–1883. Chicago: Encyclopaedia Britannica, 1968.

FIELD, JAMES A. *America and the Mediterranean World, 1776–1882.* Princeton: Princeton University Press, 1969.

FLICK, ALEXANDER C. *Samuel Jones Tilden: A Study in Political Sagacity.* Port Washington: Kennikat Press, Inc., 1963.

FLIPPER, LIEUTENANT HENRY O. *The Colored Cadet at West Point.* New York: Johnson Reprint Company, 1968.

FONER, PHILIP S. *Hstory of the Labor Movement in the United States.* New York: International Publishers, 1947.

FORD, HENRY. *My Life and Work.* Garden City, New York: Doubleday, Page, and Co., 1922.

FORD, WORTHINGTON C. ed. *Letters of Henry Adams.* Boston: Houghton Mifflin, 1930.

FOSTER, WILLIAM Z. *History of the Three Internationals.* New York: International Publishers, 1955.

FURNAS, J. C. *The Americans: A Social History of the United States.* New York: G. P. Putnam's Sons, 1969.

GLADDEN, WASHINGTON. *Working People and Their Employers.* Reprint of 1876 work. New York: Arno, 1969.

GLASER, LYNN. *Counterfeiting America.* New York: C. N. Potter, 1967.

GOLDMAN, ERIC F. *Rendezvous with Destiny.* New York: Alfred A. Knopf, 1952.

GOMPERS, SAMUEL. *Seventy Years of Life and Labor.* New York: E. P. Dutton and Co., 1925.

GROSS, IRA B. *History of the Labor Movement in California.* Berkeley: University of California Press, 1935.

HABBERTON, JOHN. *Helen's Babies.* Boston: Loring Publishers, 1876.

HALE, EDWARD E. *James Freeman Clarke.* Cambridge: Riverside Press, 1891.

HALL, LUELLA J. *The United States and Morocco, 1776–1956.* Metuchen, New Jersey: Scarecrow Press, Inc., 1971.

HARRIS, CHARLES T. *Memories of Manhattan in the Sixties and Seventies.* New York: Derrydale Press, 1928.

HARRIS, JULIA C. *The Life and Letters of Joel Chandler Harris.* Boston: Houghton Mifflin Co., 1918.

HASKINS, JAMES. *Pinckney Benton Stewart Pinchback.* New York: Macmillan, 1973.

HATTON, JOSEPH. *Today in America, Studies for the Old World and the New.* London: Chapman and Hall, 1881. 2 vols.

HAWORTH, PAUL L. *Th Hayes-Tilden Disputed Election of 1876.* Cleveland: Burrows Bros., 1906.

HAYNES, FRED E. *Third Party Movements Since the Civil War.* Iowa City: State Historical Society of Iowa, 1916.

HEARN, LAFCADIO. *An American Miscellany.* First collected by Albert Mordell. New York: Dodd, Mead, and Co., 1925.

HERESHOFF, DAVID. *American Disciples of Marx.* Detroit: Wayne State University Press, 1967.

HERRICK, WALTER R., JR. *The American Naval Revolution.* Baton Rouge: Louisana State University Press, 1966.

HESSELTINE, W. B. *The Blue and the Gray on the Nile.* Chicago: University of Chicago Press, 1961.

———. *Ulysses S. Grant, Politician.* New York: Dodd, Mead, and Co., 1935.

HEWITT, EDWARD R. *Those Were the Days.* New York: Duell, Sloan, and Pearce, 1943.

HILLQUIT, MORRIS. *History of Socialism in the United States.* New York: Funk and Wagnalls, 1910.

HIRSCH, MARK D. *William C. Whitney, Modern Warwick.* New York: Dodd, Mead, and Co., 1948.

HIRSHON, STANLEY P. *The Lion of the Lord: A Biography of Brigham Young.* New York: Knopf, 1969.

HOLBROOK, STEWART H. *The Age of the Moguls.* Garden City, New York: Doubleday and Co., Inc., 1953.

HOOGENBOOM, ARI and OLIVE, eds. *The Gilded Age.* Englewood Cliffs, New Jersey: Prentice-Hall, 1967.

HOWELLS, WILLIAM DEAN. "A Sennight at the Centennial." *Atlantic Monthly,* vol. 38 (July, 1876), pp. 92–107.

HUNTER, ROBERT. *Violence and the Labor Movement.* New York: Macmillan, 1914.

HUTCHINSON, WILLIAM T. *McCormick.* New York: The Century Co. 1935. 2 vols.

Important Events of the Century. New York: United States Century Publishing Co., 1878.

JAMES, HENRY, ed. *The Letters of William James.* Boston: Atlantic Monthly Press, 1920. 2 vols.

JARRELL, HAMPTON. *Wade Hampton and the Negro: The Road Not Taken.* Columbia: University of South Carolina Press, 1949.

JOHNSON, THOMAS H., ed. *Final Harvest: Emily Dickinson's Poems.* Boston: Little, Brown, 1961.

_____. *The Letters of Emily Dickinson,* vol. iii. Cambridge: Harvard University Press, 1958.

JORDAN, DAVID M. *Roscoe Conkling of New York.* Ithaca: Cornell University Press, 1971.

JOSEPHSON, MATTHEW. *The Politicos, 1865–1896.* New York: Harcourt, Brace, and Co., 1938.

JOYNER, CHRISTOPHER C. "The Hegira of Sitting Bull to Canada, Diplomatic Realpolitik 1876–1881." *Journal of the West,* vol. XIII, no. 2 (April, 1974), pp. 6–18.

KAPLAN, JUSTIN. *Mr. Clemens and Mark Twain: A Biography.* New York: Simon and Schuster, 1966.

KARSTEN, PETER. *The Naval Aristocracy.* New York: Free Press, 1972.

KAUFMAN, STUART B. *Samuel Gompers and the Origins of the American Federation of Labor 1848–1896.* Westport, Connecticut: Greenwood Press, 1973.

KEIR, MALCOLM. *The March of Commerce,* vol. 4, *The Pageant of America.* New Haven: Yale University Press, 1927.

KUGLER, ISRAEL. "The Trade Union Career of Susan B. Anthony." *Labor History,* vol. 2 (winter, 1961), No. 1.

KULL, IRVING S, and NELL M. *A Short Chronology of American History 1422–1950.* New Brunswick: Rutgers University Press, 1952.

LA FEBER, WALTER. *New Empire, An Interpretation of American Expansion, 1860–1898.* Ithaca: Cornell University Press, 1963.

LENG, JOHN. *America in 1876.* Dundee: 1876.

LENS, SIDNEY. *The Forging of the American Empire.* New York: Thomas Y. Crowell, 1971.

_____. *The Labor Wars from the Molly Maguires to the Sitdowns.* New York: Doubleday, 1973.

_____. *Poverty, America's Enduring Paradox.* New York: Thomas Y. Crowell, 1969.

LEYDA, JAY. *The Melville Log: A Documentary Life of Herman Melville, 1819–1891.* New York, Harcourt, 1951. 2 vols.

_____. *The Years and Hours of Emily Dickinson.* New Haven: Yale University Press, 1960.

LIGHT, JAMES F. *John William De Forest.* New York: Twayne Publications, 1965.

LINK, ARTHUR S., ed. *The Papers of Woodrow Wilson,* vol 1. Princeton: Princeton University Press, 1966.

LIPSET, SEYMOUR M., and EARL RAAB. *The Politics of Unreason: Right-wing Extremism in America, 1790–1970.* New York: Harper and Row, 1970.

LYNCH, DENIS TILDEN. *"Boss" Tweed.* New York: Boni and Liveright, 1927.

————. *The Wild Seventies.* New York: D. Appleton-Century Co., 1941.

MACK, EDWARD C. *Peter Cooper.* New York: Duell, Sloan, and Pearce, 1949.

MCJIMSEY, GEORGE T. *Genteel Partisan, Manton Marble.* Ames: Iowa State University Press, 1971.

MCNEILL, GEORGE E. *The Labor Movement, the Problem of Today.* Boston: A. M. Bridgeman and Co., 1886.

MCPHERSON, EDWARD. *A Handbook of Politics for 1876.* New York: Da Capo Press, 1972.

MANDEL, BERNARD. *Samuel Gompers.* Yellow Springs, Ohio: Antioch Press, 1963.

MARTIN, FREDERICK. *The Statesman's Yearbook, 1876.* London: Macmillan, 1876.

MAY, ERNEST R. *Imperial Democracy.* New York: Harper's, 1961.

MERRIAM, GEORGE S. *Life and Times of Samuel Bowles,* vol. 2. New York: The Century Co., 1885.

MILLER, EDWIN H. *Walt Whitman, the Correspondence,* vol. 3. New York: New York University Press, 1964.

MONAGHAN, JAY, ed. *The Book of the American West.* New York: Julian Messner, Inc., 1963.

MORGAN, H. WAYNE. *The Gilded Age: A Reappraisal.* Syracuse: Syracuse University Press, 1963.

————. *William McKinley and His America.* Syracuse: Syracuse University Press, 1963.

MORLEY, CHARLES. *Portrait of America: Letters of Henry Sienkiewicz.* New York: Columbia University Press, 1959.

MORRIS, RICHARD B. *Encyclopedia of American History.* New York: Harper and Row, 1970.

MORRISON, ELTING E., ed. *Letters of Theodore Roosevelt,* vol. 1. Cambridge: Harvard University Press, 1951–1954.

MOTT, FRANK L. *American Journalism: A History of Newspapers in the United States Through Two Hundred and Fifty Years, 1690–1940. New York: Macmillan, 1947.

MUMFORD, LEWIS. Herman Melville. New York: Harcourt Brace, 1929.

NEVINS, ALLAN. Abram S. Hewitt. New York: Harper and Bros., 1935.

———. Hamilton Fish: The Inner History of the Grant Administration. New York, Dodd, Mead, 1936.

———. John D. Rockefeller, vol 1. New York: Scribner, 1953.

NEWMAN, ERNEST. The Life of Richard Wagner, vol. 4. New York: Knopf, 1946.

NEWMARK, HARRIS. Sixty Years in Southern California, 1853–1913. New York: Knickerbocker Press, 1916.

NIBLEY, PRESTON. Brigham Young. Salt Lake City: Deseret News Press, 1936.

NORRIS, JAMES D., and ARTHUR H. SHAFFER. Politics and Patronage in the Gilded Age. Madison: State Historical Society of Wisconsin, 1970.

NYE, RUSSELL B. George Bancroft, Brahmin Rebel. New York: Knopf, 1944.

OBERHOLZER, ELLIS P. A History of the United States Since the Civil War, vol. 3. New York: Macmillan, 1926.

O'CONNOR, RICHARD. The Scandalous Mr. Bennett. New York: Doubleday, 1962.

OFFENBACH, JACQUES. Orpheus in America: Offenbach's Diary of His Journey to the New World, trans. by Lander MacClintock. Bloomington: University of Indiana Press, 1957.

Papers Relating to the Foreign Relations of the United States Transmitted to Congress. Washington: Government Printing Office, 1876.

PEEL, ROBERT. Mary Baker Eddy. New York: Holt, Rinehart, and Winston, 1971.

PENNELL, ELIZABETH R. and JOSEPH. The Life of James McNeill Whistler, vol. 2. Philadelphia: J. B. Lippincott Co., 1908.

PHILLIPS, DAVID L. Letters from California for 1876. Springfield: Illinois State Journal Co., 1877.

PINKERTON, ALLAN. Strikers, Communists, Tramps, and Detectives. New York: G. W. Dillingham Co., 1878.

POLAKOFF, KEITH IAN. The Politics of Inertia, The Election of 1876 and the End of Reconstruction. Baton Rouge: Louisiana State University Press, 1973.

POMERANTZ, SIDNEY I. "Election of 1876," in Arthur M. Schlesinger, Jr.,

The Coming to Power: Critical Elections in American History. New York: Chelsea House Publishers, 1972.

PORTER, KIRK H., and DONALD B. JOHNSON. *National Party Platforms 1840–1968.* Urbana: University of Illinois Press, 1970.

POTTER, JOHN M. *Plots Against Presidents.* New York: Astor-Honor Inc., 1968.

POWDERLY, TERENCE. *Thirty Years of Labor 1859–1889.* Columbus, Ohio: Excelsior Publishing House, 1890.

PRINGLE, HENRY F. *Theodore Roosevelt.* London: Jonathan Cape, Ltd., 1932.

PUTNAM, CARLETON. *Theodore Roosevelt: A Biography,* vol. 1, *The Formative Years.* New York: Scribner, 1958.

QUINT, HOWARD H. *The Forging of American Socialism.* Columbia: University of South Carolina Press, 1953.

RANDEL, WILLIAM PEIRCE. *Centennial, American Life in 1876.* Philadelphia: Chilton Book Company, 1969.

REWALD, JOHN. *The History of Impressionism.* New York: Museum of Modern Art, 1961.

RICHARDSON, JAMES D. *A Compilation of the Messages and Papers of the Presidents,* vol. 7. Washingon: Government Printing Office, 1898.

ROOSEVELT, THEODORE. *Theodore Roosevelt's Diaries of Boyhood and Youth.* New York: Scribner's, 1928.

ROSS, ISHBEL. *Crusades and Crinolines: The Life and Times of Ellen Curtis Demorest and William Jennings Demorest.* New York: Harper's, 1963.

_____. *The General's Wife: The Life of Mrs. Ulysses S. Grant.* New York: Dodd, Mead, 1959.

_____. *The President's Wife, Mary Todd Lincoln: A Biography.* New York: G. P. Putnam's Sons, 1973.

_____. *Silhouette in Diamonds: The Life of Mrs. Potter Palmer.* New York: Harper's, 1960.

ROWLAND, DUNBAR, ed. *Jefferson Davis, Constitutionalist: His Letters, Papers, and Speeches.* New York: J. J. Little and Ives Co., 1923.

RUHL, J. BARTLETT. *The Record of American Diplomacy.* New York: Knopf, 1952.

SANDOZ, MARI. *The Battle of the Little Bighorn.* Philadelphia: J. P. Lippincott Co., 1966.

SAVELL, ISABELLE K. *The Executive Mansion in Albany, An Informal History, 1856–1960.* Her copyright, no publisher listed, 1960.

SCHLESINGER, ARTHUR M., JR. *History of Presidential Elections.*

SEITZ, DONALD C. *The James Gordon Bennetts, Father and Son, Proprietors of the New York* Herald. Indianapolis: The Bobbs-Merrill Co., 1928.

SHANNON, FREDERICK A. *The Centennial Years.* New York: Doubleday, 1967.

SHANNON, R. T. *Gladstone and the Bulgarian Agitation of 1876.* London: Thomas Nelson and Sons Ltd., 1963.

SHEPARD, ODELL, ed. *The Journals of Bronson Alcott.* Boston: Little, Brown and Co., 1938.

SIMMONS, DAWN L. *A Rose for Mrs. Lincoln.* Boston: Beacon Press, 1970.

SIMON, JOHN Y., ed. *The Personal Memoirs of Julia Dent Grant (Mrs. Ulysses S. Grant).* New York: G. P. Putnam's Sons, 1975.

SINGLETON, ESTHER. *The Story of the White House.* 1907 work reissued in one volume. New York: Benjamin Blonn, Inc., 1969.

SINKLER, GEORGE. *Racial Attitudes of United States Presidents.* Garden City, New York: Doubleday, 1971.

SMITH, SAMUEL DENNY. *The Negro in Congress 1870–1901.* Chapel Hill: University of North Carolina Press, 1940.

SMITH, THEODORE C. *The Life and Letters of James Abram Garfield,* vol 1. New Haven: Yale University Press, 1925.

SMITH, WILLIAM ERNEST. *The Francis Preston Blair Family in Politics.* New York: Macmillan, 1933.

SPROAT, JOHN G. *"The Best Men," Liberal Reformers in the Gilded Age.* New York: Oxford University Press, 1968.

STEVENS, SYLVESTER K. *American Expansion in Hawaii, 1842–1898.* New York: Russell and Russell, 1968.

STEVENSON, ADLAI E. *Something of Men I Have Known.* Chicago: A. C. McClurg and Co., 1909.

STEVENSON, ELIZABETH. *Lafcadio Hearn.* New York: Macmillan, 1961.

STEWART, EDGAR I. *Custer's Luck.* Norman: University of Oklahoma Press, 1955.

STODDARD, HENRY L. *As I Knew Them.* New York: Harper's, 1927.

STONE, IRVING. *They Also Ran: The Story of the Men Who Were Defeated for the Presidency.* Garden City, New York: Doubleday, Doran and Company, Inc., 1944.

TAYLOR, TIM. *The Book of Presidents.* New York: Arno Press, 1972.

TEBBELL, JOHN. *From Rags to Riches: Horatio Alger Jr. and the American Dream.* New York: Macmillan, 1963.

THAYER, WILLIAM ROSCOE. *Life and Letters of John Hay*. Boston: Houghton Mifflin Co., 1915. 2 vols.

TRACHTENBERG, ALAN, ed. *Democratic Vistas 1860–1880*. New York: George Braziller, 1970.

TURNER, JUSTIN G. and LINDA L. *Mary Todd Lincoln: Her Life and Letters*. New York: Knopf, 1972.

UNITED STATES BUREAU OF THE CENSUS. *Historical Statistics of the United States . . . to 1957*. Washington: Government Printing Office, 1960.

UNGER, IRWIN. *The Greenback Era: A Social and Political History of American Finance, 1865–1879*. Princeton: Princeton University Press, 1964.

UTLEY, ROBERT M. *Frontier Regulars: The United States Army and the Indian 1866–1891*. New York: Macmillan, 1973.

VAN ALSTYNE, RICHARD W. *The American Empire: Historical Pattern and Evolution*. London: Routledge and Paul, 1960.

VESTAL, STANLEY. "The Man Who Killed Custer," *American Heritage*, vol. VIII, no. 2 (February, 1957), pp. 4–9, 90–91.

WARE, NORMAN. *The Labor Movement in the United States 1860–1895*. New York: Appleton, 1929.

WASHBURN, WILCOMB. *The Indian in America*. New York: Harper and Row, 1973.

WILLIAMS, MARY W. *Dom Pedro the Magnificent*. New York: Octagon Books, 1966.

WILLIAMS, T. HARRY, ed. *Hayes, The Diary of a President 1876–1881*. New York: David McKay, 1964.

WILLSON, BECKLES. *American Ambassadors to England (1785–1928)*. London: John Murray, 1928.

WOODWARD, C. VANN. "The Lowest Ebb," *American Heritage*, vol. VIII, no. 3 (April, 1957), pp. 53–56, 108.

————. *Reunion and Reaction*. New York: Doubleday, 1956.

NOTES

JANUARY 1, Washington: President Grant Celebrates New Year's

1. Esther Singleton, *The Story of the White House* (New York: Benjamin Blonn, 1969), pp. 147 and *passim*.

2. John Y. Simon, ed., *The Personal Memoirs of Julia Dent Grant (Mrs. Ulysses S. Grant)* (New York: Putnam, 1975), p. 175.

3. C. Vann Woodward, "The Lowest Ebb," *American Heritage* vol. VIII, no. 3 (April, 1957), pp. 53–56, 108. This is an able summary of the scandals of the Grant administration, which are mentioned in many of the books listed in the bibliography.

4. Sidney I. Pomerantz, "Election of 1876," in Arthur M. Schlesinger, Jr., *The Coming to Power: Critical Elections in American History* (New York: Chelsea House, 1972), p. 180.

5. William Peirce Randel, *Centennial, American Life in 1876* (Philadelphia: Chilton, 1969), p. 2. Also see Dee Brown, *The Year of the Century: 1876* (New York: Scribner's, 1966), p. 7. The present author is greatly indebted to these two works. The first is a mine of information and bibliography on American society in this era. The second is a racy, literate, informative treatment of major themes of the centennial year.

JANUARY 3, Chicago: Chicago *Daily News* Prints First Issue

1. Frank L. Mott, *American Journalism: A History of Newspapers in the United States Through Two Hundred and Fifty Years 1690–1940* (New York: Macmillan, 1947), pp. 462–466. This book is the main source for most of this section. Also see Brown, *op. cit.*, pp. 25, 59–61; Randel, *op. cit.*, pp. 362–64.

2. Mott, *op. cit.*, p. 416.

3. Julia C. Harris, *The Life and Letters of Joel Chandler Harris* (Boston: Houghton Mifflin, 1918).

4. Mott, *op. cit.*, p. 386.

JANUARY 4, Albany: Governor Tilden Attacks Republican Administration

1. Alexander C. Flick, *Samuel Jones Tilden: A Study in Political Sagacity* (Port Washington: Kennicat Press, 1963), pp. 277–78.

2. *Ibid.*, p. 488. See also Irving Stone, *They Also Ran: The Story of the Men Who Were Defeated for the Presidency* (Garden City: Doubleday, Doran, 1944), pp. 193–212.

3. Isabelle K. Savell, *The Executive Mansion in Albany: An Informal History* (Albany: n.p., 1960), p. 5.

4. Flick, *op. cit.*, p. 295.

5. Henry L. Stoddard, *As I Knew Them* (New York: Harper, 1927), p. 80.

6. Flick, *op. cit.*, p. 279.

7. Keith Ian Polakoff, *The Politics of Inertia, The Election of 1876 and the End of Reconstruction* (Baton Rouge: Louisiana State University Press, 1973), p. 71.

JANUARY 10, Washington: Representative Blaine Denounces Amnesty Bill

1. Polakoff, *op. cit.*, p. 16; Randel, *op. cit.*, p. 242.

2. Pomerantz, *op. cit.*, pp. 181, 194.

3. Randel, *op. cit.*, p. 221.

4. Pomerantz, *op. cit.*, p. 180.

5. *Ibid.*

6. Randel, *op. cit.*, p. 345.

7. Bunbar Rowland, ed., *Jefferson Davis, Constitutionalist, His Letters, Papers, and Speeches* (New York: J. J. Little and Ives Co., 1923), pp. 478, 483.

8. *Ibid.*, p. 486.

9. Richmond *Daily Dispatch*, January 15, 1876.

10. David M. Jordan, *Roscoe Conkling of New York* (Ithaca: Cornell University Press, 1971), p. 230. Also see Pomerantz, *op. cit.*, pp. 184–85.

11. Seymour M. Lipset and Earl Raab, *The Politics of Unreason, Right-wing Extremism in America 1790–1970* (New York: Harper, 1970), p. 75.

JANUARY 10, New York: Peter Cooper Speaks Against the Money Power

1. Samuel Gompers, *Seventy Years of Life and Labor* (New York: Dutton, 1925), p. 135.

2. Edward C. Mack, *Peter Cooper* (New York: Duell, Sloan, and Pearce, 1949), p. 361.

3. *Ibid.*, p. 376.

4. *Ibid.*, p. 374.

5. *Ibid.*, p. 376.

6. *Ibid.*, p. 366.

7. John R. Commons et al., *History of Labor in the United States,* vol. 2 (New York: Macmillan, 1918), pp. 167–69.

8. Randel, *op. cit.*, p. 278.

9. Flick, *op. cit.*, p. 280.

JANUARY 16, Madrid: Spain Fears War over Cuba

1. J. Bartlett Ruhl, *The Record of American Diplomacy* (New York: Knopf, 1952), p. 371.

2. Samuel F. Bemis, ed., *The American Secretaries of State and Their Diplomacy* (New York: Cooper Square Publications, 1963), p. 201.

3. F. E. Chadwick, *The Relations of the United States and Spain* (New York: Scribner's, 1909), pp. 375–76.

4. Ruhl, *op. cit.*, p. 371.

5. John D. Bergamini, *The Spanish Bourbons: The History of a Tenacious Dynasty* (New York: Putnam, 1974), pp. 254 ff.

6. Ruhl, *op. cit.*, p. 371.

7. Bemis, *op. cit.*, p. 194.

8. Samuel F. Bemis, *A Diplomatic History of the United States* (New York: Holt, 1950), p. 436.

9. Walter R. Herrick, Jr., *The American Naval Revolution* (Baton Rouge: Louisiana State University Press, 1966), p. 19.

JANUARY 18, Mauch Chunk: First Molly Maguire Goes on Trial

1. For general background on the Irish coal miners, see J. Walter Coleman, *The Molly Maguire Riots: Industrial Conflict in the Pennsylvania Coal Region* (Richmond, Va.: Garrett and Massie, 1936), pp. 3 ff.; Harry W. Aurand, *From the Molly Maguires to the United Mine Workers* (Philadelphia: Temple University Press, 1973), pp. 104–6; Commons, *op. cit.*, pp. 181–83.

2. Sidney Lens, *The Labor Wars from the Molly Maguires to the Sitdowns* (New York: Doubleday, 1973), p. 11.

3. Wayne G. Broehl, Jr., *The Molly Maguires* (Cambridge:Harvard University Press, 1964), p. 234.

4. Lens, *op. cit.*, p. 23.

5. Coleman, *op. cit.*, p. 103.

6. *Ibid.*, p. 112.

JANUARY 24, Hartford: Mart Twain Reads a Gloomy Tale

1. Justin Kaplan, *Mr. Clemens and Mark Twain: A Biography* (New York: Simon and Schuster, 1966), p. 175.

2. *Ibid.*, p. 193.

3. *Ibid.*

4. *Ibid.*, p. 182.

5. *Ibid.*, p. 181.

6. *Ibid.*, pp. 168–69.

7. *Ibid.*, pp. 195–96.

8. *Ibid.*, p. 18.

JANUARY 25, Washington: Congress Votes Money for the Centennial

1. Columbia, S.C., *Daily Register,* June 27, 1876.

2. Brown, *op. cit.,* pp. 10–12, 18–23.

3. Randel, *op. cit.,* pp. 283–89.

JANUARY 31, Red Cloud Agency: Deadline Passes for Hostile Indians

1. Edgar I. Stewart, *Custer's Luck* (Norman: University of Oklahoma, 1955), p. 32.

2. *Ibid.*, p. 26.

3. Robert M. Utley, *Frontier Regulars, the United States Army and the Indian 1866–1891* (New York: Macmillan, 1973), p. 53.

4. Dee Brown, *Bury My Heart at Wounded Knee* (New York: Holt, 1970), p. 293. This is a highly acclaimed account of the Indian wars from the Indians' point of view.

5. James D. Richardson, *A Compilation of the Messages and Papers of the Presidents,* vol. VII (Washington: Government Printing Office, 1898), p. 358.

6. Utley, *op. cit.,* p. 246.

7. Stewart, *op. cit.,* p. 65.

8. Brown, *Bury,* p. 283.

9. Stoddard, *op. cit.,* p. 150.

10. Utley, *op. cit.,* p. 254.

11. *Ibid.*, p. 255.

FEBRUARY 1, Washington: Congress Considers Resumption Act

1. New York *Tribune,* February 2, 1876.

2. Irwin Unger, *The Greenback Era: A Social and Political History of American Finance, 1865–1879* (Princeton: Princeton University Press, 1964), p. 144. This section is generally based on Unger's book.

3. Randel, *op. cit.,* p. 195.

4. Unger, *op. cit.,* p. 292.

5. Mack, *op. cit.,* p. 359.

FEBRUARY 8, St. Louis: Whiskey Ring Trial Involves Grant's Secretary

1. Randel, *op. cit.*, p. 205; Brown, *1876*, pp. 83–91; Simon, *op. cit.*, pp. 186–87.

2. Claude G. Bowers, *The Tragic Era: The Revolution After Lincoln* (Cambridge: Riverside Press, 1929), p. 465.

3. Brown, *1876*, p. 89; Randel, *op. cit.*, p. 204.

FEBRUARY 8, Chicago: Army Plans War on Sioux

1. Utley, *op. cit.*, p. 254.

2. *Ibid.*, pp. 51–52.

3. *Ibid.*, p. 15.

4. *Ibid.*, p. 35.

5. *Ibid.*, pp. 16 ff. Randel, *op. cit.*, p. 136.

6. Utley, *op. cit.*, p. 62.

7. *Ibid.*, p. 22.

8. *Ibid.*, p. 85.

9. *Ibid.*, p. 47.

10. *Ibid.*, p. 20.

11. *Ibid.*, p. 23.

12. *Ibid.*, p. 47.

13. *Ibid.*, p. 255.

14. *Ibid.*, p. 43.

15. *Ibid.*, p. 49.

16. Stewart, *op. cit.*, p. 85.

17. Brown, *Bury*, p. 287.

FEBRUARY 9, Boston: Henry Adams Proposes Liberal Republicanism

1. Worthington C. Ford, ed., *Letters of Henry Adams* (Boston: Houghton Mifflin, 1930), p. 273.

2. James Truslow Adams, *The Adams Family* (Boston: Little, Brown, 1930), p. 335.

3. *Ibid.*, p. 322.

4. Ford, *op. cit.*, p. 288.

5. Harold D. Cater, *Henry Adams and His Friends* (New York: Octagon Books, 1970), p. 80.

6. Adams, *op. cit.*, p. 323.

7. Ford, *op. cit.*, p. 288.

8. *Ibid.*, p. 272.

9. *Ibid.*, p. 281.

10. *Ibid.*, pp. 278–79.

11. *Ibid.*, p. 276.

FEBRUARY 14, Washington: Bell Files for Telephone Patent

1. Robert V. Bruce, *Alexander Graham Bell and the Conquest of Solitude* (Boston: Little, Brown, 1973), p. 168.

2. *Ibid.*, p. 130.

3. L. Sprague De Camp, *The Heroic Age of American Invention* (Garden City, N.Y.: Doubleday, 1961), p. 165.

4. *Ibid.*, p. 158.

5. Randel, *op. cit.*, p. 180.

6. *Ibid.*, pp. 178–79.

FEBRUARY 16, Lynn, Massachusetts: Bronson Alcott Visits Mary Baker Glover

1. Edwin Dakin, *Mrs. Eddy, the Biography of a Virginal Mind* (New York: Scribner, 1929), p. 117.

2. Robert Peel, *Mary Baker Eddy* (New York: Holt, Rinehart, and Winston, 1971), p. 8.

3. Odell Shepard, ed., *The Journals of Bronson Alcott* (Boston: Little, Brown, 1938), p. 464.

4. *Ibid.*, pp. 464–65.

5. Mary Baker Eddy, *Retrospection and Introspection* (Norwood, Mass.: The Plimpton Press, 1891), p. 13.

6. *Ibid.*, p. 15.

7. Norman Beasley, *Mary Baker Eddy* (New York: Duell, Sloan, and Pearce, 1963), p. 40.

8. Dakin, *op. cit.*, p. 115.

9. Shepard, *op. cit.*, p. 465.

10. Dakin, *op. cit.*, p. 115.

11. Peel, *op. cit.*, p. 16.

12. *Ibid.*, p. 14.

13. Jean Burton, *Lydia Pinkham Is Her Name* (New York: Farrar, Straus, 1949).

FEBRUARY 19, London: Schenck Resigns as Minister to Britain

1. Beckles Willson, *American Ambassadors to England (1785–1928)* (London: John Murray, 1928), p. 359.

2. *Ibid.*, pp. 366–67. See also Ellis P. Oberholtzer, *A History of the United States Since the Civil War*, vol. 3 (New York: Macmillan, 1926), p. 186.

3. Brown, *1876*, p. 57. See also George W. Curtis, ed., *The Correspondence of John L. Motley*, vol. II (New York: Harper, 1889) p. 390; Richard Henry Dana, *Hospitable England in the Seventies: The Diary of a Young American 1875–1876* (Boston: Houghton Mifflin, 1921).

4. Willson, *op. cit.*, pp. 367–68.

5. Richardson, *op. cit.*, pp. 370–73.

FEBRUARY 22, Princeton: Woodrow Wilson Begins Commonplace Book

1. Arthur S. Link, ed., *The Papers of Woodrow Wilson*, vol. 1 (Princeton: Princeton University Press, 1966), pp. 88–102, 227.

2. *Ibid.*, p. 242.

3. *Ibid.*, p. 217.

4. *Ibid.*, p. 28.

5. *Ibid.*, p. 135.

FEBRUARY 23, Liverpool: Sienkiewicz Sails for America.

1. Charles Morley, *Portrait of America: Letters of Henry Sienkiewicz* (New York: Columbia University Press, 1959), p. 1.

2. Frederick A. Shannon, *The Centennial Years* (New York: Doubleday, 1967), p. 4.

3. Morley, *op. cit.*, pp. 3–5.

4. *Ibid.*, p. 8.

5. *Ibid.*, p. 4.

6. *Ibid.*, p. 11.

7. *Ibid.*, p. 6.

8. *Ibid.*, p. 21.

9. *Ibid.*, p. 12.

MARCH 2, Washington: Belknap Resigns as Secretary of War

1. The Belknap scandal is treated at length in Randel, *op. cit.*, pp. 207–14; Brown, *1876*, pp. 87–94; Simon, *op. cit.*, pp. 189–92.

2. Randel, *op. cit.*, p. 215.

3. New York *Herald,* March 10, 1876.

4. Randel, *op. cit.,* p. 208.

5. Stewart, *op. cit.,* p. 125.

6. Bowers, *op. cit.,* p. 473.

7. *Ibid.,* p. 472.

8. *Ibid.,* p. 476.

MARCH 4, Camden, New Jersey: Walt Whitman Stirs Up Controversy in Press

1. Edwin H. Miller, ed., *Walt Whitman, The Correspondence,* vol. III (New York: New York University Press, 1964), p. 27.

2. *Ibid.,* p. 28.

3. *Ibid.,* p. 19.

4. *Ibid.,* p. 47.

5. *Ibid.,* p. 32.

6. *Ibid.,* p. 47.

7. *Ibid.,* p. 25.

8. *Ibid.,* pp. 48, 29.

9. *Ibid.,* p. 20.

10. *Ibid.,* p. 27.

11. Randel, *op. cit.,* p. 351.

12. *Ibid.,* p. 358.

13. Miller, *op. cit.,* p. 28.

14. *Ibid.,* p. 28, note 43.

15. *Ibid.,* pp. 30–31, notes 51–52.

MARCH 8, New York: Tweed Found Guilty of Stealing Millions

1. Alexander B. Callow, Jr., *The Tweed Ring* (New York: Oxford University Press, 1966), p. 293.

2. *Ibid.,* pp. vii, 166. See also Denis Tilden Lynch, *"Boss" Tweed* (New York: Boni and Liveright, 1927).

3. Callow, *op. cit.,* p. 10.

4. *Ibid.,* p. 300.

5. *Ibid.,* p. 268; Mott, , *op. cit.,* pp. 383–84.

6. Callow, *op. cit.,* p. 265.

MARCH 10, Boston: Bell Says First Words over Telephone

1. Bruce, *op. cit.*, p. 181; De Camp, *op. cit.*, p. 159.
2. Bruce, *op. cit.*, p. 144.
3. *Ibid.*, p. 172.
4. *Ibid.*, p. 175.

MARCH 28, Washington: Grant Falls Ill

1. Brown, *1876*, pp. 110–11.
2. *Ibid.*, p. 108.
3. Richardson, *op. cit.*, pp. 361–66.
4. Brown, *1876*, p. 109.

MARCH 29, Washington: Colonel Custer Testifies in Congress

1. Sidney Lens, *The Forging of the American Empire* (New York: Crowell, 1971), p. 7.
2. Utley, *op. cit.*, p. x.
3. Stewart, *op. cit.*, p. 167.
4. *Ibid.*, p. 58.
5. Brown, *1876*, pp. 172–73.

APRIL 2, Paris: Henry James and Mary Cassatt Admire Impressionist Exhibition

1. John Rewald, *History of Impressionism* (New York: Museum of Modern Art, 1961), p. 369.
2. *Ibid.*
3. *Ibid.*, pp. 370–72. See also Dana, *op. cit.*, p. 254.
4. Randel, *op. cit.*, p. 357.
5. Gay W. Allen, *William James, A Biography* (New York: Viking, 1967), pp. 206–7.
6. Randel, *op. cit.*, pp. 356–57.
7. Allen, *op. cit.*, p. 206.
8. David Lowe, "Mary Cassatt," *American Heritage* vol. 25, No. 1 (December 1975) p. 21.
9. *Ibid.*, Rewald, *op. cit.*, p. 409.
10. Lowe, *op. cit.*, p. 98.

11. For a general discussion of the fine arts in America, see Randel, *op. cit.*, pp. 384 ff.

APRIL 10, New York: Millionaire A. T. Stewart Dies

1. William Edmond and William E. Curtis, *Letters and Journals* (New York: Case, Lockwood, and Brainard, 1926), p. 336.

2. *Appleton's Annual Cyclopedia and Register of Important Events of the Year: 1876* (New York: D. Appleton and Co., 1877), p. 735–36.

3. Herbert Ashbury, *The Gangs of New York* (New York: Knopf, 1927), p. 218.

4. Columbia, S.C., *Daily Register,* April 21, 1876.

5. *Socialist,* April 22, 1876.

6. Stephen Birmingham, *Our Crowd: The Great Jewish Families of New York* (New York: Harper and Row, 1967), pp. 141–43.

7. Ashbury, *op. cit.*, pp. 221–22.

8. Stewart H. Holbrook, *The Age of the Moguls* (Garden City, N.Y.: Doubleday, 1953).

APRIL 15, New York: Emperor Dom Pedro Arrives in the United States

1. Mary W. Williams, *Dom Pedro the Magnificent* (New York: Octagon Books, 1966), pp. 189–91.

2. *Ibid.,* p. 188.

3. *Ibid.,* p. 191.

4. Columbia, S.C., *Daily Register,* April 9 and May 3, 1876.

5. Williams, *op. cit.*, p. 209.

APRIL 17, Pittsburgh: Labor Conference Endorses Greenbackism

1. *Socialist,* April 29, 1876.

2. Israel Kugler, "The Trade Union Career of Susan B. Anthony," *Labor History,* vol. 2 (Winter, 1961), p. 100.

3. On the general history of the NLU, see Commons, *op. cit.*, pp. 86 ff.

4. On the April conference, see *ibid.*, pp. 201–2, 236; Unger, *op. cit.*, pp. 301–2.

5. *Socialist,* April 29, 1876.

6. Norman Ware, *The Labor Movement in the United States 1860–1895* (New York: Appleton, 1929), p. 35.

7. Commons, *op. cit.*, p. 239.

8. *Ibid.,* p. 238.

APRIL 18, Washington: Grant Vetoes Salary Bill

1. Edward McPherson, *A Handbook of Politics for 1876* (New York: Da Capo Press, 1972), p. 149; Richardson, *op. cit.*, pp. 380–81.

2. Randel, *op. cit.*, pp. 262–63, 278–79.

3. For 1876 figures, McPherson, *op. cit.*, p. 238; for 1976 figures, New York *Times*, February 2, 1975, p. 22.

APRIL 24, Washington: Blaine Defends Himself in Congress

1. Pomerantz, *op. cit.*, p. 185.

2. Theodore C. Smith, *The Life and Letters of James Abram Garfield*, vol. 1 (New Haven: Yale University Press, 1925), p. 599.

3. Randel, *op. cit.*, pp. 217–18.

4. Brown, *1876*, p. 199.

5. Smith, *op. cit.*, pp. 598, 601.

6. Stoddard, *op. cit.*, p. 89.

7. Jordan, *op. cit.*, p. 233.

8. *Ibid.*, p. 232.

9. Smith, *op. cit.*, pp. 596–97; Jordan, *op. cit.*, p. 230.

10. Polakoff, *op. cit.*, p. 32.

11. *Ibid.*

12. *Ibid.*, p. 38.

MAY 4, Pottsville, Pennsylvania: Gowen Prosecutes Molly Maguires Wholesale

1. Coleman, *op. cit.*, p. 99.

2. Broehl, *op. cit.*, p. 144.

3. *Ibid.*, p. 296.

4. Coleman, *op. cit.*, p. 75.

5. *Ibid.*, pp. 73–75.

6. *Ibid.*, p. 127.

7. *Ibid.*, p. 110.

8. *Ibid.*, p. 119.

9. *Ibid.*, p. 133.

10. Broehl, *op. cit.*, p. 302.

11. Coleman, *op. cit.*, p. 129.

12. *Ibid.*, pp. 141–42.

13. *Ibid.*, p. 142.

MAY 4, Chicago: Custer Is Arrested

1. Brown, *1876*, p. 175.

2. Stewart, *op. cit.*, pp. 134–35.

3. Brown, *1876*, p. 176.

4. Mari Sandoz, *The Battle of the Little Bighorn* (Philadelphia: Lippincott, 1966), p. 27. Also, Stewart, *op. cit.*, p. 138.

5. Stewart, *op. cit.*, p. 222.

MAY 6, New York: Maestro Offenbach Arrives in America

1. Jacques Offenbach, *Orpheus in America, Offenbach's Diary of His Journey to the New World* (trans. by Lander MacClintock (Bloomington: University of Indiana Press, 1957), pp. 9–15.

2. *Ibid.*, p. 48.

3. *Ibid.*, p. 21.

4. *Ibid.*, pp. 22–23.

5. Brown, *1876*, pp. 303–5.

6. Offenbach, *op. cit.*, p. 46.

7. *Ibid.*, p. 54.

8. *Ibid.*, p. 74.

9. *Ibid.*, p. 55.

10. *Ibid.*, pp. 60–62.

MAY 10, Philadelphia: Centennial Exhibition Opens

1. Brown, *1876*, pp. 112–33. This is a detailed, very colorful account of opening day. See also Randel, *op. cit.*, p. 290 ff.

2. Morley, *op. cit.*, p. 119.

3. Brown, *1876*, p. 127.

4. Williams, *op. cit.*, p. 197.

5. Brown, *1876*, pp. 138–45.

MAY 15, New York: Free Conference of Republican Liberals Meets

1. See Polakoff, *op. cit.*, p. 140; Pomerantz, *op. cit.*, p. 184; Randel, *op. cit.*, p. 216; John G. Sproat, *"The Best Men," Liberal Reformers in the Gilded Age* (New York: Oxford University Press, 1968), pp. 90–92.

2. Brown, *1876*, pp. 203–4.

3. *Ibid.*

4. *Socialist,* June 17, 1876.

MAY 17, Philadelphia: William Dean Howells Visits Centennial

1. For a general description of the Centennial, see *Appleton's, op. cit.,* pp. 262–81.

2. William Dean Howells, "A Sennight at the Centennial," *Atlantic Monthly.* vol. 38 (July, 1876), p. 92.

3. About Howells, see Randel, *op. cit.,* pp. 92, 365 ; Brown, *1876,* pp. 51–53.

4. Howells, *op. cit.,* p. 97.

5. *Ibid.,* p. 104.

6. *Ibid.,* p. 93.

7. *Ibid.,* p. 96.

8. Allen, *op. cit.,* p. 209.

9. Howells, *op. cit.,* pp. 93–95.

10. *Ibid.,* pp. 96 ff.

11. *Ibid.,* p. 96.

12. Harris Newmark, *Sixty Years in Southern California, 1853–1913* (New York: Knickerbocker Press, 1916), p. 497.

13. Howells, *op. cit.,* p. 103.

14. *Ibid.,* pp. 100–1.

15. *Ibid.,* p. 106.

16. *Ibid.,* pp. 106–7.

MAY 18, Indianapolis: Greenbackers Hold First National Convention

1. Mack, *op. cit.,* pp. 366–67.

2. Commons, *op. cit.,* p. 170.

3. Unger, *op. cit.,* p. 306.

4. *Ibid.,* McPherson, *op. cit.,* p. 224.

5. Unger, *op. cit.,* p. 307.

6. Fred E. Haynes, *Third Party Movements Since the Civil War* (Iowa City: State Historical Society of Iowa, 1916), p. 122.

7. Unger, *op. cit.,* p. 308.

8. The pitfalls of using handbooks and almanacs are shown by the fact that Greenback candidate for Vice President is listed variously as Samuel F. Cary (correct), Samuel F. Carey, Samuel F. Perry, and Senator Booth.

9. Mack, *op. cit.,* p. 367.

MAY 23, Boston: First No-Hit Baseball Game Takes Place

1. Gorton Carruth et al., *The Encyclopedia of American Facts and Dates,* 5th

ed. (New York: Crowell, 1970), pp. 309–13. Also see Randel, *op. cit.,* pp. 319–20.

JUNE 1, St. George, Utah: Brigham Young Celebrates Birthday

1. Preston Nibley, *Brigham Young* (Salt Lake City: Deseret News Press, 1936), p. 524.

2. Stanley P. Hirshon, *The Lion of the Lord: A Biography of Brigham Young* (New York: Knopf, 1969) p. 313.

3. *Ibid.,* p. 303.

4. Williams, *op. cit.,* p. 193.

5. Hirshon, *op. cit.,* p. 182.

6. *Ibid.,* p. 189.

7. *Ibid.,* pp. 212, 311.

8. John Leng, *America in 1876* (Dundee: 1876), pp. 196–97.

9. Hirshon, *op. cit.,* p. 317.

10. *Ibid.,* p. 313.

11. Newmark, *op. cit.,* p. 498.

12. Hirshon, *op. cit.,* p. 320.

JUNE 3, New York: Herman Melville Publishes *Charel*

1. Jay Leyda, *The Melville Log: A Documentary Life of Herman Melville,* vol. 2 (New York: Harcourt, 1951), pp. 750–56.

2. Lewis Mumford, *Herman Melville* (New York: Harcourt, Brace, 1929), p. 329.

3. Leyda, *op. cit.,* p. 731.

4. *Ibid.,* p. 753.

5. *Ibid.,* p. 747.

6. *Ibid.,* p. 756.

7. Brown, *1876,* pp. 47 ff.

8. Randel, *op. cit.,* p. 352.

9. *Ibid.,* pp. 354–55.

JUNE 9, Boston: Dom Pedro Tours New England

1. Williams, *op. cit.,* p. 203.

2. *Ibid.,* p. 205.

3. *Ibid.,* p. 207.

JUNE 11, Washington: Blaine Faints at Church

1. Polakoff, *op. cit.*, pp. 51 ff.; Brown, *1876*, pp. 204–05.
2. Smith, *op. cit.*, p. 599.
3. *Ibid.*, p. 600.
4. Randel, *op. cit.*, p. 219.
5. Ford, *op. cit*., p. 286.
6. Polakoff, *op. cit.*, p. 52.
7. Smith, *op. cit.*, p. 601.

JUNE 14, San Francisco: California Adopts Anti-Chinese Ordinances

1. Ira B. Gross, *History of the Labor Movement in California* (Berkeley: University of California Press, 1935), pp. 85 ff.; Tyler Dennett, *Americans in East Asia* (New York: Macmillan, 1922), pp. 540 and *passim.*
2. Morley, *op. cit.*, p. 262.
3. David L. Phillips, *Letters from California for 1876* (Springfield: Illinois State Journal Co., 1877), pp. 35, 133.

JUNE 14, Valley of the Rosebud: Sitting Bill Has Vision of Victory

1. Stewart, *op. cit.*, pp. 193 ff.; Brown, *Bury*, p. 290.
2. *Ibid.*, p. 288.
3. *Ibid.*, p. 290.
4. Lens, *Empire*, pp. 140–41; Utley, *op. cit.*, pp. 243–44.
5. Stewart, *op. cit.*, p. 3.
6. Brown, *Bury*, p. 179.
7. Lens, *Empire*, p. 40.
8. *Ibid.*, p. 41.
9. Stewart, *op. cit.*, p. 308.
10. Utley, *op. cit.*, pp. 262–63, 269.
11. Sandoz, *op. cit.*, p. 7.

JUNE 15, Chicago: Mrs. Lincoln Is Pronounced Sane

1. Dawn L. Simmons, *A Rose for Mrs. Lincoln* (Boston: Beacon Press, 1970), pp. 184–93.
2. Ishbel Ross, *The President's Wife, Mary Todd Lincoln: A Biography* (New York: Putnam, 1973), p. 316.
3. *Ibid.*, p. 318.

4. Justin G. and Linda L. Turner, *Mary Todd Lincoln, Her Life and Letters* (New York: Knopf, 1972), p. 615.

5. Simmons, *op. cit.,* p. 190.

JUNE 16, Cincinnati: Republican National Convention Meets

1. Pomerantz, *op. cit.,* p. 187. See also the colorful description in Brown, *1876,* pp. 205–10.

2. Jordan, *op. cit.,* p. 238; Denis Tilden Lynch, *The Wild Seventies* (New York: D. Appleton-Century Co., 1941), p. 359.

3. Edward E. Hale, *James Freeman Clarke* (Cambridge: Riverside Press, 1891), p. 350.

4. Kirk H. Porter and Donald B. Johnson, *National Party Platforms, 1840–1968* (Urbana: University of Illinois Press, 1970), p. 49.

5. Brown, *1876,* pp. 148–51.

6. Porter, *op. cit.,* pp. 47–49.

7. Randel, *op. cit.,* p. 218; Brown, *1876,* p. 208.

8. Pomerantz, *op. cit.,* p. 187.

9. Jordan, *op. cit.,* p. 241; Lynch, *Seventies,* p. 359.

10. Brown, *1876,* p. 210.

11. Ford, *op. cit.,* p. 288.

12. Brown, *1876,* p. 209.

13. Pomerantz, *op. cit.,* p. 187.

JUNE 19, Philadelphia: Offenbach Gives Concert Tour

1. Offenbach, *op. cit.,* p. 96.

2. *Ibid.,* pp. 94–95.

3. *Ibid.,* pp. 82 ff.

4. *Ibid.,* pp. 69–73.

5. *Ibid.,* p. 171.

JUNE 19, Princeton: Wilson Predicts No Bicentennial

1. Link, *op. cit.,* p. 143.

2. *Ibid.,* p. 135.

3. *Ibid.,* p. 143.

4. *Ibid.,* p. 192.

5. *Ibid.,* p. 142.

6. *Ibid.*

7. *Ibid.*, p. 148.

8. *Ibid.*, p. 166.

9. *Ibid.*, p. 153.

10. *Ibid.*, p. 188.

11. *Ibid.*, p. 190.

JUNE 20, Anaheim Landing, California: Sienkiewicz Begins Commune in California

1. Morley, *op. cit.*, p. 123. For a description of the place, see Phillips, *op. cit.*, p. 120.

2. Morley, *op. cit.*, pp. 41–57.

3. *Ibid.*, p. 68.

4. *Ibid.*, p. 84.

5. *Ibid.*, p. 88.

6. *Ibid.*, p. xi.

7. *Ibid.*, p. 219. Also see Newmark, *op. cit.*, p. 494.

8. Morley, *op. cit.*, p. 221. See Hirsch, *op. cit.*, p. 146.

9. Morley, *op. cit.*, p. 216.

10. *Ibid.*, pp. 90 ff.

11. *Ibid.*, pp. 226–27.

12. *Ibid.*, p. 105.

13. *Ibid.*, p. 239.

JUNE 25, Valley of the Little Bighorn: Custer Rides to His Last Stand

1. Sandoz, *op. cit.*, p. 57.

2. Stewart, *op. cit.*, p. 316.

3. *Ibid.*, p. 240.

4. Sandoz, *op. cit.*, p. 49.

5. Stewart, *op. cit.*, p. 330.

6. *Ibid.*, p. 341.

7. Brown, *Bury*, pp. 291, 294.

8. Stewart, *op. cit.*, p. 414.

9. *Ibid.*, p. 459.

10. Stanley Vestal, "The Man Who Killed Custer," *American Heritage,* vol. VIII, no. 2 (February, 1957), pp. 4–9, 90–91.

11. Vine Deloria, *Custer Died for Your Sins: An Indian Manifesto* (New York: Macmillan, 1969), p. 149.

12. Brown, *Bury,* p. 294.

13. *Ibid.,* p. 296.

14. Stewart, *op. cit.,* p. 490.

15. Deloria, *op. cit.,* p. 149.

16. Sandoz, *op. cit.,* p. 176.

17. Stewart, *op. cit.,* p. 280.

18. Utley, *op. cit.,* p. 269.

19. Stewart, *op. cit.,* p. 6.

JUNE 25, Philadelphia: Dom Pedro Notices Bell's Telephone

1. Williams, *op. cit.,* p. 210; De Camp, *op. cit.,* p. 162.

2. *Ibid.,* p. 267, note 7.

3. Bruce, *op. cit.,* p. 197.

4. De Camp, *op. cit.,* p. 162.

5. Bruce, *op. cit.,* p. 197.

JUNE 28, St. Louis: Democratic National Convention Meets

1. Brown, *1876,* pp. 218–24.

2. William Earnest Smith, *The Francis Preston Blair Family in Politics* (New York: Macmillan, 1933), p. 474.

3. Columbia, S.C., *Daily Register,* June 25, 1876.

4. Porter, *op. cit.,* p. 49. See also George T. McJimsey, *Genteel Partisan, Manton Marble* (Ames: Iowa State University Press, 1971), pp. 176 ff.

5. Brown, *1876,* pp. 150–51.

6. *Ibid.,* p. 151.

7. Polakoff, *op. cit.,* pp. 91–93.

8. Flick, *op. cit.,* p. 295.

JUNE 30, Shanghai: American Builds First Railroad in China

1. *Papers Relating to the Foreign Relations of the United States Transmitted to Congress* (Washington: Government Printing Office, 1876), p. 73; Dennett, *op. cit.,* p. 596; Appleton's, *op. cit.,* p. 111.

2. Peter Karsten, *The Naval Aristocracy* (New York: Free Press, 1972), p. 148.

[370]

3. *Papers Relating to the Foreign* . . ., *op. cit.*, p. 43.

4. *Ibid.*, p. 51.

5. *Ibid.*, p. 45.

6. *Ibid.*, p. 46.

7. Stoddard, *op. cit.*, p. 156.

8. *Papers Relating to the Foreign* . . ., *op. cit.*, p. 47.

9. *Ibid.*, p. 58.

JULY 1, West Point: Lieutenant Flipper Enters Final Year at West Point

1. Henry O. Flipper, *The Colored Cadet at West Point* (New York: Johnson Reprint Company, 1968), pp. 166–67.

2. *Ibid.*, p. 90.

3. *Ibid.*, p. 119.

4. *Ibid.*, p. 149.

5. *Ibid.*, pp. 15, 164, 304 ff.

6. *Ibid.*, p. 2 86.

7. *Ibid.*, p. 48.

8. *Ibid.*, p. 121.

9. *Ibid.*, pp. 146–47, 175.

10. *Ibid.*, p. 121.

11. *Ibid.*, p. 170.

12. *Ibid.*, p. 245.

13. *Ibid.*, p. 282.

14. *Ibid.*, p. 271.

JULY 4, various places: Nation Celebrates Centennial Fourth

1. Thomas H. Johnson, ed., *The Letters of Emily Dickinson*, vol. 2 (Cambridge: Harvard University Press, 1958), p. 558.

2. Jay Leyda, *The Years and Hours of Emily Dickinson* (New Haven: Yale University Press, 1960), p. 253.

3. Brown, *1876*, p. 169.

4. *Ibid.*, p. 168; Randel, *op. cit.*, p. 301.

5. Brown, *1876*, pp. 152–66.

6. *Socialist*, July 8, 1876.

7. Alan Trachtenberg, ed., *Democratic Vistas 1860–1880* (New York: Braziller, 1970), p. 72.

8. *Ibid.*, pp. 81–82.

9. Newmark, *op. cit.*, p. 501.

10. *Papers Relating to the Foreign . . ., op. cit.*, pp. 10, 16, 175, 441.

11. Offenbach, *op. cit.*, p. 99.

12. Richmond, *Daily Dispatch*, July 12, 1876.

JULY 6, New York: News of Custer Disaster Stuns Country

1. Utley, *op. cit.*, p. 275; Brown, *1876*, pp. 169–70; Stewart, *op. cit.*, pp. 4–5.

2. Stewart, *op. cit.*, p. 197.

3. Richard O'Connor, *The Scandalous Mr. Bennett* (New York: Doubleday, 1962), p. 81.

4. St. Louis *Post-Dispatch*, July 7, 1876.

5. Miller, *op. cit.*, p. 53.

6. Link, *op. cit.*, p. 150.

7. Brown, *1876*, pp. 178–79.

8. Randel, *op. cit.*, p. 75.

9. *Ibid.*, p. 71.

10. Morley, *op. cit.*, pp. 55, 62–64.

11. Randel, *op. cit.*, p. 135.

JULY 8, Hamburg, South Carolina: Blacks Are Massacred in South Carolina

1. Augusta, Ga., *Chronicle and Sentinel*, July 9, 1876.

2. *Ibid.*

3. *Ibid.*

4. Augusta, Ga., *Constitutionalist*, July 9, 1876.

5. Augusta, Ga., *Chronicle and Sentinel*, July 9, 1876.

6. *Ibid.*

7. *Ibid.*

8. *Ibid.*

9. Bowers, *op. cit.*, p. 353.

10. *Ibid.*, p. 505.

11. Richardson, *op. cit.*, pp. 375–76.

12. McPherson, *op. cit.*, p. 256.

JULY 12, Washington: Comstock Anti-Obscenity Law Is Adopted

1. Ari and Olive Hoogenboom, eds., *The Gilded Age* (Englewood Cliffs, N.J., Prentice-Hall, 1967), p. 138.

2. Randel, *op. cit.*, pp. 313–14.

3. *Labor Standard*, August 19, 1876.

JULY 14, Columbus: Hayes Accepts Republican Nomination

1. The text of the letter is in McPherson, *op. cit.*, pp. 212 ff.

2. About Hayes' background, see: Brown, *1876*, p. 211; Randel, *op. cit.*, p. 221; Jordan, *op. cit.*, pp. 242–43.

3. Pomerantz, *op. cit.*, p. 191.

4. Randel, *op. cit.*, pp. 224–25.

5. George Sinkler, *Racial Attitudes of United States Presidents* (Garden City, N.Y.: Doubleday, 1971), pp. 174 ff.

6. Pomerantz, *op. cit.*, p. 175.

7. Polakoff, *op. cit.*, p. 115.

8. Pomerantz, *op. cit.*, p. 119.

9. Brown, *1876*, pp. 247–50.

10. *Ibid.*, p. 229; Polakoff, *op. cit.*, pp. 116–45.

JULY 15, Philadelphia: First International Dissolves Itself

1. George E. McNeill, *The Labor Movement, The Problem of Today* (Boston: A.M. Bridgeman and Co., 1886), p. 615.

2. Commons, *op. cit.*, p. 212.

3. Robert Hunter, *Violence and the Labor Movement* (New York: Macmillan, 1914), p. 191.

4. For the general history of the International in America, see Commons, *op. cit.*, pp. 202–15.

5. *Ibid.*, p. 222.

6. David Hereshoff, *American Disciples of Marx* (Detroit: Wayne State University Press, 1967), pp. 100–3.

7. Samuel Bernstein, *The First International in America* (New York: Augustus M. Kelley, 1962), pp. 281–83.

8. Philip S. Foner, *History of the Labor Movement in the United States* (New York: International Publishers, 1955), p. 450.

9. Gompers, *op. cit.*, p. 88.

10. Bernstein, *op. cit.*, p. 272.

11. *Socialist,* July 8, 1876.

12. Bernstein, *op. cit.,* pp. 273–74; Foner, *op. cit.,* p. 440.

JULY 18, Cleveland: Rockefeller Consolidates Oil Monopoly

1. Allan Nevins, *John D. Rockefeller,* vol. 1 (New York: Scribner, 1953), p. 225.
2. About Rockefeller tactics generally, see: *ibid.,* pp. 230 ff.; Holbrook, *op. cit.,* pp. 61–89, 131–44.
3. Randel, *op. cit.,* p. 184.
4. Holbrook, *op. cit.,* p. 131.
5. Henry Ford, *My Life and Work* (Garden City, N.Y.: Doubleday, Page, 1922), pp. 22–23.

JULY 18, War Bonnet Creek: Buffalo Bill Kills Yellow Hand

1. Brown, *1876,* pp. 181 ff.; Sandoz, *op. cit.,* p. 175; Jay Monaghan, ed., *The Book of the American West* (New York: Messner, 1963), pp. 237–38.
2. *Ibid.,* pp. 256–57.
3. *Ibid.,* p. 322; Randel, *op. cit.,* p. 115.
4. *Ibid.,* pp. 145 ff.; Monaghan, *op. cit.,* pp. 280–83.
5. Randel, *op. cit.,* pp. 137 ff.
6. *Ibid.,* pp. 113, 140–41.
7. *Ibid.,* p. 112; La Feber, *op. cit.,* p. 12.

JULY 20, Philadelphia: Workingmen's Party Is Founded

1. *Socialist,* August 12, 1876.
2. Morris Hillquit, *History of Socialism in the United States* (New York: Funk and Wagnalls, 1910), p. 195.
3. Commons, *op. cit.,* p. 227; Hereshoff, *op. cit.,* pp. 99–100.
4. Howard H. Quint, *The Forging of American Socialism* (Columbia: University of South Carolina Press, 1953), p. 12.
5. *Socialist,* April 22, 1876.
6. *Ibid.,* August 12, 1876.
7. For the general program, see Commons, *op. cit.,* pp. 270–71; Stuart B. Kaufman, *Samuel Gompers and the Origins of the American Federation of Labor 1848–1896* (Westport, Conn.: Greenwood Press, 1973), p. 61.
8. Gompers, *op. cit.,* p. 88.

9. *Ibid.*, pp. 128–29; Kaufman, *op. cit.*, pp. 61–62.

10. *Ibid.*, p. 65.

11. *Labor Standard*, September 30, 1876.

12. *Ibid.*, November 4, 1886.

13. *Ibid.*, November 25, 1876.

14. Hereshoff, *op. cit.*, p. 100.

15. *Labor Standard*, August 26, 1876.

16. Theodore Draper, *The Roots of American Communism* (New York: Viking, 1957), pp. 31, 38.

JULY 21, Saratoga, New York: College Athletes Organize

1. Carruth, *op. cit.*, p. 309; Randel, *op. cit.*, p. 319.

2. About Saratoga at its height, see Leng, *op. cit.*, pp. 38–39; Birmingham, *op. cit.*, p. 143; Ishbel Ross, *Crusades and Crinolines: The Life and Times of Ellen Curtis Demorest and William Jennings Demorest* (New York: Harper's, 1963), pp. 174 ff.

3. Offenbach, *op. cit.*, p. 130.

4. Ross, *Crusades*, p. 125.

5. Russell B. Nye, *George Bancroft, Brahmin Rebel* (New York: Knopf, 1944).

JULY 26, Cincinnati: Unemployed Demonstrate

1. *Socialist*, August 5, 1876.

2. Robert V. Bruce, *1877: Year of Violence* (Indianapolis: Bobbs-Merrill, 1959), pp. 20–25; Brown, *1876*, pp. 346–47.

3. *Labor Standard*, December 23, 1876.

4. Foner, *op. cit.*, pp. 442–43.

5. *Labor Standard*, September 9, 1876.

6. *Ibid.*, December 30, 1876.

AUGUST 1, Denver: Colorado Becomes Thirty-Eighth State

1. Proclamation in Richardson, *op. cit.*, p. 393. Also see Randel, *op. cit.*, pp. 115–16, 263–64.

AUGUST 2, Deadwood, Dakota Territory: Wild Bill Hickok Is Shot Dead

1. *Ibid.*, pp. 146–47; Monaghan, *op. cit.*, pp. 313–14.

AUGUST 4, Albany: Tilden Accepts Democratic Nomination

1. Brown, *1876*, p. 225.
2. Hirsch, *op. cit.*, p. 108.
3. Polakoff, *op. cit.*, p. 124; McPherson, *op. cit.*, p. 217.
4. Flick, *op. cit.*, p. 318.
5. *Ibid.*, p. 319.
6. *Ibid.*, p. 281; Randel, *op. cit.*, p. 223.
7. Flick, *op. cit.*, pp. 303–4; Pomerantz, *op. cit.*, p. 190; Polakoff, *op. cit.*, pp. 125 ff.

AUGUST 4, Elmira, New York: Mark Twain Starts Writing *Huckleberry Finn*

1. Kaplan, *op. cit.*, p. 197.
2. *Ibid.*
3. *Ibid.*, p. 198.
4. *Ibid.*, p. 200.
5. Randel, *op. cit.*, p. 350. Also see Brown, *1876*, pp. 54–55.
6. Kaplan, *op. cit.*, p. 180.
7. Randel, *op. cit.*, p. 350.
8. *Ibid.*, p. 349. See also James F. Light, *John William De Forest* (New York: Twayne Publications, 1965).

AUGUST 7, New York: Edward Bok Becomes Office Boy

1. Edward Bok, *The Americanization of Edward Bok* (New York: Scribner, 1923), pp. 15–16.
2. John Tebbell, *From Rags to Riches: Horatio Alger Jr. and the American Dream* (New York: Macmillan, 1963); Randel, *op. cit.*, p. 359.
3. Birmingham, *op. cit.*, p. 133.

AUGUST 15, Columbia, South Carolina: South Carolina Democrats Nominate Wade Hampton

1. About South Carolina politics generally, see McPherson, *op. cit.*, pp. 74–81; Oberholzer, *op. cit.*, pp. 221–29; Pomerantz, *op. cit.*, pp. 197–98.
2. Brown, *1876*, p. 277.
3. Bowers, *op. cit.*, p. 507.
4. *Ibid.*, pp. 506–10.
5. Brown, *1876*, p. 281.

6. Randel, *op. cit.*, p. 254.

7. Bowers, *op. cit.*, pp. 514–21.

8. *Ibid.*, pp. 515–16; Polakoff, *op. cit.*, p. 189.

AUGUST 18, Boston: Mahan Has Troubles with Navy

1. Samuel A'Court Ashe, *Papers* (Alfred Thayer Mahan Letters) (Flowers Collection, William Perkins Library, Duke University), July 23 and August 19, 1876.

2. Karsten, *op. cit.*, p. 278. See also Ernest R. May, *Imperial Democracy* (New York: Harper, 1961), p. 7.

3. Karsten, *op. cit.*, p. 288.

4. Randel, *op. cit.*, pp. 158–59, 271.

5. Oberholtzer, *op. cit.*, pp. 182–83.

6. Ashe Papers, January 27, 1876.

7. *Ibid.*, June 17 and August 21, 1876.

8. *Ibid.*, January 27 and June 17, 1876.

9. Karsten, *op. cit.*, pp. 330–31.

AUGUST 22, New York: *Times* Accuses Tilden About False Taxes

1. Brown, *1876*, pp. 232–33; Randel, *op. cit.*, p. 223.

2. Flick, *op. cit.*, p. 324.

3. *Ibid.*, p. 311.

4. Polakoff, *op. cit.*, p. 119.

5. Flick, *op. cit.*, p. 307.

6. Columbia, S.C., *Daily Register*, August 3, 1876.

7. George S. Merriam, *The Life and Times of Samuel Bowles*, vol. 2 (New York: The Century Co., 1885), p. 280.

8. Pomerantz, *op. cit.*, p. 193.

9. Flick, *op. cit.*, p. 315.

10. Brown, *1876*, p. 284.

AUGUST 24, Honolulu: Hawaii Gets News of Reciprocity Treaty

1. Richardson, *op. cit.*, pp. 394–95; Karsten, *op. cit.*, p. 148.

2. Lens, *Empire*, p. 163.

3. Walter La Feber, *New Empire, An Interpretation of American Expansion 1860–1898* (Ithaca: Cornell University Press, 1963), p. 35.

4. Randel, *op. cit.*, pp. 157–58.

5. Richard W. Van Alstyne, *The American Empire, Historical Pattern and Evolution* (London: Routledge and Paul, 1960), p. 177.

6. Karsten, *op. cit.*, pp. 171–72.

AUGUST 26, Cincinnati: Lafcadio Hearn Reports Gruesome Hanging

1. Elizabeth Stevenson, *Lafcadio Hearn* (New York: Macmillan, 1961), p. 56.

2. *Ibid.*, pp. 44–45.

3. *Ibid.*, p. 30. Also see Randel, *op. cit.*, p. 357.

4. Stevenson, *op. cit.*, p. 32.

5. *Ibid.*, p. 56.

6. Lafcadio Hearn, *An American Miscellany*, first collected by Albert Mordell (New York: Dodd, Mead, 1925), pp. 163–70.

7. *Ibid.*, pp. 171–79.

AUGUST 29, Constantinople: Americans Reveal "Bulgarian Horrors"

1. James A. Field, *America and the Mediterranean World, 1776–1882* (Princeton: Princeton University Press, 1969), pp. 365–66.

2. Robert L. Daniel, *American Philanthropy in the Near East 1820–1960* (Athens: Ohio University Press, 1970), p. 129.

3. Field, *op. cit.*, p. 365; F. L. Bullard, *Famous War Correspondents* (Boston: Little, Brown, 1914), pp. 115–54.

4. Daniel, *op. cit.*, p. 129.

5. *Ibid.*, p. 130; R. T. Shannon, *Gladstone and the Bulgarian Agitation of 1876* (London: Thomas Nelson and Sons Ltd., 1963).

6. Ashe Papers, *op. cit.*, July 23, 1876.

7. New York *Sun*, September 3, 1876.

8. *Labor Standard*, September 9, 1876.

9. Field, *op. cit.*, p. 368.

10. *Ibid.*, p. 372.

11. *Ibid.*, p. 371.

12. Daniel, *op. cit.*, p. 105; Field, *op. cit.*, pp. 345, 350.

13. *Ibid.*, pp. 330–43, 369.

14. *Ibid.*, pp. 311–14.

AUGUST 30, New York: Peter Cooper Continues Greenback Campaign

1. Mack, *op. cit.*, pp. 368–69.

2. *Ibid.*, p. 366.

3. Unger, *op. cit.*, pp. 312–13.

4. Haynes, *op. cit.*, p. 115.

5. Unger, *op. cit.*, pp. 313–14.

6. *Labor Standard,* August 12, September 30, October 7, and October 14, 1876. See also Commons, *op. cit.*, p. 171.

7. Unger, *op. cit.*, p. 317.

SEPTEMBER 6, Scranton: Powderly Joins Knights of Labor

1. Harry J. Carman et al., eds., *The Path I Trod: The Autobiography of Terence V. Powderly* (New York: Columbia University Press, 1940), pp. 44–51.

2. Allan Pinkerton, *Strikers, Tramps, Communists, and Detectives* (New York: G. W. Dillingham Co., 1878), p. 88.

3. On the Knights of Labor generally, see Commons, *op. cit.*, pp. 195 ff.; McNeill, *op. cit.*, p. 251; Foner, *op. cit.*, p. 437.

4. Carman, *op. cit.*, pp. 44–45.

5. *Ibid.*, pp. 68–69.

6. *Ibid.*, p. 38.

7. Terence Powderly, *Thirty Years of Labor, 1859–1889* (Columbus, Ohio: Excelsior Publishing House, 1890), p. 224.

SEPTEMBER 7, Northfield, Minnesota: James Gang Holds Up Minnesota Bank

1. Brown, *1876,* pp. 188–93; Randel, *op. cit.*, p. 110.

2. Randel, *op. cit.*, p. 162.

3. Monaghan, *op. cit.*, p. 272.

SEPTEMBER 11, London: Whistler Paints Peacock Room

1. Elizabeth R. and Joseph Pennell, *The Life of James McNeill Whistler,* vol. 2 (Philadelphia: Lippincott, 1908), pp. 205–9.

2. *Ibid.*, p. 198.

3. *Ibid.*, pp. 199–200.

4. *Ibid.*, pp. 213, 235–36.

5. *Ibid.*, p. 195.

6. *Ibid.*, pp. 189–90.

7. *Ibid.*, p. 194.

8. *Ibid.*, p. 189.

SEPTEMBER 12, Brussels: Central Africa Association Is Established

1. Norman R. Bennett, *Stanley's Despatches to the New York Herald 1871–1872, 1874–1877* (Boston: Boston University Press, 1970).

2. Clarence Clendenen et al., *Americans in Africa, 1865–1900* (Palo Alto: Stanford University Press, 1966), pp. 45–50.

3. Luella J. Hall, *The United States and Morocco, 1776–1956* (Metuchen, N.J.: Scarecrow Press, 1971).

4. W. B. Hesseltine, *The Blue and the Gray on the Nile* (Chicago: University of Chicago Press, 1961).

5. Sigmund Diamond, ed., *The Nation Transformed* (New York: Braziller, 1963), p. 464.

SEPTEMBER 21, Indianapolis: Ingersoll Waves the "Bloody Shirt"

1. Brown, *1876,* pp. 243–44.

2. Haynes, *op. cit.,* pp. 117–18; Polakoff, *op. cit.,* p. 145.

3. Bowers, *op. cit.,* p. 492.

4. William E. Smith, *op. cit.,* p. 477.

SEPTEMBER 27, Boston: Theodore Roosevelt Begins Harvard

1. Elting E. Morrison, ed., *Letters of Theodore Roosevelt,* vol. 1 (Cambridge: Harvard University Press, 1951–1954), p. 16.

2. *Ibid.,* p. 17.

3. Carleton Putnam, *Theodore Roosevelt, A Biography,* vol. 1, *The Formative Years* (New York: Scribner, 1958), pp. 119–26.

4. Morrison, *op. cit.,* p. 19.

5. Putnam, *op. cit.,* p. 141.

6. Morrison, *op. cit.,* p. 18.

7. Putnam, *op. cit.,* pp. 131, 141.

8. Theodore Roosevelt, *Theodore Roosevelt's Diaries of Boyhood and Youth* (New York: Scribner, 1928), p. 357.

9. Putnam, *op. cit.,* p. 143.

10. *Ibid.,* p. 138.

11. Henry F. Pringle, *Theodore Roosevelt* (London: Jonathan Cape Ltd., 1932), p. 33.

12. Putnam, *op. cit.,* p. 140.

13. *Ibid.,* p. 132.

14. Pringle, *op. cit.,* p. 26.

15. *Ibid.*, p. 36.

16. Morrison, *op. cit.*, p. 19.

17. Putnam, *op. cit.*, p. 131

SEPTEMBER 30, Hartford: Mark Twain Speaks at Republican Rally

1. Randel, *op. cit.*, pp. 225–26.

2. Brown, *1876*, pp. 248–49.

3. Randel, *op. cit.*, pp. 225–26.

4. William A. Croffut, *An American Procession, 1855–1914* (Boston: Little, Brown, 1931), pp. 169–71.

5. Kaplan, *op. cit.*, p. 211.

OCTOBER 4, Philadelphia: Melvil Dewey Begins Library Reform

1. Grosvenor Dawe, *Melvil Dewey, Seer, Inspirer, Doer* (Melvil Dewey Biografy, Lake Placid Club, Essex County, New York, 1932), p. 287.

2. *Ibid.*, p. 127.

3. *Ibid.*, pp. 78, 165.

4. Randel, *op. cit.*, pp. 425 ff.

5. Dawe, *op. cit.*, p. 145.

6. *Ibid.*, pp. 146, 176.

7. *Ibid.*, p. 277.

OCTOBER 9, Boston: Bell Phones Long Distance

1. Bruce, *Bell*, p. 104.

2. De Camp, *op. cit.*, pp. 163–67.

3. Malcolm Keir, *The March of Commerce*, vol. 4, *Pageant of America* (New Haven: Yale University Press, 1927), p. 265.

OCTOBER 10, Indianapolis: Indiana Elections Go Democratic

1. Polakoff, *op. cit.*, p. 198.

2. Theodore C. Smith, *op. cit.*, p. 613.

3. T. Harry Williams, ed., *Hayes, The Diary of a President 1875–1881* (New York: David McKay, 1964), p. 343.

4. Brown, *1876*, pp. 237–38.

5. *Ibid.*, p. 244.

6. *Ibid.*, pp. 236–37.

7. Polakoff, *op. cit.*, p. 198.

8. *Ibid.*, pp. 157–58.

9. Bowers, *op. cit.*, p. 494.

10. T. Harry Williams, *op. cit.*, p. 370.

OCTOBER 10, Amherst, Massachusetts: Helen Hunt Jackson Visits Emily Dickinson

1. Leyda, *Dickinson*, pp. 258–59.

2. *Ibid.*, p. 245.

3. *Ibid.*, p. 265.

4. *Ibid.*, pp. 258–59.

5. Thomas H. Johnson, ed., *Final Harvest: Emily Dickinson's Poems* (Boston: Little, Brown, 1961), pp. vii–viii.

6. *Ibid.*, p. vi.

7. Leyda, *Dickinson*, p. 240.

8. *Ibid.*, p. 253.

9. *Ibid.*, pp. 275–76.

10. *Ibid.*, pp. 258, 260.

11. Johnson, *Letters*, p. 586.

12. *Ibid.*, pp. 559, 561.

13. *Ibid.*, pp. 251, 260. Leyda, *Dickinson* pp. 251, 260.

14. Johnson, *Final*, p. 278.

15. *Ibid.*, p. x.

16. Johnson, *Letters*, p. 570.

17. Leyda, *Dickinson*, p. 273.

OCTOBER 11, Kirkwood, New Jersey: Walt Whitman Writes Admirer

1. Miller, *op. cit.*, p. 62.

2. Randel, *op. cit.*, p. 16.

3. Miller, *op. cit.*, p. 67.

4. *Ibid.*, p. 68.

5. *Ibid.*, pp. 86–87

6. *Ibid.*, p. 71.

7. *Ibid.*, p. 77.

8. *Ibid.*, p. 70.

OCTOBER 16, Pottsville, Pennsylvania: Nineteen Molly Maguires Are Sentenced

1. Coleman, *op. cit.*, p. 147.
2. *Ibid.*, p. 150.
3. *Ibid.*, p. 158.
4. Lens, *Labor*, p. 9.
5. Coleman, *op. cit.*, p. 164.
6. Lens, *Labor*, p. 11.
7. *Ibid.*, p. 29.
8. Aurand, *op. cit.*, p. 25.
9. Coleman, *op. cit.*, p. 138.
10. Anthony Bimba, *The History of the American Working Class* (New York: International Publishers, 1927), p. 81. See also Powderly, *op. cit.*, p. 253.
11. Broehl, *op. cit.*, p. 350.

OCTOBER 17, Cainhoy, South Carolina: Election Violence Grows in South Carolina

1. Bowers, *op. cit.*, p. 519.
2. *Ibid.*, pp. 511–12.
3. Brown, *1876*, pp. 280–81.
4. Richardson, *op. cit.*, p. 396.
5. Bowers, *op. cit.*, p. 519.
6. Brown, *1876*, p. 282.
7. *Ibid.*, p. 520.

OCTOBER 23, Red Cloud Agency: Sioux Surrender at Agencies

1. Utley, *op. cit.*, pp. 280–81.
2. Brown, *Bury*, p. 299.

OCTOBER 27, Boston: Harvard Students Rally for Hayes

1. Pringle, *op. cit.*, pp. 31–32.

NOVEMBER 7, Nationwide: Tilden Wins Popular-Vote Majority

1. Polakoff, *op. cit.*, p. 200.
2. Richmond *Daily Dispatch,* November 6, 1876.
3. Unger, *op. cit.*, pp. 318–20.

4. Pomerantz, *op. cit.*, pp. 193–94.

5. Polakoff, *op. cit.*, p. 205.

6. Brown, *1876*, p. 288; Randel, *op. cit.*, p. 227.

7. Polakoff, *op. cit.*, p. 200.

NOVEMBER 7, Springfield, Illinois: Counterfeiters Attempt to Steal Lincoln's Remains

1. John M. Potter, *Plots Against Presidents* (New York: Astor-Honor Inc., 1968), pp. 122–37; Lynn Glaser, *Counterfeiting America* (New York: C. N. Potter, 1967), p. 135.

NOVEMBER 8, New York: Republicans Plot to Steal Election

1. Pomerantz, *op. cit.*, pp. 193–94; Randel, *op. cit.*, pp. 227 ff.

2. Oberholtzer, *op. cit.*, p. 281; Mott, *op. cit.*, p. 486.

3. Brown, *1876*, pp. 317–18.

4. *Ibid.*, p. 318.

5. *Ibid.*, p. 319.

6. Link, *op. cit.*, pp. 222–24.

7. *Ibid.*, p. 228.

8. *Ibid.*, pp. 231–32.

9. Brown, *1876*, p. 290.

NOVEMBER 10, Philadelphia: Grant Closes Centennial Exhibition

1. Brown, *1876*, p. 290.

2. Randel, *op. cit.*, pp. 187–88.

3. *Socialist*, July 22, 1876.

4. *Ibid.*, July 15, 1876.

5. Bruce, *1877*, p. 9.

6. Randel, *op. cit.*, pp. 4, 304.

NOVEMBER 23, New York: Tweed Is Brought Back to the United States

1. Lynch, *Tweed*, pp. 398–404.

2. Callow, *op. cit.*, p. 291.

3. Lynch, *Tweed*, p. 401.

4. Brown, *1876*, p. 234.

5. Lynch, *Tweed*, p. 404.

6. Callow, *op. cit.*, p. 292.

7. *Ibid.*, p. 297.

8. Hirsch, *op. cit.*, pp. 103–4.

NOVEMBER 23, Springfield, Massachusetts: Collegians Agree on Football Rules

1. Carruth, *op. cit.*, p. 313.

NOVEMBER 28, Columbia, South Carolina: Rival Governments Are Established in South Carolina

1. Pomerantz, *op. cit.*, pp. 197–98.

2. McPherson, *op. cit.*, pp. 74 ff.

3. Brown, *1876*, p. 326.

4. Bowers, *op. cit.*, p. 540.

DECEMBER 1, Columbus, Ohio: Hayes Meets with Roberts of South

1. Polakoff, *op. cit.*, p. 244; Brown, *1876*, p. 323; Pomerantz, *op. cit.*, p. 202.

2. Theodore C. Smith, *op. cit.*, pp. 624–25.

3. Arthur M. Schlesinger, Jr., *History of American Presidential Elections* (New York: Chelsea House, 1971), pp. 1456–57.

4. Pomerantz, *op. cit.*, p. 195.

DECEMBER 5, Washington: Grant Delivers Last Message to Congress

1. Richardson, *op. cit.*, p. 399.

2. Jesse Grant Cramer, *Letters of Ulysses S. Grant* (New York: Putnam, 1912), pp. 125–28.

3. Brown, *1876*, p. 342.

4. Richardson, *op. cit.*, pp. 399–400.

5. Columbia, S.C., *Daily Register*, November 2, 1876.

6. Richardson, *op. cit.*, p. 408. See Allan L. Damon, "Impoundment," *American Heritage*, vol. XXV, no. 1 (December, 1973), pp. 22–23, 89–91.

7. Richardson, *op. cit.*, p. 401.

8. *Ibid.*, p. 412.

9. *Ibid.*, p. 401.

10. *Ibid.*, p. 413.

11. Cramer, *op. cit.*, p. 127.

DECEMBER 5, Brooklyn: Brooklyn Theater Burns

1. Randel, *op. cit.*, p. 330.

DECEMBER 6, Washington: Electoral College Vote Is Indefinite

1. Pomerantz, *op. cit.*, pp. 196–97; Brown, *1876*, pp. 319–20, 324.
2. Pomerantz, *op. cit.*, pp. 195–96.
3. Brown, *1876*, p. 325.
4. William Ernest Smith, *op. cit.*, p. 480.

DECEMBER 17, St. Louis: General Shelby Rejects Appeal to Arms

1. Brown, *1876*, p. 329.
2. Rowland, *op. cit.*, p. 526.
3. Turner, *op. cit.*, p. 623.
4. Brown, *1876*, p. 330.
5. James D. Norris and Arthur H. Shaffer, *Politics and Patronage in the Gilded Age* (Madison: State Historical Society of Wisconsin, 1970), p. 175.
6. Mott, *op. cit.*, p. 458.
7. Brown, *1876*, p. 321.
8. Pomerantz, *op. cit.*, p. 201.
9. Polakoff, *op. cit.*, p. 222; Randel, *op. cit.*, pp. 231–33.
10. William Ernest Smith, *op. cit.*, p. 205.

DECEMBER 18, Redwater Creek: Sitting Bull Is Defeated in Skirmish

1. Utley, *op. cit.*, p. 297.
2. *Ibid.*, p. 285.
3. *Ibid.*, pp. 57, 193. See also Sandoz, *op. cit.*, p. 173.
4. Utley, *op. cit.*, p. 296.
5. *Ibid.*, p. 299.
6. Sandoz, *op. cit.*, p. 178.

DECEMBER 22, Washington: Congress Compromises on Electoral Dispute

1. Brown, *1876*, p. 330.
2. *Ibid.*, p. 333.
3. William Ernest Smith, *op. cit.*, p. 486.
4. Randel, *op. cit.*, pp. 235–36.

5. Brown, *1876,* p. 339.

6. Pomerantz, *op. cit.,* p. 223.

DECEMBER 29, Ashtabula, Ohio: Great Train Crash Occurs in Ohio

1. Bruce, *1877,* p. 28.

2. Offenbach, *op. cit.,* p. 136.

3. Randel, *op. cit.,* p. 61.

4. *Ibid.,* pp. 163–68.

5. Brown, *1876,* p. 258.

6. Bruce, *1877,* p. 36; Randel, *op. cit.,* pp. 169–70.

7. Columbia, S.C., *Daily Register,* June 22, 1876.

8. Bruce, *1877,* p. 34 and *passim.*

DECEMBER 30, Lynn, Massachusetts: Mary Baker Glover Decides to Marry Mr. Eddy

1. Dakin, *op. cit.,* p. 123.

2. Peel, *op. cit.,* pp. 18–19.

3. *Ibid.,* p. 12.

4. *Ibid.*

5. Eddy, *op. cit.,* p. 42.

6. Dakin, *op. cit.,* p. 121.

7. Peel, *op. cit.,* p. 16.

8. Dakin, *op. cit.,* pp. 127–29.

9. *Ibid.,* p. 141.

10. Peel, *op. cit.,* p. 17.

DECEMBER 31, New York: James Gordon Bennett Gets Drunk

1. Donald C. Seitz, *The James Gordon Bennetts, Father and Son, Proprietors of the New York* Herald (Indianapolis: Bobbs-Merrill, 1928), p. 267.

2. O'Connor, *op. cit.,* p. 136.

3. *Ibid.*

Index

Colfax, Schuyler, 89, 147
Colorado, statehood, 225–26, 319
Columbia University, 221, 312; School of Library Science, 279
Columbia (S.C.) *Daily Register*, 41–42, 103, 178
Comanche Indians, 44
Combahee, S.C., race riots, 296
Communist Club of New York, 205
Communist Societies (Nordhoff), 167
Comstock, Anthony, 200–1
Comstock Law, 201
Conkling, Roscoe, 80, 90, 110–11, 112, 123, 127, 157–58, 159, 160, 240, 272
Constantinople Conference, 251
Contes d'Hoffmann, Les (Offenbach), 163
Cooper, Edward, 230
Cooper, Mrs. James S., 288
Cooper, Peter, 26–29, 50, 219, 221, 230, 259; as Independent Party candidate, 133–35, 253–55, 300–1
Cooper Union, 26–27, 253
Cornell University, 221; journalism program, 20
"Cotton Exchange in New Orleans, The" (Degas), 95
Cousins, Phoebe, 179
Cox, Samuel S. "Sunset," 24
Crazy Horse, Chief, 44, 45, 47, 55, 58, 118, 153–54, 170, 174, 196, 298, 327, 328
Crédit Mobilier scandal, 89–90, 232, 317, 333–34
Cremation, 322
Crook, George, 47, 55, 59, 94, 118, 153–54, 170, 171, 175, 298, 326, 327
Croquet, 136
Crow Indians, 44, 46, 152, 154, 171
Cuba, 30
Currency issue, 228–29. *See also* Greenbacks; Resumption Act
Cushing, Caleb, 30, 32
Custer, Boston, 171
Custer, Elizabeth, 93, 194, 195
Custer, George Armstrong, 47, 48, 56, 59, 60, 91–94, 117–19, 151, 152, 193, 194–96, 200, 213, 227, 291, 299, 327, 328, 338; last stand, 169–76

Custer, Tom, 171, 175
Customs House Ring, 52, 142, 160

Dana, Charles A., 18
Dana, Richard Henry, 70, 158
"Dancing at the Moulin de la Galette" (Renoir), 95
Dartmouth College, 221
Darwin Charles, 275
Davis, David, 134, 301, 329
Davis, Jefferson, 24–25, 324; amnesty grant, 23, 24
Davis, Jim, 291
Davis, John M., 106, 107, 258
"Death Song for Custer, A" (Whitman), 194
De Forrest, John, 232
Degas, Edgar, 95, 96
Democratic Campaign Book, 230
Democratic Party, 20, 22, 23 ff., 29, 35, 48–49, 50–51, 52, 56, 90–91, 92, 94, 109, 125, 196, 199–200, 228–30, 235 ff., 240 ff., 253, 270, 281 ff., 296–98, 299, 311; Convention, 171, 177–80; National Committee, 236; election dispute, 304–7, 313 ff., 316 ff., 322–26, 329–31
Democratic Vistas (Whitman), 83
Denver, Colo., 191
De Palm, Baron, 322
Dewey, Melvil, 278–80
Dewey Decimal Classification, 278–80
Dickel's Riding Academy, 136
Dickinson, Austin, 287, 288
Dickinson, Edward, 287
Dickinson, Emily, 188, 285–90
Dickinson, Lavinia, 287
Dickinson, Susan, 287, 288
Dispatch Number 266, 30, 31, 32
Disraeli, Benjamin, 250, 251
"Dolly, An Idyl of the Levee" (Hearn), 248–49
Donnelly, Ignatius, 133
Dorsheimer, W. D., 179
Douglass, Frederick, 123
Doyle, Michael J., 33, 36–37
Doyle, Peter, 291
Dracula (Stoker), 83
Draw Poker (Schenck), 69

Grant, Orvil, 79, 92

Grant, Ulysses S., 13–16, 20, 24, 38, 41, 42, 46, 47, 59, 63, 68, 71, 72, 77, 94, 98, 99, 104, 105, 110, 111, 126, 136, 138, 144, 158, 160, 175, 177, 183, 189, 190, 191, 199, 200, 202, 203, 205, 214, 222, 223, 229, 230, 233, 236, 239, 244, 270, 276, 297, 308, 311, 313, 315, 323; and Cuba, 29, 31; expansionist policy, 32; Indian affairs, 47, 55, 320; economic policies, 50, 51; and Whiskey Ring, 51–54; Emma Mine scandal, 69, 70; illness, 89–91; salary, 108; opens Centennial, 123, 124; and Colorado statehood, 225; 1876 presidential election, 306–7, 323, 325, 329; last message to Congress, 318–20

Gray, Elisha, 63, 89, 176–77, 281

Great Britain, 71–72, 249, 250, 251, 320

Great Campaign, The, 255

Great Cuban Insurrection (1868), 30

Greeley, Horace, 18, 126, 134

Greenback Club, 254, 259

Greenback Party, 28–29; Convention, 133–35. *See also* Independent Party

Greenbacks, Greenbackism, 27, 105, 106–7, 217, 220, 223, 243, 253–55, 283–84, 300–1, 329

Groom, Wallace, 133, 134, 254

Grouard, Frank, 152

Habberton, John, 143

Hague Congress (1872), 207

Haldeman, H. R., 52

Half-breed Republicans, 110

Hamburg Massacre, 196–200, 235, 315

Hampton, Wade, 235–38, 296, 297, 306, 313–15, 316

Hancock, Winfield Scott, 23, 178, 180

Hantranft, Governor (Pennsylvania), 157, 159–60

Hard money, 48 ff.

Harper's Monthly, 19, 62

Harper's Weekly, 19, 86, 97, 178, 249, 308, 310

Harris, Joel Chandler, 19

Harrison, Benjamin, 281, 282–83, 284

Harrison, William Henry, 282

Harte, Bret, 231, 232, 267

Hartford *Evening News*, 41

Harvard University, 62, 221, 272 ff., 312–13; library, 278, 279; Medical School, 145

Hawaii, Reciprocity Treaty with, 244–45, 320

Hawley, Joseph, 41–43, 124, 125, 171, 276–77, 307, 308

Hawthorne, Nathaniel, 141

Hayes, Lucy Webb, 203

Hayes, Ruddy, 301

Hayes, Rutherford B., 110, 111–12, 127, 147, 157–58, 159–60, 189, 222, 228, 229, 231, 238, 240, 253, 254, 255, 259, 270, 276, 283, 284–85, 299, 309; presidential nomination, 164, 201; campaign, 202–5, 241–44, 284–85; disputed election, 300–2, 304–7, 314, 316–18, 319, 322–24, 329–31

Helena *Daily Herald*, 193

Helen's Babies (Habberton), 143

Hearn, Lafcadio, 246–49

Hearst, William Randolph, 20

Hendricks, Thomas A., 24, 178, 179, 180, 220, 228–29, 282, 283, 301

Henry, Joseph, 176

Henry V (Shakespeare), 103, 121

Hewitt, Abram S., 229–30, 241, 243, 253, 275, 305, 323, 325, 330

Hickok, Wild Bill, 226–27

Higginson, Thomas W., 126, 222, 286–87, 289, 290

Hill, Benjamin H., 24, 316

Hilton, Henry, 100

Hires, Charles E., 132

History of an Attempt to Steal the Body of Abraham Lincoln (Powers), 303

History of the United States (Bancroft), 222

Holland, Josiah, 83, 291

Holmes, Oliver Wendell, 62, 143, 189, 232, 275

Homer, Winslow, 97

Honest Money League, 255

Hopkins, John, 303–4

Wolff, Albert, 94–95
Women's Christian Temperance Union, 68
Women's Pavilion, 124–25
Women's rights movement, 179, 189–90, 218. *See also* Suffragists
Wood, Fernando, 56
Wooden Leg, 59
Woodhull, Victoria, 101, 206–7, 208, 335
Woodhull and Claflin's Weekly, 206
Woolsey, Theodore Dwight, 125
Woosung Road Company, 182
Woosung Railroad, 183
Worden, John L., 31, 252
Workingmen's organizations. *See,* Knights of Labor; Junior Sons of '76; Trade unionism
Workingmen's Party of the United States, 217–18
Workingmen's Trade and Labor Union of San Francisco, 150
Wounded Knee, Battle of, 328
Wyoming, statehood, 226

Yale University, 221, 275, 313
Yachting, 136
Yellow Hand, 213
Yost, Benjamin, 113, 114, 115, 292
Young, Brigham, 137–40
Young, Brigham, Jr., 140
Younger brothers, 260, 262

DATE DUE			
OC 26 '81			
IIA			
GAYLORD			PRINTED IN U.S.A